Thinking about the Emotions

MIND ASSOCIATION OCCASIONAL SERIES

This series consists of carefully selected volumes of significant original papers on predefined themes, normally growing out of a conference supported by a Mind Association Major Conference Grant. The Association nominates an editor or editors for each collection, and may cooperate with other bodies in promoting conferences or other scholarly activities in connection with the preparation of particular volumes.

Director, Mind Association: Julian Dodd
Publications Officer: Sarah Sawyer

Recently published in the series

The Epistemic Life of Groups: Essays in the Epistemology of Collectives
Edited by Michael S. Brady and Miranda Fricker

Reality Making
Edited by Mark Jago

The Metaphysics of Relations
Edited by Anna Marmodoro and David Yates

Thomas Reid on Mind, Knowledge, and Value
Edited by Rebecca Copenhaver and Todd Buras

Foundations of Logical Consequence
Edited by Colin R. Caret and Ole T. Hjortland

The Highest Good in Aristotle and Kant
Edited by Joachim Aufderheide and Ralf M. Bader

How We Fight: Ethics in War
Edited by Helen Frowe and Gerald Lang

The Morality of Defensive War
Edited by Cécile Fabre and Seth Lazar

Metaphysics and Science
Edited by Stephen Mumford and Matthew Tugby

Thick Concepts
Edited by Simon Kirchin

Thinking about the Emotions

A Philosophical History

EDITED BY

Alix Cohen & Robert Stern

UNIVERSITY PRESS

OXFORD
UNIVERSITY PRESS

Great Clarendon Street, Oxford, OX2 6DP,
United Kingdom

Oxford University Press is a department of the University of Oxford. It furthers the University's objective of excellence in research, scholarship, and education by publishing worldwide. Oxford is a registered trade mark of Oxford University Press in the UK and in certain other countries

First Edition published in 2017

Impression: 2

Published in the United States of America by Oxford University Press
198 Madison Avenue, New York, NY 10016, United States of America

British Library Cataloguing in Publication Data
Data available

Library of Congress Control Number: 2016962766

ISBN 978–0–19–876685–8

Printed and bound by
CPI Group (UK) Ltd, Croydon, CR0 4YY

Contents

Notes on Contributors

LILLI ALANEN is Professor emerita of History of Philosophy at Uppsala University, Sweden. She is the author of *Descartes' Concept of Mind* (2003), and has published a number of articles on early modern theories of mind, epistemology, and moral psychology, focusing primarily on Descartes, Spinoza, and Hume. She currently works on self and reason in early modern naturalist accounts of the passions.

CHRISTOPHER BENNETT is a Reader in the Philosophy Department at the University of Sheffield. He is the author of *The Apology Ritual* (2008), which sets out an expressive theory of punishment; and is currently working, among other things, on the topic of action expressive of emotion.

ALIX COHEN works at the University of Edinburgh. She is the author of *Kant and the Human Sciences: Biology, Anthropology and History* (2009), the editor of *Kant's Lectures on Anthropology: A Critical Guide* (2014), *Kant on Emotion and Value* (2014), and Associate Editor of the *British Journal for the History of Philosophy*.

DANIEL GARBER is Stuart Professor of Philosophy at Princeton University, and Associated Faculty in the Program in the History of Science and the Department of Politics. He specializes in the history of philosophy and science in the early-modern period, and is also interested in issues in epistemology and the philosophy of science. In addition to numerous articles, he is the author of *Descartes' Metaphysical Physics* (1992), *Descartes Embodied* (2001), *Leibniz: Body, Substance, Monad* (2009), and is the co-editor (with Michael Ayers) of *The Cambridge History of Seventeenth-Century Philosophy* (1998).

SACHA GOLOB is a Lecturer in Philosophy at King's College London; prior to that he was a Junior Research Fellow at Peterhouse, Cambridge. His research focuses on the intersection between Kantian/Post-Kantian Philosophy and contemporary work on the philosophy of mind, on aesthetics, and on philosophical methodology. He is the author of *Heidegger on Concepts, Freedom and Normativity* (2014), and the editor of the forthcoming *Cambridge History of Moral Philosophy* (2017).

ANTHONY HATZIMOYSIS is Associate Professor of Philosophy at the History and Philosophy of Science Department of the University of Athens. His main interests are in the theory of value, the analysis of emotion, and the nature of the self. He is currently working on the distinction between self-consciousness and self-knowledge, and on the nature of emotions that involve one's assessment of oneself. He is the editor of *Philosophy and the Emotions* (2003), *Self-Knowledge* (2011), and the author of *The Philosophy of Sartre* (2011).

T. H. Irwin is Professor of Ancient Philosophy in the University of Oxford and a Fellow of Keble College. From 1975 to 2006 he taught at Cornell University. He is the author of Plato's *Gorgias* (translation and notes), Clarendon Plato Series (1979), Aristotle's *Nicomachean Ethics* (translation and notes, 1999), *Aristotle's First Principles* (1988), *Classical Thought* (1989), *Plato's Ethics* (1995), and *The Development of Ethics*, 3 vols (2007–9).

Laurent Jaffro is Professor of Moral Philosophy at Pantheon-Sorbonne University, Paris. He is a fellow of the Ecole Normale Supérieure and the Institut universitaire de France. His research focuses on moral judgement and motivation, and the history of moral philosophy, especially in the eighteenth century. His most recent publications include *Croit-on comme on veut? Histoire d'une controverse* (ed., 2013) and papers on Shaftesbury and Reid.

Christopher Janaway is Professor of Philosophy at the University of Southampton. He has written extensively on the philosophy of Nietzsche and Schopenhauer and on aesthetics. His books include *Self and World in Schopenhauer's Philosophy* (1989), *Images of Excellence: Plato's Critique of the Arts* (1995), *Schopenhauer: A Very Short Introduction* (2002), and *Beyond Selflessness: Reading Nietzsche's* Genealogy (2007). He has also edited several collections of articles: *Willing and Nothingness: Schopenhauer as Nietzsche's Educator* (1998), *The Cambridge Companion to Schopenhauer* (1999), *Better Consciousness: Schopenhauer's Philosophy of Value* (with Alex Neill, 2009), and *Nietzsche, Naturalism, and Normativity* (with Simon Robertson, 2012).

Kevin Mulligan has filled the chair of analytic philosophy at the University of Geneva since 1986. He publications are mainly in analytic metaphysics, the philosophy of mind and the history of Austro-German philosophy from Bolzano to Wittgenstein. His book *Wittgenstein et la philosophie Austro-Allemande* (2012) has recently been published in Italian and Spanish.

Dominik Perler is Professor of Philosophy at Humboldt-Universität, Berlin. His research focuses on medieval and early modern philosophy. He is the author of *Theorien der Intentionalität im Mittelalter* (2002), *Zweifel und Gewissheit. Skeptische Debatten im Mittelalter* (2006), *Transformationen der Gefühle. Philosophische Emotionstheorien 1270–1670* (2011), and most recently editor of *The Faculties: A History* (2015).

Elizabeth S. Radcliffe is Professor of Philosophy at the College of William & Mary. Her research interests lie in Hume on the passions, motivation, practical reasoning, and morality; and in contemporary action theory and the Humean theory of motivation. Radcliffe is past co-editor of *Hume Studies* and editor of *A Companion to Hume* (2008).

Amy M. Schmitter is Professor of Philosophy at the University of Alberta, an editor of the *Canadian Journal of Philosophy*, and co-editor of *Hume Studies*. She works mostly in the history of early modern philosophy (particularly on Descartes and Hume) and the philosophy of art, but has teaching and research interests in a number of areas. Recent publications include works on Descartes, and on passions and affections, as well as a series of articles for the *Stanford Encyclopedia of Philosophy* (2012).

Robert Stern is a Professor in the Department of Philosophy at the University of Sheffield. His publications include *Hegel and the Phenomenology of Spirit* (2nd edn, 2013), *Hegelian Metaphysics* (2009), *Understanding Moral Obligation* (2012), and *Kantian Ethics* (2015).

Fabrice Teroni is Associate Professor in philosophy at the University of Geneva. He works in the philosophy of mind and epistemology, with a marked interest in the philosophy of memory, of perception, and of affective states. He is the author of several articles and monographs on the general theory of emotions (*The Emotions: A Philosophical Introduction*, 2012), on the nature of shame (*In Defense of Shame: The Faces of an Emotion*, 2011), and on memory.

Introduction

Alix Cohen and Robert Stern

It is now commonplace to say that, until recently, philosophical research in the emotions was meagre if not nonnexistent. While for much of the twentieth century philosophers of mind and psychologists tended to neglect the study of emotions, in recent years they have become the focus of vigorous interest in philosophy, in particular through the proliferation of increasingly fruitful exchanges between researches of different stripes. However, less acknowledged is the fact that many if not most of the great philosophers of the tradition have developed highly sophisticated accounts of emotion that often reflect their differing philosophical perspectives.

This volume proposes to investigate the philosophical history of the emotions by bringing together leading historians of philosophy and covering a wide spectrum of schools of thought and epochs, from ancient philosophy up to twentieth-century accounts. It provides resources that should enable its readers to step back from the contemporary perspective and ask fundamental questions that will stimulate philosophical reflection on the topic.

As demonstrated by the contributions in this volume, philosophers and their commentators have used a wide variety of terms to refer to our affective states, from 'affects', 'affections', 'passions', 'feelings', 'sentiments', and 'agitations' to the more contemporary term 'emotions'. The term 'emotion' is of course a rather late invention as far as the history of philosophy is concerned. While there is some disagreement regarding the history of the term, the word itself dates from the sixteenth century for the French and the seventeenth century for the English.[1] Lisa Shapiro and Martin Pickavé talk about a 'family resemblance between a range of terms and their referents', but given the immense diversity of the accounts of emotion presented in this volume, we can safely conclude that the issue of the nature and unity of emotions remains an open question.[2]

A number of contemporary theorists of the emotions lay claim to a historical heritage, trace back their views to historical predecessors, or identify philosophical precursors. Aristotle is of course a common source: he is cited by both Anthony Kenny and Magda Arnold, who are in many ways precursors in their respective fields, and his account of virtue is a focal point of most if not all virtue-based approaches of the emotions.[3] The Stoics are also an important reference in Martha

Nussbaum's account of emotions as judgements, and of cognitivist accounts in general.[4] Hume is often referred to in feeling theories of emotion, as in Richard Wollheim or Irwin Goldstein's hedonic theory.[5] William James remains a ubiquitous inspiration for theories that put the body at the centre of their accounts, as do Jesse Prinz or Jenefer Robinson.[6] Finally, less familiar references are found to Nietzsche and Sartre in Robert Solomon, and Spinoza in Aaron Ben-Ze'ev and Antonio Damasio. Yet overall, as Amélie Rorty already noted over twenty years ago, philosophers of the emotions tend not to think historically about their topic, nor do they show much interest in previous theories.[7]

Nonetheless, as Peter Goldie noted in his Introduction to the *Oxford Handbook of Philosophy of Emotion*, 'how much there is still to be learned from a careful study of the history of philosophical work in the emotions: without this kind of study, the history of philosophy, like history, is bound to repeat itself, often with little or no gain on what has gone before'.[8] This volume is a contribution to this task. Inspired by the burgeoning field of the history of the philosophy of the emotions, it offers the first overview of the emotions in the history of philosophy.[9] Far from being limited to determining how emotions are situated within broader theories of the mind, the essays in this volume tackle a wide range of questions about the nature of emotions as well as their contribution to human life.

However, given the breadth of the material under consideration, the aims of this volume remain limited. It does not aspire to put forward a narrative that would account for the historical development of the notion from ancient philosophy onwards.[10] Nor can it hope to be exhaustive. While we have attempted to cover a wide array of views, many are still missing. As is unavoidable for such collections, exhaustiveness is impossible and a number of issues are too briefly covered if at all. We chose not to emphasize particular periods or topics but rather give our authors some leeway in selecting their angle to tackle this notion within their period of choice.

The collection opens with a paper by Daniel Garber, which sets the scene for what follows by asking what role the historian of philosophy can play in relation to current research. Garber begins by highlighting what he sees as two distinctive features of the recent 'analytic' approach to the emotions as this has developed from the 1960s onwards. First, most of this literature has been largely ahistorical in its approach; and second, it has emerged as a rather self-contained sub-field. It is this second feature which Garber then contrasts with three key early modern philosophers from the tradition: Descartes, Spinoza, and Malebranche. For Descartes, he argues, his account of the passions connected not just to Cartesian natural philosophy, but also to moral issues. The latter is said to be equally true of Spinoza, in a way that had theological implications, while such implications were also important to Malebranche. While Garber does not intend any direct criticism of contemporary analytic philosophy by drawing this contrast in approach, he nonetheless argues that it is suggestive, and may perhaps indicate that we should expect this current work on emotions to be less self-contained than is generally supposed.

Subsequent papers then focus on specific historical thinkers and periods, beginning with a discussion of Aristotle by T. H. Irwin, and particularly his division of the soul into a rational and non-rational part. As Irwin brings out in detail, Aristotle's account of this issue is complex and subtle, and bears importantly on his account of the virtue of character. Irwin defends a reading whereby Aristotle attributes rational desires to the rational part of the soul, and that virtue of character requires the correct rational desires. Irwin also explores how these issues play out in Aquinas's account of the passions, and why they are subjects of virtue. We thus find in Aristotle and Aquinas important contributions to debates concerning the relation between reason and the emotions, and the place of both within theories of the virtues.

This issue is further developed in the next chapter by Dominik Perler, in which he considers the Thomistic position in more detail, and in particular Aquinas's claim that the emotions 'are subject to the commandment of reason and will' and are to be located in the sensory faculty. Perler contrasts this view with the alternative proposed by William of Ockham, who argued for rational emotions. He explores the background to this difference in approach between the thinkers, and the assumptions on which each account relies. He also looks at the implications of the two views, particularly as regards the unity or disunity of the soul, questions concerning responsibility, and the problem of irrational emotions.

In her paper, Lilli Alanen brings us back to a discussion of Spinoza, and in particular to his account of how we can turn passive affects into active emotions, in a way that constitutes a 'therapy of the passions'. Alanen considers how far this picture draws Spinoza into a kind of rationalism that stands in tension with his naturalism, by attributing a rational power to the mind in relation to these affects, which would then seem to set it apart from the body. This difficulty can be addressed, Alanen suggests, if we see this 'therapy' as consisting in forming a clear and distinct idea of the cause of the affect, which while it does not free us from it, may nonetheless give it a different place in the order of our thoughts, and the way it influences our behaviour.

One theme all these papers raise implicitly, alongside others in the collection, is how to categorize the various passions and emotions: this issue is explicitly addressed by Amy Schmitter, particularly in relation to Descartes and Hobbes. As she argues, such categorization issues are usually more than merely taxonomic or matters of intellectual house-keeping, but can tell us a great deal about the assumptions underlying the proposed classifications. She explains how Descartes set 'wonder' at the head of his scheme, while for Hobbes 'glory' received prominence, and she shows the significance they gave to each; both claims were innovative in their time, and likely to strike us as curious today. Schmitter suggests that this indicates how far our understanding of the emotions, and indeed emotions themselves, are mediated by their historical and social context.

A phenomenon that not everyone might classify as an emotion is laughter. In his paper, Laurent Jaffro discusses it as a 'moral emotion', and how this conception of laughter plays an important role in the thought of Shaftesbury and Hutcheson. While arguing that they shared some common ground, Jaffro nonetheless points to a significant difference of emphasis between them: while Hutcheson saw laughter as primarily a response to a value, Shaftesbury focused more on its social role, and how it can be used against 'enthusiasm'. This then raises questions concerning our ability to control laughter, and what norms should govern its use. As Jaffro shows, for both Hutcheson and Shaftesbury, laughter forms an important and interesting part of their conception of a liberal society, but while Hutcheson favours regulation, for Shaftesbury it is seen as a self-regulating form of human interaction, with its own immanent system of normative control.

In her paper, Elizabeth S. Radcliffe turns to Hume, and his account of contrary passions. As Radcliffe shows, Hume provides an elaborate and perhaps not fully consistent taxonomy of the passions, while they are central to his account of sympathy and function according to the principles of Hume's associationist psychology. This enabled him to offer a complex account of how various passions interrelate, and how they also might be used to control one another. In this way, Hume could allow for this control while avoiding rationalism, and at the same time escape the implication that our passions are merely chaotic and disordered.

The question of the relation between reason and the affective states is also at the heart of Kant's philosophy, where Alix Cohen considers this issue as it relates to his account of morality. She counters the common view that he rejects any role for such states, emphasizing instead the significance Kant attached to their cultivation. Cohen considers how Kant made this cultivation an indirect duty, and how doing so is still compatible with his account of freedom. In general, she argues, taking these issues seriously shows how Kant recognized our embodied natures, and what this meant for the proper fulfilment of morality in human terms. To this extent, Kant's account of feelings and emotions can stand as a corrective to a common perception of his ethics as failing to come to terms with these phenomena.

One post-Kantian who helped fuel this perception is Friedrich Schiller, who forms the focus of the article by Christopher Bennett. Bennett argues that in his conception of grace, Schiller recognized what he saw to be an important issue for Kant's theory of freedom: if spontaneous action is action responsive to principles of practical reason, how can this be reconciled with the fact that we sometimes act expressively, out of emotion, as in the case of graceful actions. Bennett shows how Schiller was looking for ways in which to reconcile reason and sensibility, and saw the expression of emotion in these terms, where it is from this reconciliation that his distinctive conception of freedom arises, one that puts pressure on the standard Kantian view while also pointing forward to more rationalistic conceptions of the emotions.

In his paper, Christopher Janaway discusses both Schopenhauer and Nietzsche, contrasting the way each see the relation between emotions and cognition: whereas Schopenhauer argues that the former impair the latter, Nietzsche holds that they are required in order to make cognition possible. Janaway explores the background to this difference, relating to their respective epistemologies and metaphysical views, as well as their conceptions of the emotions. He also considers possible challenges to Nietzsche's account, and how it can best be understood, showing that the position can be made plausible and attractive.

William James is the focus of the next chapter, by Kevin Mulligan, who considers the criticism offered of James's very influential view of the emotions by thinkers in the nineteenth-century Austro-German tradition, particularly Carl Stumpf, Edmund Husserl, and Max Scheler, where all were variously influenced by Franz Brentano. On James's account, emotions are to be identified with the feeling of bodily changes; Mulligan shows how this was challenged by these heirs of Brentano, while contrasting their critique of James with one also offered by Wittgenstein. In doing so, he shows how James's position stood at the centre of these debates, and provides some assessment on the effectiveness of the critique that was offered.

Turning now to the twentieth century, Sacha Golob presents Heidegger's treatment of the emotions against the background of his distinctive challenge to traditional philosophical approaches and thinking. He focuses on Heidegger's account of 'moods', and shows that while his work bypasses some standard issues in accounts of the emotions, it connects with others—particularly the normative significance of the emotions in relation to agency, and the role emotions can play in how we relate to the world around us. Golob considers Heidegger's account of 'anxiety' in this light, and discusses some of the difficulties that it raises.

The next chapter, by Anthony Hatzimoysis, discusses Sartre's position, and in particular his treatment of the emotions in two key texts: the *Sketch for a Theory of the Emotions* of 1939, and *The Imaginary*, which was published the following year. Hatzimoysis shows how each text seems to offer a contrasting view of the emotions—as actions and as perceptions respectively—and thus raises worries about consistency. However, Hatzimoysis argues, Sartre's view in each text is more complex than this implies, while suggesting that they can be made consistent if we think of each work as operating from a different theoretical standpoint: the *Sketch* from the third-person standpoint, and the *Imaginary* from a first-personal one.

The volume concludes with a paper by Fabrice Teroni, which takes us back to William James but also forward to the contemporary analytic tradition, which James did so much to shape and to influence, both positively and negatively. Teroni brings out how far James broke with previous traditional approaches, while we continue to struggle with finding a fully successful alternative to his bodily account in attempting to assimilate emotions to beliefs on the one hand or to perceptions on the other. As Teroni suggests, this remains a live debate, and one which philosophers will doubtless continue to take forward as the history of our engagement with the emotions develops further.[11]

Acknowledgements

This collection of papers is based on the inaugural conference of CHiPhi, the Centre for the History of Philosophy, which took place at the University of York, 13–15 May 2011. The Centre was originally founded by Mike Beaney, Alix Cohen, and Robert Stern to support and enhance research in the history of philosophy in Yorkshire thanks to a grant from the White Rose University Consortium. Although Mike Beaney and Alix Cohen have now left Yorkshire,

CHiPhi continues to flourish under the guidance of Robert Stern together with Keith Allen and Gerald Lang.

This volume would not have been possible without the help of many people. First, we would like to thank Peter Momtchiloff for helping us bring the project to completion—his constant support throughout the process is very much appreciated. We also want to express our gratitude to all the contributors for making our lives much easier by providing excellent contributions. Particular thanks go to Mike Beaney, who worked behind the scenes to organize the original conference in York and supported us throughout. Thanks also go to James Lewis for preparing the index. Finally, we would like to thank the Mind Association, the White Rose Consortium, the British Society for the History of Philosophy, and Oxford University Press for enabling us to organize the inaugural conference on which this volume is partly based.

Notes

1. Contrast, for instance, Thomas Dixon, '"Emotion": The History of a Keyword in Crisis', *Emotion Review* 4 (2012): 338–44, with Amy M. Schmitter, 'Passions, Affections, Sentiments: Taxonomy and Terminology', in *The Oxford Handbook of British Philosophy in the Eighteenth Century*, ed. James A. Harris (Oxford: Oxford University Press), pp. 197–225. While Dixon notes that the modern acceptance of the term as a psychological category dates from the nineteenth century, Schmitter points to Lord Kames's definition of 'emotion' as a mental term in 1762. Baldwin's *Dictionary of Philosophy and Psychology* states that 'The use of the word emotion in English psychology is comparatively modern. It is found in Hume, but even he speaks generally rather of passions or affections. When the word emotion did become current its application was very wide, covering all possible varieties of feeling, except those that are purely sensational in their origin' (J. M. Baldwin, 'Emotion', in *Dictionary of Philosophy and Psychology* (London: Macmillan, 1901), I, p. 316).
2. Lisa Shapiro and Mark Pickavé, 'Introduction', in *Emotion and Cognitive Life in Medieval and Early Modern Philosophy*, ed. Lisa Shapiro and Mark Pickavé (Oxford: Oxford University Press, 2012), p. 7.
3. Magda Arnold, *Emotion and Personality* (New York: Columbia University Press, 1960); A. J. P. Kenny, *Action, Emotion and Will* (New York: Humanities Press, 1963). For virtue-based approaches, see for instance Christine Swanton, *Virtue Ethics: A Pluralistic View* (Oxford: Oxford University Press, 2003) and Linda Zagzebski, *Virtues of the Mind* (Cambridge: Cambridge University Press, 1996).
4. Martha C. Nussbaum, *Upheavals of Thought: The Intelligence of Emotions* (Cambridge: Cambridge University Press, 2001); Robert Solomon, 'Emotions and Choice', in *Explaining Emotions*, ed. Amélie Rorty (Los Angeles: University of California Press, 1980), pp. 251–81.
5. Richard Wollheim, *On the Emotions* (New Haven: Yale University Press, 1999); Irwin Goldstein, 'Are Emotions Feelings? A Further Look at Hedonic Theories of Emotions', *Consciousness and Emotion* 3 (2002): 21–33.
6. Jesse J. Prinz, *Gut Reactions: A Perceptual Theory of the Emotions* (Oxford: Oxford University Press, 2004). Jenefer Robinson, *Deeper than Reason* (Oxford: Oxford University Press, 2007).
7. Amélie Rorty, 'From Passions to Emotions and Sentiments', *Philosophy* 57 (1982): 172.

8. Peter Goldie (ed.), *Oxford Handbook of Philosophy of Emotion* (Oxford: Oxford University Press, 2009), p. 5. Interestingly, as Fabrice Teroni pointed out to us, Aristotle is by far the most cited historical figure in this volume.
9. See in particular Susan James's *Passion and Action: The Emotions in Seventeenth-Century Philosophy* (Oxford: Oxford University Press, 1997), Richard Sorabji's *Emotion and Peace of Mind: From Stoic Agitation to Christian Temptation* (Oxford: Oxford University Press, 2000), and William Reddy's *The Navigation of Feeling: A Framework for the History of Emotions* (Cambridge: Cambridge University Press, 2001), Thomas Dixon's *From Passions to Emotions: The Creation of a Secular Psychological Category* (Cambridge: Cambridge University Press, 2003), Simo Knuuttila, *Emotions in Ancient and Medieval Philosophy* (Oxford: Oxford University Press, 2004), and Lisa Shapiro and Martin Pickavé (eds) *Emotion and Cognitive Life in Medieval and Early Modern Philosophy* (Oxford: Oxford University Press, 2012).
10. Contrast with Thomas Dixon's *From Passions to Emotions* or Solomon's *The Passions: Emotions and the Meaning of Life* (Garden City, N. Y: Doubleday, 1976).
11. Thanks to Anthony Hatzimoysis, Amy Schmitter, and Fabrice Teroni for their helpful feedback on the introduction.

Bibliography

Arnold, Magda. *Emotion and Personality* (New York: Columbia University Press, 1960).

Baldwin, J.M. 'Emotion', in *Dictionary of Philosophy and Psychology* (London: Macmillan, 1901).

Dixon, Thomas. *From Passions to Emotions: The Creation of a Secular Psychological Category* (Cambridge: Cambridge University Press, 2003).

Dixon, Thomas. '"Emotion": The History of a Keyword in Crisis', *Emotion Review* 4 (2012): 338–44.

Goldie, Peter (ed.). *Oxford Handbook of Philosophy of Emotion* (Oxford: Oxford University Press, 2009).

Goldstein, Irwin. 'Are Emotions Feelings? A Further Look at Hedonic Theories of Emotions', *Consciousness and Emotion* 3 (2002): 21–33.

James, Susan. *Passion and Action: The Emotions in Seventeenth-Century Philosophy* (Oxford: Oxford University Press, 1997).

Kenny, A. J. P. *Action, Emotion and Will* (New York: Humanities Press, 1963).

Knuuttila, Simo. *Emotions in Ancient and Medieval Philosophy* (Oxford: Oxford University Press, 2004).

Nussbaum, Martha C. *Upheavals of Thought: The Intelligence of Emotions* (Cambridge: Cambridge University Press, 2001).

Prinz, Jesse J. *Gut Reactions: A Perceptual Theory of the Emotions* (Oxford: Oxford University Press, 2004).

Reddy, William. *The Navigation of Feeling: A Framework for the History of Emotions* (Cambridge: Cambridge University Press, 2001).

Robinson, Jenefer. *Deeper than Reason* (Oxford: Oxford University Press, 2007).

Rorty, Amélie. 'From Passions to Emotions and Sentiments', *Philosophy* 57 (1982): 159–72.

Schmitter, Amy M. 'Passions, Affections, Sentiments: Taxonomy and Terminology', in *The Oxford Handbook of British Philosophy in the Eighteenth Century*, ed. James A. Harris (Oxford: Oxford University Press, 2013), pp. 197–225.

Shapiro, Lisa and Mark Pickavé. 'Introduction', in *Emotion and Cognitive Life in Medieval and Early Modern Philosophy*, ed. Lisa Shapiro and Mark Pickavé (Oxford: Oxford University Press, 2012), pp. 1–8.

Solomon, Robert. *The Passions: Emotions and the Meaning of Life* (Garden City, N.Y.: Doubleday, 1976).

Solomon, Robert. 'Emotions and Choice', in *Explaining Emotions*, ed. Amélie Rorty (Los Angeles: University of California Press, 1980), pp. 251–81.

Sorabji, Richard. *Emotion and Peace of Mind: From Stoic Agitation to Christian Temptation* (Oxford: Oxford University Press, 2000).

Swanton, Christine. *Virtue Ethics: A Pluralistic View* (Oxford: Oxford University Press, 2003).

Wollheim, Richard. *On the Emotions* (New Haven: Yale University Press, 1999).

Zagzebski, Linda. *Virtues of the Mind* (Cambridge: Cambridge University Press, 1996).

1

Thinking Historically/Thinking Analytically

The Passion of History and the History of Passions

Daniel Garber

The main theme of this volume is the history of philosophical thinking about the passions and emotions. This is a subject that needs no justification: like other topics in the history of philosophy, it is of clear and obvious interest to those of us who enjoy living in the past, at least philosophically speaking. But even if we spend most of our time in past centuries, we also live in the present, and teach in departments with colleagues whose intellectual lives are centred on current philosophical thought. And for most of us, that means dealing on a regular basis with current Anglo-American analytic philosophy. This raises an interesting question: how is the study of the passions in the early modern period different from the way in which they are studied now? In what ways is it similar, but in what ways are our ancestors involved in a different kind of project?

Not surprisingly, I will begin historically. Not as one might suspect, though, with the history of the passions in the distant past, but with the question of how the passions came to be established as a subject in current Anglo-American analytic philosophy. This will give us some insight into its current status within the Anglo-American tradition. I will then turn to three central historical figures, Descartes, Spinoza, and Malebranche, and examine some aspects of the way they treated the passions and the emotions. I will end with some thoughts about how the earlier project relates to what is currently understood as the philosophical study of the passions.

Before we begin, though, I would like to make some preliminary remarks. First, I have no rigorous definition of analytic philosophy or the contemporary Anglo-American philosophical tradition. I'm using it here in a rough-and-ready way, as a category more sociological than intellectual, for what's taught in departments of philosophy in the Anglophone world. Though different varieties of analytic philosophy may only bear a family resemblance to one another, I think it is safe to say that we all know it when we see it. That's good enough for me, at least at this first pass. And secondly, I will not make a radical distinction between the study of the passions and the study of the emotions. The distinction will certainly come up from time to time in what follows, particularly in connection with Descartes and Spinoza. But in general I will use the word 'emotions' in a broad enough way so as to include everything generally treated within the domain.

One last preliminary remark. It would be nice if this exercise eventuated in some salient lessons for the philosophy of the passions that we might be able to learn from studying their history. But as an historian of philosophy, I cannot tell my analytic colleagues how to do their business. Instead, I would like to point out what seem to be some interesting and salient differences between the way in which the subject was handled back then, and what I can gather of the present state of the question, at least as it is reflected in the materials that I have examined. I leave it to others to draw conclusions about what lessons should be drawn from historical practice for contemporary theories.

1.1 Theories of the Passions: The Analytic Tradition

The emotions and passions are prominent in philosophical discussions from the ancients on down. But surprisingly enough, interest in the emotions comes very late to Anglo-American analytic philosophy. First, my sources. I began by going where we all do these days, to the *Stanford Encyclopedia of Philosophy*, where there is an excellent review article by Ronald de Sousa, one of the recent philosophers who is a major contributor to the area.[1] His article was most recently revised in January 2013. I also consulted a review article by Peter Goldie ('Emotion') published in the *Philosophy Compass* in 2007,[2] and the introduction to the 2004 edition of Robert Solomon's Oxford University Press anthology, *Thinking about Feeling: Contemporary Philosophers on Emotions.* I also looked again at the important anthology that Amélie Rorty published in 1980, *Explaining Emotions.*[3] Finally, and most recently, there is the essay by Fabrice Téroni published in this volume, 'In Pursuit of Emotional Modes: The Philosophy of Emotion after James'.[4] This is, of course, far from a complete survey of the study of the passions and emotions as it is currently practised in analytic departments of philosophy. But that's not my intention here. For the moment, at least, I would like to chart the beginnings of the study of the passions and emotions as a domain in Anglo-American departments. These sources paint a pretty consistent picture of the pioneers and the conception of the project that emerged out of these early efforts.

Now, in the twentieth century, one can certainly find interest in the emotions in the so-called Continental philosophical tradition, in Heidegger and especially in Sartre. But interest in the emotions in the analytic tradition comes rather late in the game. Solomon writes:

> . . . the philosophy of emotion is by one measure quite recent. In the Anglo-American tradition, the subject of emotion was for a considerable period disreputable, typically dismissed as 'mere subjectivity' or, worse, as nothing by physiology plus dumb sensation. . . . It was only with occasional pieces by Princeton philosopher George Pitcher and Edinburgh philosopher Errol Bedford and then a book by Anthony Kenny that the subject started to become noticed at all, although it was several years more before it began to attract an audience and deserve recognition as a 'field'.[5]

De Sousa largely agrees, noting Bedford and Kenny at the founding, adding Irving Thalberg but forgetting poor George Pitcher.[6] Errol Bedford's founding piece, 'Emotion' was published in the *Proceedings of the Aristotelian Society* in 1957. Pitcher's article, 'Emotion' appeared in *Mind* in 1965, and Kenny's book, *Action, Emotion and Will* was published in 1963. A quick glance at Amélie Rorty's 1980 bibliography confirms this view.[7] Her bibliography is divided into sections: (I) General and Historical Studies; (II) Physiological Studies; (III) Biological Studies; (IV) Psychological Studies; (V) Psychoanalytic Studies; (VI) Anthropological Studies. She ends with '(VII) Philosophical Studies', separated off from the others. Leaving aside Sartre and Stanislavski's *An Actor Prepares* (1936), which somehow insinuated itself into this list, and a few other items like Ryle's *Concept of Mind* that don't really belong, there is almost nothing before 1960 beside Bedford. Between 1960 and 1965 there are only a handful of articles. And then the field begins to take off.

Among the pioneers in the field, Anthony Kenny certainly takes an historical approach to his topic. *Action, Emotion and Will* begins with a chapter focused on Descartes' *Passions de l'âme*, and the rest of the book is heavily leavened with discussions of Aristotle and St Thomas. But Bedford and Pitcher don't show any such interest in the historical background to the question.

Bedford begins as follows: 'The concept of emotion gives rise to a number of philosophical problems. The most important of these, I think, concern the function of statements about emotions and the criteria for their validity.'[8] The paper starts out with a quick reference to McTaggart and Russell, a couple of brief nods at Stout's *Manual of Psychology* and William James's *Principles of Psychology*, and later, a nod to Aristotle in passing.[9] But the emphasis is on refuting what he calls 'the traditional theory of the emotions', the view that 'an emotion is a feeling, or at least an experience of a special type which involves a feeling'.[10] After the introduction, the paper takes a quick turn to the linguistic. Bedford is interested in correcting 'the logical mistake of treating emotion words as names, which leads in turn to a misconception of their function'.[11] He asks: 'Does the truth of such a statement as "He is afraid" logically require the existence of a specific feeling?'[12] The view that he substitutes for the 'traditional theory' is a kind of behavioural view on which statements about emotions interpret behaviour.[13] For example, Bedford notes that the statement 'He raised his voice and began to thump the table' is evidence for the statement 'He was very angry.'[14] The view is not as crude as that might suggest. Bedford ends by noting that 'emotions concepts . . . are not purely psychological: they presuppose concepts of social relationships and institutions, and concepts belonging to systems of judgment, moral, aesthetic and legal'.[15] But it is framed clearly in terms of terms and statements, their referents, and their truth conditions.

George Pitcher's treatment is no more historical than Bedford's is. He begins by referring to the same passage in William James that Bedford cites, and he refers to Bedford as well.[16] Hume enters briefly, but only in order to be quickly dismissed.[17] In Pitcher's essay, Bedford's 'traditional theory', the position that emotion words refer to feelings, becomes the 'Traditional View', now capitalized. Like Bedford, Pitcher advances a dispositional view of emotions, but he also focuses on emotion as having an object (involving an apprehension or misapprehension) and involving an evaluation of that object.[18] Like Bedford, Pitcher focuses on the use of emotion words, and their functions in language, though he employs a complex Wittgensteinian conception of language.[19]

So the discussion of emotion begins. From this acorn, grew a mighty oak. Or, if not a mighty oak, at least a pretty sturdy shoot. Over the intervening years, the study of the emotions has emerged as lively sub-area within contemporary analytic philosophy.

The area as it is presently constituted is nicely summarized in Peter Goldie's 2007 review article of work in the field. Goldie's article is divided into two parts: a presentation of 'the facts that an account of emotion needs to accommodate' and an organized list of the principal theories that have been proposed to account for those facts.[20]

The following are the 'facts':

(1) *Diversity*: Goldie notes here that emotions can be different in duration, in focus and specificity, in complexity, in physical manifestation or lack thereof, in consciousness, in 'degree of development' (mild annoyance vs full anger), their connection with action.
(2) *Evolution*: At least some emotions seem to be connected with human evolution, are shared by all humans in all cultures, and presumably contribute to the survival of the species.
(3) *Beasts and Babies*: Some higher non-human creatures seem capable of emotions, as do babies, and 'an acceptable account of emotion must accommodate this fact'. (This, of course, is connected with the evolutionary 'facts'.)
(4) *Intentionality*: Emotions are characteristically intentional in the sense that they have an object (an object of anger, an object of love, etc.). This seems central.
(5) *Feelings and Phenomenology*: Emotions often (though not always) have a characteristic 'feel'. (There is much debate about how relevant feelings are, as we saw in Bedford and Pitcher.)
(6) *Importance*: 'Your emotions are about things that matter to you.'
(7) *Rationality*: One makes judgments of rationality with respect to emotions. It can be rational to be angry or irrational to be proud.
(8) *Connection to action*: 'Emotions seem to motivate us to do things.'
(9) *Responsibility for emotions*: Some emotions we are responsible for, some we are not. We are not characteristically responsible for surprise, but we can be held responsible for a feeling of loathing of foreigners.[21]

So much for the facts. Goldie divides theories of the emotions into three groups: non-cognitive feeling theories, cognitive theories, and perceptual theories.[22] Non-cognitive feeling theories, as Goldie understands them, are the kinds of theories that Bedford and Pitcher opposed in their articles, theories deriving broadly from William James on which emotions are associated with characteristic non-cognitive feelings. Cognitive theories, on the other hand, see emotions as kinds of appraisals and value judgments. Perceptual theories see emotions as a kind of perception or analogous to perceptions: emotions are reactions to the world around us and the people in it in just the way that our perceptions are.

This is not the place to go more deeply into contemporary theories of the emotions; the literature is vast at this point, and my goal is not to provide yet another general survey of the field.[23] But what I want to emphasize is a very general feature of the current philosophical approaches to the question that the twentieth and twenty-first century history of the field and these surveys suggest. What is notable here is that the theory of the emotions as it has emerged in the last fifty or sixty years constitutes a coherent and autonomous domain of philosophical inquiry with its own phenomena to be explained, problems to be explored, and set of alterative theoretical frameworks. It is a field, or, at least, a subfield of philosophy with a pretty robust identity.[24]

At this point I would like to turn to treatments of the passions among three central figures in the history of philosophy: Descartes, Spinoza, and Malebranche.[25] There are many other historical figures that could be examined in this context, including ancient and medieval figures, not to mention later eighteenth- and nineteenth-century philosophers.[26] But these three will be sufficient to show us an interestingly different way of thinking about the passions and emotions than what we found in the brief examination of recent writings. Unlike what appears to be the dominant trend in recent studies, the passions and emotions as treated in these three figures are deeply intertwined with other intellectual domains and larger philosophical projects, and are not taken to constitute an autonomous discipline.

1.2 Descartes

Let me begin with some remarks about Descartes' account of the emotions in his *Passions de l'âme* (1649).[27] In the letters to an unknown friend that constitute a kind of preface to the work, Descartes tells his friend and the reader what the point of the treatise is: 'My intention was to explain the passions only as a natural philosopher [*en physicien*], and not as a rhetorician or even as a moral philosopher.'[28] It is clear enough what it means to examine the passions as a rhetorician, who wants to teach how to arouse certain passions in his listeners. It is a bit less clear what it means to examine the passions as a moral philosopher, though this is an issue that I want to talk about shortly. But what does Descartes mean when he talks about explaining the passions 'en physicien'?

First, a word about natural philosophy or physics. Any educated person in Descartes' day would have studied natural philosophy or physics as part of the standard 'arts' curriculum, what we would have called the undergraduate years. Physics was usually divided into two parts, the general and the particular. In the Aristotelian framework, the general part of physics included such things as the three principles of physics, matter, form and privation, space and time, the four causes, etc. Special physics began with cosmology, then terrestrial physics, minerals, and ended with living things, plants, animals, and man. The study of living things, though, generally begins with an account of the soul, the principle of life, that which differentiates the dead or inanimate from the living thing. In this way the study of the soul is part of physics, properly speaking.[29]

Now, Descartes' physics was not Aristotelian, of course. But the large-scale structure shared a lot. In his *Principia philosophiae,* after part I, 'The Principles of Human Knowledge', Descartes begins the physics proper in Part II with what might be read as an update of the general part of physics: his account of notions like body, space, time, motion, and the laws of motion. Part III offers a cosmology, and then Part IV a terrestrial physics. Descartes had intended a Part V and a Part VI, where he would deal with living things, including man.[30] Unfortunately, Descartes died before writing them, but in the beginning of Part I of the *Passions de l'âme* we get some of what he might have included in those unwritten sections.[31] On Descartes' view, many of the life functions that the Aristotelians attributed to a soul are really a function of the size, shape, and motion of the smaller parts that make up bodies. Many, but not all: thought, sensation, volition, and reason all pertain to a soul, an immaterial substance that is distinct from body. But the study of this soul and its relation to the organic body presumably remains a part of natural philosophy or physics.

To treat the passions of the soul 'en physicien' presumably means, then, to study the way the soul is acted on by the body to which it is attached: when Descartes talks about passions of the soul, he means them in this literal sense, passions, or actings-upon that are coordinate with actions of the body.[32] Understood broadly, passions include sensations and imaginations as well as emotions, states of the soul that are caused by the sense organs or the activity of the brain, and are 'referred' to things outside of ourselves, like the state that the soul is in when we are perceiving an apple through our senses. But in the *Passions de l'âme*, Descartes particularly concerns himself with those passions that we 'refer' to the soul itself.[33]

An example of the kind of account that Descartes gives in the *Passions de l'âme* is the case of fear. Descartes imagines that we see a fierce animal approaching us. The light reflected from the animal's body forms images on the retina of each of the eyes, which are then transmitted as motion through the optic nerves to the pineal gland in the centre of the brain, where the motions that trace back to the two retinas merge in the gland.[34] This merged impression in the pineal gland has two consequences. On the one hand, it causes a particular passion in the soul, a characteristic kind of feeling:

If... this shape is very strange and terrifying—that is, if it has a close relation to things which have previously been harmful to the body—this arouses the passion of anxiety in the soul, and then that of courage or perhaps fear and terror, depending upon the particular temperament of the body or the strength of the soul, and upon whether we have protected ourselves previously by defense or by flight against the harmful things to which the present impression is related.[35]

But, in addition, it may also cause certain things to happen in the body, for example, it may cause the legs to move in such a way that it flees the animal:

...in certain persons these factors dispose their brain in such a way that some of the spirits reflected from the image formed on the gland proceed from there to the nerves which serve to turn the back and move the legs in order to flee.[36]

It is important here that this motion does not derive in any way from the soul; it is simply a result of the makeup of the body: 'the body may be moved to take flight by the mere disposition of the organs, without any contribution from the soul'.[37] This may suggest that the passion of the soul is just a feeling that accompanies the physiological state of the body that causes the motion of the legs that carries us away from the perceived danger. But the feeling, the passion in the soul has a role to play as well. Descartes writes:

...it must be observed that the principal effect of all the human passions is that they move and dispose the soul to want the things for which they prepare the body. Thus the feeling of fear moves the soul to will [*vouloir*] to flee, that of courage to will [*vouloir*] to fight, and similarly with the others.[38]

The initial perception of the frightful animal directly causes the body to flee in many people. In those people it may also cause the passion of fear in the soul. This passion of fear *in the soul* will then cause *the soul* voluntarily, through its will, to do that which reinforces the initial impulse to flee. This secondary impulse, caused by the passion, which, in turn, influences the volition, is fundamentally different in kind from the non-thinking impulse to flee. (Descartes also envisions that there are others for whom the initial perception of the animal causes them to stand and fight, and then have a passion of courage which reinforces the initial impulse.[39])

For Descartes, then, the point of the passions of the soul is to reinforce through an act of will the impulse that the body naturally is inclined to do by virtue of its physical configuration. This is an example of treating the passions 'en physicien'. Regarded in this way, the project is to understand how the passions of the soul function within the context of living things as understood by Cartesian physics. The project is to understand what they are, and what they do. But it is important to keep in mind the centrality of Cartesian physics in this enterprise. Descartes' account of the passions is fundamentally shaped by the physics in which it sits: *it is an account of the passions appropriate for the Cartesian man*, the union of an incorporeal thinking substance and an extended body governed by mechanistic laws of nature. Taken outside of the context of this conception of man, the enterprise makes no sense. It is precisely because in his larger programme for (natural) philosophy Descartes is introducing a new conception of the human being that he must offer a new conception of the passions, and cannot use the one inherited, through St Thomas, from the Aristotelian tradition.

In Descartes I have emphasized the way in which the Cartesian theory of the passions is situated in the context of the Cartesian natural philosophy. But there is also a moral dimension to the project. At the end of the *Passions de l'âme* Descartes writes:

> Now that we are acquainted with all the passions, we have much less reason for anxiety about them than we had before. For we see that they are all by nature good, and that we have nothing to avoid but their misuse or their excess, against which the remedies I have explained might be sufficient if each person took enough care to apply them.[40]

In the postil of the last section, Descartes asserts that 'it is on the passions alone that all the good and evil of this life depend'. The last sentence of the section, the last sentence of the book then advises that:

> ...the chief use of wisdom lies in its teaching us to be masters of our passions and to control them with such skill that the evils which they cause are quite bearable, and even become a source of joy.[41]

The central goal of Descartes' morality in the *Passions de l'âme* is the proper control of the passions: good in themselves, when excessive they lead to trouble. In this way the treatment of the passions 'en physicien' in Descartes is in the service of a moral project. It is interesting here to remember Descartes' tree of philosophy, whose roots are metaphysics, whose trunk is physics, and whose branches, growing out of the trunk, include morals.[42] The account of the passions grows out of the trunk of physics; it yields fruit in morals when we come to understand the true good in this life. But again, I would want to emphasize that the tree of philosophy in question is the centrepiece of the *Cartesian* garden, and the ethics in question a fruit that issues from a *Cartesian* conception of philosophy and the world: it is an ethics for the Cartesian man.

1.3 Spinoza

The moral dimension of the theory of the passions and the emotions is central in Spinoza's account. First a word about vocabulary and about texts. While Descartes does use the term 'emotion' with some regularity in the *Passions de l'âme* and other writings, his focus is on the passions.[43] An emotion (*émotion*, *commotio*) is a general term that designates 'an alteration or motion excited in the humours, spirits or the mind', to quote the definition given in the 1762 Académie Française dictionary. (This is the oldest dictionary definition I could find.) But Descartes' focus is on the passions strictly speaking: those states of mind (emotions) that are the consequences of something external acting on the mind. Spinoza's usual term in the *Ethica* is 'affect' ('*affectus*'). While it could certainly be translated as 'emotion', it is usually translated as 'affect'. Occasionally he uses the term '*commotio animi*', or what is more naturally interpreted as 'emotion'.[44] But Spinoza makes a clear distinction between active affects (actions) and passive affects (passions, strictly speaking).[45]

I noted that Spinoza's account of the affects is connected with his moral philosophy. In fact, it is, in a way, the centrepiece.[46] We should of course remember that the title of

Spinoza's main philosophical work is the *Ethica*. As in Descartes, the ethical project is conceived of in terms of attaining a highest good. The ethical project conceived in this way is set out most clearly in the opening sections of the *Tractatus de intellectus emendatione* (TdIE). The TdIE begins as follows:

> After experience had taught me that all the things which regularly occur in ordinary life are empty and futile, and I saw that all the things which were the cause or object of my fear had nothing of good or bad in themselves, except insofar as [my] mind was moved by them, I resolved at last to try to find out whether there was anything which would be the true good, capable of communicating itself, and which alone would affect the mind, all others being rejected—whether there was something which, once found and acquired, would continuously give me the greatest joy, to eternity.[47]

After considering wealth, honour, and sensual pleasure, Spinoza finally finds what he is looking for:

> But love toward the eternal and infinite thing feeds the mind with a joy entirely exempt from sadness. This is greatly to be desired, and to be sought with all our strength.[48]

This, in brief, is the goal of the *Ethica*: to lead us to this highest kind of love, a love of God, what he calls in E5 beatitude.

And how is this state to be attained? For Spinoza, beatitude comes through understanding: it is through having more and more adequate ideas that we attain this state of beatitude. But having adequate ideas, for Spinoza, is the same as being active as opposed to being passive, having power as opposed to lacking power, having virtue as opposed to lacking virtue. All of these concepts travel together for Spinoza: having adequate ideas, having power, acting, and having inadequate ideas, lacking power, and being acted upon.[49] In a number of texts, Spinoza characterizes the path that we have to travel to beatitude in terms of coming closer and closer to a model of human nature that we choose for ourselves. In the preface to E4, Spinoza advances the thesis that 'good' and 'evil' must be understood in relation to a model that we have in mind in terms of which things are judged by the extent to which the agree with or fail to agree with the model. He then continues:

> For because we desire to form an idea of man, as a model of human nature which we may look to, it will be useful to us to retain these same words with the meaning I have indicated. In what follows, therefore, I shall understand by good what we know certainly is a means by which we may approach nearer and nearer to the model of human nature that we set before ourselves. By evil, what we certainly know prevents us from becoming like that model. Next, we shall say that men are more perfect or imperfect, insofar as they approach more or less near to this model.[50]

Later in E4 this model of human nature is plausibly identified with what Spinoza calls the 'free man', 'i.e., one who lives according to the dictate of reason alone', that is, one all of whose ideas are adequate.[51]

And here is where Spinoza's account of the affects enters. Before undergoing Spinoza's programme, we are subject to the passions. Part III of the *Ethica* is called 'On the

Origin and Nature of the Affects', and part IV, 'Of Human Bondage, and the Powers of the Affects'. Spinoza's account of the passions is very different from Descartes'. Descartes is concerned with passions of the *soul*: he conceives of the soul as a substance distinct from the body, and the passions of the soul are the result of something bodily acting on the soul. For Spinoza, on the other hand, the passions are passions of the *person as a whole*, whether conceived of as body or as mind (where, of course, the mind is the idea of body). Passions are actings-upon due to something impinging on the person from the outside, and causing changes.

Spinoza's account of the passions is grounded in his idea of *conatus*: 'Each thing, as far as it can, strives to persevere in its being.'[52] This striving is basic, and is what we call will, appetite, or desire:

> When this striving is related only to the Mind, it is called Will; but when it is related to the Mind and Body together, it is called Appetite. This Appetite, therefore, is nothing but the very essence of man, from whose nature there necessarily follow those things that promote his preservation. And so man is determined to do those things. Between appetite and desire there is no difference, except that desire is generally related to men insofar as they are conscious of their appetite. So *desire* can be defined *as appetite together with consciousness of the appetite*.[53]

Two other passions that are especially important to Spinoza are joy and sadness:

> We see, then, that the Mind can undergo great changes, and pass now to a greater, now to a lesser perfection. These passions, indeed, explain to us the affects of Joy and Sadness. By *Joy*, therefore, I shall understand in what follows that *passion by which the Mind passes to a greater perfection*. And by *Sadness*, that *passion by which it passes to a lesser perfection*.[54]

It is in terms of these three passions that all the others can be explained: 'apart from these three I do not acknowledge any other primary affect'. For I shall show in what follows that the rest arise from these three.'[55]

Now, some passions are better than others. It is obvious that joy is better than sadness, for example, though they are both passions. But, Spinoza argues, we should seek to eliminate the passions as much as is possible. Corresponding to at least some of the *passive* affects (passions), there are *active* affects: 'Apart from the Joy and Desire that are passions, there are other affects of Joy and Desire that are related to us insofar as we act.'[56] These active affects correspond to adequate ideas. And insofar as we are guided by reason, we should seek more and more adequate ideas: 'What we strive for from reason is nothing but understanding: nor does the Mind, insofar as it uses reason, judge anything else useful to itself except what leads to understanding.'[57] And therefore, insofar as we are guided by reason, we should seek to transform passive affects into active affects as much as possible. This leads us directly to the intellectual love of God that constitutes beatitude, and is our greatest good. This is one of the main goals of the *Ethica*. He summarizes this theme in a passage from E5, just before the famous discussion of the eternity of the mind:

> ...the power of the Mind is defined by knowledge alone, whereas lack of power, *or* passion, is judged solely by the privation of knowledge, i.e., by that through which ideas are called inadequate. From this it follows that that Mind is most acted on, of which inadequate ideas constitute the greatest part....On the other hand, that Mind acts most, of which adequate ideas constitute the greatest part...From what we have said, we easily conceive what clear and distinct knowledge...can accomplish against the affects. Insofar as the affects are passions, if clear and distinct knowledge does not absolutely remove them..., at least it brings it about that they constitute the smallest part of the Mind....And then it begets a Love toward a thing immutable and eternal..., which we really fully possess..., and which therefore cannot be tainted by any of the vices which are in ordinary Love, but can always be greater and greater..., and occupy the greatest part of the Mind..., and affect it extensively.[58]

Let me offer a couple of brief remarks on this. Although the goal in principle is to eliminate *all* of the passions and become completely active, this is impossible. When he wrote the TdIE, Spinoza claimed that 'man conceives a human nature much stronger and more enduring than his own, and at the same time sees that nothing prevents his acquiring such a nature'.[59] But by the time of the *Ethica*, he came to realize that only an infinite creature could hope to have all and only adequate ideas: 'It is impossible that a man should not be a part of Nature, and that he should be able to undergo no changes except those which can be understood through his own nature alone, and of which he is the adequate cause.'[60] And secondly, I have left out another important theme that leads us to convert passions into active affects. Basic to Spinoza's politics is the idea that only humans are of use to other humans, and they are more so to the extent that they are alike. And they are alike to the extent that they have active affects (adequate ideas) and eliminate the passions (inadequate ideas). For the sake of a stable society, we should all seek to transform our passions into active affects, and help and encourage others to do so too. This is connected to the other theme in an interesting and deep way. Since we know that we need the protection and comforts of society in order to be able to perfect the intellect and reach beatitude, we want to do that which will encourage others to perfect their intellects as well: 'The good which everyone who seeks virtue wants for himself, he also desires for other men; and this Desire is greater as his knowledge of God is greater [i.e., as he is more rational].'[61]

In this way, to understand Spinoza's account of the passions and emotions, we must understand it as part of a larger programme. His interest is not in the passions and emotions in themselves, but as they contribute to this larger programme. Spinoza's philosophy takes us on a dramatic path from bondage to beatitude, from wandering in the desert to the realization of our greatest good, the intellectual love of God that gives us true happiness. The study of the passions and emotions is important to Spinoza largely in the context of this central Spinozistic project.[62]

Before leaving Spinoza, let me add one further observation.[63] One of the interesting and surprising doctrines on the emotions that Spinoza advances in the *Ethica* is about humility: 'Humility is not a virtue, that is, it does not arise from reason.'[64] This follows almost directly from the very definition of humility Spinoza offers: 'Humility is a sadness which arises from the fact that a man considers his own lack of power.'[65] Since a sadness is 'that passion by which [the mind] passes to a lesser perfection', it is a passion, and not an action, a consequence of an inadequate idea and not an adequate idea.[66] And thus, it is something that Spinoza thinks we should eliminate, if we are to seek to be like the free man, the model of human nature that he thinks that we are emulating. At the same time, though, for the rationally imperfect many, those who may be unable to attain the full rationality that the philosopher seeks, humility (and other passive emotions) have their place. In a passage slightly later in the text Spinoza writes:

Because men rarely live from the dictate of reason, these two affects, Humility and Repentance, and in addition, Hope and Fear, bring more advantage than disadvantage. So since men must sin, they ought rather to sin in that direction. If weak-minded men were all equally proud, ashamed of nothing, and afraid of nothing, how could they be united or restrained by any bonds? The mob is terrifying, if unafraid. So it is no wonder that the Prophets, who considered the common advantage, not that of the few, commended Humility, Repentance, and Reverence so greatly. Really, those who are subject to these affects can be guided far more easily than others, so that in the end they may live from the guidance of reason, i.e., may be free and enjoy the life of the blessed.[67]

Though the philosopher should avoid humility and other related emotions, there is a way in which they should be encouraged in the mob.

Julie Cooper discusses the critique of these passages among contemporaries. (She notes especially Pierre Poiret, a French Protestant, François Lamy, a Benedictine Monk, and the Dutch Cartesian theologian, Christoph Wittich.)[68] Nor should such critical reactions be surprising. As Cooper emphasizes, humility is a central Christian virtue. Looking at Spinoza's theory of the passions from the viewpoint of these critics reminds us of what was at stake with a theory of the passions in that period: Spinoza is not presenting a neutral scientific theory, but entering into a charged theological context. What he is doing, in essence, is denying the importance of a central theological doctrine in Christianity, and arguing that humility (and by implication, Christianity itself) is not a genuine good, but only a means of controlling the unruly masses.

1.4 Malebranche

The theological dimension is also very important for understanding the theory of the passions that Nicolas Malebranche advances in book V of his *Recherche de la vérité*.[69] Right from the opening sentences of Malebranche's Preface, it is clear that there is a theological agenda in the book:

The mind of man is by its nature situated, as it were, between its Creator and corporeal creatures, for, according to Saint Augustine, there is nothing but God above it and nothing but bodies below it. But as the mind's position above all material things does not prevent it from being joined to them, and even depending in a way on a part of matter, so the infinite distance between the sovereign Being and the mind of man does not prevent it from being immediately joined to it in a very intimate way.[70]

As a result of Original Sin, Malebranche argues, our minds have become especially closely connected with our bodies:

...Original Sin has so strengthened our soul's union with our body that it seems to us that these two parts of us are but one and the same substance...[71]

Malebranche, of course, wants us to return to the prelapsarian state, loosen the connection by which the mind is bound with the body, and return to the proper connection between the mind and God. For Malebranche, this can be done by withdrawing the mind from the senses, and returning to reason and clear and distinct perception:

The body... fills the mind with so many sensations that it becomes incapable of knowing things that are at all hidden. Corporeal vision dazzles and distracts the mind's vision so that there is great difficulty in clearly seeing a given truth with the soul's eyes while we are using the body's eyes to know it. This shows that it is only by the mind's attention that any truths are discovered are any sciences acquired, because the mind's attention is in fact only its conversion and return to God, who is our sole Master...[72]

In this way, Descartes' fundamental rule to believe only that which we can clearly and distinctly perceive turns out to be a theological maxim by which we are enjoined to turn our minds away from the body, and towards God.

But there is another way in which we can turn away from the corrupt corporeal world to which we have become bound in Original Sin, and return the mind to its proper connection with God: through the rejection of the passions. Malebranche defines the passions as follows: 'The passions of the soul are impressions from the Author of nature that incline us toward loving our body and all that might be of use in its preservation.'[73] As in Descartes' conception of the passions, they are given to us in order to 'incline... us to will what seems to be useful to the body'.[74] Thus they make us slaves of the body. But, Malebranche argues,

Only God makes us see clearly that we should yield to what He wishes of us; therefore, we should be slaves of Him alone. There is no certainty in the charms and endearments, in the threats and terror that the passions cause in us; they are only confused and obscure sensations to which we should not yield. We must wait until a purer light illumines us, until this time of passion passes away and God speaks. We must withdraw into ourselves and there search out Him who never leaves us and who enlightens us always.... But our passions continually draw us away from ourselves, and by their clatter and shadows they prevent us from being instructed by His voice and illumined by His light.[75]

In that way, the passions bind us to the material world, and prevent us from reuniting with God and returning to the prelapsarian state.

In this way, Malebranche's account of the passions is closely linked to his central philosophical and theological project: it is an account of the passions that will help us to understand how it is that we have become separated from God. More than that, it is an account of the passions that will help lead us *back* to God.

1.5 Some Concluding Thoughts

I began with a few words about what the contemporary theory of the passions looks like, before my brief excursus into a few historical discussions of the passions. At this point I would like to venture some comparisons between the two.

Modern theorists seem to take it for granted that the emotions and passions form a kind of autonomous domain of phenomena that can be studied on their own terms. Certainly it bears connections with other domains, such as psychology and psychoanalysis, or moral theory. But even so, there is such a subject as the theory of the passions which can be pursued as its own kind of specialty in philosophy. That is to say, the domain of the theory of the passions seems to be largely independent of other philosophical projects: it is a philosophical project of its own.[76]

But one of the very interesting facts about the earlier accounts that we briefly examined is precisely the way in which the accounts of the passions were thoroughly interconnected with other questions in other domains, and with the larger projects that the philosophers we have been examining were undertaking. For Descartes, the account of the passions of the soul is thoroughly connected with his radical new conception of the human soul and body, and how it fits into his radically new conception of the physical world. In a very related way, it is also connected with his revisionist conception of what constitutes moral philosophy. For Descartes, the theory of the passions constitutes a central piece of the explanation of how the science of morals fits into the account he gives of the tree of knowledge, where the science of moral philosophy is one of the branches attached to the trunk of the tree of philosophy, which is physics. Though influenced by Descartes, to be sure (and Hobbes as well), Spinoza's account of the passions and affects (emotions) bears a different relation to his larger programme for philosophy, though it is, in its way, as integrated as it is in Descartes' programme. For Spinoza, the account of the passions and their transformation into actions is a central part of the developmental narrative that forms the core of his thought. They are interesting not in themselves, but in the role that they play in the liberation narrative at the heart of his thought, the path from human bondage to beatitude. They are not a neutral and autonomous domain of inquiry, as they seem to be in contemporary analytic thought, but very much a charged part of the philosopher's journey to enlightenment and genuine happiness. This is not altogether unlike the role that the passions and emotions play in Malebranche's *Recherche de la vérité*, where they are an important part of the Augustinian drama in which we are trying to free ourselves from the body and return to the close connection with God that constitutes our prelapsarian state. In this way, the theories of the passions we have been examining are very closely linked with very particular historical projects in the figures involved: we are dealing with accounts of the passions appropriate to a Cartesian, or Spinozistic, or Malebranchist philosophical project.

What does this all mean? What consequences can we draw from this study for contemporary theories of the passions? As I said at the beginning, as a simple historian of philosophy I hesitate to tell my analytic colleagues how to pursue their projects. But I would like to end with a question. The earlier theories of the passions and emotions we examined are embedded in a rich web of philosophical context; modern theories are more autonomous. Descartes, Spinoza, and Malebranche are interested in the passions and emotions not in and of themselves, but as part of larger philosophical projects; contemporary theorists, on the other hand, seem to regard the theory of the passions as an autonomous philosophical problem, one that can be treated independently of any larger project. Why? Is the philosophy of the passions as treated by our contemporaries really as autonomous as it appears to be? What is it that is different about contemporary discussions that allows us now to treat the domain in a coherent theoretical way without having larger metaphysical, or ethical, or theological questions relevant to the issues? The contrast between the historical accounts of the passions that we have examined and contemporary accounts suggest that it may be interesting to look for the larger context and connections that may be hidden in our contemporary theories.

When investigating historical figures and their ideas, the historian of philosophy naturally turns to larger intellectual (and sometimes social and political) context to make intelligible ideas that may be obscure to us. But even we historians swim in the same waters as our analytical colleagues in the departments in which we teach. In this way, our common context of philosophical assumptions can be largely invisible to us. Their philosophical accounts of the passions may well bring with them philosophical assumptions and connections with other philosophical programmes that we cannot see simply because we are too close to them, that is, because we take them for granted without even noticing that we do. It is one virtue of history that it may lead us to look at ourselves in a different, and, in a sense, more analytic way.

Notes

1. Ronald de Sousa, 'Emotion', in The Stanford Encyclopedia of Philosophy (Spring 2014 edition; revised January 31, 2013), ed. Edward N. Zalta, URL = <http://plato.stanford.edu/archives/spr2014/entries/emotion/>.
2. Peter Goldie, 'Emotion', *Philosophy Compass* 2 (2007), pp. 928–38. Robert C. Solomon, ed., *Thinking about Feeling: Contemporary Philosophers on Emotions* (Oxford: Oxford University Press, 2004).
3. Amélie O. Rorty, ed., *Explaining Emotions* (Berkeley: University of California Press, 1980).

4. This volume, pp. 291–313.
5. Solomon, *Thinking about Feeling*, p. 3. See Errol Bedford, 'Emotions', *Proceedings of the Aristotelian Society* N.S. 57 (1956–57), pp. 281–304; George Pitcher 'Emotion', *Mind* N.S. 74 (1965), pp. 326–46; and Anthony Kenny, *Action, Emotion and Will* (London: Routledge and Kegan Paul, 1963).
6. See de Sousa, 'Emotion', pp. 4–5 and Irving Thalberg, *Perception, Emotion, and Action: a Component Approach* (Oxford: Blackwell, 1977).
7. See Rorty, *Explaining Emotions*, pp. 537–43.
8. Bedford, 'Emotions', p. 281.
9. Ibid., pp. 281, 282, 294.
10. Ibid., p. 281. It is referred to as the 'traditional theory' on p. 291.
11. Ibid., p. 282.
12. Ibid., p. 283.
13. Ibid., p. 288.
14. Ibid.
15. Ibid., pp. 303–4.
16. Pitcher, 'Emotion', pp. 326, 329.
17. Ibid., pp. 330–1.
18. Ibid., pp. 333–4.
19. Ibid., pp. 342ff.
20. De Sousa, 'Emotion' is similar, though he focuses on the theories at much greater length and leaves the facts to fend for themselves.
21. Goldie, 'Emotion', pp. 928–33.
22. Ibid., pp. 933–6. De Sousa, 'Emotion', divides them a bit more finely, but that won't matter for our purposes.
23. Téroni, 'Pursuit', provides a good guide to the most recent material, organized around responses to problems that arise out of William James's account of the emotions. Téroni's essay takes up many of the earlier twentieth-century figures I mentioned, including Bedford, Pitcher, Kenny, and Thalberg in this context.
24. This is not to deny that some philosophical discussions of the emotions do connect these questions with other fields, particularly the cognitive sciences. Even so, the literature I have discussed here strongly suggests that it is generally assumed that there are some characteristically *philosophical* questions we can ask about the emotions, even if they can be illuminated by other domains.
25. For some general background on the question of the emotions and passions in seventeenth century philosophy, see, e.g. Susan James, *Passion and Action: The Emotions in Seventeenth-Century Philosophy* (Oxford: Oxford University Press, 1997) and Amy Schmitter, '17th and 18th Century Theories of the Emotions', in *Stanford Encyclopedia of Philosophy*, ed. E. N. Zalta (Spring 2014 edition; revised October 15, 2010). URL=http://plato.stanford.edu/archives/spr2014/entries/emotions-17th18th/. On the relations among these three particular philosophers, see Paul Hoffman, 'Three Dualist Theories of the Passions', *Philosophical Topics* 19 (1991): 153–200.
26. Indeed, at the same time as there has been an increase of interest in the emotions among contemporary analytic philosophers, historians of philosophy have been increasingly attending to the views of figures from past centuries. For a sampling of some of the recent

work on the emotions in medieval and early-modern philosophy, see, e.g., Martin Pickavé and Lisa Shapiro, eds, *Emotion and Cognitive Life in Medieval and Early Modern Philosophy* (Oxford: Oxford University Press, 2012).

27. Denis Kambouchner, *L'homme des passions: commentaire sur Descartes*. 2 vols (Paris: Albin Michel, 1995) provides an extensive commentary on Descartes' *Passions de l'âme*. But see also Deborah J. Brown, *Descartes and the Passionate Mind* (Cambridge: Cambridge University Press, 2006), Lisa Shapiro, 'Descartes's *Passions of the Soul*'. *Philosophy Compass* 1 (2006): 268–78, Gary Hatfield, 'The *Passions of the Soul* and Descartes's Machine Psychology', *Studies in History and Philosophy of Science* 38 (2007): 1–35, and the supplement to Schmitter, '17th and 18th Century Theories', 'Descartes on the Emotions'. See also Amy Shmitter's essay, '"I've Got a Little List": Classification, Explanation, and the Focal Passions in Descartes and Hobbes', this volume, pp. 109–29.
28. René Descartes, *Œuvres de Descartes*, ed. C. Adam and P. Tannery, 11 vols (Paris: J. Vrin, 1996), vol. XI, p. 326. (Abbreviated by 'AT', with references given by volume number (in Roman) and page number (in Arabic).)
29. See, for example, the treatment in the 'Physica' in Eustachius à Sancto Paulo, *Summa philosophiae quadripartita* (Paris: Carolinus Chastellian, 1609), a typical scholastic textbook that was widely used both in Catholic and Protestant countries.
30. See *Principia* 4.188.
31. See *Passions de l'âme* §§ 4–26. There is a somewhat fuller account of the functioning of the human body in *La description du corps humain* (AT XI 223ff), left incomplete at the time of Descartes' death. Both of these accounts, of course, draw on material in the *Traité de l'homme*, part of the early *Le monde*, which Descartes abandoned in 1633, when he learned of the condemnation of Galileo.
32. *Passions de l'âme* § 1.
33. *Passions de l'âme* §§ 19–29.
34. See Descartes, *Traité de l'homme*, AT XI 175–76, translated in René Descartes, *The Philosophical Writings of Descartes*, eds and trans. John Cottingham, Robert Stoothoff, Dugald Murdoch, and Anthony Kenny (vol. 3), 3 vols (Cambridge: Cambridge University Press, 1984–1991), vol. I pp. 105–6. (*Philosophical Writings* is abbreviated by 'CSM' followed by volume number (in Roman) and page number (in Arabic).)
35. *Passions de l'âme* § 36, trans. CSM I, 342.
36. Ibid.
37. *Passions de l'âme* § 38, trans. CSM I, 343.
38. *Passions de l'âme* § 40, trans. CSM I, 343.
39. See *Passions de l'âme* §§ 39–40.
40. *Passions de l'âme* § 211, trans. CSM I, 403.
41. *Passions de l'âme* § 212, trans. CSM I 404.
42. *Les principes de la philosophie*, 'Lettre de l'autheur...' AT IXB 14, trans. CSM I 186.
43. See, e.g., *Passions de l'âme* §§ 27, 28, 29, 46, etc; *Principia* 1.48, etc.
44. In his widely used translation of the *Ethica* in Benedictus de Spinoza, *The Collected Works of Spinoza*, 2 vols., ed. and trans. E.M. Curley (Princeton: Princeton University Press, 1985), E.M. Curley renders it in that way.
45. I should note before digging into Spinoza that I will stick to the *Ethica*. The emotions and passions are central to the *Korte Verhandeling* as well, an early work that tracks many of the

themes of the later *Ethica*, but the treatment there is interestingly different from the treatment in the *Ethica*, though the differences are not relevant to the points that I would like to make.

46. For general accounts of Spinoza on the affects, see, e.g., Michael Della Rocca, 'Spinoza's Metaphysical Psychology', in *The Cambridge Companion to Spinoza*, ed. D. Garrett (Cambridge: Cambridge University Press, 1996), pp. 192–266; Genevieve Lloyd, 'Rationalizing the Passions: Spinoza on Reason and the Passions', in *The Soft Underbelly of Reason: The Passions in the Seventeenth Century*, ed. S. Gaukroger (London and New York: Routledge,1998), pp. 34–45; Steven Nadler, *Spinoza's* Ethics*: An Introduction* (Cambridge: Cambridge University Press, 2006), ch. 7; and Michael LeBuffe, 'The Anatomy of the Passions', in *Cambridge Companion to Spinoza's Ethics*, ed. O. Koistinen (Cambridge: Cambridge University Press, 2009), pp. 188–222. See also Lilli Alanen, 'Affects and Ideas in Spinoza's Therapy of Passions', in this volume, pp. 83–108.
47. TdIE § 1. All translations of Spinoza are taken from Spinoza, *Collected Works*.
48. TdIE § 10.
49. See E3p1, E3p3, E4d8, E4p23, E4p24. References to the *Ethica* are given in standard form. 'E3' indicates part 3, 'p1' proposition 1, 'p1d' the demonstration of proposition 1, etc.
50. E4pref. See also TdIE § 13. Below we shall return to this passage from the TdIE and note a crucial difference between the context of the TdIE and that of the *Ethica*.
51. E4p67d. It should be noted that the identification of the model of human nature in E4pref with the free man who appears at the end of E4 is somewhat controversial. For an alternative view, see, e.g., Steven Nadler, 'On Spinoza's "Free Man"', *Journal of the APA* 1 (2015): 103–20.
52. E3p6.
53. E3p10s.
54. E3p11s.
55. Ibid.
56. E3p58.
57. E4p26.
58. E5p20s.
59. TdIE § 13.
60. E4p4.
61. E4p37. The argument of this paragraph is summarized in E4p18s and demonstrated in the propositions following.
62. Here I differ fundamentally from the approach to the passions taken by Michael Della Rocca. He writes: 'Spinoza is a metaphysician. I emphasize this fact here... because one can discover what is most exciting and important about Spinoza's psychology only by seeing it as emerging from his metaphysics.' (Della Rocca, 'Metaphysical Psychology', p. 192). I would argue, instead, that while the metaphysics is important, it is secondary to a project focused on understanding the proper way in which to live our lives, what he means by an ethics. It is in the context of this project that we must understand his account of the affects, I argue.
63. My comments here draw on very illuminating discussions with Julie Cooper, and on her recent book, *Secular Powers: Humility in Modern Political Thought* (Chicago: University of Chicago Press, 2013). I thank her for calling to my attention some usually overlooked aspects of Spinoza's thought.
64. E4p53.
65. E4p53d.

66. E4p11s.
67. E4p54s.
68. See Cooper, *Secular Powers*, ch. 3 for a detailed development of her reading.
69. The literature on Malebranche on the passions and emotions is rather small. For some accounts, see, Geneviève Rodis-Lewis, *Nicolas Malebranche* (Paris: Presses universitaires de France, 1963), pp. 218–26; Craig Walton, *De la recherche du bien: A Study of Malebranche's Science of Ethics* (The Hague: Nijhoff, 1972), ch. 5; and Sean Greenberg, 'Malebranche on the Passions: Biology, Morality and the Fall,' *British Journal for the History of Philosophy* 18 (2010): 191–207.
70. Nicolas Malebranche, *Œuvres complètes*, ed. A. Robinet, 22 vols (Paris: Vrin, 1954–84), vol. I, p. 9. (The *Œuvres complètes* is abbreviated 'MOC,' and references are given to volume number (in Roman) and page number (in Arabic).) The translation is from Nicolas Malebranche, *The Search after Truth* and *Elucidations of the Search after Truth*, ed. and trans. Thomas Lennon and Paul J. Olscamp (Cambridge: Cambridge University Press, 1997), p. xxxiii. (The *Search* is abbreviated 'MLO.')
71. MOC I 11; trans. MLO, p. xxxiv.
72. MOC I 17; trans. MLO, p. xxxviii.
73. MOC II 128; trans. MLO, p. 338.
74. MOC II 128–9; trans. MLO, p. 338.
75. MOC II 158–9; trans. MLO, p. 357.
76. This, in a way, is characteristic of much of mainstream analytical philosophy more generally, which, certain naturalists aside, sees philosophy as a kind of autonomous domain, distinct from the special sciences and the other humanities. In this respect, I think it differs quite interestingly from the subject as it was practised in the early-modern period, for example, where what we consider philosophical questions and questions in what we consider natural science were of a piece.

Bibliography

Bedford, Errol. 'Emotions', *Proceedings of the Aristotelian Society* N.S. 57 (1956–57): 281–304.

Brown, Deborah J. *Descartes and the Passionate Mind* (Cambridge: Cambridge University Press, 2006).

Cooper, Julie E. *Secular Powers: Humility in Modern Political Thought* (Chicago: University of Chicago Press, 2013).

de Sousa, Ronald. 'Emotion', *The Stanford Encyclopedia of Philosophy* (Spring 2014 edition; revised January 31, 2013), ed. E. N. Zalta, URL = <http://plato.stanford.edu/archives/spr2014/entries/emotion/>. [Pagination is in the downloaded PDF version.]

Della Rocca, Michael. 'Spinoza's Metaphysical Psychology', in *Cambridge Companion to Spinoza*, ed. Don Garrett (Cambridge: Cambridge University Press, 1996), pp. 192–266.

Descartes, René. *Oeuvres de Descartes*, 11 vols., Charles Adam and Paul Tannery (eds.) (Paris: J. Vrin, 1996). Abbreviated 'AT'. References are given by volume number (in Roman) and page number (in Arabic).

Descartes, René. *The Philosophical Writings of Descartes*. 3 vols., John Cottingham, Robert Stoothoff, Dugald Murdoch (eds.), vol. 3, Anthony Kenny (ed.). (Cambridge: Cambridge University Press, 1984–1991). Abbreviated 'CSM'.

Eustachius à Sancto Paulo, *Summa philosophiae quadripartita* (Paris: Carolinus Chastellian, 1609).

Goldie, Peter. 'Emotion', *Philosophy Compass* 2 (2007): 928–38.

Greenberg, Sean. 'Malebranche on the Passions: Biology, Morality and the Fall', *British Journal for the History of Philosophy* 18 (2010): 191–207.

Hatfield, Gary. 'The *Passions of the Soul* and Descartes's Machine Psychology,' *Studies in History and Philosophy of Science* 38 (2007): 1–35.

Hoffman, Paul. 'Three Dualist Theories of the Passions', *Philosophical Topics* 19 (1991): 153–200.

James, Susan. *Passion and Action: The Emotions in Seventeenth-Century Philosophy* (Oxford: Oxford University Press, 1997).

Kambouchner, Denis. *L'homme des passions: commentaire sur Descartes*, 2 vols (Paris: Albin Michel, 1995).

Kenny, Anthony. *Action, Emotion and Will* (London: Routledge and Kegan Paul, 1963).

LeBuffe, Michael. 'The Anatomy of the Passions', in *Cambridge Companion to Spinoza's Ethics*, ed. Olli Koistinen (Cambridge: Cambridge University Press, 2009), pp. 188–222.

Lloyd, Genevieve. 'Rationalizing the Passions: Spinoza on Reason and the Passions', in *The Soft Underbelly of Reason: The Passions in the Seventeenth Century*, ed. Steven Gaukroger (London and New York: Routledge, 1998), pp. 34–45.

Malebranche, Nicolas. *Œuvres complètes*, ed. A. Robinet. 22 vols (Paris: Vrin, 1958–84). Abbreviated 'MOC'.

Malebranche, Nicolas. *The Search after Truth* and *Elucidations of the Search after Truth*, ed. and trans. T. Lennon and P. J. Olscamp (Cambridge: Cambridge University Press, 1997). Abbreviated 'MLO'.

Nadler, Steven M. *Spinoza's Ethics: An Introduction* (Cambridge: Cambridge University Press, 2006).

Nadler, Steven. 'On Spinoza's "Free Man"', *Journal of the APA* 1 (2015): 103–20.

Pickavé, Martin and Lisa Shapiro (eds). *Emotion and Cognitive Life in Medieval and Early Modern Philosophy* (Oxford: Oxford University Press, 2012).

Pitcher, George. 'Emotion', *Mind* N.S. 74 (1965): 326–46.

Rodis-Lewis, Geneviève. *Nicolas Malebranche* (Paris: Presses universitaires de France, 1963).

Rorty, Amélie (ed.). *Explaining Emotions* (Berkeley: University of California Press, 1980).

Schmitter, Amy. '17th and 18th Century Theories of the Emotions', in *Stanford Encyclopedia of Philosophy*, ed. E. N. Zalta (Spring 2014 edition; revised October 15, 2010). URL=http://plato.stanford.edu/archives/spr2014/entries/emotions-17th18th/.

Shapiro, Lisa. 'Descartes's *Passions of the Soul*', *Philosophy Compass* 1 (2014): 268–78.

Solomon, Robert C. (ed.). *Thinking about Feeling: Contemporary Philosophers on Emotions* (Oxford: Oxford University Press, 2004).

Spinoza, Benedictus de. *The Collected Works of Spinoza*, 2 vols, ed. and trans. E.M. Curley (Princeton: Princeton University Press, 1985–2016).

Téroni, Fabrice. 'In Pursuit of Emotional Modes: The Philosophy of Emotion after James'. Chapter 14, this volume.

Thalberg, Irving. *Perception, Emotion, and Action: A Component Approach* (Oxford: Blackwell, 1977).

Walton, Craig. *De la recherche du bien: A Study of Malebranche's Science of Ethics* (The Hague: Nijhoff, 1972).

2

The Subject of the Virtues

T. H. Irwin

2.1 Parts of the Soul and Subjects of Virtue

Aristotle divides the soul into a rational and a non-rational part. This division underlies his ethical theory, and specifically his theory of the virtues. My main aim is to discuss the extent to which, and the sense in which, the virtues of character are virtues of the non-rational part. Mediaeval students of Aristotle express this view in the claim that the passions are the subject of the virtues; they disagree about whether the claim is true. I want to ask what the claim means and how we should decide whether it is true.

To answer these questions, we need to understand Aristotle's conception of the non-rational part of the soul, and especially what it means to call it non-rational. Aristotle clarifies his view through two comparisons with inter-personal relations. Sometimes he says that the non-rational part is capable of listening to reason, of obeying it, and of agreeing with it, as well as of the contraries. Once he compares the rule of intellect (*nous*) over desire (*orexis*) with royal or political rule, as opposed to the despotic rule of the soul over the body (*Politics* 1254b2–9). But Aristotle does not say much to explain this comparison, and he does not connect it with his remarks about the non-rational part listening to reason. How should we understand these remarks on the non-rational part? Do they tell us anything useful about the contribution of the passions to virtue of character?

The philosophical questions that arise are large, but we can grasp Aristotle's answers to them only if we are willing to examine his argument in detail. In this paper I have space only for the first step in his argument. I will examine *Nicomachean Ethics (EN)* I 13. In any sensible division of the *EN* into books, this chapter would be the first chapter of Book II. It introduces the whole argument of Books II to VI. Aristotle's meaning in this chapter is not always immediately obvious. But a little patience with the details allows us to see how he answers some of our questions.[1] This chapter presents some of the foundations of Aristotle's conception of the virtues. It is not a crude, or rough, or inaccurate statement of the view that Aristotle develops in the following books; nor does it state a view that he later rejects. It tells us how the passions are the subject of the virtues.

Though I will spend most of this paper on a discussion of *EN* I 13, I will also try to show, much more briefly, that the doctrine of this chapter fits the rest of the *EN* and the relevant parts of the *De Anima*. Moreover, at some points I will turn to Aquinas' exposition of Aristotelian doctrine. His fuller discussion often reveals implications of Aristotle's position, and often suggests some questions that can be asked about it.

2.2 Does Aristotle Believe in Parts of the Soul?

First, how seriously ought we to take parts of the soul? Aristotle's reference to the rational and non-rational parts recalls Plato's division of the soul. But in *De Anima* III he questions the Platonic partition, and in *EN* I 13 he expresses doubts about the status of the different parts he mentions. One might infer that he does not take partition seriously. This argument needs a brief answer.

In the *De Anima* Aristotle asks how we should speak of parts of the soul and how many parts there are.[2] Platonic tripartition and bipartition ignore many other parts of the soul. In particular, it would be absurd to tear apart the desiring part (*to orektikon*); for wish (*boulêsis*) occurs in the rational part, and appetite and spirit in the non-rational part, but if the soul has three parts, desire will be in each part (432b3–7). If we split desire in three, and we suppose that the Platonic tripartition is uniquely correct, we ignore the desiring part.

We avoid this unwelcome conclusion, however, one we recognize that different psychic functions justify different partitions for different purposes. The Platonic tripartition is mistaken not because tripartition is illegitimate, but because it is not the one partition to which all other partitions are subordinate. Aristotle rejects any partition that denies or obscures the integrity of the desiring part, but he agrees that the soul has rational and non-rational desires, and that the different types of desire belong to different parts.

And so he both affirms that desire is the only mover and accepts the partition of desire. Hence he reaffirms that wish is rational desire (433a21–4),[3] and he asserts that incontinence is the overcoming of wish by non-rational desire (434a11–14). Nothing in these chapters excludes different parts that contain the different types of desire that also belong to the desiring part.

In the *EN* Aristotle contrasts the rational (*logon echon*) and the non-rational part. He believes that, for his present purposes, it does not matter whether these two parts are distinct in the way the parts of the body are, or are inseparable, and two only in account, as the convex and the concave are (1102a26–32). He casts no doubt on the reality of the two parts, or on their importance for ethics.

2.3 Reason and Impulse

What do these parts consist of? Aristotle speaks of one part as 'having reason', and as 'having <reason> and thinking' (*dianooumenon*, 1098a5). He also calls it the reasoning (*logistikon*) part. Does it consist, then, of thought, and is it the faculty or capacity of thought and reasoning? If so, perhaps Aristotle separates thought, or some type of thought, from desire. This is why some modern readers refer to the rational part as 'reason'. In *De Anima* III, however, Aristotle ascribes wish, a type of desire, to the rational part, so that this part includes both reason and desire. The relevant desire does not belong to the reasoning itself, but it essentially depends on reasoning. In *EN* I 13 Aristotle describes the rational part very briefly, arguing more fully for a non-rational part of the soul that shares in reason.

He describes the role of a non-rational part in continent and incontinent agents. To illustrate the conflict in these agents, he refers to bodily movements.

> (A) But another nature in the soul would also seem to be non-rational, though in a way it shares in reason. (B) For in the continent and the incontinent person we praise their reason and the <part> of the soul that has reason, because it exhorts them correctly and towards what is best; but they evidently also have in them some other <part> that is by nature something aside from (*para*) reason, that fights and opposes reason. (C) For just as parts of a body that are loosened aside (*paralelumena*), when one decides to move them to the right, on the contrary move aside (*parapherontai*) to the left, the same is true of the soul; for incontinent people have impulses towards contrary things. (D) But in bodies we see the <part> that moves aside, whereas in the case of the soul we do not see it; nonetheless, presumably, we should suppose that the soul also has something aside from reason, contrary to and opposing reason. The way it is different does not matter. (1102b13–25)

In (A) Aristotle makes three claims: (i) that there is something non-rational in the soul, (ii) that this is 'another nature' in addition to the non-rational part that belongs to plants, and (iii) it shares in reason in a way. Let us call this part *indirectly* rational, and the part that has reason *directly* rational. Aristotle clarifies this difference later (see §12.7 below). His third claim gives his reason for the second claim, but he does not defend this third claim until later (in (E), at 1102b25, *logou de*...; see §12.5 below).

In (B) he supports his first claim. In (C) he supports (B) through the comparison with parts of the body, and in (D) he answers an objection to the comparison in (C).[4] Let us consider, then, how (C) is meant to support (B).

I have drawn attention to a puzzle in (C) by choosing a barely intelligible translation, 'loosened aside', to describe the condition of the limbs that do not go in the direction that the agent intends. If we translate by 'paralysed', we obscure the main point. If my legs are paralysed and I decide to stand up, I will not be able to stand up. But Aristotle speaks not of inability to move, but of moving to the left when we decide to move to the right. He does not refer to paralysis, which results in no movement, but to a movement in the wrong direction. 'Loosened aside' (*paraluesthai*) suggests that something is detached from its normal attachments; hence it can be used both for the literal removal of a part, and more generally for weakening or undermining. Paralysis, as we usually understand it, is one way of being detached from the normal sort of control, but it is not the only way. Aristotle may have in mind something more like the effects of some cerebral palsy, which results in apparently random and uncontrolled movements.[5]

This explanation of the illustration in (C) allows us to clarify the description of continence and incontinence in (B).[6] In the incontinent and the continent person something fights and resists reason (*machetai kai antiteinei tô(i) logô(i)*, 1102b16–17), while the part that has reason exhorts correctly and towards the best things (1102b15–16). If one's limbs are uncontrolled (*paralelumena*), one decides (*prohairoumenôn*) to move the parts of one's body to the right, but they move to the left. The same is true of the soul; 'for the impulses of incontinent people are towards contrary things' (1102b21–2).

To grasp Aristotle's point about incontinent people, we need to decide between two possible paraphrases:

(a) 'The impulses of incontinent people are contrary to the instructions of the rational part.'[7] The plural 'impulses' agrees with the plural subject. Each incontinent person has an impulse that conflicts with the instructions of the rational part.

(b) 'The impulses of incontinent people are contrary to each other.'[8] The plural is to be explained by reference to the plural impulses in one incontinent person.

If the first view is right, only one impulse is ascribed to the uncontrolled agent in the illustration, and therefore to the incontinent agent. If the second view is right, however, the agent in both cases has two impulses, and the deviant one determines his action. In the illustration the adverbial singular *tounantion* indicates the contrariety of the deviant limb to the direction we decide to take. In the case illustrated the plural *epi tanantia* indicates the contrariety of impulses in incontinent agents. We might argue that the change to the plural indicates that Aristotle attributes two impulses to each incontinent agent.

We might be able to answer this question about incontinence if we knew what Aristotle means by 'impulse' (*hormê*) in this context. If both the agent with the wayward limb and the incontinent agent have just one impulse, Aristotle uses 'impulse' to refer to the effective tendency to motion. In that case, though the agent may try to move one way, his only actual impulse is to go in the direction in which he actually moves. Aristotle's use of '*hormê*', however, does not support this claim. He uses it rarely in the *EN*.[9] It is more frequent in *EE* and *MM*. Sometimes he attributes two contrary impulses (*enantias hormas*) to both the incontinent and the continent (*EE* 1224a32–3). The normal use of '*hormê*', therefore, does not imply that each of the agents described in (C) has only one impulse.

In the illustration the agent decides (*prohairoumenôn*)[10] to move to the right, but the wayward limb moves to the left. Should we carry this feature of the illustration over to the incontinent agent, so that he also decides? Aristotle says there is something aside from reason (*para ton logon*), but he does not say it is aside from decision (*para tên prohairesin*). Does he none the less assume a decision in the incontinent?

In the illustration something is visible that is not visible in the case illustrated. We see that the wayward limb deviates ('moves aside', *parapheromenon*), whereas we do not see the deviant element in the soul of the incontinent. We see the incontinent agent act; and so his taking an extra piece of cake (for instance) is visible. The invisible feature of the action is its deviant and incontinent character, because it results from some conflict within the agent. But how, we may ask, is this feature visible in the case of the wayward limb? If we only saw the movement to the left, the illustration would be no clearer than what it illustrates. But we also see that the movement is deviant, because we can see the agent trying to move to the right when his limb moves to the left; the rest of his body moves to the right, but its movement is checked. This movement is not visible in the case of incontinence.

The illustration clarifies the 'impulses' in incontinent agents. The agent who lacks complete control over his limbs tries visibly to move them in the direction he decides on, though he fails. The attempt is visible in the illustration and invisible in the case illustrated. Since the agent in the illustration has two impulses, the incontinent agent also has two impulses, and so the 'contrary impulses' are contrary to each other.

If incontinent agents have two impulses, one impulse is probably a decision. For a decision is a type of desire (*orexis*), and therefore a type of impulse. The second impulse is the agent's appetite (*epithumia*), his non-rational desire for the object that he eventually pursues. Since Aristotle often treats a desire as identical to, or the source of, an impulse, he probably treats the incontinent's decision as one of the two contrary impulses.

2.4 Continence, Incontinence, and Decision

Are these remarks on continence and incontinence consistent with the fuller account in Book VII? The fuller account does not speak of rational and non-rational parts, or of contrary impulses. It explains incontinence by reference to ignorance, which has no place in I 13. Has Aristotle moved beyond the bipartition of the soul to a different explanation of incontinence? We might explain any inconsistency by saying that the present chapter states Aristotle's earlier views, or by saying that it is a rough and ready statement of views that he states more accurately elsewhere.

In fact, however, our present chapter is consistent with what Aristotle says later. For in Book VI the bipartition of the soul is the starting point for Aristotle's discussion of the intellectual virtues (1138b36–1139a6). We cannot treat the bipartition as a mere preliminary to the argument.[11] We have no good reason, therefore, to suppose that Aristotle changes his mind about bipartition, or that he does not take it seriously. On the contrary, his remarks elsewhere tend to confirm our conclusions about our present chapter. I have just argued that he attributes two impulses to both the continent and the incontinent person, and that one of these two impulses is a decision, just as it is in the example of the wayward limb. Similarly, Book VII affirms that both the incontinent and the continent have not only the correct belief about what to do, but also the correct decision (e.g. 1151a29–35). And if we discount Book VII, on the ground that it is a Eudemian book, we should at least attend to Book III. In this book Aristotle says that continence involves decision, which fits Book I.[12]

2.5 Decision and the Rational Part

We can now identify the contents of the rational part. This part has reason, and it exhorts the continent and incontinent agents correctly and towards the right things. The non-rational part opposes the rational part by having an impulse in a direction contrary to what the rational part judges to be correct. Aristotle's description mentions only one of the two impulses in each of these agents. The other impulse is the correct one that belongs to the agent's decision.

Decision is inappropriate for the non-rational part. According to Aristotle, we praise the rational part in the continent and the incontinent, because it exhorts them correctly. The non-rational part, however, opposes reason. If, however, the correct decision were in the non-rational part, one element of the non-rational part would agree with reason, contrary to Aristotle's assertion. If the correct decision were in neither part, it would be a further praiseworthy aspect of the agent. But Aristotle recognizes no such aspect in this context; for he says only that we praise the rational part of continent and incontinent agents. Probably, then, their decision belongs to the rational part. If so, this part contains desires as well as beliefs and judgments.

To see why decision probably does not belong to the non-rational part, we can consider Aristotle's description of how the non-rational part is indirectly rational.

> (E) However, this <part> as well <as the rational part> appears, as we said, to share in reason. At any rate, in the continent person it obeys reason, and in the temperate and the brave person it presumably listens still better to reason; for there it agrees with reason in everything. (1102b25–8)

In 'as well' (*kai*) Aristotle recalls his previous reference to the directly rational part, which has (*echei*) reason.[13] He has mentioned an indirectly rational part, which shares in reason 'in a way' (*pôs*). He now explains 'in a way'. When he introduced this part he first argued that it is distinct from the rational part, and sometimes opposes it. Now he argues that it is indirectly rational.

First, he distinguishes obedience to reason from listening better to reason and so agreeing with reason in everything. In continent agents the non-rational part does not agree with reason, because they have appetites that disagree with their correct decision; but it obeys reason, since they do what reason tells them to do. This obedience falls short of the better listening that leads the non-rational part of the virtuous person to agreement with reason. The non-rational part that agrees with reason has only the desires that reason allows.

In Aristotle's division between the non-rational part and reason, it is not clear where he puts the rational desire that he mentions in his remarks on decision and impulses. But he probably does not put it in the non-rational part that shares in reason. If this part included all desires, its relation to the rational part would be puzzling. Aristotle observes that in the continent person the non-rational part obeys reason, and that in the virtuous person it agrees with reason. He assumes that in the incontinent person the non-rational part does not obey reason. He is right to assume this if the non-rational part includes only appetite and spirit. But he is wrong to assume it if the non-rational part includes all desires. For since the incontinent person has two impulses, and since one of them is his correct decision, he has one desire that obeys reason, just as the continent person has.

And so, when Aristotle contrasts the non-rational parts of the incontinent, the continent, and the virtuous person, he does not say that the non-rational part includes the correct rational desire that they all share. His silence would be strange if he attributed this rational desire to the non-rational part. It is intelligible if he attributes it to the rational part.

Aquinas accepts this argument. In his view, Aristotle attributes a correct decision to the rational part of both the continent and the incontinent person, and the sensory desire in the non-rational part 'obstructs reason, that is to say, impedes it in carrying out its election'[14] (*in EN* §237). Since election is an act of the will (§486; 1a q83 a3; 1–2 q13 a1), Aquinas implies, on behalf of Aristotle, that the will (*boulêsis, voluntas*) belongs to the rational part. He sees that in the present section Aristotle says what we expect him to say if he ascribes impulses and desires to the rational part.

2.6 The 'Appetitive and in General Desiring' Part

The next section, however, is more difficult.

(F) The non-rational <part>, then, as well <as the whole soul> apparently has two parts. For the plant-like <part> shares in reason not at all, but the appetitive and in general desiring <part> shares in reason in a way, in the respect that it listens to reason and obeys it. (1102b28–1103a3)

In (F) Aristotle returns to his claim in (A). He has said that the soul has two parts, the rational and the non-rational, and that the non-rational soul part has two parts. He now reaffirms, on the basis of B)-(E), that the non-rational part has two parts, because the part with non-rational desires, in contrast to the plant-like part, is indirectly rational. He describes this part as 'appetitive, and in general desiring' (*epithumêtikon kai holôs orektikon*, 1102b30). Aristotle's usual term for the desires of the lowest part of the soul is 'appetite' (*epithumia*), and so it is intelligible that he calls the non-rational part appetitive. He refers to appetite because he has discussed continence and incontinence in relation to appetites.[15]

But what does Aristotle mean when he mentions desire in general? His usual three types of desire (*orexis*) are appetite, spirit, and wish. If he refers to all of these, the non-rational part includes wish and decision. The *De Anima* says that one part of the soul is the desiring part, and that this is the only thing that initiates motion (433a21). We might infer that he is talking about the same part in our present passage, by calling it 'desiring', and that this is the part that shares in reason.[16]

This is the simplest interpretation of the passage, taken by itself. It is also Aquinas' interpretation (*in EN* §240–1).[17] Though he recognizes that elsewhere Aristotle places rational desires (*boulêsis, voluntas*) in the rational part (*Summa Theologiae* 1a q82 a1 obj2), he believes that in our present passage Aristotle places will in the non-rational part that 'participates in a way in reason'. And so he often claims that the will is 'rational by participation'.[18]

This attempt to place the will in the non-rational part conflicts with Aquinas' remarks on the previous passage on continence and incontinence. Continent and incontinent agents have two contrary impulses, and one of these two impulses is the correct decision. Since the conflicts between contrary impulses distinguish the rational from the non-rational part, the conflicting impulses should belong to these two parts. Aquinas believes correctly that Aristotle ascribes decision, and therefore will, to the rational part. But how, in that case, can the will belong to the non-rational part, and not to the rational part?

This contradiction in Aquinas exposes a difficulty in our passage. If we want to avoid the conclusion that Aristotle's position contains the same contradiction, we might try different solutions:

1. Aristotle has no stable account of rational desire. In so far as it is rational, he is inclined to place it in the rational part. But since it is a type of desire, he is inclined to place it in the desiring part, which is distinct from the rational part. He does not decide between these two conflicting inclinations.
2. Despite our earlier arguments, the previous section does not ascribe desires to the rational part. The relevant conflict between the rational part and the non-rational is simply the conflict between the exhortation of reason and the wayward desire. This conflict results in contrary impulses of the non-rational, desiring part. The non-rational part, therefore, includes the desires that result from the exhortations of reason.
3. The present passage does not put all desire in the non-rational part. 'In general desiring' indicates not that all desire belongs to the non-rational part, but that the non-rational part is simply a desiring part.[19] The rational part is not simply a desiring part, but has distinctively rational desires, so that not all desire belongs to the non-rational part.[20]

How can we choose between these three answers? We might appeal to what Aristotle says elsewhere, in the *EN* or in other works, on the desiring part. But it would be better if we could find a reason in the immediate context for taking 'in general desiring' one way or the other. I have already given reasons to believe that the third answer is the most plausible if we consider this sentence in the light of what precedes. But we still have to consider it in the light of what follows.

2.7 Direct and Indirect Rationality

In the next sentence Aristotle returns to 'having reason' and to its relation to the 'appetitive and in general desiring' part.[21]

(G) In this way, indeed, we also say we 'have reason' (*echein logon*) from father and friends, and not as in mathematics. And that the non-rational <part> is persuaded in a way by reason is shown by correction, and by every sort of reproof and exhortation. (1102b31–1103a1)

The introductory particle 'indeed' (*dê*) in (G) helps us to connect this sentence with the previous one.[22] Aristotle has contrasted 'having reason', which belongs only to the rational part, with 'sharing in reason', which belongs to the non-rational part. Having explained how the non-rational part shares in reason in a way (*metechei pôs*, 1102b30–1), he now acknowledges that the contrast between having reason and sharing in reason may not capture his point precisely. We may paraphrase: 'Indeed one may go further and say that this is a case of having reason, not only of sharing in reason.' Aristotle plays on two senses of '*echein logon*' in Greek. No phrase in English has the same two senses, but we might try to capture Aristotle's point with 'listening to reason' and 'having reason', or with 'taking account' and 'having (or giving) an account'. A part of the soul is in the first relation to reason if it is indirectly rational. It is in the second relation to reason if it has reason 'fully'[23] and in itself', and hence is directly rational.[24]

Once he has acknowledged that the non-rational part takes account of reason, Aristotle reinforces the claim that this part 'has' reason. He mentions admonition, reproof, and exhortation as three sources of being persuaded 'in a way' (*peithetai pôs*) by reason. Just as the non-rational part shares in reason only 'in a way' (*metechein pôs*), it is also persuaded only in a way. In this context 'in a way' implies not that this is really a species of persuasion, but that it is only persuasion to some degree. In both instances 'in a way' (*pôs*) has an alienating force that marks a contrast with 'strictly' or 'fully' (*kuriôs*'). If we were strictly persuaded by reason, the reasonableness of the advice or instruction would persuade us. But this is not what happens when the non-rational part is persuaded 'in a way'; it is quasi-persuaded.

Aristotle's conception of quasi-persuasion deserves more exploration, and in section 2.8 I explore it. As we will see (in §2.9), a clear idea of quasi-persuasion will help us to understand the way in which the 'appetitive and in general desiring' part can be indirectly rational, and hence to understand the sorts of desires that Aristotle intends to attribute to it.

2.8 How Do We Listen to Reason?

Aristotle speaks of quasi-persuasion through obeying, listening, and agreeing, and he takes the rational part to communicate with the non-rational part through admonition, reproof, and exhortation. Listening to one's father and one's friends illustrate the attitude that he attributes to the non-rational part. These are characteristics of indirectly rational attitudes. Sometimes reason might issue a simple command that demands obedience, but at other times it might offer advice or instruction that is based on some sort of reason. Exhortation (*paraklêsis*) may include more or less elaborate reasoning.[25] Commands and exhortations are different forms of quasi-persuasion by reason. We may do as we are told, as the non-rational part in the continent person does, without having a view on whether what we are being told to do is right; we might be reluctant or indifferent. If we listen to, and agree with, the exhortation we are given, we come to believe that what we are told to do is the right thing to do. These different forms of quasi-persuasion mark the difference between the continent and the virtuous person.

The non-rational part includes the various passions on which pleasure and pain follow (1105b19–23). That is why pleasure and pain are so prominent in the first stages of habituation. We might suppose, then, that Aristotle's account of indirect rationality is fairly simple. If we are punished for failing to do what reason approves of, and rewarded for doing what it approves of, we gradually come to connect the pleasure and pain with the good or bad actions themselves, so that we enjoy doing them even when we get no further reward. This is how we can become indirectly rational.

This simple mechanism, however, is too simple to cover the varieties of indirect rationality. To see how other types of indirect rationality are possible, we may refer to Aquinas' description of the passions, which amplifies Aristotle's briefer remarks. As Aquinas describes them, passions are similar to the will, in so far as they respond to an apparent good. But they respond only to particular goods, and only in so far as they are 'pleasant from the point of view of sense and suitable to nature' (1a q82 a5). The sensory desire that belongs to the passions aims at good only 'under a determinate character of good' (*in De Anima* III 14 (§804). In non-rational animals sensory desire is moved by the estimative capacity (1a q78 a4).[26] A human being has the cogitative capacity or 'particular reason' in the place of the estimative capacity (1a q81 a3; *De Veritate* q18 a7 ad7). The will, however, pursues the universal good (1a q82 a5; 1–2 q1 a2 ad3),[27] because it regards the good 'under the common character of good' (1a q82 a5).

Each passion, therefore, attends exclusively to its proper goods, but is indifferent to the overall good. The will, however, relies on a comparison of the goodness of different objects. Our passions follow our sensory judgment, which may be an immediate judgment without comparison (1–2 q45 a4; q17 a7c, ad1).[28] This is why the passions are in some way non-rational; they are not directly rational in the way the will is. We cannot enlist the support of passions by pointing out to them that a particular action will secure a good, but will also cause a greater evil in the future. The passions may be indifferent to such comparisons because they rely on immediate rather than reflective judgments. If I am angry because I have been insulted, my knowing that it would be better to restrain the anger is not directly relevant to what makes me angry. It does not change the fact that my anger responds to, and so it does not necessarily prevent me from responding to the insult.

None the less, Aquinas believes that the particular reason belonging to the passions is moved by universal reason (1a q81 a3.) Attention affects the passions. My anger at one person may be diverted if someone else makes me angrier; so that the new insult absorbs the anger that would have concentrated on the old insult. Similarly, one passion is weakened if my attention is turned to an object that provokes another passion. If I am brooding on my anger about something, but I face some immediate and life-threatening danger, my sudden fear overshadows my anger.[29] Similarly, if something pleasant captures my attention, it may divert me from my anger by presenting me with something more urgent.

We can also divert our attention by deliberately attending to something, without waiting for circumstances to capture our attention. I may recognize I have no good reason to be as angry as I am, but I may none the less stay angry until I turn my attention to something else. My anger fades not because I am persuaded that it is unjustified, but because I have something else to absorb me. Since we can attend to things as a result of deciding to consider them, and since will and reason cause these decisions, will and reason can direct my attention and thereby modify my passions.

Aquinas alludes to this effect of attention. Just as undirected or misdirected passions can absorb our attention with bad results, proper direction of our passions can absorb our attention in the right objects with good results (1–2 q77 a1). Directed attention may have different effects: (1) If we think about the future effect of our proposed action, we may choose to act differently. Sometimes we are not affected by the prospect of future goods because we find it difficult to attend to them if present or shorter-term goods and evils capture our attention. If, however, we can be trained to think about the future, our passions can be diverted from the shorter term to the longer term. (2) If our attention can be diverted from what we normally enjoy to other things, we may come to enjoy these other things as well, and if we enjoy them, we will be more inclined to attend to them. We may not want to face danger or discomfort, but if we help other people who are grateful to us afterwards, the appropriate passions may be strengthened.

The motives that we acquire by turning our attention and modifying our passions in these ways are not the distinctive motives of the virtuous person. If the passions were capable of taking pleasure in virtuous action precisely because it is virtuous, they would also value the virtuous action irrespective of whether it appealed to passions. This evaluation, however, belongs to the rational part rather than the non-rational part. The enjoyment that Aristotle takes to be essential to virtue is the enjoyment of virtuous action because it is virtuous. This enjoyment is an effect on the non-rational part of motives that belong to the rational part; we could not have these motives unless we valued virtue for its own sake apart from its being pleasant. Motives that arise from the passions are no less characteristic of the virtuous person.

Listening to reason causes agreement with reason, but without direct rationality. The rational outlook does not reject the characteristic satisfactions of the appetitive part; it directs them to some objects and away from others, according to circumstances. This direction is characteristic of the virtuous person. Nor do we have to give up the concerns for honour, status, and self-image that are characteristic of the spirited part; we find different ways to satisfy these concerns.

The deliberate direction of attention is a task, as Aquinas sees, for will and deliberation. At earlier stages of moral development we need someone else's will and deliberation to direct our attention so as to modify our passions. But eventually we direct ourselves through our own will and deliberation. If Aristotle did not recognize desires of the rational part of the soul, he would have no account of how we can form our own passions in the way a virtuous person forms them.

This excursus through Aquinas' views on passions and attention helps us to understand Aristotle's remarks on the different forms of indirect rationality. His examples of listening to one's parents and friends show that indirect rationality includes more than the results of simple training by reward and punishment. The examples suggest various indirectly rational responses: (1) Sometimes it seems to us that the advice of parents or friends is good advice, and we can see the point of it. (2) We are disposed to take their advice seriously because they are parents and friends. Our affective connexions incline us to think they are good advisers. (3) Sometimes we do not see the point of their advice, but we follow it anyhow, because we think they are in general sensible, or because we trust them to think of our best interests. (4) Sometimes we do not see the point of their advice, but we none the less want to please them, because they are parents and friends; we act simply out of friendship or out of the love of children to parents. (6) We may suppose that parents, and to some extent friends, are entitled to tell us what to do; we attach some authority to their wishes, apart from any judgment about whether the wishes are sensible or not.

These interactions with friends and parents require only indirect rationality. In none of these cases do our friends or parents simply inform us of all the reasons that seem to them to be good reasons for their advice so that we can appreciate, on the same grounds, that these are good reasons and act on them. If we accepted their advice in this way, we would be directly rational. We are indirectly rational in so far as we grasp considerations that are connected to the merits of their advice, but we do not grasp all of them, and we do not grasp them precisely in so far as they determine the merits of the advice.

2.9 The Place of Rational Desire

We can now return to the text of EN I 13, to see whether we can reach a more definite view about Aristotle's conception of the 'appetitive and in general desiring' part. He now adds a comment on 'having reason'.

(H) But if we ought to say that this also is having reason,[30] then what has reason, as well <as the non-rational>, will be twofold—one having <reason> fully and within itself, and the other <having it> as listening in some respect[31] <to reason> as to a father. (1103a1–3)

Aristotle asks whether quasi-persuasion is a case of 'having reason' (*echein logon*), so that the part that has reason (the *logon echon*) would include quasi-persuasion. He replies that if we say that, we need to distinguish two things that have reason; one has it fully and in itself, whereas the other has it as something that listens to reason as to a father in some respect. 'In some respect' (*ti*) has the alienating force of 'in a way' in the previous sections. 'In itself' indicates direct rationality.

What, then, are the two subjects that 'have reason'? Could Aristotle mean that the second subject, the one that does not have reason fully and in itself, is the part of the soul that includes all desires?[32] If he meant this, he would create serious difficulties for himself. The present division between having reason within itself and listening to reason as to a father marks the division between direct and indirect rationality; and so, if we put all desires in the part that listens to reason as to a father, we deny that any desires are directly rational. But Aristotle has already recognized directly rational desires; these are the decisions on which the continent and the virtuous person act. Since these decisions do not merely listen to reason as to a father, they do not belong to the part that is only indirectly rational. Hence they do not belong to the 'appetitive and in general desiring' parts, which is indirectly rational and is quasi-persuaded by reason. The rational part is directly rational, and so 'having reason' needs to be qualified in order to mark this vital difference.

We can now understand 'in general desiring' in (F). In (G)–(H) Aristotle allows only indirect rationality to the 'appetitive and in general desiring' part. He is right, if this part consists only of non-rational desires. But he would be wrong if it also included rational desires. Rational desire responds to reason as such, and is not simply quasi-persuaded. Since quasi-persuasion is the mark of the 'appetitive and in general desiring' part, this part does not include rational desire. Hence rational desire belongs to the rational part. There is no room for directly rational desire within the non-rational part, as Aristotle describes it. If the text both before and after (F) supports the narrower interpretation of 'in general desiring', this interpretation is preferable. Part (F) conforms to the view that we have defended from the previous part of the chapter, that Aristotle attributes rational desires to the rational part of the soul.

That view fits the *De Anima* as well. In the passage where Aristotle asserts that the desiring part is the only source of animal motion, he also mentions rational desire.

And so there is one mover, the desiring part. For if there were two—intellect and desire—they would move us in so far as they had a common form. In fact, however, intellect evidently does not move anything without desire; for wish is desire, and whenever <an agent> is moved in accordance with reasoning, he is moved in accordance with wish. But desire moves us against reasoning as well <as in accordance with it>, since appetite is a kind of desire. (*De Anima* 433a21–6)

According to the *De Anima,* some desires are in accordance with reasoning, and therefore are wishes. Aristotle does not suggest that their only source is quasi-persuasion or that they share in reason only 'in a way'. Hence the 'appetitive and in general desiring part' in the *EN* is not the same part as the desiring part in the *De Anima*.

How, then, are we to compare the two divisions? If neither of the parts described in the *EN* is the desiring part described in the *De Anima*, how are we to connect this desiring part within the division in the *EN*? Since the desiring part is partly rational and partly non-rational, it must be found both in the rational part and in the non-rational part.

This conclusion would be unwelcome if it 'tore apart' (*diaspan*, *De Anima* 432b3–7) the desiring part. We would tear it apart by placing it in both the rational and the non-rational part, if a part of the soul were a single spatial item with its unique place; for in that case the desiring part would need to have both its own unique place and the unique places of the rational and the non-rational parts, so that it would have no unique place.

Aristotle does not believe, however, that his partition of the soul implies this absurdity, and so he allows that a single part can also be in several other parts without losing the appropriate sort of unity. And so the argument in this chapter of the *EN* implicitly endorses the view stated in the *De Anima*, that the desiring part is both rational and non-rational.[33]

2.10 Parts of the Soul and Their Virtues

The next sentence, however, raises doubts about our conclusions so far.

(I) Virtue is also distinguished in accordance with this difference. For we say that some of them are virtues of thought, others virtues of character; <we say> wisdom, comprehension, and prudence are virtues of thought, generosity and temperance virtues of character. (1103a3–7)

Aristotle tells us that virtues can be divided in accordance with 'this difference', the division between parts of the soul. Some are virtues of thought or 'intellectual virtues', and others are virtues of character. The virtues of thought are virtues of pure thought that do not include rational desire. They are states of the rational part alone, and the rational part seems to consist of thought. But this conclusion conflicts with our previous conclusion that the rational part includes both thought and rational desire.

Similarly, we might suppose, virtues of character should be states of the non-rational part that listens to reason but is not directly rational. If virtues of thought are states of the rational part alone, virtues of character should be states of the non-rational part alone. That is why the virtues of thought are acquired mostly by teaching and experience, whereas the virtues of character are acquired by habituation, which involves the passions and especially pleasure and pain. This route to virtues of character seems to place them in the non-rational part. Moreover, Aristotle remarks later that bravery and temperance seem to be the virtues of the non-rational parts (1117b13–14). His reference to 'the non-rational parts' in connexion with the two virtues, and his use of the definite article in 'the virtues', indicate that appetitive and spirited desire constitute the two non-rational parts.

This alignment of the parts of the soul with the different types of virtues needs to be compared with our account of the previous sections of the chapter. On the one hand, the remark about bravery and temperance attributes only appetitive and spirited desires to the non-rational part, since these desires are proper to these two virtues. On the other hand, if the purely intellectual virtues are in the rational part, this part seems to include no desires; for if it includes some desires, why do no virtues belong to them? If rational desires are neither in the rational part nor in the non-rational part, Aristotle seems to have no room for them. He now seems to suppose that the rational part consists only of reasoning, and that the non-rational part consists only of non-rational desires that can become indirectly, but not directly, rational. He does not mention directly rational desires.

2.11 The Role of Rational Desire in the Virtues

But this may not be the right way to understand the division between types of virtue. Aristotle does not say in *EN* I 13 or in II 1 that the virtues of character are all virtues of the non-rational part.[34] Nor does he say so when he remarks that the division between the virtues corresponds to the division of the soul (*kata tên diaphoran tautên*). Though he agrees later on that bravery and temperance seem to be the virtues of the two non-rational parts, he does not say this about all the virtues of character.

But even if the virtues of character were all virtues of the non-rational part, it would not follow that they consist only in conditions of the non-rational part. This latter claim tells us that virtue of character depends only on facts about the non-rational part. But Aristotle may not mean this. He may mean only that these virtues are essentially states that perfect the non-rational part. They are its virtues—aspects of its goodness—in so far as they make it good. But the perfection of the non-rational part may involve the perfection of some of the rational part as well. If something's perfection essentially consists in its playing its part in some system that functions well, it achieves this perfection only in so far as the rest of the system functions well. If the rest of the body is unhealthy enough, it may cause excessive strain on the heart, so that the heart does not function properly. If a rugby team is no good, the scrum half cannot carry out the appropriate role.

Aristotle may believe, therefore, that the virtues of character perfect the non-rational part because they relate it to the right conditions of the rational part. Though the virtue that results from this relation is not strictly a virtue of the rational part, because it is not directed towards the perfection of the rational part, it may still involve the rational part. Rational desires may both belong to the rational part and contribute to the perfection of the non-rational part.

The earlier part of this chapter gives Aristotle a good reason to hold this view.[35] For he takes the rational part of the virtuous, the continent, and the incontinent person to be praiseworthy, and he regards the correct decision as an impulse in the rational part. If a decision is a praiseworthy impulse in all these people, it contributes to virtue of character. In the virtuous person the non-rational part agrees with reason. It does not simply agree with the judgments of the rational part; it also agrees with correct decision, which is an impulse of the rational part. If Aristotle allows virtues of the non-rational part to consist partly in conditions of the rational part, this chapter offers a consistent and intelligible description of the parts of the soul and their role in virtue.

2.12 Why the Passions Are Subjects of Virtue

These aspects of Aristotle's position help to explain why Aquinas believes that the passions are subjects of some of the virtues of character (*ST* 1a q59 a4 ad3; 1–2 q56 a4 sc). He might reasonably rely on Aristotle's assertion that the division of the virtues corresponds to the division between rational and non-rational parts, and on his assertion that bravery and temperance seem to be the virtues of the non-rational parts (quoted in 1–2 q56 a4 sc).

When Aquinas claims that the passions are the subject of the virtues, he goes beyond the modest claim that they are somehow involved in the virtues. The body is the subject of health and strength, but it is not the subject of bravery and temperance, even though these virtues of the soul require training of the body. Similarly, the mere fact that the virtues of character require the training of passions does not make the passions their subject. If the passions are subjects of moral virtues, they cannot merely provide suitable material or support.

Aquinas believes that the passions are more than mere material for the virtues, partly because he agrees with Aristotle's view that the rational part exercises political rule over the passions (1–2 q56 a4 ad3).[36] Citizens in a state have a will of their own that has to be persuaded and not simply coerced or commanded. The non-rational parts of the soul cannot have a will of their own, strictly speaking, but they have something close enough to it to be treated as subjects of virtue.

This comparison of rule over the non-rational part with political rule is more than a metaphor or a vague claim about similarity. We can give it a fairly precise content by reference to quasi-persuasion and indirect rationality. Political rule does not rely simply on coercion or on giving orders for thoughtless acceptance. It offers reasons and considerations that present the rulers' instructions as deserving assent. If we are indirectly rational, we can accept these instructions on the basis of reasons that are brought to our attention. To that extent we are similar, because we are guided by the passions of an indirectly rational non-rational part, to citizens who are guided by their will.

The non-rational part, therefore, is the subject of virtue of character because it is the part that needs to be perfected. The virtue of character consists in, and does not simply depend on, the appropriate perfection of the non-rational part through the education of its indirectly rational capacities.

Since this is how the passions are the subject of virtues of character, Aquinas believes that the will is also relevant to them. The non-rational part achieves the appropriate perfection only in so far as it is subordinate to and agrees with the will, and hence with rational desire. Though the passions are the subject of the virtues, the virtues require the right relation to the will (1–2 q56 a4c).

Aquinas states in his own terms the conception of virtue of character that Aristotle states through his reference to the correct decision. Neither Aristotle nor Aquinas implies that the virtues consist wholly in a condition of the passions. Aristotle attributes an essential role in virtue of character to the rational part and to the rational desire that belongs to it. The same is true of Aquinas, if we set aside his mistaken remarks on the desiring part in I 13 and concentrate on his other views. The remarks on indirect rationality and the direction of attention explain how both rational and non-rational desires are essential for virtue of character. Aquinas exploits Aristotle's remarks on political rule over the non-rational part more effectively than Aristotle ever exploits them, to explain Aristotle's view on how the non-rational part is indirectly rational.

What I have said is incomplete, because I have discussed only the first stage of Aristotle's discussion of the virtues of character. One might object that this first stage is only a rough and preliminary sketch, and that the division between parts is abandoned or revised in the later discussions of reason, action, and virtue in the later books of the *EN*.[37] I do not believe that this objection is justified. On the contrary, attention to the first stage, set out in I 13, shows that it is not at all rough. It is brief and in places obscure, because it needs to be clarified by the further explanations that come later. But it offers a reasonable account of a virtue of character and of its relation to the rational and non-rational parts.

Moreover, I believe that a wider examination of the *EN* confirms the view that we have reached on the basis of our discussion of this chapter. I have no space for a full examination of the other relevant parts of the *EN*, let alone for a discussion of Aquinas' instructive treatment of them. But it may be helpful to sketch briefly how one might understand them in the light of what I have said about the first stage of the discussion. The following sections offer a few remarks to amplify the view that I have defended so far.

2.13 Decision, Wish, and the Rational Part

So far I have argued:

1. In I 13 Aristotle maintains a conception of directly rational desire that is both consistent throughout the chapter and consistent with his views in the *De Anima*.

2. This directly rational desire belongs to the rational part of the soul.
3. Virtue of character, which perfects the non-rational part of the soul, essentially includes a state of the rational part.

The third claim may provoke some doubts, especially about inclusion. Even if we grant that some condition of the rational part is necessary for virtue of character, why should we also agree that it is included in virtue of character? We might wonder why an intellectual condition could not be similar to a bodily condition. As Aquinas remarks, a bodily condition may be necessary for a state of character without being part of it. The bodily condition itself is no part of the perfection of the non-rational part of the soul. If we could have the other elements of virtue of character without the right bodily condition, they would still constitute a virtue of character. Though a bodily condition may be necessary for a virtue of character, it is not essential to it. Might we not say the same about conditions of the rational part?

The role of decision helps to answer this question. Aristotle has implicitly ascribed a correct decision to the continent and to the incontinent person, and has placed this decision in the rational part; for he takes agreement with reason to be agreement with the decision in the rational part. In II 4 Aristotle asserts that a virtue of character includes a decision to do the virtuous action for its own sake from a firm and unvarying state (1105a31–3). He distinguishes the earlier stages of moral education, in which we are trained to do brave (e.g.) actions, from the terminus, at which we have reached the virtue. We have not reached the terminus if we have simply learned to do the brave actions on the right occasions; we must also decide on them for their own sakes.

If we were right to say that in I 13 Aristotle treats decision as a desire of the rational part of the soul, and if he holds the same view of decision in II 4, he maintains that a desire of the rational part is essential to a virtue. Since a virtue is a 'state that decides' (*hexis prohairetikê*),[38] it includes a state of the rational part.

In Book III Aristotle begins his formal analysis of decision by denying that action on decision is voluntary action, and that decision is appetite, or spirit, or wish, or wish or some kind of belief (111b10–12), but it is not always clear what he is denying. He affirms that actions on decision are a proper subset of voluntary actions. But he denies that actions on decision are a proper subset of actions on appetite or spirit. It is less clear whether he denies that they are a proper subset of actions on wish. If we wish for, but do not decide on, things that we cannot bring about, it follows that not all wishes are decisions, but the converse does not follow.

Wish is about the end more (*mallon*) than the means, but decision is about the means to the end.[39] It is not appropriate to say that we decide to be healthy and happy, because decision is about things that are up to us, and therefore about means (1111b26–30). Aristotle offers examples of things that we can wish for but not decide on. He offers no examples of things that we can decide on but cannot wish for. He affirms that decision is about the means and that wish is for the end (1113a12–17), but neither of these claims excludes the possibility of wish for the means.[40]

These passages cannot be straightforwardly compared with the *De Anima*, because the latter work does not use 'decision', but affirms that whenever someone is moved in accordance with reasoning, he is moved in accordance with wish (433a24–5). Here Aristotle speaks of wish in places where we might expect a reference to decision. Incontinence, for instance, is a conflict between non-deliberative desire and wish (434a11–14).[41] Since the *EN* discusses decision at length, it tends to use 'wish' to refer specifically to ends.[42] But it does not reject the assertions about wish in the *De Anima*. Aristotle neither affirms nor denies that decision is a type of wish. He still implicitly agrees that there is desire in the rational part, and that this desire is wish.

But even if Aristotle intends to confine wish to the desire for the end, decision should still belong to the rational part, for two reasons: (1) Decision is a directly rational desire that responds directly to deliberation; that is why it is a deliberative desire (1113a11). Nothing that was said about the indirectly rational 'appetitive and in general desiring part' applies to decision. (2) Not every desire that results from deliberation is a decision, because a decision must also result from a wish. When Aristotle says that the end is an object of wish (1111b26–30, 1113a15, b3), he does not mean that every end that one might try to achieve must be an object of wish rather than of either of the other types of desire; he means that the end that originates a decision is an object of wish. When we decide, we desire as result of deliberation, in accordance with our wish for the end.[43]

This analysis of decision, therefore, does not actually say that decision is a desire of the rational part, since it does not discuss the rational part. But Aristotle has not changed his mind about the place of decision in the soul, since he still believes it is directly rational.

2.14 The Division of the Rational Part

Book VI discusses the rational part more fully, and we can usefully compare this discussion both with the previous sections of the *EN* and with the *De Anima*.[44] Aristotle returns to his earlier division between the rational and the non-rational part. He now divides the rational part into the sub-parts that deal, respectively, with necessary and with contingent truths (1139a3–15). We look for the virtue of each of these sub-parts, by reference to their proper functions (1139a15–17).

The origins of action are thought (*nous, dianoia*) and desire. Pursuit and avoidance are the operations of desire that correspond to assertion and denial in thought (1139a17–22). Since virtue of character is a state that decides, and since decision is deliberative desire, a virtuous decision requires true reason to agree with correct desire, so that desire pursues what reason asserts (1139a22–6). Acting well requires the appropriate origins of action, and we can find these by analysing the correct decision, which includes both thought and desire.

Given these facts about action, virtue, and decision, the truth in practical intellect is the truth that agrees with correct desire. Practical intellect is at work if our deliberation tells us that the best way to get the better of our neighbours is to deceive them; this practical judgment is true, but it is not the sort of truth that it is the function of practical intellect to discover. The truth that properly-functioning practical reason has to discover is the truth that (e.g.) the best way to protect our fellow-citizens is to stand firm in certain kinds of dangers. We have a virtue of character in so far as we stand firm in these dangers (1139a26–31). Practical truth consists of the truths that are appropriate for correct desire.

Aristotle has now introduced desire into his discussion of the calculative (*logistikon*) part of the rational part. But should this desire be placed within the rational part or outside it? If truth in agreement with correct desire fulfils the function of the rational part, does correct desire also fulfil this function? We might reasonably understand 'correct desire' as the correct desire of the part that achieves the relevant truth; for Aristotle has just said that decision is a deliberative desire.

The origin of decision is desire and goal-directed reasoning (*logos ho heneka tinos*, 1139a31–3). That is why decision requires intellect and thought, on the one hand (because these are needed for goal-directed reasoning), and a state of character, on the other hand (because this is needed for the right desire). Without the right combination of thought and desire we cannot act well (1139a33–5). To initiate action, we need thought for the sake of something, which is practical thought; for acting well is the end, and this is the object of desire (1139a35–b4).[45] The relevant kind of thought is thought about the unqualified end (the *telos haplôs*, 1139b2), which is not an end by being a means to some further end.

These facts about thought, desire, and action are offered to explain why decision is either desiring intellect or thinking desire (*ê orektikos nous ê orexis dianoêtikê*, 1139b4–5). The correct decision is the origin of good action, and so it requires both true belief about what good action is and the appropriate desire for that good action. Truth about action, therefore, will be truth about what ought to be done, which is the proper object of correct desire.

What are the contents of the practically-rational part (i.e., the part of the rational part that is about action)? Does it consist only of beliefs and inferences, sometimes expressed in exhortations (*parakalein*)? Or does it also include desires? We might say that when Aristotle analyses decision and takes it to require both thought and desire, only the thought, and specifically the deliberation, belongs strictly to the rational part, whereas the desire is outside the rational part. Alternatively, we might take him to mean that both aspects of decision belong to the rational part.[46]

Thought forms the correct decisions through deliberation that begins from wish. The origin of decision is 'desire and reason for the sake of something'. If the relevant desire is wish for the end, we might suppose that the reason is deliberative reasoning about means to ends. In that case we will take 'for the sake of something' to refer to reasoning about means. The alternative possibility is that the relevant sort of thought and reason is the thought that forms the wish rather than the thought that directly forms the decision. Which sort of thought has Aristotle in mind?

The relevant sort of thought is practical rather than productive; it is about the unqualified end of acting well, rather than the qualified end that guides production. Action (*praxis*), and hence acting well (*eupraxia*, 1139b3, 1140b6–7), is an unqualified end that is not simply a means to some further end. The relevant reasoning, then, is about this unqualified end of acting well. It is not simply reasoning about means.[47] The result of this reasoning about the unqualified end will be a conclusion about what acting well is like. My conception of acting well forms the conception of the end that I assume in further deliberation. If I think living well requires pleasure and freedom from insecurity, for instance, and I see that money helps towards these ends, I will want to make money. My desire for pleasure and security fixes the end that begins further deliberation. My desire for this end is a wish.

We can now recall Aristotle's claim in the *De Anima* that whenever one is moved in accordance with reasoning, one is moved in accordance with wish. This claim is true in so far as decision is deliberative desire that rests on a wish. But the discussion of decision did not tell us how wish for the end could be a rational desire. In our present passage Aristotle implies that the wish that begins deliberation and leads to decision is the result of thought about the unqualified end. Hence he implies that both the decision to pursue the means and the wish for the end are desires resulting from reason. They are both wishes, as the *De Anima* understands wish.

Does Aristotle place these desires in the practical part of the rational part, or in the non-rational part? If we want to assign them to the non-rational part, we might rely on the fact that Aristotle speaks of them as desires, and recall that in I 13 Aristotle described the non-rational part as 'in general desiring'. In that case, we may suppose that VI 2 describes the interactions between the rational part and the desiring part. The agreement between true judgment and correct desire will then exemplify the agreement between the rational and the non-rational parts that is mentioned in I 13.[48]

But this attempted reconciliation of the present chapter with I 13 conflicts with the description in that earlier chapter of the non-rational part. None of the desires of this part is a deliberative desire of the sort that is described in VI 2. The non-rational part in I 13 can only be quasi-persuaded by reason, and therefore is only indirectly rational, whereas deliberative desire is directly rational and is persuaded, not just quasi-persuaded, by reason. In VI 2 Aristotle does not allude to his description of the non-rational part in I 13, and does not suggest that the deliberative desire that he discusses here has the features of non-rational desire that he mentioned in I 13. Hence in VI 2 he ascribes some desires to the rational part.

We might question this conclusion, if we recall that a correct decision requires both a state of character (*êthike hexis*) and thought (*nous* and *dianoia*), because acting well requires both thought and character (1139a33–5). The reference to character reminds us of the virtues of character that were taken to belong to the non-rational part. We might infer that the virtues of the non-rational part ensure the correctness of desire, and that the rational part supplies only the correct thought.[49]

It does not follow, however, that no correct desires belong to the rational part; for, as we have seen, the virtues of character are not states of the non-rational part alone. They perfect the non-rational part through the appropriate connexion to states of the rational part. Hence, whenever Aristotle refers to virtues of character, he refers to states of the rational part as well as the non-rational part. Since good character does not involve only the non-rational part, the correct desire that springs from good character does not belong only to the non-rational part. And since the virtues of character include the correct decision, they include the correct wish, which is a state of the rational, part. To form the right wish, we need the rational aspect of virtue of character. To execute it, we need the non-rational aspect.[50]

If the rational part does not consist only of thought, and if some desires are directly rational and do not belong to the non-rational part, they ought to belong to the rational part. If they belonged to neither part, desire would be in the strange position of belonging in part to one of Aristotle's two parts, and in part to neither of them. We would have reason to attribute this strange position to desire only if we had reason to deny that rational desire could belong to the rational part, as Aristotle describes it; but we have no reason to deny this. Therefore we should attribute rational desire to the rational part.

Aristotle affirms this view in the *De Anima*, since he places wish in the rational part. So far we have found nothing equally explicit in the *EN*. But the present chapter comes close to an explicit affirmation. This may be the point of the claim that decision is either desiring intellect or thinking desire. Thought can cause desire in many different ways, only one of which causes the desire to be based on the thought. I may think it would be good to write a paper over which I have procrastinated. This thought may put me in mind of the difficulty of writing it and of the attractions of reading a novel instead. And so I may start reading a novel because I thought it would be good to write a paper. The reverse might also happen; when I feel like reading the novel, it may occur to me that I am doing this instead of writing a paper I ought to write, and so I may write the paper because I wanted to read the novel. In both cases 'because' would refer to a real causal and psychological connexion, but it would be potentially misleading if it were taken to refer to my reason for reading the novel or writing the paper.

When Aristotle describes decision as thinking desire or desiring thought, he refers to a rational connexion. My decision is not only the result of my wish and deliberation, but it is also rationally responsive to them. If my wish and deliberation no longer gave a good reason for the decision, the decision would disappear. Hence decision is desire that responds to thought and thought in so far as they purport to justify the desire. This relation between thought and desire makes a decision directly rational. It gives a good reason for treating the relevant thought as a constituent, rather than simply a causal condition, of the decision. If the decision is thought and desire, combined in the way we have described, it belongs in the rational part in virtue of the fact that it is thought. Similarly, since it is desire responsive to thought, its direct rationality places it in the rational part.

A decision is a rational desire not only because it depends on deliberation about the means but also because it depends on a wish, which is also a directly rational desire. Aristotle has something more to say about the thought on which wish depends. As we have seen, the 'reason for the sake of something' (*logos ho heneka tou*, 1139a32–23) and 'thought for the sake of something and about action' (*dianoia... hê heneka tou kai praktikê*, 1139a35–6) is the thought that forms our wish. In Aristotle's view, thought by itself initiates no motion, but only this kind of thought initiates motion. Some take him to be saying that thought moves nothing unless it is about some desired object, so that 'by itself' means 'without desire'.[51] But Aristotle may not mean to commit himself to this. He says that thought moves if it is goal-directed and, specifically, directed towards *praxis* and *eupraxia*. Goal-directed thought may be directed either towards a desired object or towards a desirable object, an object that deserves to be desired. Since we are capable of wish, which is desire that responds to reason, the discovery that something is desirable produces the appropriate wish.

This is what Aristotle means when he says that acting well is the end and desire is for this end. The desire in question is the wish that responds to the recognition of the desirability of the end. Thought about the good would not move us to action if we could not form desires that are responsive to this sort of thought; but thought may still move us even if it does not thinks about an object of some actual antecedent desire. If Aristotle allows that thought about acting well results in action, the rational part itself is a source of desire and action. It does not have to present some attractive object to the non-rational desiring part.

2.15 How Thought and Desire Originate Action

It is worth comparing this conclusion about *EN* VI 2 with the passage in *De Anima* that mentions practical intellect (433a15–a26). Aristotle says, as we would expect, that it differs from purely theoretical intellect 'in the end', in other words, because it reasons with reference to an end. Desire is also goal-directed; 'for what desire is of, this is the origin of practical intellect' (433a15–16).[52] The exact point depends on the sense of 'what desire is of' (*hou hê orexis*). Does Aristotle refer to an object of actual desire, or to the sort of object that is desired? In the latter case, he may be referring to a desirable object rather than to an actually desired one. Aristotle next refers, apparently, to the same thing as 'the object of desire' (*to orekton*), and says that this is what initiates motion, and that thought initiates motion because the origin of the relevant thought is the object of desire (433a17–20). The use of 'object of desire' does not help us, since this may refer either to the desired or to the desirable end.

In Aristotle's view, this is why one can plausibly (*eulogôs*) say that both desire and practical thought are movers. But then he seems to suggest that this plausible claim is false:

> The mover, then, is some one thing, the desiring <part> (*orektikon*); for if there were two movers, intellect and desire, they would move in accordance with a common form, but in fact

intellect does not appear a mover without desire—for wish is a desire, and when one is moved in accordance with reasoning, one is also moved in accordance with wish—but desire moves even against reasoning—for appetite is also a type of desire. (433a11–15)

The claim that there are two movers, intellect and desire, seems to conflict with the claim that there is just one mover, the desiring part. But the reason Aristotle gives for rejecting two movers is that intellect does not move us without desire. He seems to agree that intellect may move us in combination with desire. And so, when he denies that there are two movers, he denies that intellect and desire are two independent movers. He affirms that there is one mover, the desiring part, and in his support he observes that when we are moved in accordance with reason, we are also moved in accordance with wish, which is a desire.

These arguments for a single mover do not imply that all practical thought presupposes an independent desire to which it seeks means. If our explanation of the object of desire was correct, Aristotle's arguments allow thought about the desirable to produce a wish. The wish is the origin of action, but the thought about the desirable is the origin of the wish. This conclusion matches the claim in *EN* VI that decision is the origin of action, but goal-directed reasoning and desire are the origin of the decision.

If this is at least a plausible account of what Aristotle means in the *De Anima*, it answers the objection that our account of the *EN* clearly conflicts with the *De Anima*. Aristotle believes that the desiring part is the mover, but he allows some desires to depend essentially on reason. Some desires, therefore, belong both to the desiring part and to the rational part. Cross-membership in two parts raises no difficulty for Aristotelian parts of the soul.[53]

2.16 Full Virtue

Aristotle returns to the partition of the soul in the last chapter of Book VI, which discusses the relation of prudence to virtue of character. He mentions the doxastic part of the soul and its two conditions, cleverness and prudence. He compares these with two conditions of the ethical part, natural virtue and full (or strict: *kuria*) virtue (1144b14–17).[54] The doxastic part is the practically-rational part of the rational part, according to the division in VI 1–2. The ethical part is the seat of character; it is the non-rational part that shares in reason in a way. In the doxastic part cleverness is an intellectual ability that can be used badly or well; it is used well when it is guided by prudence. In the ethical part natural virtues are desirable tendencies that make habituation easier, but they can also mislead us. Full virtue of character requires prudence (1144b1–17).

Virtue of character is not an intermediate condition between natural virtue and the full virtue that requires prudence. On the contrary, Aristotle identifies virtue of character, discussed in the earlier books of the *Ethics*, with full virtue. He introduced virtue of character as the virtue of the non-rational part; he now calls this the ethical part, which has two conditions, natural and full virtue. Since virtue of character is not natural virtue, it is full virtue. Hence the virtue of the non-rational part requires prudence, a condition of the rational part. This conclusion fits our previous discussion of the two parts and their virtues.

We have seen why virtue of character includes affective conditions of the non-rational part, cognitive conditions of the rational part, and directly rational desires. To see whether Aristotle includes all of these in full virtue, we should consider the division between natural and full virtue. He reminds us that virtuous people decide on the right action for its own sake, and that therefore they have the correct decision (1144a13–20). Virtue makes the decision correct, and some other capacity is needed to find what is to be done for the sake of the decision (1144a20–1). To clarify this remark Aristotle discusses prudence and cleverness. He applies this discussion to his division between natural and full virtue. Eventually he returns to the question about what makes the decision correct. He answers that virtue makes us achieve the end and prudence makes us achieve the means to the end (1145a2–6).[55]

We have now learnt that the virtue that makes the end correct is the full virtue that requires prudence. The correct decision, therefore, is the one that follows prudence. Its relation to practical reason fits Aristotle's description of decision as either desiring intellect or thinking desire (1139b4–5). He reminds us that virtue of character requires the directly rational desires of the rational part.

To explain how virtue of character agrees with correct reason, Aristotle recalls the difference between mere conformity with virtue and acting on the right decision. The view that virtue is 'in accordance with correct reason' needs to be modified, because it does not distinguish conformity to reason from responsiveness to reason. Since virtue is directly rational, because it responds to reason, it is not only in accord with correct reason, but also with (*meta*) correct reason. This correct reason is prudence (1144b21–8).[56]

The end of Book VI, therefore, confirms our conclusion from other remarks on the two parts of the soul. The ascription of virtues of character to the non-rational part does not undermine our account of the parts of the soul.

2.17 How the Passions Are the Subject of Virtue

Aristotle has now answered some of our earlier questions: (1) He attributes rational desires to the rational part of the soul. The desires he attributes to the non-rational part are only indirectly rational, but decision rests on wish, which is a directly rational desire. (2) Virtue of character requires not only correct non-rational desires, but also the correct decision, and therefore the correct thought and the correct rational desires. (3) He therefore has a consistent view about the attributes of the rational and the non-rational parts of the soul in the *EN* and in the *De Anima*.

Aquinas is right, therefore, to maintain that Aristotle takes the passions to be the subject of the virtues of character. His formulation captures Aristotle's view that the indirectly rational part of the soul is the part that is perfected by the virtues of character. But Aquinas' formulation captures Aristotle's view only if we see that it does not make virtue of character depend exclusively on states of the non-rational part of the soul. The virtues belong to the non-rational part only in so far as it agrees with the correct decision in the rational part. Since the correct decision is part of the virtue, and since decision is a desire of the rational part, the virtue has to include a state of the rational part. Virtue of character is both a state that decides and a state of the non-rational part, because the correct decision is needed to perfect the non-rational part.

Aristotle's explanation of the relation between his partition of the soul and his conception of virtue is complex, and can easily be misunderstood. We would misunderstand it if we thought that the desires that are characteristic of virtue of character are all desires of the non-rational part. Similarly, critics of Aquinas who supposed that his description of virtue of character underestimates the role of the will misunderstood his claim about the subject of virtue. Once we grasp what Aristotle says and does not say in his introductory discussion (in I 13), we can see that his account of virtue in the EN is both careful and reasonable.

Notes

1. I discussed this chapter briefly in 'Who Discovered the Will?', *Philosophical Perspectives* 6 (1992): 453–73. Some more recent discussions of questions about this chapter, or questions relevant to it, are Jennifer Whiting, 'Locomotive Soul', *Oxford Studies in Ancient Philosophy* 22 (2002): 141–200; Hendrik Lorenz, 'Virtue of Character in Aristotle's *Nicomachean Ethics*', *Oxford Studies in Ancient Philosophy* 37 (2009): 177–212; Jessica Moss, *Aristotle on the Apparent Good* (Oxford: Oxford University Press, 2012).
2. *De Anima* 432a22–b7.
3. 433a21–4.
4. I have rendered '*para*', both alone and in compounds, by 'aside' to mark its presence in *para ton logon, paralelumena,* and *parapherontai*. '*Para*' may sometimes mean simply 'alongside', 'in addition to'. (Cf. Aristotle's description of the universal as *hen para ta polla* (e.g. *Posterior Analytics* 100a7).) This is a plausible rendering of *para ton logon*, which may simply mean that this part is something additional to reason. But '*para*' can also connote deviation, going off to one side, as when we say that something is beside the point. From deviation it can readily pass into opposition. Since Aristotle has just one preposition, he does not tell us the precise connotation in each instance, but since no one preposition is equally natural in English, we have to think more carefully about what is intended. In this passage it is helpful to bear in mind that when x is *para* y, x is to one side of y.
5. See A.W.H. Adkins, 'Paralysis and akrasia', *American Journal of Philology* 97 (1976): 62–4.
6. What is the force of '*kai*' ('and') in *ton logon kai tês psuchês to logon echon* ('their reason and the <part> of the soul that has reason')? Is this a genuine conjunction, so that Aristotle means we praise two distinct things? Or is it epexegetic, so that we might render it 'that is to say' or 'or in other words'? The fact that Aristotle continues with the singular 'exhorts' may

incline us towards the second view. He does not sharply distinguish logos from the part of the soul that has it.

7. This is the view of Aquinas (§237), Burnet, Dirlmeier, and Natali, 460n91. Crisp renders 'the impulses of incontinent people carry them off in the opposite direction', apparently supplying *parapherousi* from *parapheretai* above. Stewart's view is not clear.

   I cite the following by the name of the commentator or translator: Aquinas, *in Decem Libros Ethicorum Aristotelis ad Nicomachum Expositio*, 3rd edn., ed. R.M. Spiazzi (Turin: Marietti, 1964). J.A. Stewart, *Notes on Aristotle's Ethics* (Oxford: Clarendon Press, 1892). John Burnet, *Aristotle's Ethics* (London: Macmillan, 1900). H.H. Joachim, *Aristotle: Nicomachean Ethics* (Oxford: Oxford University Press, 1951). Franz Dirlmeier, *Aristoteles: Nikomachische Ethik* (Berlin: Akademie-Verlag, 1969). René-Antoine Gauthier and Jean-Yves Jolif, eds, *Aristote: L'Ethique à Nicomaque*, 2nd edn., 4 vols (Louvain: Publications universitaires de Louvain, 1970). C. Natali, *Aristotele: Etica Nicomachea* (Bari: Laterza, 1999). Roger Crisp, *Aristotle: Nicomachean Ethics* (Cambridge: Cambridge University Press, 2000). Sarah Broadie and C.J. Rowe, *Aristotle: Nicomachean Ethics* (Oxford: Oxford University Press, 2002).
8. This is the interpretation of Gauthier and Rowe, who actually include 'to each other' in their translations. See also Moss, *Apparent Good*, 101n.
9. Only 1116b30, 1180a23.
10. Or 'is deciding', if we want to emphasize the use of the present rather than the aorist participle.
11. Aristotle does not mark any explicit connexion between Books VI and VII, except for one possible backward reference (1152a7–8), but at least the presence of the bipartition in VI should lead us to hesitate to attribute an inconsistent view to Aristotle.

    These remarks about Books VI and VII have ignored their probable origin in the *EE* rather than the *EN*. But their origin makes no difference to the main point. For Aristotle introduces bipartition in *EE* II 1 (1219b26–1220a12), at the stage of his argument that is parallel to *EN* I 13, so that any inconsistency in the *EN* is no less present in the *EE*. The same is true of the *MM*.
12. See 1111b10–15. We ought not to be surprised that I 13 assumes some familiarity with Aristotle's moral psychology. This is one of the three references to decision that precede the analysis in Book III (see also 1094a1, 1105a32). He introduces decision before he has analysed it, and introduces continence and incontinence without telling us how they are related to decision.
13. In *EE* 1219b28–31 the rational and non-rational parts share in reason in different ways.
14. 'Electio' renders Aristotle's '*prohairesis*'.
15. Stewart and Burnet take '*holôs orektikon*' to cover all desires. Aquinas also takes this view. Gauthier, on the contrary, takes Aristotle to be alluding only to *thumos* as well as *epithumia*, not to *boulêsis* as well. See also Broadie, 295, 314 (in the light of which her remarks at 43 are puzzling; see Lorenz, 'Virtue', p. 183).
16. EE 1219b23 speaks of *to aisthêtikon kai orektikon*, referring to two parts (as the following plural *atelê* shows).
17. In *The Development of Ethics* vol. 1 (Oxford: Oxford University Press, 2007) §257, I have tried to explain more fully how Aquinas' view creates difficulties for the rest of his doctrine of the will.

18. See *ST* 1–2 q56 a6 ad2; q59 a4 ad2; a61 a2c, ad2; 2–2 q58 a4 ad3.
19. On this view, the sense of '*holôs*' in this context is close to that of '*haplôs*'. Eustratius takes it to imply some degree of generality without extending to all desires (*epêgage de tô(i) epithumêtikô(i) to kai holôs orektikon dia to mê monon tên epithumian alla kai ton thumon orektikên einai dunamin*). See *Commentaria in Aristotelem Graeca*, vol. 20, 118.33–5).
20. Some of the Greek commentators take the non-rational part to consist only of *epithumia* and *thumos*. See Heliodorus, *CAG* 19.1, 24.40; (*thumikon kai epithumêtikon*); Aspasius, *CAG* 19.2, 35.22, 36.2 (*to orektikon kai pathêtikon*), 36.13 (*orektikon kai hormêtikon*). These remarks do not comment directly on *holôs orektikon*.
21. Gauthier rearranges the whole passage in his translation, without justification but not without excuse. See his n ad 1102b33.
22. Natali renders '*dê*' as 'then' (allora). Similarly Crisp has 'so'. Dirlmeier has 'denn'.
23. Or 'strictly', *kuriôs*.
24. Persuasion requires reason; *De Anima* 428a23.
25. We can compare the different speeches by generals to their troops before battles, as composed by Thucydides. Some are brief and imperative, but others are long and argumentative. See also *EE* 1229a30–1 (some incentives are not part of genuine bravery, but are useful for exhortations).
26. See 1a q78 a4; q81 a3; 3a Supp. q92 a2; *De Veritate* q25 a2. H.H. Price, *Perception* (2nd edn. London: Methuen, 1950), pp. 139–42, speaks of 'perceptual acceptance'. After completing this paper, I read Dominik Perler's chapter in this volume, which explains some aspects of Aquinas' view in more detail.
27. Cf. 1a q59 a4; *De Ver.* a1; a3. On passions see 1–2 q23 a1, a2).
28. Cf. *in De Anima* iii 16 (§842–3).
29. Kant offers an example of overshadowing fear in his comment on the threatened execution. See *Critique of Practical Reason*, tr. L. W. Beck, 3rd edn. (New York: Macmillan, 1993), p. 30 (5:30 in the Akademie pagination).
30. One might take the subject of *touto* to be *to alogon* (from b34) (so Gauthier, Crisp) or (perhaps better) the quasi-persuasion that has just been described.
31. Or 'something listening' (making *ti* qualify *akoustikon*).
32. According to Whiting, 'Locomotive Soul', p. 175n, 'the ethical works describe the practical (as opposed to the theoretical) part of *to logon echon*—somewhat surprisingly—in the same way that they describe the non-nutritive part of *to alogon* (i.e., as obeying reason) (*NE* 1103a1–3)'. She is right to find this view surprising; for it implies that the practical part of *to logon echon* is only indirectly rational.
33. Gauthier's diagram (n ad 1103a1–3) correctly labels the desiring part (of the *De Anima*) as 'mi-irrationelle, mi-rationelle', though his accompanying discussion undertakes the hopeless task of identifying this desiring part with the 'obedient' part.
34. Contrast *EE* 1220a10, *MM* 1185b6, both of which say that the virtues of character are virtues of the non-rational part.
35. Contrast Moss, *Apparent Good*, p. 165.
36. 1a q81 a3 ad2; 1–2 q17 a7; q56 a4 ad3; q58 a2.
37. According to Joachim, p. 69, the final form of Aristotle's division of the virtues 'is very different from the crude and simple division suggested by the present chapter'. This is because he takes I 13 to accept the assumption about virtue of character that I have said Aristotle does not accept.

38. Or 'a state that produces decisions'.
39. This sentence is ambiguous in two ways: (1) We might render '*mallon*' here by 'more than', so that x may be more F than y, even though both x and y are F. (Gauthier ad 1111b27; Crisp: Rowe.) But we might also render it by 'rather than', so that if x rather than y is F, x is F, and y is not F. (Stewart.) (2) We might connect '*mallon*' either (a) with '*tou telous*', so that Aristotle says wish is the attitude we take to ends more than (rather than) to means, or (b) with '*boulêsis*', to say that wish more than (or rather than) decision is the attitude we take to ends.
40. Stewart ad 1111b26 cites this passage in support of his view that Aristotle confines decision to means and wish to ends.
41. In 434a11–14 I assume that *tên boulêsin* should remain in the text. Some mss omit it, but most editors retain it.
42. Aristotle has some support in ordinary Greek for this specialized use of '*boulêsis*'. See Gauthier ad 1111b26–7.
43. This point is confirmed by the preferable reading, *kata tên boulêsin*, in 1113a12. Some mss have *bouleusin* instead of *boulêsin*.
44. We need not be put off by the probable origin of this book in the *EE*; for the earlier parts of the *EE* do not disagree with the *EN* on the points I have examined.
45. I am inclined to treat '*hautê gar... alla to prakton*', 1139b1–3, as a parenthesis, so that '*he gar eupraxia*' in b3 explains '*he heneka tou kai praktikê*' in a36. Stewart on a31 discusses various ways of analysing this passage. Gauthier transposes the whole of a31–b11 to go just after a20.
46. The translation that makes Aristotle describe decision as 'desiring intellect' and 'thinking desire' may be an over-translation. These descriptions are probably not meant to give us new information about decision. Aristotle normally uses 'that is why' (*diho*) not to introduce an unfamiliar truth that he claims to have proved, but to introduce a familiar fact that is intelligible in the light of what he has said. If he uses 'that is why' in the normal way here, these two descriptions of decision should mention something we are already familiar with, and should explain it by what he has just said. The adjectives should probably be taken more loosely, so as to mean 'intellect connected with desire' and 'desire connected with intellect'. When he calls decision 'deliberative desire' (*bouleutikê orexis*) both here and in Book III (1113a10), he does not mean that the desire itself deliberates; he means that it is the result of deliberation (*ek tou bouleusasathai gar krinantes oregometha*, 1113a11–12). Since in our present chapter he first speaks of decision as *bouleutikê orexis* and then then calls it *orexis dianoêtikê*, we might try to give the adjective the same force both times, and so take '*dianoêtikê*' to refer to the fact that thought produces decision. But can we ascribe the same force to '*orektikos nous*'? Aristotle's previous remarks have not prepared us for a causal understanding of this phrase; he has not said that decision is some form of thought that is caused by desire. If we want to explain the phrase from what has already been said, we should take *orektikos nous* to be intellect resulting in desire. The adjectives, then, refer to opposite directions of causation; *orexis dianoêtikê* is desire caused by thought, and *orektikos nous* is thought that causes desire. (This may also be the sense of the '*-ikos*' termination in the description of virtue as a *hexis prohairetikê*.) In that case, the two phrases say the same thing about decision.
47. One might object that there are instrumental means to good action as well as to more specific ends, so that Aristotle may still be talking about purely instrumental reasoning. If this were what he meant, however, the contrast with productive reasoning would not be

as significant as he takes it to be. Suppose I decide that I want to make money or to form useful friendships because this is instrumental to acting well. This is no different from deciding that I want to build a house because this is instrumental to acting well. Making money or making friends becomes my qualified end; but it depends on some conception of acting well.

48. See Stewart ad 1139a26, who cites '*homophônei tô(i) logô(i)*' and '*metechein logou*', from I 13.
49. Is this what Aristotle means? The dual preconditions of decision are taken to be another familiar fact, introduced by 'that is why' (*diho*, 1139a33–5). We might look for an explanation in what precedes and in the clause that follows, introduced by 'for'. Before 'that is why' Aristotle says that the origin of decision is desire and reason for the sake of something; and so we might infer that the desire is the product of the state of character and the goal-directed reasoning is the product of the rational part. But the 'for' that follows offers a different explanation; Aristotle remarks that acting well requires both thought and character. He does not say here that character is necessary for the right desire, but that it is necessary for the execution of the desire. If this is his main point, he does not imply that a well-trained non-rational part is the only possible source of the right desire.
50. This is over-simplified. The formation and preservation of the right wish also requires the non-rational aspects of character. See 1140b12–20, 1144a29–b1.
51. See Burnet ad loc.
52. This is the most plausible text, though there are variants.
53. Joachim, p. 168, insists that Aristotle's talk of parts of the soul must not be pressed: 'We know already that Aristotle did not recognize different parts of the soul, though he insists on difference of function. The soul, on his view, is a one-of-many-functions, not a one-containing-many-parts.' Joachim probably thinks we know this because of I 13.
54. Or 'virtue strictly speaking', *kuria arête*.
55. I am assuming that 'achieve' is an acceptable rendering of '*prattein*' here. But the text may be open to question.
56. This interpretation of the passage agrees with the division between '*kata*' and '*meta*' that the *MM* presents more fully in 1198a15–21. An alternative is offered by J.A. Smith, 'Aristotelica', *Classical Quarterly* 14 (1920): 16–22, at pp. 19–22.

Bibliography

Adkins, A.W.H. 'Paralysis and akrasia', *American Journal of Philology* 97 (1976): 62–4.

Aquinas, Thomas. *in Aristotelis De Anima*, ed. A.M. Pirotta (Turin: Marietti, 1936).

Aquinas, Thomas. *De Veritate* in *Quaestiones Disputatae*, 2 vols, ed. R. Spiazzi et al. (Turin: Marietti, 1949).

Aquinas, Thomas. *Summa Theologiae*, 3 vols, ed. P. Caramello (Turin: Marietti, 1952).

Aquinas, Thomas. *in Decem Libros Ethicorum Aristotelis ad Nicomachum Expositio*, 3rd edn., ed. R.M. Spiazzi (Turin: Marietti, 1964).

Aristotle. *De Anima*.

Aristotle. *Ethica Nicomachea*.

Aristotle. *Ethica Eudemia*.

Aristotle. *Magna Moralia*.

Aspasius, in *Commentaria in Aristotelem Graeca* vol. 19.2.
Broadie, Sarah and C.J. Rowe. *Aristotle: Nicomachean Ethics* (Oxford: Oxford University Press, 2002).
Burnet, John. *Aristotle's Ethics* (London: Macmillan, 1900).
Commentaria in Aristotelem Graeca. 23 vols (Berlin: Reimer, 1882–1907).
Crisp, Roger. *Aristotle: Nicomachean Ethics* (Cambridge: Cambridge University Press, 2000).
Dirlmeier, Franz. *Aristoteles: Nikomachische Ethik* (Berlin: Akademie-Verlag, 1969).
Eustratius, in *Commentaria in Aristotelem Graeca*, vol. 20.
Gauthier, René-Antoine and Jean-Yves Jolif? *Aristote: L'Ethique à Nicomaque*, 2nd edn, 4 vols (Louvain: Publications Universitaires de Louvain, 1970).
Heliodorus, in *Commentaria in Aristotelem Graeca*, vol. 19.1.
Irwin, T.H. 'Who Discovered the Will?', *Philosophical Perspectives* 6 (1992): 453–73.
Irwin, T.H. *The Development of Ethics* vol. 1. (Oxford: Oxford University Press, 2007).
Joachim, H.H. *Aristotle: Nicomachean Ethics* (Oxford: Oxford University Press, 1951).
Kant, Immanuel. *Critique of Practical Reason*, trans. L. W. Beck, 3rd edn. (New York: Macmillan, 1993).
Lorenz, Hendrik. 'Virtue of Character in Aristotle's *Nicomachean Ethics*', *Oxford Studies in Ancient Philosophy* 37 (2009): 177–212.
Moss, Jessica. *Aristotle on the Apparent Good* (Oxford: Oxford University Press, 2012).
Natali, Carlo. *Aristotele: Etica Nicomachea* (Bari: Laterza, 1999).
Price, H.H. *Perception* 2nd edn. (London: Methuen, 1950).
Smith, J.A. 'Aristotelica', *Classical Quarterly* 14 (1920): 16–22.
Stewart, J.A. *Notes on Aristotle's Ethics* (Oxford: Clarendon Press, 1892).
Whiting, Jennifer. 'Locomotive Soul', *Oxford Studies in Ancient Philosophy* 22 (2002): 141–200.

3

Emotions and Rational Control

Two Medieval Perspectives

Dominik Perler

3.1 Emotions and Faculty Psychology: Three Problems

Imagine that you are going home late at night and that you need to cross a dark and empty park in order to reach your apartment. Suddenly a masked man leaps out from behind a bush and threatens you with a knife. You are immediately gripped by fear. Can you control this emotion? Or are you a helpless victim of the fear that takes possession of you? There seems to be a simple and fairly plausible answer. In the first moment, you are utterly unable to be in control. Fear naturally and spontaneously arises as soon as you see the man with the knife. But you can try to get a hold on this emotion by evaluating the situation. When taking a closer look at what is threatening you, you will soon realize that the seemingly dangerous knife is nothing but a plastic toy and that the seemingly brutal mugger is simply your neighbour who is playing a bad trick on you. As soon as you come to this conclusion, your fear disappears. In a nutshell, your rational analysis of the whole situation enables you to control and eventually overcome your fear.

Many medieval philosophers in the Aristotelian tradition would have agreed with this answer, and they would have justified it with an explanatory model that appeals to faculties of the soul that are responsible for our emotional reactions. In their view, emotions are 'passions of the soul' that arise in the lower sensory faculty.[1] They are usually brought about by perceptions and imaginings, which also emerge in that faculty. Thus, it is the perception of a threatening object that immediately produces fear. However, the higher rational faculty, responsible for judgments and volitions, can control the naturally produced emotions and mitigate them or eventually make them disappear; as soon as we understand that there is no reason to be afraid, our emotional reaction changes. We therefore crucially differ from brute animals, which like us have a sensory faculty and hence also emotions, but differ in having no rational faculty and consequently no means to control what is naturally produced in them. Since we are rational animals, we are not purely passive creatures that are completely in the grip of emotions. Thomas Aquinas made this point very clear, stating that emotions 'are subject to the commandment of reason and will'.[2] They might not always be immediately controllable as they often resist this commandment, but in principle they do obey reason and can be regulated. That is why we are responsible for them. When we neglect to control them we can be blamed for being passive, because we do not use the rational faculty we could and should use.

Simple and convincing as this explanatory strategy may seem, it poses at least three problems. First, one might ask how the hierarchical relationship between sensory and rational faculties is to be understood. Aquinas describes it metaphorically, saying that the rational faculty 'gives orders' to the lower sensory one, and that the sensory faculty 'follows' or 'executes' the orders.[3] However, he also points out that there is only one soul in a human being and therefore only one acting principle.[4] So how can there be a commanding and an obeying entity if there is, strictly speaking, just one active thing? Does an appeal to interacting faculties not amount to the introduction of various principles or even homunculi that somehow act inside a human being? As long as the status of the commanding and obeying faculties is not explained, the talk about rational control remains rather obscure.

Second, it is unclear how far the rational control is supposed to go. It seems as if it were basically concerned with moderating or eliminating emotions that naturally arise in the sensory faculty. Sometimes this control can also lead to a strengthening of the emotions. Should you realize that it is not your silly neighbour but a real mugger with a real knife who is standing in front of you, your rational insight would intensify your fear. Aquinas is aware of this fact, stating that the purpose of the rational control is to calm or to incite an emotion.[5] But is it plausible to limit its function to this regulating activity? Imagine a writer who has only written a few pages of a book manuscript he ought to send to his publisher within a month. The mere thought of the dreadful deadline produces fear or even panic. Or imagine a person who is thinking about the upcoming visit of her closest friend and is immediately filled with joy. Here again, the mere thought produces an emotion. How can an explanatory model that takes all the emotions to be products of the sensory faculty and that assigns only a regulating function to the rational faculty give an account of these cases? Emotions fully produced by the rational faculty seem to be impossible.

Finally, this model seems hardly convincing with respect to cases in which emotions cannot be controlled despite the best possible rational insight. Suppose you have realized that it is indeed only your neighbour that you are encountering in the park. Yet the sensory impression of a fierce looking person is so strong and persistent that you cannot overcome your fear. You keep trembling and sweating even though you know that you no longer need to be afraid. Or imagine a person who suffers from arachnophobia. Despite knowing that spiders are harmless little creatures, she is in a state of panic as soon as she sees spiders in her bathroom. Her fear is 'cognitively impenetrable,' as philosophers and psychologists nowadays say, and therefore immune to rational control.[6] How can there be such a phenomenon if emotions in the lower sensory faculty are always subject to the commands of the rational faculty and hence always under rational control?

Given these problems, it is hardly surprising that the explanatory model defended by Aquinas (and following him a large number of authors) came under attack in the later Middle Ages. William of Ockham was one of the most outspoken critics.[7] He stressed that we should not simply assume that emotions in the sensory faculty can be directly influenced by the rational faculty, and he pointed out that we need to introduce a category of emotions in the rational faculty if we want to speak about rational control in the strict sense. In fact, he held that 'there are passions in the will, because love, hope, fear and joy are in the will, and they are usually considered to be passions'.[8] Since the will is part of the rational faculty, these emotions are clearly rational ones. This appeal to special higher emotions gives rise to the questions of how exactly they are produced, how they can be controlled, and how they are related to the lower sensory ones.

In the following I will examine this cluster of problems by first exploring Aquinas' model that takes some kind of interaction between sensory and rational faculties for granted. Then I will discuss Ockham's model and analyse the reasons that led him to introduce rational emotions. Finally, I will point out the consequences each of these models has for dealing with seemingly irrational emotions.

3.2 Thomas Aquinas: Emotions as Sensory-Appetitive States

We can most easily reconstruct Aquinas' explanatory model by focusing on fear as a paradigmatic emotion. Aquinas introduces it as one of the eleven basic emotions.[9] It is of crucial importance to him that fear is not simply a feeling, comparable to tickling and pain, but an intentional state that can be distinguished from all other emotions with respect to its specific object. This object has three distinctive features: (i) it is bad, (ii) imminent in the near future, and (iii) very difficult to resist.[10] Let me briefly look at each of these features.

Feature (i) is the most basic one and responsible for the fact that fear is a negative emotion. It is to be noted, however, that the object does not need to be intrinsically bad. All that matters is that it is bad for the person facing it. Should you encounter a real mugger, not your neighbour, he would be bad for you, but not for the children he supports with the money he makes with his criminal activity. It is therefore important to look at the object in relation to a given person and to characterize its being bad as a relational property. Feature (ii) distinguishes the object of fear from that of negative emotions that are directed at objects that are or have been present. If the mugger has already taken your money and run away, you may be in shock or feel humiliated, but you are no longer afraid of him. What makes you afraid is the fact that he is about to attack you. Finally, feature (iii) makes your object a particularly dangerous one and sets it apart from other bad objects that can be resisted or avoided. If you were not approached by a mugger, but by a barking poodle, you would most probably be annoyed without being afraid, because you could easily step aside or defend yourself with a stick. It is the fact that you are completely in the mugger's hands that gives rise to your fear—the more you realize that you cannot escape, the more intense your fear will be.

The three features make clear that it is a certain type of object that determines a certain type of emotion. It is therefore not surprising that Aquinas does not characterize and classify emotions with respect to bodily expression or behaviour. To be sure, he stresses that they always involve a bodily change, and in the case of fear he points out that this change consists in a 'contraction' occurring in the body, which typically gives rise to trembling.[11] But this is simply the bodily change that normally takes place; other kinds of change are possible. No matter what kind of behaviour a person shows, whether she starts trembling or not, what accounts for the fact that she is in fear is her being intentionally directed at a bad and threatening object.

But what makes it possible for a person to be directed at this kind of object? Aquinas is not at a loss for an answer: it is usually a perception that fixes the intentional relation. This is possible because perceptions also arise in the sensory faculty. They are, technically speaking, sensory-apprehensive states that cause emotions, which are sensory-appetitive states. Imaginings are also sensory-apprehensive states and can therefore also give rise to emotions.[12] This is quite plausible. Suppose that the dark trees in the park are moving in the wind, triggering an imagining of a huge man who is approaching you. This imagining alone can cause fear. Moreover, Aquinas points out that fear itself can become the object of fear.[13] In that case there is meta-fear: we are afraid of fear itself which we imagine to be something bad, imminent, and hardly avoidable. This can easily be illustrated. Suppose that you have often crossed the park and repeatedly become afraid because you have repeatedly imagined the trees in the wind to be persons threatening you. Now you no longer want to walk through the park—not because you are afraid of the trees, but because you are afraid that the trees will inevitably cause you to imagine dangerous persons, which in turn will inevitably give rise to fear. You are then afraid of the fear that is threatening you.

Aquinas' reference to sensory-apprehensive and sensory-appetitive states may give rise to the impression that no rational activities are at stake. But this impression would be misleading. In his entire discussion of emotions Aquinas takes it for granted that all the faculties of the soul form a unity and work together.[14] And faculties are not inner agents or homunculi but powers of the soul, which are activated when there is an appropriate input. Strictly speaking, it is not a faculty that produces perceptions, emotions or other states, but the soul or even the entire human being, i.e. the hylomorphic compound that makes use of all the faculties.[15] Since human beings are complex animals, they have vegetative, sensory, and rational faculties and use all of them at once. This means that they always make use of their rational faculty when they see or hear things around them. Unlike non-rational animals, they conceptualize the sensory objects and make judgments about them. This crucial difference can be illustrated with an example Aquinas himself adduces.[16] When a sheep stands in front of a wolf, it has sensory impressions and therefore perceptions of this wild animal. It even spontaneously grasps the dangerous character of the wolf. But it is utterly unable to produce the concepts 'wolf' and 'danger' and to come up with the predicative judgment 'This wolf is dangerous'. Its sensory apprehension of the dangerous character is nothing more than an inner alarm bell that starts ringing when it receives a certain sensory input. The sheep has no means to stop the alarm bell, say by carefully evaluating the wolf and producing the judgment that it is not as bad as it looks at first sight. By contrast, human beings can and in fact do conceptualize the wolf they see thanks to their rational faculty, and they make a judgment about it. They are also able to change their judgment by re-evaluating what they see. The better they evaluate the situation, the better they produce an accurate judgment.

It is important to note that the rational faculty is not simply a faculty that is eventually added to the sensory one, working independently. It rather joins the lower sensory faculty and influences it in its activity. Aquinas stresses this point by claiming that human beings have a 'particular reason' that distinguishes them from other animals.[17] This is a power belonging to the sensory faculty and therefore not reason in the strict sense. But it is a power that is always influenced by the rational faculty: it structures the sensory images in the light of the concepts provided by the rational faculty. Thus, when you see the wolf you immediately structure the image you receive by using concepts such as 'animal' and 'dangerous'. That is why you see the wolf in front of you as an animal, even as a dangerous animal. To put it generally, you do not only see something, you rather see something *as* something.[18] This is the case because you have a rational faculty that is active together with the sensory faculty and that has an impact on your seeing. Aquinas even goes so far as to claim that the rational faculty somehow 'flows' into the sensory faculty and that human beings therefore have a unique sensory faculty that should not be conflated with the faculty to be found in non-human animals: it is perfected by the rational faculty.[19]

This has an important consequence for an explanation of the origin of emotions. It first seemed as if emotions were pure products of the lower sensory faculty and as if the higher rational faculty was intervening at a later moment, regulating and eventually moderating them. It also seemed as if the two faculties were more or less independent entities interacting with each other. This simple picture can now be corrected. Sensory and rational faculties are well-coordinated powers used by a person, and they are normally used *simultaneously* so that all the objects present to the senses are rationally categorized and assessed.[20] Perceptions and emotions are, as it were, imbued with reason. This has the following consequence in the example of fear: at the very moment at which you see the dark man in the park as a bad and threatening object, you rationally categorize and evaluate what you see. It is therefore not a purely sensory activity, but a perception involving rational activity that gives rise to your fear.

If we take this basic fact into account, it becomes clear that the question concerning the impact reason has on emotions is not simply the question of how the rational faculty can eventually intervene after emotions have been produced on a purely sensory level. The question Aquinas poses is rather how we ought to use our rational faculty right from the beginning. How should we conceptualize and evaluate the objects present to us so that we come up with the appropriate emotional reaction? The answer is clear: we should perceive and evaluate them as accurately as possible, and this requires full use of the rational faculty. Since this faculty consists of two powers, intellect and will, both of them have to be used. But what exactly does it mean to use them? And how can our use change or even improve our emotional reaction? It is in his answer to these questions that Aquinas spells out his theory of rational control. Let us look at some of the details.[21]

The intellect can bring about an emotional change by producing new and better judgments, which will lead to a new assessment of the object. This will immediately shape the emotional reaction. Aquinas appeals to personal experience to make this point: 'This is something everyone can experience for himself: by using certain general considerations one moderates anger, fear, etc., or one incites it.'[22] So, after spontaneously assessing the man in the park as a bad and threatening object, you can try to better evaluate what you see by coming up with more detailed observations and general considerations. You can say to yourself that the park is absolutely safe and that there has never been a single case of robbery. Or you can come up with the thought that a dark silhouette is most likely a tree in the wind. This will lead to a new evaluation of the situation and consequently to a moderation or perhaps even the disappearance of your fear.

Yet this explanation seems to be too simple and far too optimistic. It may well be that rational considerations sometimes have an immediate effect. But there are striking cases in which the appeal to general considerations does *not* moderate one's emotions. The case of the arachnophobic person who correctly judges that spiders are harmless little creatures and nevertheless cannot overcome her fear has already been mentioned. There are also less spectacular cases. Suppose that you see a wolf and spontaneously take it to be a dangerous animal. Then you realize that you are protected by a fence and that wild animals behind fences do not mean danger. But the visual as well as auditory impression of this terrible looking, howling animal is so strong and persistent that you remain in the grip of fear. The general judgment that wild animals behind fences are not to be feared will by no means change your spontaneous emotion. Aquinas seems to be working with an overly rationalist framework when he assumes that a rational judgment is like a magic wand that touches emotions and transforms them.

However, a closer examination of his texts shows that he does not subscribe to a naïve rationalist position. He explicitly holds that reason has no absolute power over the emotions. There is no 'despotic rule' but only a 'political rule' that can always be restricted and resisted. Aquinas explains the resistance as follows:

For the sensory appetite can not only be moved by the estimative power, as it is the case in other animals, and by the cogitative power, as it is the case in human beings, where this power is directed by universal reason. It can also be moved by the imaginative power and by the senses. This is the reason why we experience that the irascible or the concupiscible power resists reason, namely when we sense or imagine something enjoyable that reason forbids, or something sad that reason demands.[23]

This statement makes clear that many faculties or powers are responsible for the emergence and lasting effect of an emotion. And there can be a clash between them: what the senses present does not always coincide with what reason judges. Thus, your sensory impression of something grey and howling does not match your judgment about the wolf; consequently you do not overcome your fear. This is possible because the cause of an emotion has both rational and sensory elements, and the stronger the sensory element is, the more it will determine what kind of emotion arises or persists. Of course, the sensory element does not always need to play a negative role, as my example suggests.[24] All that matters is that there can be a conflict, but in some situations the senses can very well contradict a false or an incomplete rational judgment. Suppose that the fence is quite low so that the wolf can easily jump over it. In that case the impression of a wild animal, which keeps your fear in existence, is an important correction of the far too general judgment about animals behind fences. And even if your judgment happens to be complete and correct, it does not directly change your emotion. It only has an effect when it elicits new sensory-apprehensive states, which will then lead to an emotional change. Thus, your general judgment that animals behind a fence are not dangerous can make you look more carefully at the wolf and at yourself, and you will then have a sensory state presenting yourself as being well protected. It is only this sensory change initiated by reason that will bring about an emotional change. Aquinas himself adduces a telling example for the importance of a sensory change. When we want a religious person to be afraid of punishment in hell, he says, we should not simply make him produce general judgments about the torments he will suffer there. We should rather make him produce vivid pictures of the torments, because 'when he imagines burning fire, a gnawing worm and similar things, the passion of fear will arise in the sensory appetite'.[25] Fear will then arise as the appropriate emotion, and there will be no conflict between a 'commanding' rational faculty and an 'obeying' sensory one, because the general judgment that eternal life in hell is horrible and the vivid pictures of the torments will be in accordance with each other.

Given the crucial function Aquinas assigns to imaginings, it would be inadequate to accuse him of naïve rationalism. He clearly sees that reason is not a magic wand that immediately touches emotions and changes them. There is nothing but an *indirect* relation: rational activity sets the senses in motion, and the imaginings they produce then give rise to an emotional change. The important point is that imaginings, not rational judgments, present particular things in a detailed way, thus providing an intentional object for an emotion. Rational judgments alone only yield general insights, but they never particularize these insights.[26] The example of the believer who is afraid of punishment illustrates this point quite nicely. If he were only making rational judgments, he would simply come to the conclusion that torments in hell are horrible and that hell is therefore to be avoided. But this would be a general conclusion, applicable to every human being. It would not make *him* afraid. What he needs is an application of the conclusion to himself: he needs to realize what life in hell would be for *him*, not just for human beings in general. It is precisely the power of imagination that provides this first-person approach. Or generally speaking, imaginings particularize general judgments and turn them into first-person assessments of a given situation.

I already pointed out that it is not only the intellect that is responsible for judgments, but also the will that needs to be used for a control or change of emotions. What exactly is the function of the will? Aquinas describes it by saying that 'the sensory appetite is also subject to the will, namely with respect to execution, which takes place by means of a moving power'.[27] He illustrates the execution he has in mind by returning to the example of the wolf. A sheep seeing the wolf has no means to stop or influence the processes that occur; sensory impressions naturally cause fear, which naturally causes fleeing. By contrast, human beings can control their reaction by means of their will. When facing the wolf, we can say to ourselves: 'Wait a moment, I do not want to be overwhelmed by fear, and I do not want simply to run away. Let me try to defend myself, even if it seems hopeless.' In coming up with this volition, we can stop a causal chain that would lead to fleeing. To be sure, it is not the will alone that makes this change possible. Just like the intellect, the will is no magic wand that immediately touches an emotion—nobody can stop or delete an emotion by sheer force of the will. It is precisely the overly rationalist idea that we can extirpate emotions at our will that Aquinas intends to refute.[28] His aim is to show that the will can play an important role in a process involving many activities. In initiating a re-evaluation of the situation and in stopping the 'execution' of a seemingly unavoidable emotion it makes new judgments possible, which will then lead to new emotions. And here again, imaginings play a crucial role. For the will does not only give rise to new judgments, but also to new imaginings. Thus, when we say to ourselves that we want to resist, we will come up with vivid pictures of the way in which we are going to defend ourselves. These pictures together with general judgments will turn fear into courage.

Aquinas mentions yet another function the will has in the process of controlling or changing emotions. He points out that they can be transformed 'through an overflow' (*per modum redundantiae*).[29] That is, the will can produce a positive or a negative rational attitude towards an object, from which a corresponding positive or negative emotion will 'flow out' or follow. How does this work? Imagine two persons on different continents who have been corresponding with each other for many years without ever meeting. Thanks to their letters they have a very positive impression of each other. Since they have never seen each other, their positive attitude is purely rational; they appreciate and value each other as intellectual companions. One day they have the chance to meet and instantly feel affection for each other. Why is that? The sensory emotion immediately flows out, as it were, from the rational appreciation. The more someone wants to be with the intellectual companion he highly esteems, the more spontaneously he comes up with a positive emotion when he stands in front of her. This 'overflow' of a rational attitude shows that the emotion is hardly a state that is deliberately and consciously produced. It is not the case that the person meeting his pen friend for the first time says to himself: 'Now I want to feel affection for her!' Affection arises quite naturally. It is only the earlier appreciation and the decision to meet the pen friend that is consciously produced. But once this rational attitude is in place, the emotion emerges spontaneously.

My example of the pen friend shows that it is not only an existing emotion that can be strengthened or weakened by the rational faculty. Reason can also give rise to a completely new emotion. It can even do so consciously and deliberately. Aquinas explicitly mentions this possibility, emphasizing that an emotion can be created 'by means of a choice' (*per modum electionis*).[30] In producing a judgment, we can deliberately produce an emotion, without there being sensory input. At first sight, this claim looks quite suspicious and poses exactly the third problem I mentioned at the beginning. How can there be an emotion caused by reason alone if all emotions are sensory-appetitive states? Consider again the example of the writer who should turn in his book manuscript but will not meet the deadline. How can thinking about the dreadful deadline produce fear? The answer is clear: thinking alone does not produce fear. But one can deliberately come up with a thought, which will give rise to a number of imaginings, which in turn will cause an emotion. Thus, the writer's thinking about the deadline he will miss will give rise to the painfully vivid picture of many unpleasant phone calls and letters from his publisher, and this imagining will immediately cause fear. This example shows that rational activity cannot only moderate a given emotion, but also create a new one. The important point is, however, that only rational activity mediated by the senses can achieve that.

I hope it has become clear that the interplay between rational and sensory faculties plays a crucial role in Aquinas' theory. It is not simply a rational 'command' that makes emotional change possible. This command is executed, so to speak, by means of perceptions and imaginings that have an immediate impact on the emotions. This close connection between rational, sensory-apprehensive, and sensory-appetitive states is possible because all of these states are produced by a single soul. To put it briefly, the unity of the soul makes the interaction of various faculties and hence the connection between various states possible.

3.3 William of Ockham: Emotions as Sensory or Rational States

It was precisely the unity thesis that came under attack among Aquinas' successors.[31] One of the most fervent critics was William of Ockham, who claimed that there are not just various faculties in a human being. Rather, there are two distinct souls, and each of them has its own emotions: the sensory soul brings about sensory emotions, whereas the rational soul produces higher emotions, so-called 'passions of the will'.[32] The latter 'passions' or emotions are real emotions, not simply emotions in a loose or metaphorical sense, and ought to be taken as seriously as the sensory emotions. In fact, they should be even more valued than the sensory emotions since they are the only ones that are directly guided by volitions and therefore directly controllable. And only these higher emotions are distinctively human, whereas the sensory ones are the lower emotions we share with brute animals.

At first sight, this claim looks quite astonishing. Why should there be two types of emotions? Even if there are two souls that somehow coexist in a human being, as Ockham suggests, it is far from evident that there should be emotions in each of them. One could still argue that it is only the lower sensory soul that produces emotions, whereas the higher rational soul is responsible for purely rational activities, such as conceiving and judging, and perhaps for controlling sensory emotions. Why should there be love, fear, joy, and many other emotions in the rational soul? Ockham adduces two basic reasons for this claim.

His first reason is rooted in the characterization of the two souls. Just like Aquinas, he claims that a soul has both apprehensive and appetitive states. The apprehensive states of the sensory soul are perceptions and imaginings, while the appetitive states are 'passions' or emotions that have two characteristic features: they are directed at good or bad objects and make us go for the good ones and flee from the bad ones. To put it in modern terms, one could say that they have an intentional and a motivational component. Now the rational soul displays the same basic structure, i.e. it also has apprehensive and appetitive states. Its apprehensive states are conceptions and judgments, whereas the appetitive states are volitions. And volitions also have an intentional and a motivational component. That is why volitions can very well be 'passions' or emotions. The crucial point is that the bodily component, which played an important role in Aquinas' theory, is no longer considered a necessary component. This is most evident in Ockham's definition of emotions. He claims that 'a passion is a form that is distinct from a cognition, that exists in the appetitive power as its subject, and that requires a cognition for its existence'.[33] Quite obviously, all that is required is (i) that the emotion be based on a cognition, i.e. on an apprehensive state, in order to have an intentional component, and (ii) that it be the state of an appetitive power in order to have a motivational component. But it does not need to be triggered by some sensory impression, nor does it need to involve a bodily component. It can be produced by the rational soul alone, which is, according to Ockham's metaphysical programme, an immaterial substantial form.[34]

But why should there be emotions in the immaterial rational soul? It may well be that angels or other purely immaterial beings have these disembodied states as some kind of substitute for the missing sensory emotions. But isn't it evident that human beings always have a body and therefore emotions that include a bodily component? How could there be human joy without smiling or other bodily expressions and human fear without trembling? An answer to these questions immediately leads to the second reason Ockham presents for the existence of rational emotions. In his view, an analysis of emotions that is limited to those arising in the sensory soul neglects some important cases. In particular, it fails to consider the emotions human beings will have in the afterlife. When seeing God face to face they will experience perfect joy. This will be a purely rational form of joy because God is clearly not a material object that will give rise to sensory states. In the theological literature, this joy was usually called '*fruitio*' and distinguished from mundane forms of joy that involve a bodily component.[35] Ockham discusses it at great length and uses it as a paradigm case for purely rational emotions.[36] He takes this case to be highly relevant, for if the rational soul can be in a state of rational joy after death, it can be in that state before death as well since it does not change its basic structure; after death it simply loses its connection with the body. And once we understand how rational joy is possible after death, we will also understand how it can arise before death, even if we cannot see it in its purest form in this life.

Given the structural similarity of the rational soul before and after death, it is clear that Ockham has much more than a theological interest in the joy human beings will experience when contemplating God. He considers it a test case for the existence of purely rational emotions that are not triggered by sensory impressions and not bound to a bodily process. But we may also think about more mundane cases in order to see what kind of phenomenon he has in mind. Imagine a mathematician who has just found the proof for a theorem. She is in a state of perfect joy when contemplating the proof. This joy is not caused by perceptions, imaginings, or some other sensory states, but by a purely rational activity. And it does not necessarily involve a bodily change. Of course, the mathematician may become so excited that she will blush. But this need not be the case. Perhaps she feels a purely rational joy, some form of intellectual satisfaction that motivates her to do more research. To use Ockham's terminology, we could say that her rational soul is in an appetitive state that is exclusively based on an apprehensive state in that soul. No special activities in the lower sensory soul are necessary for its existence. Nor do such activities necessarily go along with it.

The two reasons Ockham adduces for the existence of rational emotions make clear why he thinks that it would be inappropriate to locate all emotions in the lower sensory soul. To be sure, he does not pursue a reductionist strategy that would limit all emotions to purely rational states. On the contrary, his aim is to show that there are sensory as well as rational emotions and that we cannot give a full picture of the emotional life of a human being unless we take both kinds into account. But how exactly do they arise? And how can they be controlled?

Let us first look at sensory emotions.[37] They are, technically speaking, sensory-appetitive states that are caused by objects which affect the body. Ockham stresses, however, that they are not directly caused by these objects. There is only an indirect causal relation: the objects cause sensory cognitions, which in turn cause sensory emotions. This claim is, of course, perfectly in line with the already mentioned definition of emotions, according to which every emotion presupposes some cognition. Why does Ockham emphasize this point? The reason is simple. The mere presence of an object does not give rise to an emotion. Thus, the mere presence of a wolf does not cause fear in a person in its vicinity. It could very well be that the person is asleep or not paying attention to the wolf. Only the act of seeing or otherwise perceiving the wolf will cause fear. The external object is therefore only 'the cause of the cause', as Ockham remarks.[38] He illustrates this point by appealing to the hypothesis of divine intervention. It could very well be that someone is in a state of fear when no object is present, for God could cause an act of seeing something horrible and thereby cause fear. Thus, the external 'cause of the cause' could always be replaced by God. All that matters is that the person has a sensory cognition, which is the immediate and necessary cause of an emotion.

How exactly does this cognition give rise to an emotion? This is a natural and spontaneous process that occurs in the body. Ockham claims that sensory cognitions are images that are literally impressed on the internal senses and give rise to an emotion. Just like Aquinas, he mentions the classic example of the sheep to explain this point.[39] The sensory cognition it has of the wolf is nothing but an image of an object with a certain colour, size, and shape. This image is impressed on its internal senses, which are located in the brain, and causes fear. The important point is that no special evaluation or assessment takes place. Nor is there any reflection upon the appropriate reaction to the image. Fear is, as it were, a hardwired reaction to the image—there is nothing the sheep can do about it. In human beings, there is a similar hardwired process. When they have a sensory cognition, they also receive an image that is impressed upon them and followed by an emotional reaction. Given this natural causal chain, it is not surprising that Ockham compares sensory emotions to sensations like pain and hunger.[40] Of course, there is a considerable difference between them because emotions are intentional, whereas sensations are not. But they share an important feature: they are all bodily reactions to bodily changes and occur without any rational control. Ockham even thinks that they can block rational activity under certain circumstances. He cites the example of the adulterer who enjoys sexual pleasure. This sensory emotion, caused by a purely bodily process, can be so strong and dominant that it turns off, as it were, the higher rational soul and makes every act of thinking and willing impossible.[41]

This has an important consequence for the problem of controllability and responsibility. Since sensory emotions are the inevitable outcome of a natural process, they cannot be controlled—at least not directly. Consequently, we cannot be made responsible for them, for we only have responsibility for things that are in our power. Ockham is very clear about this point, claiming that sensory emotions are nothing we can be praised or blamed for.[42] They are as natural and unavoidable as pain, hunger, and thirst. To be sure, this does not mean that there is absolutely nothing we can do about them. We can very well avoid the situation in which they naturally arise, thus choosing a preventive strategy. Or as Ockham would say, we can avoid the 'cause of the cause' of a sensory emotion. The adulterer who feels sexual pleasure can avoid meeting the sexual partner. In doing so, he can prevent the natural causal process from arising. Or the person suffering from arachnophobia can avoid going to places where she would eventually see spiders. That is why human beings (unlike animals) are in some sense even responsible for a sensory emotion. But strictly speaking, they are only responsible for exposing themselves to a causal process, not for having the emotion as the end-product of this process once it has started.

It is quite significant that Ockham does not consider the possibility that the sensory cognition could be modified by some kind of rational control, so that the sensory emotion would then change. Unlike Aquinas, he does not think that reason could directly create an imagining, which would then alter the emotion. Why not? The main reason lies in the metaphysical setting Ockham chooses. Since he takes sensory and rational souls to be really distinct, each of them being an active principle, he rules out the possibility of a direct intervention. Of course, the two souls are well coordinated and often interact. But they cannot manipulate or directly change each other's activities. Each of them produces its own activities or states. Thus, the sensory soul produces its own emotions on the basis of a natural process triggered by external things. All the rational soul can do is prevent that process from starting or use the result of this process for its own activity. Thus, the adulterer can either use his rational soul in order to come up with a decision to prevent this pleasure (e.g., by saying to himself: 'Don't meet the seductive person ever again!'), or he can use it in order to morally evaluate his pleasure (e.g., by producing guilt or shame). But there is nothing he can do about the causal process producing pleasure.

If we had just sensory emotions, we would be like brute animals that are in the grip of natural processes. Like every medieval author, Ockham wants to avoid this fatal conclusion and therefore insists on the fact that we also have rational emotions. It is precisely our metaphysical constitution—our having a rational soul in addition to the sensory one—that sets us apart from brute animals and enables us to have higher emotions. How do they arise? Ockham's answer is clear. They must be caused by cognitions, and since they arise in the rational soul, they must be caused by intellectual cognitions, which are acts of conceiving and judging. Here again, it is important that it is not the external object that immediately brings about an emotion, but the cognition of an object. The theological example of the enjoyment of God nicely illustrates this point. Not even God as the best possible object can directly cause joy. All he can cause is an act of conceiving of him as the best possible object to contemplate, and it is this intellectual cognition that will then give rise to rational joy. This emphasis on the external object as the mere 'cause of the cause' could give rise to the impression that there is a perfect analogy between sensory and intellectual emotions: both are directly caused by cognitions, and both relate us to external objects as their indirect causes. However, it would be misleading to see a perfect analogy, for Ockham stresses that the intellectual cognition alone does not suffice for the emergence of an emotion in the rational soul. What is also required is an act of the will. Why is that? Ockham's answer is clear: one could have the best possible cognition, yet without approving or disapproving of what it presents one would not show the slightest emotional reaction. It is precisely the act of the will that provides this additional element. That is why it is in the end this act that is responsible for the emergence of love and joy (in the case of an approval) or of hate and sadness (in the case of a disapproval); an intellectual cognition alone does not suffice.[43]

Ockham illustrates this point with the example of the joy human beings will experience when they contemplate God. In that situation they will have a complete understanding of God, i.e. they will conceive of him as the highest and most perfect being. But this intellectual cognition alone does not cause joy. It is only the approval of the perfect being and some kind of personal engagement that gives rise to joy: human beings in the beatific state *want* God to be the way he is, thus appreciating what they intellectually grasp, and therefore produce perfect joy. This kind of reaction can also be illustrated with the more mundane example of the mathematician who has proved a theorem. It is not just her understanding of the proof that gives rise to joy. Any other competent mathematician who will later check the correctness of the proof will also reach this understanding but not necessarily feel joy. What makes her joyful is the fact that she approves of the proof as her innovative solution to a difficult problem: she *wants* it to be the way it is, thus appreciating what she understands as a special achievement. Moreover, she wants it to be *her* proof, thus valuing it as her own achievement. It is exactly this volition that makes her feel joyful. Similar things can be said about negative emotions. Ockham mentions the example of Christ who felt sadness when he was crucified.[44] What made him feel sad? It was not just the intellectual cognition of the fact that he had been betrayed and that crucifixion meant pain. What immediately caused sadness was a strong disapproval: he did *not want* this horrible event to take place, and certainly not as an event affecting *him*. These examples show that it is always a positive or a negative volitional attitude regarding something happening to oneself that is responsible for the emergence of a rational emotion.

It is to be noted that this attitude is a rational activity a person consciously and deliberately produces. The joy of the person in the beatific state and Christ's sadness are therefore not 'passions' in the narrow sense, i.e. states one is simply affected by and cannot resist. Ockham makes this point very clear, saying that these emotions are, strictly speaking, acts that have the same status as other acts produced by the rational soul.[45] He thereby draws a clear line between sensory emotions, which are the end-product of a natural process and therefore passions in the strict sense (the adulterer is inevitably overcome by pleasure), and rational emotions, which do not result from a natural process (the person in the beatific state is not simply overcome by joy). They are rather states we deliberately bring about by approving or disapproving of certain situations. This means, of course, that we are responsible for them, for we can choose between approving and disapproving. We even have the choice between three options: we can produce a positive volition, a negative volition, or no volition at all. The will is, as Ockham remarks, a free power that is not determined in its choice.[46] It is therefore in our power to come up with a positive emotion, a negative emotion or no emotion at all.

But how far does our freedom go? Imagine that the person in the beatific state does in fact have a perfect understanding of God. Is she then not compelled to produce joy and even love for this perfect being? Is it really possible for her to come up with a negative volition? Or think again about the successful mathematician. Does the fact that she understands the proof as her original solution to a difficult problem not compel her to become joyful? Would it be possible for her to understand this great achievement and not to come up with a positive volition? This hardly seems plausible. Perhaps she could refuse to use her intellectual capacity and to reach a full understanding of the proof as her own contribution to mathematical research. But once she has reached it, she seems to have no choice. She then has to come up with the appropriate volition and hence with the appropriate emotion. In a nutshell, she is under a cognitive constraint.

Ockham would clearly reject this conclusion. He repeatedly remarks that the will is a free power that is not under any constraint.[47] With respect to beatific joy he unmistakably holds that a human being always has the freedom *not* to want union with God and therefore *not* to enjoy and love him.[48] At first sight, this statement looks quite puzzling. One might have the impression that Ockham takes the will to be a power that arbitrarily wants or rejects things—a power that ignores all intellectual judgments about a given situation and does whatever it wants. But this would be a caricature of the voluntarist position he defends. When explaining the freedom of the will, he makes it clear that the will is guided by reason and that it is 'inclined' to follow intellectual judgments.[49] But being inclined is not the same as being necessitated. A person who has a perfect understanding of God is not like an automaton that immediately and necessarily produces love. She rather brings about love because she uses her intellectual judgments as a reason for the production of a specific emotion. That is why she is an active and *free* cause as opposed to a natural cause that is simply triggered by an input.[50] For instance, she can say to herself: 'I want to accept all the positive judgments that speak in favour of being united with God as my reason for loving God.' And she can very well not accept the judgments, even if they look very strong. It is up to her to choose or reject them. Similar things can be said about the mathematician. Her understanding certainly makes her strongly inclined to become joyful. But there is no necessary causal chain. She is not an automaton that cannot but react with joy when some intellectual judgments are present. She can say to herself: 'I want to accept all the judgments about the successful proof and my authorship of that proof as my reason for becoming joyful.' Of course, she may not say that explicitly. Perhaps her acceptance of the judgments is so swift that she does not notice it. But the decisive point is that there is an acceptance and that it is not necessitated. As a free cause, she can accept or reject the judgments. Consequently, she is free to become joyful. If there is some kind of constraint or necessity, it is only conditional: *if* she accepts the judgments, *then* she must become joyful. But there is no necessity that the condition be fulfilled.

This shows that Ockham defends a strong thesis about the controllability of higher emotions. Not only can we control them because we can reflect upon and eventually change the intellectual judgments that provide the cognitive basis for these emotions, we can also freely accept or reject the judgments as our reasons for coming up with emotions. Even those judgments that may seem absolutely decisive and compelling to another person need not be chosen as our good reasons. Consequently, we never have to come up with a specific higher emotion. In fact, we do not even have to come up with any higher emotion. Since we can also stay neutral with respect to intellectual judgments, we can withhold every emotional reaction. Even the person in the beatific state can simply acknowledge that God is indeed the highest and best possible being, but not accept this judgment as her reason for becoming joyful. Nor does she need to reject it. It is only some kind of personal commitment that gives rise to joy, and it is up to every person to make this commitment or not.

The fact that Ockham stresses the importance of higher emotions that are anchored in a purely rational soul, without any bodily implementation, shows that he transforms the traditional concept of emotion. Unlike Aquinas, he does not take an emotion to be a state that necessarily includes a bodily change. Consequently, on his view an emotion does not necessarily involve a bodily feeling. Only the lower sensory emotions that are present in the body have a feeling component. But the higher emotions, produced by the will, have no such component. They are purely rational states—fleshless states even angels can have.[51] Using a modern expression, one could say that they are nothing but pro- or con-attitudes that have nothing to do with bodily reactions to external things that affect us. Higher emotions are rational reactions and therefore much closer to evaluative judgments than to feelings. In emphasizing their importance, Ockham shifts the attention from the lower animal-like emotions to the higher angel-like emotions and stresses their purely rational character. What makes us distinctively rational is the possession of freely produced emotions that are not subject to bodily constraints.

3.4 Conclusion: Two Ways of Dealing with Irrational Emotions

I hope it has become clear that Aquinas and Ockham present two rather different accounts of the way we can deal with our emotions. Aquinas takes all emotions to be sensory states that are naturally caused by perceptions and imaginings but can always be controlled by rational judgments and volitions. This is possible because rational activities have an immediate impact on perceptions and imaginings, the immediate causes of emotions. Since these causes are somehow infused with reason, emotions are open to rational guidance. By contrast, Ockham clearly separates sensory emotions, which are not under direct rational control, from higher rational emotions, which can be controlled because they involve a volitional element. Higher emotions can even be fully controlled because the will is never coerced to react positively or negatively to a given situation.

Given this difference between the two explanatory models, it is clear that the two authors would have reacted quite differently to the problem of irrational emotions, one of the most vexing problems I mentioned at the beginning of this paper. How can it be that we sometimes produce emotions and persist in having them even though we know that we should not have them? How can it be that you are afraid of the man in the park although you know that he is simply your neighbour who is playing a bad trick on you? Aquinas would give an answer along the following lines. In principle, your rational faculty should make your fear disappear, for when you judge that the seemingly dangerous mugger is your silly neighbour you no longer see him as a threatening person. The fact that you nevertheless remain afraid is a sign that your judgment is not clear and determined enough. Hence, it does not have a decisive influence on your perception. You only assume or guess that the mugger might be your neighbour. Therefore, you alternate between seeing him as a mugger and a harmless person, and as long as you are still inclined to see him as a mugger your fear persists. So, strictly speaking, there is no irrational emotion, for there is no emotion that would stand in opposition to a rational judgment. There is simply some kind of vagueness or openness in the judgment, which leads to an unstable perception. This is the reason why your initial emotion persists. But once you have reached a clear and determined judgment, your fear will disappear.[52]

Ockham would give a rather different answer. Sensory fear is a natural reaction to a sensory cognition and persists as long as this cognition is present. So, as long as you have the image of a dark, fierce-looking man and as long as this image is haunting you, your fear will not disappear. When your rational soul then comes up with the judgment that the man is your neighbour, you are in some kind of conflict: what you judge to be harmless does not correspond to what is present in the sensory image. But the judgment does not simply wipe out the image; hence fear persists. Of course, you can also make the judgment that your neighbour is playing a funny game and you can even approve of this game. Then you come up with a positive volition and consequently with a positive emotion. Perhaps you enjoy the game the neighbour is playing with you, and this is an emotion you can fully control because you can decide whether or not you want to give your approval. But even if you do approve of it, your sensory fear will not simply disappear. It will persist as a deep gut feeling as long as the sensory image is present. You will therefore experience two emotions at the same time: sensory fear and rational enjoyment. But even in this case, you do not have an irrational emotion, because sensory fear is not against reason or in conflict with reason. It is simply a natural reaction to a natural process, comparable to pain and other sensory experiences. Only what belongs to the realm of reason can be in conflict with reason. Strictly speaking, there could only be an irrational higher emotion, namely one that is opposed to judgments produced by the rational soul. How could it occur? You could make the best possible judgments about the harmless man in front of you and still *not* take them to be your decisive reason for an emotional reaction. Thus, you could refuse to become amused by your neighbour although you judge that he is joking. For Ockham, this would be possible because the will is only 'inclined' to follow judgments but not necessitated by them—rejecting the best possible judgments is always an option. If there is irrationality, it has its root in this freedom of the will that is not limited by rational judgments.

It is precisely the different accounts Aquinas and Ockham give of the interplay between rational and sensory activities that is responsible for their different analysis of rational as well as irrational emotions. It is therefore to their entire architecture of the soul that we need to turn if we want to understand how they explain the control—or the lack of control—of emotions.[53]

Notes

1. A large number of medieval authors, ranging from Albert the Great to Francisco Suárez, defended this claim. For an overview, see Simo Knuuttila, *Emotions in Ancient and Medieval Philosophy* (Oxford: Clarendon Press, 2004), ch. 3, and Peter King, 'Emotions in Medieval Thought', in *The Oxford Handbook of Philosophy of Emotions*, ed. Peter Goldie (Oxford: Oxford University Press, 2010), pp. 167–87. On the framework of faculty psychology, see Dominik Perler, 'Faculties in Medieval Philosophy', in *The Faculties: A History*, ed. Dominik Perler (Oxford: Oxford University Press, 2015), pp. 97–139. Note that medieval authors always used the term '*passio*' when talking about emotions. However, this term was meant to refer to a wide range of phenomena, including hunger and thirst. I will use the modern expression 'emotion' to make clear that only a sub-class of *passiones* is at stake here, namely those that have an intentional character (for a more detailed characterization see section 3.2).
2. *Summa theologiae* (= *STh*), ed. Petrus Caramello (Turin and Rome: Marietti, 1952), I–II, q. 24, art. 2, corp. (All translations from Latin are mine.)
3. *STh* I, q. 81, art. 2; *STh* I–II, q. 17, art. 7; *Quaestiones disputatae De veritate* (= *QDV*), ed. Leonina 22 (Rome and Paris: Commissio Leonina and Cerf, 1970–75), q. 25, art. 4.
4. *STh* I, q. 75, art. 1 and 4. For a concise analysis of the unity thesis, see Robert Pasnau, *Thomas Aquinas on Human Nature. A Philosophical Study of Summa theologiae Ia 75–89* (Cambridge: Cambridge University Press, 2002), pp. 79–99.
5. *STh* I, q. 81, art. 3, corp.
6. Emotions are therefore characterized as products of 'encapsulated modules' that cannot be directly changed by other modules, say by the module of reason. For a discussion of this thesis, see *The Modularity of Emotions*, ed. Luc Faucher and Christine Tappolet, *Canadian Journal of Philosophy*, supplementary volume 32 (2006).
7. He was by no means the first critic. A number of thirteenth-century authors were already dissatisfied with Aquinas' model that assumed some kind of harmonious interaction of faculties inside a single soul. For a discussion, see Bonnie Kent, *Virtues of the Will: The Transformation of Ethics in the Late Thirteenth Century* (Washington, D.C.: The Catholic University of America Press, 1995).
8. *Quodlibeta* (= *Quodl.*), in *Opera Philosophica* (= OPh) and *Opera Theologica* (= OTh), ed. Gedeon Gál et al. (St. Bonaventure, N.Y.: The Franciscan Institute, 1967–88), II, q. 17 (OTh IX, p. 187). Ockham was not the first medieval author to make this claim. Earlier authors, most prominently John Duns Scotus, already appealed to emotions in the will. See Olivier Boulnois, 'Duns Scot: existe-t-il des passions de la volonté?', in *Les passions antiques et médiévales*, ed. Bernard Besnier et al. (Paris: Presses Universitaires de France, 2003), pp. 281–95, and Ian Drummond, 'John Duns Scotus on the Passions of the Will', in *Emotion and Cognitive Life in Medieval and Early Modern Philosophy*, ed. Martin Pickavé and Lisa Shapiro (Oxford: Oxford University Press, 2012), pp. 53–74.

9. *STh* I–II, q. 23, art. 4; *QDV*, q. 26, art. 4. For an extensive discussion of all eleven emotions and the classificatory system as a whole, see Robert Miner, *Thomas Aquinas on the Passions: A Study of Summa Theologiae Ia2ae 22–48* (Cambridge: Cambridge University Press, 2009), and Dominik Perler, *Transformationen der Gefühle. Philosophische Emotionstheorien 1270–1670* (Frankfurt am Main: S. Fischer, 2011), pp. 66–91.
10. *STh* I–II, q. 42, art. 1 and 5; *QDV*, q. 26, art. 5. Note that these features are not necessarily those the object really has. It is simply *perceived* as having them, and perceptual errors are always possible.
11. *STh* I–II, q. 41, art. 1, corp., and q. 44, art. 3, corp. In *STh* I–II, q. 22, art. 3, corp., Aquinas emphasizes that 'there is a passion in the strict sense where there is a bodily change'. Emotions can therefore not be purely intellectual states. Aquinas makes this clear by pointing out (ibid., ad 3) that the emotional states often attributed to God and angels are not real passions since they lack the bodily component. Peter King, 'Aquinas on the Passions', in *Aquinas's Moral Theory: Essays in Honor of Norman Kretzmann*, ed. Scott MacDonald and Eleonore Stump (Ithaca: Cornell University Press, 1998), p. 105 (pp. 101–32), aptly calls them 'pseudopassions'. For an extensive analysis of these intellectual states, see Norman Kretzmann, *The Metaphysics of Theism: Aquinas's Natural Theology in Summa contra Gentiles I* (Oxford: Oxford University Press, 1997), ch. 8, and Peter King, 'Dispassionate Passions', in *Emotion and Cognitive Life in Medieval and Early Modern Philosophy*, ed. Martin Pickavé and Lisa Shapiro (Oxford: Oxford University Press, 2012), pp. 9–31.
12. Imaginings are based on earlier perceptions and produced by one of the internal senses; see *STh* I, q. 78, art. 4. For an account of their origin and function in the cognitive process, see Pasnau, *Thomas Aquinas on Human Nature*, pp. 278–95.
13. *STh* I–II, q. 42, art. 4, corp.
14. He stresses that this unity will never be destroyed or dissolved. Even after death, when the lower sensory faculties will no longer be present in a body and therefore remain inactive, they will not be lost. They will still be united with the higher rational faculty and eventually reactivated on resurrection day; see *STh* I, q. 77, art. 8.
15. Aquinas endorses Aristotle's view that it is the entire person that becomes afraid or gets angry, not one of its parts; *Sentencia libri De anima* I.2, ed. Leonina 45/1 (Rome and Paris: Commissio Leonina and Cerf, 1984), p. 10. Moreover, he insists on the fact that faculties are nothing but proper accidents of the soul; *STh* I, q. 77, art. 2, ad 5, and art. 6, corp. They are therefore not agents but the means an agent, i.e. a person, uses.
16. *STh* I, q. 78, art. 4, corp. For a detailed discussion, see Dominik Perler, 'Why is the Sheep Afraid of the Wolf? Medieval Debates on Animal Passions', in *Emotion and Cognitive Life in Medieval and Early Modern Philosophy*, ed. Martin Pickavé and Lisa Shapiro (Oxford: Oxford University Press, 2012), pp. 32–52.
17. *STh* I, q. 78, art. 4, corp.
18. Moreover, particular reason can also collect different items and establish an order among them, as Aquinas claims in *STh* I, q. 78, art. 4, corp. Thus, when seeing the wolf you can compare it to other wild animals you saw in the past and come up with the assessment that this wolf looks more dangerous than the wolf you saw last year. This is clearly an activity that requires the presence of a rational faculty.
19. See *STh* I, q. 78, art. 4, ad 5; *Quaestiones disputatae De anima*, ed. Leonina 24/1 (Rome & Paris: Commissio Leonina & Vrin, 1996), q. 11, ad 12, and ad 15.

20. Note that this is normally the case. Aquinas acknowledges that there are special situations in which human beings are unable to make use of their rational faculty. He refers to people who cannot come up with rational assessments because of drunkenness or illness. Their reason is 'totally absorbed by a passion' and they behave like non-rational animals; see *STh* I–II, q. 10, art. 3, ad 2. However, these are exceptional cases that do not cast any doubt on the basic fact that human beings in a healthy and sober state can and in fact do make use of their rational faculty.
21. For a comprehensive analysis, see Claudia Eisen Murphy, 'Aquinas on Our Responsibility for Our Emotions', *Medieval Philosophy and Theology* 8 (1999): 163–205, and Elisabeth Uffenheimer-Lippens, 'Rationalized Passion and Passionate Rationality: Thomas Aquinas on the Relation between Reason and the Passions', *The Review of Metaphysics* 56 (2003): 525–58; for a concise account, see Miner, *Thomas Aquinas on the Passions*, pp. 100–8.
22. *STh* I, q. 81, art, 3, corp.
23. *STh* I, q. 81, art. 3, ad 2.
24. This has already been noticed by Miner, *Thomas Aquinas on the Passions*, p. 107, who corrects earlier interpretations that assign a mere obstructive role to the senses.
25. *QDV*, q. 26, art. 3, ad 13.
26. Generally speaking, the rational faculty only deals with general concepts and general judgments, not with particulars. Hence a person always needs to 'turn to phantasms', i.e. to images of particulars, in order to have cognitive access to particulars. See *STh* I, q. 84, art. 1.
27. *STh* I, q. 81, art. 3, corp.
28. In fact, he explicitly criticizes the Stoics for assuming that emotions can be completely extirpated by rational activity; see *STh* I–II, q. 24, art. 2, corp. The Stoics (at least according to his interpretation) endorse a far too rationalist view. They neglect to see that emotions can successfully resist rational control.
29. *STh* I–II, q. 24, art. 3, ad 1; *QDV*, q. 26, art. 3, ad 13.
30. *STh* I–II, q. 24, art. 3, ad 1.
31. This thesis was already rejected by some of his contemporaries and became the subject of a controversy in the late thirteenth century. For an overview, see Robert Pasnau, *Metaphysical Themes 1274–1671* (Oxford: Oxford University Press, 2011), pp. 574–96.
32. On the plurality of souls, see *Quodl.* I, q. 10–11 (OTh IX, pp. 156–64), and a detailed analysis in Marilyn McCord Adams, *William Ockham* (Notre Dame: Notre Dame University Press, 1987), pp. 633–69. Ockham defends the thesis that different emotions are to be assigned to different souls in *Quodl.* II, q. 17 (OTh IX, pp. 186–8). On the metaphysical framework of this thesis, see Dominik Perler, 'Ockham on Emotions in the Divided Soul', in *Partitioning the Soul. Debates from Plato to Leibniz*, ed. Klaus Corcilius and Dominik Perler (Berlin: Walter de Gruyter, 2014), pp. 179–98.
33. *Quodl.* II, q. 17 (OTh IX, p. 186).
34. On the immateriality thesis, see *Quodl.* I, q. 10 and q. 12 (OTh IX, pp. 62–5 and pp. 68–71).
35. See Arthur S. McGrade, 'Ockham on Enjoyment—Towards an Understanding of Fourteenth Century Philosophy and Psychology', *The Review of Metaphysics* 34 (1981): 706–28, and Severin V. Kitanov, *Beatific Enjoyment in Medieval Scholastic Debates: The Complex Legacy of Saint Augustine and Peter Lombard* (Lanham: Lexington Books, 2014).

36. *Ordinatio* (= *Ord.*) I, dist. 1, q. 2–3 (OTh I, pp. 394–428).
37. *Quodl.* III, q. 17 (OTh IX, pp. 268–72) and *Quaestiones variae* (= *QV*) q. 6, art. 9 (OTh VIII, pp. 251–72). For an extensive discussion, see Vesa Hirvonen, *Passions in William Ockham's Philosophical Psychology* (Dordrecht: Kluwer, 2004), pp. 75–106.
38. *QV*, q. 6, art. 9 (OTh VIII, p. 252).
39. *Ord.* I, dist. 3, q. 2 (OTh II, p. 411).
40. He opens the entire discussion by referring to 'states of pleasure, pain and sadness' and later adds hunger and thirst to the list; see *QV*, q. 6, art. 9 (OTh VIII, p. 251 and p. 261).
41. *QV*, q. 6, art. 9 (OTh VIII, p. 262).
42. *Quodl.* II, q. 17 (OTh IX, p. 188).
43. *Quodl.* II, q. 17 (OTh IX, pp. 186–7) and *Ord.* I, d. 1, q. 2 (OTh I, pp. 395–400). Ockham cites a number of examples of higher emotions, both positive and negative ones, but never works out a detailed classification. For an attempt to classify them, see Hirvonen, *Passions in William Ockham's Philosophical Psychology*, pp. 167–70.
44. *QV*, q. 6, art. 9 (OTh IX, p. 252 and p. 256).
45. *Quodl.* II, q. 17 (OTh IX, p. 187). To be precise, he claims that some emotions (e.g. love) are nothing but acts of the will, while others (e.g. sadness) immediately follow these acts.
46. *Quodl.* I, q. 16 (OTh IX, pp. 87–9), *Ord.* I, d. 1, q. 2 (OTh I, p. 399).
47. *Reportatio* (= *Rep.*) IV, q. 16 (OTh VII, p. 358), *Quodl.* I, q. 11 and q. 16 (OTh IX, pp. 67–8 and p. 87), *Expositio in libros Physicorum* II, cap. 8 (OPh IV, pp. 319–20).
48. *Ord.* I, d. 1, q. 6 (OTh I, pp. 504–5).
49. *Rep.* III, q. 5 and q. 12 (OTh VI, p. 158 and p. 396); *QV*, q. 8 (OTh VIII, p. 448). In *Quodl.* II, q. 17 (OTh IX, p. 187) he explicitly says that the will producing an emotion 'can be guided by right reason'. Moreover, he points out that the will is also guided by habits; see *Rep.* III, q. 7 and q. 11 (OTh VI, 209–10 and 354–6). On the role of inclinations, see Marilyn McCord Adams, 'Ockham on Will, Nature, and Morality', in *The Cambridge Companion to Ockham*, ed. Paul V. Spade (Cambridge: Cambridge University Press, 1999), pp. 255–6; on the guiding function of habits, see Matthias Perkams, 'Der schwache Wille. Ockhams Theorie der Unbestimmtheit des Willens als Auseinandersetzung mit dem Problem der Willensschwäche', in *Das Problem der Willensschwäche in der mittelalterlichen Philosophie*, ed. Tobias Hoffmann et al. (Leuven: Peeters, 2006), pp. 307–29 (pp. 309–11).
50. In *Quodl.* II, q. 17 (OTh IX, p. 187) Ockham emphasizes that love and hope are 'acts immediately produced by the will and by habits of the will', without there being any other immediate cause. In *Quodl.* I, q. 16 (OTh IX, p. 87–9) he clearly characterizes the will as a free cause that should not be conflated with a natural cause.
51. Aquinas explicitly rules out that angels, which clearly lack a body, can have emotions in the strict sense; see *STh* I–II, q. 22, art. 3, ad 3. By contrast, Ockham does not hesitate to ascribe emotions to angels; see *QV*, q. 6, art. 9 (OTh VIII, p. 267–70).
52. Of course, this is only the case when a person makes full use of his or her rational faculty. As has already been pointed out (see note 20), Aquinas acknowledges that in cases of drunkenness or illnesses there is no use of a rational faculty and hence no control. In these cases there are no irrational emotions, but only non-rational ones, i.e. sensory states untutored by reason, similar to those of brute animals.
53. Earlier versions of this paper were presented at Princeton University, Harvard University, and the Max Planck Institute for the History of Science in Berlin. I am grateful to the audience

in all three places for stimulating questions, and to Stephan Schmid and two anonymous referees for detailed written comments.

Bibliography

Adams, Marilyn McCord. *William Ockham* (Notre Dame: Notre Dame University Press, 1987).

Adams, Marilyn McCord. 'Ockham on Will, Nature, and Morality', in *The Cambridge Companion to Ockham*, ed. Paul Vincent Spade (Cambridge & New York: Cambridge University Press, 1999), pp. 245–72.

Aquinas, Thomas. *Summa theologiae*, ed. P. Caramello (Torino & Roma: Marietti, 1952).

Aquinas, Thomas. *Quaestiones disputatae De veritate*, ed. Leonina 22 (Roma & Paris: Commissio Leonina & Cerf, 1970–75).

Aquinas, Thomas. *Sentencia libri De anima*, ed. Leonina 45/1 (Roma & Paris: Commissio Leonina & Vrin, 1984).

Aquinas, Thomas. *Quaestiones disputatae De anima*, ed. Leonina 24/1 (Roma & Paris: Commissio Leonina & Vrin, 1996).

Boulnois, Olivier. 'Duns Scot: existe-t-il des passions de la volonté?', in *Les passions antiques et médiévales*, ed. Bernard Besnier et al. (Paris: Presses Universitaires de France, 2003), pp. 281–95.

Drummond, Ian. 'John Duns Scotus on the Passions of the Will', in *Emotion and Cognitive Life in Medieval and Early Modern Philosophy*, ed. Martin Pickavé and Lisa Shapiro (Oxford & New York: Oxford University Press, 2012), pp. 53–74.

Eisen Murphy, Claudia. 'Aquinas on Our Responsibility for Our Emotions', *Medieval Philosophy and Theology* 8 (1999): 163–205.

Faucher, Luc and Christine Tappolet. *The Modularity of Emotions, Canadian Journal of Philosophy* supplementary volume 32 (2006).

Hirvonen, Vesa. *Passions in William Ockham's Philosophical Psychology* (Dordrecht: Kluwer, 2004).

Kent, Bonnie. *Virtues of the Will: The Transformation of Ethics in the Late Thirteenth Century* (Washington, D.C.: The Catholic University of America Press, 1995).

King, Peter. 'Aquinas on the Passions', in *Aquinas's Moral Theory. Essays in Honor of Norman Kretzmann*, ed. Scott MacDonald and Eleonore Stump (Ithaca & London: Cornell University Press, 1998), pp. 101–32.

King, Peter. 'Emotions in Medieval Thought', in *The Oxford Handbook of Philosophy of Emotions*, ed. Peter Goldie (Oxford & New York: Oxford University Press, 2010), pp. 167–87.

King, Peter. 'Dispassionate Passions', in *Emotion and Cognitive Life in Medieval and Early Modern Philosophy*, ed. Martin Pickavé and Lisa Shapiro (Oxford & New York: Oxford University Press, 2012), pp. 9–31.

Kitanov, Severin V. *Beatific Enjoyment in Medieval Scholastic Debates: The Complex Legacy of Saint Augustine and Peter Lombard* (Lanham: Lexington Books, 2014).

Klubertanz, George P. *The Discursive Power. Sources and Doctrine of the Vis Cogitativa According to St. Thomas Aquinas* (St. Louis: The Modern Schoolman, 1952).

Knuuttila, Simo. *Emotions in Ancient and Medieval Philosophy* (Oxford: Clarendon Press, 2004).

Kretzmann, Norman. *The Metaphysics of Theism: Aquinas's Natural Theology in Summa contra Gentiles I* (Oxford & New York: Oxford University Press, 1997).

McGrade, Arthur S. 'Ockham on Enjoyment—Towards an Understanding of Fourteenth Century Philosophy and Psychology', *Review of Metaphysics* 34 (1981): 706–28.

Miner, Robert. *Thomas Aquinas on the Passions. A Study of Summa Theologiae 1a2ae 22–48* (Cambridge & New York: Cambridge University Press, 2009).

Ockham, William of. *Opera Philosophica et Theologica*, ed. G. Gál et al. (St. Bonaventure: The Franciscan Institute, 1967–88).

Pasnau, Robert. *Thomas Aquinas on Human Nature. A Philosophical Study of Summa theologiae Ia 75–89* (Cambridge & New York: Cambridge University Press, 2002).

Pasnau, Robert. *Metaphysical Themes 1274–1671* (Oxford & New York: Oxford University Press, 2011).

Perkams, Matthias. 'Der schwache Wille. Ockhams Theorie der Unbestimmtheit des Willens als Auseinandersetzung mit dem Problem der Willensschwäche', in *Das Problem der Willensschwäche in der mittelalterlichen Philosophie*, ed. T. Hoffmann et al. (Leuven: Peeters, 2006), pp. 307–29.

Perler, Dominik. *Transformationen der Gefühle. Philosophische Emotionstheorien 1270–1670* (Frankfurt a.M.: S. Fischer, 2011).

Perler, Dominik. 'Why is the Sheep Afraid of the Wolf? Medieval Debates on Animal Passions', in *Emotion and Cognitive Life in Medieval and Early Modern Philosophy*, ed. Martin Pickavé & Lisa Shapiro (Oxford & New York: Oxford University Press, 2012), pp. 32–52.

Perler, Dominik. 'Ockham on Emotions in the Divided Soul', in *Partitioning the Soul: Debates from Aristotle to Leibniz*, ed. Klaus Corcilius & Dominik Perler (Berlin & New York: W. de Gruyter, 2014), pp. 179–98.

Perler, Dominik. 'Faculties in Medieval Philosophy', in *The Faculties: A History*, ed. Dominik Perler (Oxford & New York: Oxford University Press, 2015), pp. 97–139.

Uffenheimer-Lippens, Elisabeth. 'Rationalized Passion and Passionate Rationality: Thomas Aquinas on the Relation between Reason and the Passions', *Review of Metaphysics* 56 (2003): 525–58.

4

Affects and Ideas in Spinoza's Therapy of Passions

Lilli Alanen

Central to Spinoza's projects—his secular salvation project as well as his political reform project—is the examination of the passions and the tools we have for moderating them undertaken in the *Ethics Demonstrated in the Geometrical Fashion* (1677). Like many of its predecessors, the emancipation and control of passions proposed in the *Ethics* is based on true or adequate cognition. This paper focuses on what acquiring clear and distinct ideas of the passions entails and how they turn passive affects into active emotions, as Spinoza argues [in E5p3d,c].[1] We are unable to remove the causes of a passion, say of sadness, affected as we are by forces infinitely surpassing our own, yet we can change it from a passive state of confusion into an active emotion of joy merely by *understanding* its causes.[2] This raises questions about the identity both of the mind that is striving to free itself from the passions, and of particular passions themselves, which are defined as confused and inadequate, partial ideas, and whose very form or being seems to depend on their confusion and inadequacy considered as ideas.[3] Spinoza also teaches that 'affects of hate, anger, envy, etc.' are subject to the 'universal laws and rules of nature', so follow 'the same necessity and force of nature as other particular things'.[4] Is this to say, then, that the therapy of passions proposed in the *Ethics*, not unlike that of the Stoics, is in the end a matter not of changing things to the better but of changing our beliefs about them and our attitude to the events causing them—accepting and enduring rather than mastering the passions? While Spinoza distances himself from the Stoics in the preface to Part Five, some of the things he says elsewhere in the *Ethics* point in this direction.[5] Yet as many readings emphasize, acceptance for Spinoza is supposed to come with love, joy, and immersion in nature rather than detachment and resignation, where the intellectual activity of understanding by itself causes a joy that can keep any sorrows and disappointments in check.

Whichever line of reading one favours, it is not clear how the account given of the passions as natural phenomena in the *Ethics* can ground the kind of emancipation through intellectual understanding that Spinoza is seeking, without introducing a duality in the doctrine that is hard to reconcile with a consistent naturalism to which he seems committed.[6] This paper focuses on Spinoza's original account of ideas and affects and discusses some difficulties that his very theory of emotions poses for the therapy he proposes, difficulties that so far as I know have not been addressed in the literature. Section 4.1 takes up the aspects of Spinoza's cognitive psychology and notion of ideas relevant for understanding his definition of passions as passive affects. Section 4.2 gives a summary of his account of affects as modifications of striving or desire, and Section 4.3 discusses the power of imagination and passions. The role Spinoza gives to reason and 'active affects' in the mastery of passions is discussed in the last Sections (4.4–6) where the problematic arguments Spinoza offers for selling the active affects as tools for moderating the passions, and the power he attributes to reason, are examined more in detail.

4.1 Ideas and Modes of Thinking

Spinoza's theory of passions is often presented as a cognitive theory, and as a forerunner of contemporary cognitive therapy.[7] Such labels should not be used without the greatest circumspection, for cognitive terms in the framework of Spinoza's original and controversial metaphysical theory of nature, and of the human mind as part of it, take on a meaning of their own. Spinoza's term for what Descartes referred to as passions and emotions is 'affect', and affects, which can be active or passive, are a subclass of what he calls 'affections'.[8] The latter are, literally, impressions or 'traces'—patterns of motion—in the fluid parts of the finite and determinate system of forces constituting the human body. They are the joint product of the interaction of movements caused in part by the body's own striving to persist in being, and in part by the forces of external objects acting on it according to necessary and unchanging laws of nature. Like anything else in Spinoza's universe, these bodily affections are paralleled by ideas. It follows from Spinoza's explanatory or conceptual dualism that these 'ideas of affections' (with more familiar terms that Spinoza also uses, 'sensations', 'perceptions', 'images'), are not *qua* psychological or mental caused and explained by physical processes, but by other, more or less clearly perceived antecedent ideas and perceptions.[9] The dualism here, however, is merely explanatory or conceptual, for the affections themselves are neither purely mental nor purely physical, but as much mental as physical. The ways ideas of affections are linked to and follow each other not only reflect the ways the body is affected; they *are* expressions of the very same changes that the body's affections are expressions of under the attribute of extension. It is through the medium of ideas that we perceive or are aware of ourselves and of how we *qua* embodied, or the bodies we are, are affected by other things. Yet these ideas are not, *qua* ideas, effects of the body's affections but of other ideas and are, ultimately, determined by God or nature considered as thinking.[10] Thus, in the case of an individual finite human mind, the contents of the thoughts it processes, including the ideas of the affects it experiences, depend not only on the (ideas of the) external objects causing them but on the whole set of any other ideas simultaneously present to it, forming the context in which they are perceived. This explains in part why Spinoza could think that changing the larger idea-context within which affects are perceived through understanding, can transform those affects.

Spinoza's psychophysiology and naturalist ethics is based on the 'conatus' principle—his version of the law of inertia—according to which each thing in the universe (whether considered as a mind or body, as a complex idea or as an extended system of forces) strives towards self-preservation and depends on other systems concurring with or opposing its striving (3p4–p7).[11] Since the human mind—its very being—is the idea of the actually existing human body, it is also driven by the same conatus or striving, yet because of attribute dualism this striving is manifested and understood in two different ways.[12] In this chapter, I will not be concerned with the physical conatus-principle or its interpretation, but with its psychological counterpart, appetite or desire, and its role in Spinoza's cognitive and moral psychology.[13]

First however, we must briefly consider Spinoza's account of mind as thinking and his distinction between, on the one hand, adequate or distinct, and on the other, inadequate and confused, ideas. When setting out to examine in Part Two of the *Ethics* the things supposed to lead to knowledge of the human mind and its highest blessedness, Spinoza defines 'idea' as 'the concept of the Mind that the Mind forms because it is a thinking thing' (2d3), explaining that he uses 'concept' rather than 'perception' because the latter 'seems to indicate that the mind is acted on by the object', whereas 'concept seems to express an action of the mind' (2d3expl). It is important to keep this distinction in view, though Spinoza himself does not always observe it and uses 'ideas' in both senses.

None of the terms 'thought', 'intellect', or 'reason', however, is properly defined. That we are thinking, for Spinoza as for Descartes, is a self-evident fact of experience introduced as an Axiom in Part Two of the *Ethics* (2ax2). Already in this earliest work Spinoza declares that it follows from the nature of thought that it forms true ideas (TdIE 106 C, 43 cf. TdIE 73). Thinking is a cognitive activity and true ideas are said to arise 'from the very power of the mind' by contrast to false or inadequate ones arising from external causes. Spinoza contrasts the intellect to the imagination in the same terms. The intellect, moreover, involves certainty—it knows that it knows, and it forms, through its own power as it were, adequate ideas, whereas the soul or mind in imagining is said 'to have the nature of something acted on' (TdIE 84 II/32 C 37).[14]

If the intellect for Spinoza is a mode of adequate, active thinking (an infinite mode as a matter of fact), imagination—the current mode of thinking of finite human minds—is always inadequate or confused, as are the sensory perceptions that its ideas or images are based on. This is not to say that they are false or unimportant. The human being—*qua* thinking—is said to sense (*sentit*) 'a certain body affected in many ways' (E2ax4). In sensing as in imagining, the mind registers in more or less confused ways the many affections of the particular body whose idea it is together with their external causes. Although in sensing it does not grasp their causal interconnections distinctly, it still has certain cognition of being affected thus and so.

Spinoza's use of the term 'thought' is at least as broad as Descartes', since, in addition to the above mentioned, he also lists among modes of thinking, 'love, desire, or whatever is designated by the word affects of the mind', and like his predecessor, he takes the latter to have specific intentional objects: 'the idea of the thing loved, desired, etc.' (2ax3). As is well known, it is even broader, since all things in the universe are in some sense of these terms, thinking or sensing 'in different degrees' (2p13s). Singular things differ through their complexity and degree of power, so thoughts or ideas differ among themselves (in their degree of objective reality) as their objects do formally. Spinoza writes: '…and so to determine what is the difference between the human mind and the others, and how it surpasses them, it is necessary for us…to know the nature of its object, i.e., of the human body' (2p13 s). The more complex the structure and workings of the bodily organism are, the greater its capacity to think, and to understand the latter we need to know something of the nature and complexity of the thinking body we are concerned with.[15]

That Spinoza should start his account of the nature of the human mind with a sketch of physiology is noteworthy. It marks another crucial departure from Descartes' theory of cognition: nothing comes into the human mind except through the body whose idea it is. So the human being thinks yes, through the body that she immediately senses, and whatever she thinks, has affections of her body as the direct contents of her thoughts.[16]

The definitions given at the beginning of Part Two, where Spinoza explains the nature of the human mind, suggest a distinction between on the one hand, ideas as concepts or conceptions that express its activity and, on the other, ideas of affections or sensory perceptions that are externally caused so manifest its passivity (e.g., 2d3exp). But it must also be noted that any ideas—like the physical phenomena they are ideas of—are themselves, to greater or lesser degrees, active or dynamic states. Ideas are never 'mute pictures' but come with a determinate force of affirmation.[17]

So it is not quite clear what Spinoza has in mind when, in contrasting ideas to passive perceptions, he defines them as concepts that the mind forms *because* it is a thinking thing. Even obscure sensory affections come with a force of their own and thus include some activity it seems.[18] More precisely, the force with which they affirm themselves is always a joint effect of the mind's power of thinking and the body's conatus or power to persevere, which reflects the actual force of the external things affecting them through the organs of the body. Yet the distinction between what actions or activity in a mind is its own doing and what depends on external forces is crucial for Spinoza's therapy of passions. As appears from the account of the affects that we shall look at next, there seems to be a fundamental ambiguity relating to this point in his theory to which I return at the end of the paper.

4.2 Affects as Modifications of Vital Force or Striving

Passions proper, that Spinoza calls passive 'affects,' are transitional changes caused in the body's force of persisting by the action of external things. They are a subclass of affections marked specifically by their impact on its striving, by concurring and strengthening its power to persist or by hindering and weakening it.[19] This is how affects in general are defined:

By affects (*affectus*) I understand the affections of the body (*corporis affectiones*) by which the body's power to act (*corporis agendi potentia*) is increased or diminished, aided or restrained, together with the ideas of these affections. (3d3)

Affects—and their ideas—are thus essentially dynamic processes, whereby a body (and its mind) passes from any given state to an increased or weakened power of self-preservation, and they have, as will be seen, their determinate effect on its desires, thoughts, and actions.

They come in two kinds, active and passive. The definition in 3d2 stipulates that the affects, when we are their adequate cause, are to be understood as actions (*actiones*), and as passions (*passiones*) when we do not cause them. The latter consist in those transitional states whereby our fundamental striving (*conatus*) to persist—or its actual force—is changed, not by our own power alone, but through external forces acting on it in ways that are not distinctly perceived. When, one may ask, are we, transitory and dependent collections of modes as we are, ever the adequate cause of any effect?

Any change a thing undergoes is the joint effect of its own power or conatus and that of the external things acting on it. By Spinoza's identity theory, an action in the mind is an action in the body, and similarly for passions.[20] When the effects of some external force concur with our own power to persist, the latter is enforced, strengthening the body's power to act and, presumably, the mind's power to think (as when you after hard exercise benefit from the intake of a suitable amount of healthy drink or food).[21] When external causes oppose or hinder your own striving (say you are deprived of food, sleep, or company for long times), your active power (mental-cum-physical) is inhibited or weakened. Affects are thus fluctuations in the degree of force or activity with which the striving that constitutes the actual essence of a human being is manifested in the effects it produces.

This striving, 'the very essence of man', is called 'appetite' when referring to the human body and mind together, and desire when referring to the mind, i.e., to our awareness of this appetite and where it directs us to.[22] Desire, as I read Spinoza, is the more or less clear idea or cognitive registering of the immediate effects that any change (i.e., affect) in one's basic appetite causes in one's thoughts and behaviour, including changes in the muscles and motor nerves in the body.[23] Desire is thus any determinate modification of one's appetite or striving to persevere registered in more or less clear (i.e., conscious) ideas of what one wants or where one is heading. If bodily affects and their ideas (e.g., joy or sorrow, pain or pleasure) consist in determinate fluctuations of the striving to persist, they also direct this striving or appetite to specific ends. The appetite thus specified, to the extent that we notice or are conscious of it, is what Spinoza calls desire (e.g., your wish to hang on to whatever causes you joy or to destroy or avoid what gives you pain). Desire thus, on the reading here defended, is the mind–body's striving rendered conscious by more or less distinct perceptions of its needs and behavioural inclinations with their various objects or targets. What we perceive as good or as evil and thereby our actions are determined by our current desires (3p9s).

Summing up, if joy and its derivatives consist in an increase or augmentation of the mind–body's power of activity, sadness and its derivatives express its weakening or diminishing. Good or perfection is measured by degree of activity, so increased power of activity means increased perfection.[24] Joy unfailingly produces a desire to preserve any current increase of one's power of activity and make it last, directing one's thoughts to whatever object or action appears to do so, while sadness causes a desire to destroy or avoid what is perceived as the cause of the present weakening of one's power.[25] While this holds generally, Spinoza makes a distinction between different kinds of joy and sorrow that turns out to be important for the therapy of passions. It is based on whether they affect the whole of the human body or only some part of it. Pleasure (*titillatio*) and pain (*dolor*) reflect local changes in the bodily constitution that are due to the stimulation of specific sensory organs and their effects, whereas cheerfulness or joy (*hilaritas*) or its contrary sadness or sorrow (*melancholia*) reflect or express changes affecting the whole body. *Hilaritas* turns out to have a crucial role for its well-being, ensuring a healthy equilibrium of its parts and increasing its power to act and think (4p42).[26] All other passions, love, hate, pride, fear, and others, are combinations of these three primary affects of joy, sadness, and desire, with accompanying ideas of their different specific external objects (3p 57d).

The remarkable effects that passions have on our thoughts follow from a special psychological application of the conatus principle announced in 3p12: 'The mind, as far as it can, strives to think of those things that increase or assist the body's power of acting (*corporis agendi potentiam*).' Self-preservation directs our thoughts and actions automatically to the ways of keeping present whatever causes us joy and pleasure, and to avoid or hinder us from thoughts that sadden us. This principle is central to Spinoza's account of the mechanisms of passions and the ways to control them, though it is not very clear how it is grounded, nor indeed what exactly it is supposed to imply.[27] I will not discuss its derivation or proof but in order to get clearer about how the principle works, the theory of imagination alluded to earlier must now be considered more closely.

4.3 The Power of Imagination

The human body in being affected retains impressions or images of the external thing acting on it. While depending on the nature of my body and its current state or constitution, such impressions also depend, and hence, as Spinoza puts it, 'involve', the nature of the external body (3p12d see also 2p16). As long as the body is thus affected, its mind will imagine the body that caused it 'as present to itself' (2p17,d). This holds both for fresh impressions caused by external objects actually present to one's senses (e.g., my visual and tactile impressions of the white cat lying on my keyboard as I am trying to work), as well as of re-actualized past impressions or traces made by things or beings now absent (like that of a much beloved cat-chasing dog who passed away years ago (1p17c)). This is all according to Spinoza's account a matter of the random course and connections of patterns of 'fluids' in the body's softer parts, of what impressions or traces they leave in impinging on their surfaces (2p17c,d), and of how these traces (and their ideas) get associated (2p18d,s).

The reviving of memory traces caused by events or beings mattering to me can affect me in the same ways as current impressions would.[28] Depending on the current state of my body and the set of ideas being revived by mechanical association I may get stuck on traumatic or saddening events whose images disrupt or block my normal power of acting and thinking. It is an important element of this theory that any ideas of current impressions in my body are always confused because of their double origin, involving the nature and present dispositions of the body affected together with the nature of the external body acting on it (2p16). Because they indicate the 'constitution' or 'the actual physical state of our own body rather than the nature of the external body' causing them,[29] they hinder us from knowing the latter—a fact that we, in suffering these affects, are seldom aware of and don't like to be reminded of. A person madly in love with some dubious character does not appreciate her friends reminding her it is just a surge of hormones that makes the guy attractive to her, or some random feature, like a superficial resemblance of traits to earlier objects of love, whose impressions revive old traces with their associated pleasant or joyful affects. Knowledge of the true character—or lack thereof—of a present object of passion does not by itself alter the affect. It depends wholly on how the fluids in the lover's body happen to be affected by images of the object loved and their traces. The only thing that can counteract (and correct) imaginings (or false beliefs based on imagination) 'are other imaginings that are stronger' and 'exclude the present existence of the thing imagined' (4p1s, referring back to 2p17).[30]

What, then, are we to make of Spinoza's claim that we by nature tend to think more of, and seek out, what gladdens, and so benefits us (increasing our perfection), than of what saddens us and so makes us weaker? Is Spinoza implying that there is no independent scale of value apart from the changes in the striving to persist or power that we are driven by? Are we bound to consider good or useful whatever it is that presently seems to increase our power and evil whatever seems to hinder it? Spinoza writes: 'Cognition of good and evil is nothing other than the affect of joy or sadness in so far as we are conscious of it' (4p8). In the proof of this proposition Spinoza argues, referring to 4d1–d2, that 'We call good or evil what is favourable or contrary to the preserving of our being, i.e., what increases or diminishes, helps or restrains our power of acting' (by 3p7). The idea of good or evil is the idea of the affect itself, and since the affect and its idea are not really but merely conceptually distinguished, the cognition of good and evil consists in this very affect, that is, in our pleasant or painful more or less obscure awareness of the current transition in our vital power and its cause or object (4p8d).[31] Does it follow then that we inevitably tend to pursue whatever happens to make us feel good or stronger/upbeat at any given moment? Spinoza would not endorse this conclusion.

The conatus driving a singular thing is, as we saw, its essential power to act, the power that constitutes its determinate nature from which 'alone or in conjunction with other things' all the effects it can produce, i.e., its actions, follow (3p7d). The power that it strives to preserve is its determinate individual essence, so there is a matter of fact of what actually benefits or harms it. What truly preserves the being or power to act of an individual human being is, however, obscured by her current passive affects with their trains of inadequate ideas of their objects and causes. Spinoza devotes much of Parts 3 and 4 of the *Ethics* to showing how the confused ideas of passive affects (i.e., passions proper) keep us, through their own dynamics and mechanical associations, in 'bondage', enslaved in the accidental run of things, tossed about like waves on the sea, driven by contrary winds.[32] His salvation project is about setting us right in our search for a true and certain good, to free us—our minds—from this miserable state. Let us now turn to the active affects and the role given to them in this process of perfecting the mind, and—by identity—the mind–body.

4.4 From Passive to Active Affects

What Spinoza calls our actual essence can be considered in two ways: as the (actual) essence relative to mind and body as it persists in temporal duration, and the (eternally actual) essence relative to mind alone. I am only concerned with the first.[33] The actual striving of the mind is supposed to express that of the body: the mind strives to affirm the existence and striving of its body. Spinoza also argues that the mind strives to persist in its being both 'in so far as it has clear and distinct ideas and in so far as it has confused ideas', and is conscious of 'this striving it has' (3p9). These strivings together are said to constitute the actual essence of the mind (3p3 and 3p7)—the actual given essence by which it causes whatever effects are in its power.[34] But how exactly are its strivings related in having these two kinds of ideas? Are we to think of them as one and the same striving, manifested only partially in inadequate thinking—through whatever element of truth inadequate ideas affirm? The latter would then be separated from the former only by negation, i.e., the striving of the mind, in having inadequate ideas, would differ from its striving in adequate thinking only by what it lacks or by its limitations (See 3p3s).

In 3p9s we saw that Spinoza distinguishes two notions of desire or conscious appetite, one relating to mind and body together, and one relating to the mind alone that he calls will.[35] This distinction is merely nominal or conceptual, yet we must ask what work it is supposed to do and how it squares with the strivings of two kinds of ideas. The notion of a striving proper to the mind comes up again in 3p54, where the mind is said to strive to imagine (*imaginari conatur*) what posits its own power of acting. This striving is identified with the mind's essence that 'affirms only what the Mind is and can do' (3p7).[36] Imagination, as we have seen, is the processing of ideas of images or affections of the body, so whatever the mind strives to *imagine* must depend on the body and its affections, and these again depend on external causes. If, as Spinoza argues, the first and principal striving of our mind is to affirm the existence of our body, then presumably, whatever it wills and does from its own power is to affirm its body's striving to persist and what supports or strengthens it (3p7 and 3p10).[37] Towards the end of Part Three, in 3p57d, referring back again to the desire which is 'the very nature or essence of every single individual' (3p9), Spinoza describes this desire as 'the striving to persevere in one's being in so far as it is related to mind and body at once'.

It might be useful to dwell on the distinction between two kinds of conscious appetite, desire and will, that Spinoza makes in 3p9s. On the one hand, there is the striving of the individual mind *qua* sensing and thereby registering the current affections of its individual body with ensuing desires. The cognitive awareness here is a matter of more or less confused beliefs based on imagination. On the other hand, there is the striving of the mind *qua* understanding or conceiving the body and its affections adequately in its larger context of causal networks and laws. What Spinoza calls 'desire' are affirmations of inadequate ideas of the current motive tendencies of the body, which are reactions to the fluctuations in your given actual appetite caused by the action of external things (other individuals) on your body. (As when you find yourself tired or distracted and set out for yet another cup of tea or whatever else you can think of as picking you up.) What Spinoza calls 'will' (3p9s) and relates to the mind alone, would be desire restricted to the activity of affirming adequate ideas of the body and of how it fares in its transactions with surrounding bodies according to the laws of nature. This desire manifesting itself in affirming true adequate ideas, described in a more familiar terminology, would be a desire to understand (3p58d). Conceiving true adequate ideas for Spinoza involves activity. The puzzle this leaves us with is that this striving to understand, which involves activity, would be an instance of the same striving that manifests itself in affirming confused and truncated ideas that express its passivity. The mind in a sense causes nothing without the body whose idea it is and which it is wholly dependent on. Yet it is said to be active in understanding how adequate ideas follow from other adequate ideas, and this activity is not a mere epiphenomenon. It presupposes and builds on imagination—the lower and more passive level of cognition. It is also supposed to come with some real increase of force or perfection independently of imagination and its passive affects.[38]

In this context, from the end of the scholium to 3p57d considered above, Spinoza introduces his account of active affects (3p57s to 3p58), which are 'related (*referuntur*)' to us in so far as we act, and are caused by the mind when it conceives adequate ideas. In conceiving adequate ideas, the mind is aware not only of affirming them, but in affirming them it is said to 'contemplate' (be aware of) itself *qua* active, something that unfailingly gives it joy and comes with desires of its own—desires, it seems, that are purely intellectual, for all they tend to is affirming or deducing more adequate ideas. Spinoza does not use the term intellectual, but he sees it as a desire relating (*referuntur*) to us 'only in so far as we understand', so to our mind alone (3p58d, 3p59s, cf. 4app4).

This seems to suggest that the mind has resources—an essence or striving—of its own that is not directly dependent on current changes in the body's striving to persist in being, but only depends on its own activity in so far as it understands, which causes affects of its own. By contrast with the passive affects which relate to desire, joy and sadness, the active affects never have any negative effects: '. . . no affects of sadness can be related (*referuntur*) to the Mind in so far as it acts, but only affects of Joy and Desire' (3p59d).[39] Active affects thus unfailingly increase the mind's power or perfection, and though this is nowhere explained, in so far as they increase the mind's power or perfection, they should have the same effect in the body.

The following line of thinking should support this assumption. As mentioned before, Spinoza takes an individual's power to act to vary with the complexity of his/her body. The power to understand (i.e., to affirm adequate ideas and distinguish truth from falsity) presumably requires highly complex bodies of the human kind—bodies so structured that they can be acted on and act or react in many different ways. The striving of an appropriately structured human body to maintain its being can then also, whatever else it directs it to, like satisfying its basic vital needs, naturally take the form of a desire to understand, to form and affirm more adequate ideas. In 4app32 Spinoza argues that in so far as we understand (*intelligimus*), we desire and find contentment in nothing but truth, that is, in the necessary order of things. In understanding this rightly, the striving of 'our better part agrees (or is in harmony) with the order of the whole of nature'. For Spinoza, not only is understanding part of our nature but it represents our better part! According to the last Part 5 of the *Ethics*, it is also our highest contentment. Spinoza seems to assume that the joy that active reasoning and understanding gives a human being manifests itself in an increased power of his/her body-object as well.[40]

The *Ethics* from the end of Part 3 is a dialectics of back and forth between passivity and activity of the mind, between its passive and active affects, between the power through which an individual acts on its own and the power of external things acting on it. An important question for Spinoza is exactly how much of the force with which an individual asserts its power comes from the concurring action of external things on which it is necessarily dependent, and how much depends on its own being or nature. To get a better grip on how we should understand the mind's activity and the contrast between passivity and activity, it will be useful to return once more to Spinoza's definition of affects and in particular to look at the general definition of affects at the end of Part Three.

4.5 The Mind in Bondage

The definition of affects considered earlier in 3d3 related to affections of the body (transitions in the body's power to persist) *with* their ideas, and covered active as well as passive affects. Having treated both kinds of affects, devoting two propositions to active affects and then listing his definitions of particular affects (3p58–59), Spinoza closes Part 3 by what he calls a 'general definition of the affects', but which is, specifically, of passive affects:

> An affect (*affectus*) that is said to be a passion (*pathema*) is a confused idea by which the mind affirms a greater or lesser force of existing of the body or some of its parts than before, whereby the mind is determined to think of this rather than of that. (3 Gen Def Aff)

It is worth noting that this definition is limited to the affects 'in so far as they are related only to the mind' (*quatenus ad solam mentem referentur* II/203, l. 27, C 54). It is of *passive* affects, in particular those primary passions (desire, joy and sadness) of which all other innumerable passions are variations, and it concerns the ways the passions affect its thinking.

Considering their effects on the mind alone, passive affects are confused ideas and so are cognitive states, consisting in partial representations of their external causes as they affect the body.[41] That Spinoza now, at the end of Part Three, focuses on affects *qua* mental is thus not to say that their bodily aspect is ignored. On the contrary, as before, their idea is said to *affirm* the particular increasing or diminishing of the power to persevere in the body that is its primary object. In affirming their objects, passions also 'determine the mind to think of this rather than that'. This is what I want to focus on here: the effects of the passions in changing the direction of the mind's ideas, keeping its thoughts in bondage by setting off brute chains of associations, where ideas are combined in quasi mechanistic ways, according to a random course of nature rather than the order of reason.

For instance, hate and anger come with a desire to harm the object hated and hinders us from thinking of anything else. Pride inflates our self-esteem to the point of blinding us from foibles and weaknesses that others have no difficulty noticing. Love unavoidably makes us rejoice at the thought of the object loved, causing a desire to have it and keep it present, whether or not its present object actually is good for one.[42] Or take the confused idea that anger or rage consists in. Its affective content includes the awareness of a sudden change caused by a surge of adrenaline in the blood, a contraction of muscles, and an urge to harm or destroy the object causing it. Becoming aware of this urge and affirming it is what a desire for revenge consists in (Def. of Affects 36 Cf. 3p39). *Qua* idea, the anger and desire for revenge follow from other ideas (e.g., the pain or harm being done to us). *Qua* confused, it follows from other inadequate ideas (e.g., the mistaken belief that the pain was caused by the person you now desire to hit).

The ideas of affects are typically disconnected and fragmented, presenting themselves in an order we do not wholly understand and are unable to predict while suffering them. I take it this is why Spinoza emphasizes their confusion here (3 Gen Def Aff). That these ideas are said to 'affirm of its body or some part of it an increased or diminished force of existing,' I take to mean simply that they are actual cognitive expressions of the changes/fluctuations of power that the body undergoes. The transition from weaker to stronger or from stronger to weaker power is here at once physical and mental. It would make little sense, however, to characterize these transitions as passive or confused when considering only their physical aspect. Since they are externally caused, they are passive processes only from the point of view of the finite mind who suffers them, because it lacks distinct perceptions of their true causes.[43] Their very confusion as cognitive states hinders the mind's own activity and disrupts or perhaps even inhibits its desire to understand.

Spinoza thus has reasons for focusing on the mental aspect of the passive affects. The general definition of passive affects as confused ideas serves to remind the reader that the passions, whether they actually hinder or, on the contrary, increase our body's power of acting, always express the passivity rather than the activity of the mind, and thereby constrain its power.[44] Their confused and partial ideas manifest its finitude and utter dependence on infinitely many other things beyond its cognition and control. So even when affected with passive Joy, although relatively speaking the power (of the mind–body) to persist is increased because this increase is due to inadequately perceived external causes, this affect does not necessarily count as an increase of perfection in the very power of the mind itself.[45]

Turning back to the account of active affects in 3p58–p59d, I can now state what worries me about it. It is presented as continuous with and following from the account of passive affects, and yet active affects seem to presuppose a total change in perspective. Thus, in the demonstration of 3p58, Spinoza argues, based on 3p53, that the mind rejoices when *conceiving* itself and its power of acting.[46] In 3p53 it was argued, in continuity with the account of passive affects leading up to it, that the mind rejoices all the more the more distinctly it *imagines* itself and its power. Imagining, as we have seen, works with inadequate ideas depending on external causes, and as such belongs to the lowest degree of cognition. Distinctly *imagining* ourselves as active (e.g., doing something we are pleased with and proud to show off) might give us a vivid and pleasant sense of our self, as Spinoza argues in 3p53c. Yet such imaginings, which are externally caused and confused, tend to mislead us to a false or exaggerated sense of our power of acting, not comparable to the kind of distinct cognition of self which is supposed to cause active joy. Imagining sets and keeps our thoughts on the wrong course so to speak. True self-knowledge (knowledge of your 'true' self), as argued in 2p43, comes only with rational activity in conceiving adequate ideas and grasping their interconnections, not by imagining your power on grounds of fragmentary, confused ideas of imagined deeds or accomplishments.[47]

Spinoza notoriously gives little help for determining what adequate ideas consist in precisely.[48] But it helps to know that he calls the capacity to form common notions—his example of adequate ideas—reason. To form or conceive adequate ideas, from which only adequate ideas follow, is to exercise one's reason (2p40s2). To reason, then, is to know oneself *qua* active self-dependent cause, which gives one joy and increase's one's perfection. Not unsurprisingly, on the picture that emerges here, the true self, the mind considered on its own, is reason, and its true power is its capacity to understand. Is this to say that the argument in 3p53–p54 turns on an ambiguity in Spinoza's use of the term mind? I argue that it does.

The puzzling claim in 3p53 that the Mind rejoices the more distinctly it imagines itself and its own power of acting is based on 2p19 and 2p23, where it is shown that a man cognizes himself only through affections of his body; e.g., in being affected by joy or pleasure, for instance because he finds himself, his actions or his possessions praised by others, something that pleases him so increases his self-esteem and makes him feel stronger. The argument in 3p58 seems to suggest that a man, or by analogy, his mind, will be empowered in a similar way merely by rational activity or understanding. However, what bodily affections could come into play or do the work here, e.g., the work that the affect of pride in the vainglorious who is praised by others does for increasing his self-esteem and joy? Or consider the claim that 'the mind strives to imagine (*imaginari*) only those things that posit its power of acting' (3p54). How can imagining, i.e., inadequate thinking, work in this context? Should we understand this as saying that we strive or desire by nature to think of nothing else than what nurtures and strengthens our reason or rational capacity? We are still in Part 3 of the *Ethics* so this is not a normative claim or a claim about the model of a free man. Nor does it strike me as an obvious fact of common sense psychology. It is, rather, offered as a true proposition derived from considering emotions like a scientist of human nature, according to the geometric method. By contrast, in Part 4, normative claims are derived from the model Spinoza sets for us, based on an ideal standard of goodness or perfection. As we read in the 4app5, a rational life comes only with understanding, 'and things are good only insofar as they aid man to enjoy the life of the mind, which is defined by understanding' (II/266, C 588–589).[49] But we are not there yet.

4.6 From Bondage to Freedom: Hitting the Road to Salvation

Let us step back and reflect on where Spinoza has led us. He defines the human mind as the idea of the human body early on in the *Ethics*. This does not in itself tell us much about its nature, except that it is representational and that it depends on the nature or essence of its object, the singular body, which consists in its actual striving to persist in being. So the mind depends both for its power of thinking and the content of its thoughts on the constitution of its body object, its striving and its actual affections. Part 1 of the *Ethics* developed a vision or doctrine of one infinitely powerful substance, God or Nature, which as eternally actual expresses itself in infinitely many attributes or essences, of which we, *qua* finite modes, perceive only two: the attribute of thought and the attribute of extension. The task Spinoza set himself in Parts 2 and 3 was 'to determine the powers of the affects and the power of the mind over the affects', more precisely, the power whereby the mind can 'moderate and restrain the affects' (E3p56sch C 527 II/185). But what he really shows in Part 3 and the first half of Part 4 is how utterly dependent the human mind is on external forces concurring with its own.[50] He argues that a passive affect 'in so far as it relates to the mind', that is, in so far as the mind suffers from it (*conflictatur*), depends on the corresponding affection of the body. It cannot, therefore, be modified or repressed 'except by a bodily cause'. (This follows from the attribute dualism and 2p6, 4p7d.) The force of persistence of the affect depends on the force of its cause, and can be reined in or destroyed only by a cause strong enough to affect the body with a contrary affect stronger than the one it suffers from.[51]

While demonstrating to us the power of passions, and through them, of external things over our own, Spinoza also gives some hints or elements of an underlying vision of the mind's own power of activity as related to reason. He argues that rational activity comes with a joy that is supposed to increase its power (the power of the mind considered in itself). We are led to see not only that reason is essential to the mind or to us (our better part!) but that its activity is in some important sense independent of the external forces ruling its imagination and passions. These sound like familiar claims from earlier traditional versions of rationalist salvation projects, at times echoing more Stoic and at other times more Aristotelian themes. But can Spinoza ground the rationalist ideals he seems committed to within his naturalist project without inconsistency?

Consider the argument we looked at above, which goes directly from a claim about the effects of passive joy (3p53) to a similar claim (in 3p58) about the effects of active joy, from an increase in power that is externally conditioned to one that is internally caused. What entitles Spinoza to move from the sentient and desiring mind as it expresses the externally caused changes in its body's power of acting, to consider the mind alone or the mind as it were in itself, which, as it now turns out, has rational desires and priorities of its own, which are not directly dependent on the ways it is affected by the things in its immediate environment? He seems to argue both that the thinking or understanding mind (i.e., the mind in so far as it acts) stands by its nature over sorrows and other affects diminishing the power of the body whose idea it is, and, at the same time, that it is, by the identity thesis, affected by them. But what power, if any, can the mind or its power to reason have, independently of the other forces it depends on as the idea of the body? And how is this power supposed to work against the force of external powers that do not concur with but are opposed to it (3p59sc C530 II/180)?

This question is directly addressed in Part 5 where Spinoza announces a new way leading to freedom (5pref. C, 594), explaining what the 'power of reason' consists in, and 'what reason in itself can do' in so far as affects are concerned:

> Here…I shall treat only of the power of mind or reason, foremost I shall show how much ruling power (*imperium*) and what kind of ruling power, reason has over the affects to reduce and moderate them. (5pref)

Spinoza famously starts by ridiculing the views of the Stoic who attributed this power to an absolute freedom of will. He does not miss the occasion to poke fun at Descartes, who likewise pretended to explain how the free will works to change the passions with his pathetic theory of the animals spirits and the pineal gland, presupposing a comparison between incommensurable things: the force of mind or will and that of corporeal motions. The Preface to Part 5 ends by stating that, since the power of the mind, as Spinoza implies he has shown before, is defined by understanding alone (*intelligentia*), the remedies against the affects are to be determined by the mind's cognition alone.

Spinoza himself as well as many of his followers take the therapy he proposes to be superior to those of his predecessors in the rationalist tradition precisely because it does not pitch reason directly against passive affects, but rather works on the latter through cognition and the active, self-generated affects that come with it. Yet he continues to use mechanical or quasi mechanical analogies, describing the matter as a struggle of opposing forces, where the active affects are supposed to be stronger than the passive affects themselves (5p6–7). Reason by itself cannot oppose an affect but works only through the more powerful active affects it produces.

Consider the claim quoted before that 'An affect that is a passion ceases to be a passion as soon as we form a clear and distinct idea of it' and its proof, which is another source of puzzlement (5p3). It argues that a clear and distinct idea of the affect is only conceptually distinct from the affect itself when it is referred to the mind alone.[52] If the idea is distinguished from the affect conceptually or by reason, it is really identical to the affect. Now the clear and distinct idea that has the affect as its object is supposed to transform the affect from passive to active. More precisely, as Spinoza himself puts it: the affect ceases to be a passion when we form a clear and distinct idea of it. What he presupposes is that considered in relation to the mind, the idea, *qua* distinct, expresses activity. The activity of clear and distinct thought replaces a confused idea of a bodily affection, a passion of the mind. But how can a clear and distinct idea be of the same object as a confused idea of an affect, which consists in a particular change or fluctuation of the power to persist of the individual affected with its given cause? Rather, what happens seems to be that the clear and distinct idea of the passive affect replaces the latter with an active affect of its own, caused by the mind's own activity. Is this to say then that the bodily affect vanishes with its confused idea, while the joy of the distinct idea prevails? The clear and distinct idea of, say, arthritis, replaces the pain you were suffering from with pleasure or joy, counteracting its devastating effects on your power?

This cannot be the right way to understand 5p3 and its proof. In discussing errors of sense and imagination, Spinoza argued that nothing can counteract (and correct) imaginings (or false beliefs based on imagination) except stronger imaginings or images, i.e., ideas or images that 'exclude the present existence of the thing imagined' (4p1s, referring back to 2p17). He discusses two famous examples: the idea of the size and distance of the sun as a visual object, and the image of the sun reflected in water. In both cases, the error of the corresponding beliefs, say that the sun is 200 feet distant from you, or, in the second case, that the sun is in the water, vanishes as soon we know the true distance of the sun, or the laws of light and refraction. However, as Spinoza points out, in neither case does the imagining cease by the mere knowledge of the truth. The sun continues to appear as it always did 200 feet away. He bases himself on a point established earlier:

> For it is not our ignorance of its true distance that causes us to see the sun to be so near; it is that the affection of our body involves the essence of the sun only to the extent that the body itself is affected by it. (2p35s)

In other words, we perceive the sun as near us 'because the mind conceives' its magnitude only 'in so far as the body is affected by it' (4p1s). You will continue to suffer from your pain as long as its cause, say arthritis or being bitten by a dog, continues to affect some of your body parts. So applying what Spinoza says about the affections of imagination to the affects, it seems that you continue to suffer a passion as long as what caused it continues to affect your body. Your pain is the same even when you know that it is caused by the deterioration of your joints, or hip, or as long as your wound has not healed.

Now if a passive affect does not disappear—and it is hard to see how it could on Spinoza's account of the matter—he may still have some grounds for the claim that it ceases to be a passion with respect to the mind as a whole. For even if the clear and distinct idea of the cause of an affect does not by itself free you from it, it may localize and thus neutralize it to some extent, by disconnecting it from its imagined cause and thereby diminishing its conative and behavioural effects. The pain continues but it does not unravel or upset the order of your thoughts in the same way it did before, nor does it have the same effects on your behaviour. The clear and distinct idea of its causes gives you more options to view and perhaps deal with the affect you are suffering from. I won't reach for the sun in the water when I know its true location and the laws of refraction, and once I know the true cause of my pain, if it has one, I will be inclined to seek proper treatment.

The distinct cognition of the causes of the pain frees up my power of thinking for other subjects than the pain and its imagined cause I was obsessing about. The knowledge of the causes of one's passions more generally (or perhaps more correctly when speaking of finite minds: the knowledge of one's lack of knowledge of their causes) may give one a wider perspective from which their impact can start to look somewhat insignificant, perhaps even a matter of indifference. But here one might ask what help Spinoza's therapy gives us that was not suggested by the Stoics or their followers before? Instead of indifference towards our passive affects and their particular causes, Spinoza, in Part 5, preaches love of God or nature. Love of God is the joy caused by the contemplation of the infinite causal power of which human beings *qua* finite modes of thinking are parts.

Is this new kind of freedom a freedom *from* the bondage of passions we were promised? The freedom to which Spinoza leads us in the *Ethics* is, at best, a freedom *within* bondage, freedom, that is, not of action in any current sense of the word, but of thought or intellectual activity, the freedom to align our thoughts to the necessary order of things. Whether we can also be active in some other sense all depends on the circumstances concurring, independently of it, with our own power. The human mind, one is tempted to say, remains in bondage, while its best part enjoys freedom to the extent it participates through adequate thinking in the eternal activity of God's infinite intellect.[53]

Notes

1. Spinoza declares in Part 5 of the *Ethics* that a passive affect ceases to be passive 'as soon as we form a clear and distinct idea of it' 5p3 d (C, p. 598). He adds in the Corollary to the Proof of 5p3: 'The more an affect is known to us, then, the more it is in our power, and the less the Mind is acted on by it'. The extraordinary power Spinoza attributes to the understanding appears also from the following: '... insofar as we understand the causes of Sadness, it ceases (by P3) to be a passion, i.e. (by IIIP59), to that extent it ceases to be Sadness. And so, insofar as we understand God to be the cause of Sadness, to that extent we rejoice' 5p18c, s. References are to *The Collected Works of Spinoza*, ed. Edwin Curley (Princeton, N.J.: Princeton University Press, 1985) vol. 1, p. 598, cited hereafter as C. Citations of passages from the *Ethics* are in the following form: the initial number indicates the Part of the *Ethics*; 'p' indicates a proposition, 'a' indicates an axiom, 's' indicates a scholium, 'c' indicates a corollary, and 'd' indicates a definition (when immediately following a part number) or a demonstration (when immediately following a proposition number).
2. For an insightful discussion of the complexities and problematic aspects of Spinoza's theory see Herman de Dijn, 'Spinoza's Theory of Emotions and its Relation to Therapy', in *Oxford Studies of Early Modern Philosophy*, ed. D. Garber and S. Nadler (Oxford, Clarendon Press, 2010), pp. 71–90. For a comparison of Spinoza's views to the Stoics see Firmin De Brabander, 'Psychotherapy and Moral Perfection: Spinoza and the Stoics on the Prospect of Happiness', *Stoicism: Tradition and Transformation*, ed. Steven K. Strange & Jack Zupko (Cambridge: Cambridge University Press, 2004), pp. 198–213. Cf. Donald Rutherford, 'Salvation as a State of Mind: The Place of *Acquiescentia* in Spinoza's Ethics', *British Journal for the History of Philosophy* 7 (1999): 447–73. See also Anthony A. Long, 'Stoicism in the Philosophical Tradition: Spinoza, Lipsius, Butler', in *The Cambridge Companion to the Stoics*, ed. Brad Inwood (Cambridge, Cambridge University Press, 2003), pp. 365–92.
3. I discuss the first of these questions in 'Spinoza on Passions and Self-Knowledge: The Case of Pride', in *Emotion & Cognitive Life in Medieval & Early Modern Philosophy*, ed. Martin Pickavé and Lisa Shapiro (Oxford, Oxford University Press, 2012) pp. 234–54, and in 'Spinoza on the Human Mind', in *Midwest Studies in Philosophy–Early Modern Philosophy Reconsidered*, Essays in Honor of Paul Hoffman, ed. Peter A. French, Howard K. Wettstein and John Carriero, XXXV (2011), pp. 4–25. I discuss the nature of passions in Spinoza's system in 'The Metaphysics of Affects and the Unbearable Reality of Confusion', in *The Oxford Handbook of Spinoza*, ed. Michael Della Rocca (Oxford, Oxford University Press, forthcoming).
4. He bases his naturalist programme on this assumption, treating 'the nature and force of the affects', and the mind's power over them, 'by the same method' as the one applied in the first two parts of the *Ethics* to God and mind, the famous 'geometrical' method—however that is to be understood. GII/138; EIII Pref., C, 492.
5. See, e.g., 4p73s, II/265, C, 587, and 4App 32 C, 593.

6. I explore this question in a sequel to this paper, 'Affectivity and Cognitive Perfection' (in progress). The naturalism attributed to Spinoza comes in many versions, from reductive mechanistic materialism to more complex and liberal 'Aristotelian style' naturalisms. For recent discussions see John Carriero, 'Spinoza on Final Causality', in *Oxford Studies in Early Modern Philosophy*, ed. Daniel Garber and Steven Nadler (Oxford: Oxford University Press, 2005), vol. 2, pp. 105–47, Don Garrett, 'Representation and Consciousness in Spinoza's Naturalistic Theory of the Imagination', in *Interpreting Spinoza: Critical Essays*, ed. Charlie Huenemann (Cambridge: Cambridge University Press, 2008), pp. 4–25, and John Carriero, 'Conatus and Perfection', in *Midwest Studies in Philosophy*, XXXV (2011), pp. 69–92.
7. See, e.g., Jerome Neu, *Emotion, through and Therapy: A Study of Hume and Spinoza and the Relationship of Philosophical Theories of the Emotions to Psychological Theories of Therapy* (Berkeley and Los Angeles: University of California Press, 1977), and Herman de Dijn, 'Spinoza's Theory of Emotions', pp. 77–9. Antonio Damasio sees Spinoza's theory as anticipating contemporary brain research in *Looking for Spinoza, Joy, Sorrow and the Feeling Brain* (New York: Harcourt, 2003). But it is also part of a salvation project foreign to the spirit of enlightenment humanism. For a sober scepticism with regard to contemporary readings and appropriations of Spinoza's project, see Yitzhak Melmed, 'Charitable Interpretations and the Political Domestication of Spinoza, or, Benedict in the Land of the Secular Imagination', in *The Methodology of the History of Philosophy*, ed. Eric Schlisser, Mogens Laerke and Justin Smith (Oxford: Oxford University Press, 2013), pp. 258–79.
8. Spinoza had studied Descartes' *Les Passions de l'âme* (1649) that he read in its Latin translation (*Passiones animae*, Amsterdam: Elzevier, 1650) with great care, reacting to many of its claims (most notoriously his doctrines of mind–body interaction and free will) and radically modifying some of its central ideas.
9. To explain an effect (according to 1ax4 and 5) is to understand it in terms of its causes, for knowledge of the effect 'involves the knowledge of the cause' (1ax4, see also 1ax5).
10. As modes thoughts, just like the modes of body or bodily processes constituting their objects, ideas are determined through their relations to other modes of their kind: whatever transitory being they have *qua* modes is structured by and contingent on their interactions with other modes of the same attribute. See my 'Spinoza on the Human Mind', pp. 12–13. Cf. Tad Schmaltz, 'Spinoza and Descartes', in *The Oxford Handbook of Spinoza*, ed. Michael Della Rocca (Oxford: Oxford University Press, forthcoming).
11. Nature, as Spinoza conceives it, is an infinitely extended and inherently dynamic plenum of forces, where every singular mode or system of modes expressing it has its share of this power or force by means of which it, 'in so far as it is in itself, strives to preserve itself in its being', and that determines all its actions (3p6d.). This power which Spinoza calls *conatus* (striving or endeavour) constitutes its actual essence or being (3p7d9).
12. 2p11–12. Mind and body are in a sense identical: they express the same reality in different ways. But this is a complex issue, and one needs to determine what kind of identity one is talking about here. Spinoza sometimes uses the technical terms of objective and formal reality—the idea, as a representation of its object, the thing actually or formally existing, has the very same reality objectively—not formally. The scholastic distinction between objective and formal reality is suggestive, but its interpretation in the framework of Spinoza's monistic ontology is a delicate matter, and I am not sure how helpful it is. But for an interesting reading see Karolina Huebner, 'Spinoza on Essences, Universals, and Beings of Reason', *Pacific Philosophical Quarterly*, forthcoming.

13. In his so-called physical excursus in 2p13, Spinoza introduces the idea of a fixed ratio or proportion of motion and rest between the parts of complex bodies. Particular bodies would be unified by a specific ratio of motion or rest prevailing between their parts, each of which, presumably, have a ratio and striving of their own. The ratio of motion and rest is sometimes described as the 'form' of the body (2p13L4), which determines (and sets limits) to the activities of the thing and the effects it can produce. For a helpful account of Spinoza's metaphysics of force and nature see John Carriero, 'Spinoza, The Will, and the Ontology of Power', in *The Young Spinoza: A Metaphysician in the Making,* ed. Yitzhak Y. Melamed (Oxford: Oxford University Press, 2015), pp. 160–82 and his works cited below. If the ratio is the 'form' of the body, whose essence is said to be its actual striving to persist in being, then this striving can be thought of as a striving to maintain the characteristic ratio structure of the body. The being of the mind whose nature is to think or perceive the body would then be characterized by a corresponding appetite affirming the striving of its object, the body. (I return to this below in Section 4.4 See also 3p7d quoted below note 34, and end of 4pref, II/209, C, 546.)

    Some other things Spinoza says suggests that individual for him is a relative notion (after all, individual things are mere transitory modes of one substance). Singular things are defined in 2d7 as 'things that are finite and have a determinate existence. And if a number of Individuals so concur in one action that together they are all the cause of one effect, I consider them all, to that extent, as one singular thing.' (See also *Short Treatise* Part Two Preface I/52, Curley 95, *Ethics* 2p13 Axioms L3 A1–A3 and L4–7, and Spinoza's remarks on the Spanish Poet whose identity changed after brain injury (4p39s)). For recent discussions of Spinoza's challenging and elusive ontology and notion of essence see Don Garrett, 'Spinoza on the Essence of the Human Body and the Part of the Mind That Is Eternal', in OlliKoistinen (ed.) *The Cambridge Companion to Spinoza's Ethics* (Cambridge: Cambridge University Press, 2009), pp. 284–302; Valtteri Viljanen, *Spinoza's Geometry of Power* (Cambridge: Cambridge University Press, 2011); John Carriero, 'Conatus and Perfection', *Midwest Studies in Philosophy–Early Modern Philosophy Reconsidered*, Essays in Honor of Paul Hoffman, ed. Peter A. French, Howard K. Wettstein and John Carriero, vol. No. XXXV, (2011), pp. 69–92; 'Spinoza on Three Kinds of Cognition: Imagination, Understanding and Essence', unpublished manuscript; and more recently Karolina Huebner, 'Spinoza on Essences, Universals, and Beings of Reason', and 'Spinoza on Being Human and Human Perfection', in *Essays on Spinoza's Ethical Theory*, ed. Matthew Kisner and Andrew Youpa (Oxford: Oxford University Press, 2014), pp. 124–42.

14. Ideally, though this is speculative, there is complete parallelism between the intellect *qua* infinite mode and (the face of) the universe (the infinite mode of motion and rest). The intellect, in forming adequate ideas, reproduces or expresses the true structure and nature of the processes in the world, while imagination, whose images or ideas are never adequate, represents or records these same processes partially and in fragmented or disconnected ways, from the limited point of view of this one body and its current affections. Adequate ideas are true and self-evident (2def4), whereas inadequate ones are the basis of falsity and error—yet, even while misleading they may still contain some truth that, because of their confusion and random order, is not distinctly perceived. Imagining and sensing proceed in series of partial and disconnected, fragmentary and externally caused ideas that Spinoza calls images but also refers to as 'ideas of affections' or simply 'ideas'.

15. In laying out this doctrine Spinoza develops his excursus on physics that will not retain us here since the focus is on his theory of ideas (2p13s).
16. Ideas or modes of thought—distinct (adequate) perceptions of the intellect, or confused sensory perceptions or images—all have objects. The singular things that human minds sense or perceive are either bodies or 'modes of thinking' (2ax5). To the perplexity of many readers, it follows from the definition of the human mind as the idea of the body that whatever we perceive we perceive through the body whose idea our mind is. It does not follow, though, that the human mind does not perceive other objects than its body, only that these external (or internal) objects are always perceived/represented through the traces or marks that they leave in the body's cognitive organs. For discussion of this see Alan Donagan, *Spinoza* (Hertfordshire: Harvester Wheatsheaf, 1988), Margaret Wilson, 'Objects, Ideas and Minds: Comments on Spinoza's Theory of Mind', reprinted in her *Ideas and Mechanism* (Princeton, N.J.: Princeton University Press, 1999), pp. 126–40, and Don Garrett, 'Representation and Consciousness' and the literature referred to there.
17. Spinoza criticizes Descartes' separation between intellect and will, and opposes the ensuing view that ideas would be static, 'mute pictures' as well as the doctrine of a free will (2p49d,s 2). Cf. how Della Rocca, 'The Power of Ideas', spells out this view. For interesting recent discussions of Spinoza's rejection of the will and its radical consequences see Carriero, 'Spinoza, the Will and the Ontology of Power', and Karolina Huebner, 'Spinoza's Unorthodox Metaphysics of the Will', in *The Oxford Handbook on Spinoza,* ed. Michael Della Rocca (Oxford: Oxford University Press, forthcoming).
18. John Carriero draws attention to this in 'Spinoza on Three Kinds of Cognition'.
19. Not all affections change the body's power of striving according to Spinoza. See 3d3post1. There are affections or impressions that are emotionally indifferent. Cf. below end of note 23. But see Lisa Shapiro, 'Spinoza on Imagination and the Affects', in *Emotional Minds: Passions and the Limits of Pure Enquiry II: The Seventeenth Century*, ed. Sabrina Ebbersmeyer (Berlin: DeGruyter, 2012), pp. 89–104, and 'How We Experience The World: Passionate Perception in Descartes and Spinoza', in Martin Pickavé and Lisa Shapiro (eds) *Emotion & Cognitive Life in Medieval Early Modern Philosophy* (Oxford: Oxford University Press, 2012), pp. 193–216.
20. Contrast this to the distinction between activity and passivity of Descartes, who introduces the Aristotelian distinction between action and passion as relative notions from the point of view of the agent cause or the patient subject in the first article of *Les passions,* and applies it to the mind–body composite: what is an action in the body—neural movements in the sensory organs and brain—is a passion in the mind, and vice versa. See *The Passions of The Soul,* in *The Philosophical Writings of Descartes*, trans. John Cottingham, Robert Stoothoff and Dugald Murdoch (Cambridge: Cambridge University Press, 1985), Vol. 1, p. 328 (AT XI, 327–8). Spinoza, who would have no truck with mind–body interaction, takes the sameness or identity that for Descartes is a brute fact of experience as a real metaphysical identity of what is manifested or perceived in two ways—*qua* thinking or *qua* extended.
21. I say presumably because any increase in bodily force or well-being is not automatically translated into greater power of the mind to think.
22. 'This striving (*conatus*), when related to the mind alone, is called will (*voluntas*); but when it is related to the mind and body together, it is called appetite (*appetitus*), which is therefore nothing but the very essence of man, from whose nature necessarily follow those things that promote his preservation; and by which man is determined to do them. Between

appetite and desire there is no difference, except that desire is generally related to men insofar as they are conscious of their appetite. So desire can be defined as appetite together with consciousness of the appetite. (*Cupiditas est appetitum cum ejusdem conscientia*)' (3p9s, C 500. Cf. 4p8).

23. Does Spinoza suggest that desire as consciousness of one's appetite is a specifically human phenomenon, presupposing some determinate, minimum degree of distinct and perhaps reflexive thinking? For discussion see Don Garrett, 'Representation and Consciousness', and Michael LeBuffe, 'Theories about Consciousness in Spinoza's Ethics', *Philosophical Review* 119 (2010): 531–63. As I read it, consciousness in the passage above is the mere awareness or noticing of what we presently want and are heading for—our appetite as determined and made conscious by actual affects. I would thus not take it in the sense of some phenomenal awareness proposed by Steven Nadler, 'Spinoza on Consciousness', *Mind* (2008): 575–601. I also disagree with the reading of Michael LeBuffe, who identifies striving with the fixed ratio of motion and argues that conscious desire is consciousness of the ratio of motion and rest defining the form of the body. See Michael LeBuffe, 'The Anatomy of Passions', in *The Cambridge Companion to Spinoza's Ethics*, ed. Olli Koistinen (Cambridge: Cambridge University Press, 2009), pp. 188–222, p. 209, and LeBuffe, *From Bondage to Freedom: Spinoza on Human Excellence* (Oxford: Oxford University Press, 2010). I discuss Spinoza's view on this more in detail in 'Affectivity and Cognitive Perfection', N. Naaman Zauderer and Tom Vinci (eds), *Freedom and the Passions in Spinoza*, forthcoming, Sections 4–6.

    Spinoza distinguishes between affections of the body that make no difference to its striving and the affects that do. Cf. above note 19. Peter Myrdal points out to me it is not clear that there could be any affection that would not affect the conatus in one way or another. Leibniz did not see any difference here other than in degree (see, e.g., *Discourse on Metaphysics* §33; *New Essays* II.20, p. 162; and *New Essays*, Preface, p. 53). Spinoza as I read him seems to single out affections that have a strong enough effect on our striving to shape it into determinate appetites involving some more or less confused cognition of its object or target. These are what he calls desire. I get back to this point in the last section of the paper.

24. 'We see that the mind can undergo great changes, and can pass now to a greater or lesser perfection. These passions (*passiones*) explain to us the affects of joy and sadness. By joy (*Laetitia*), therefore, I shall understand in what follows the passion (*passionem*) by which the mind passes to a greater perfection (*perfectionem*) and by sadness the passion by which it passes to a lower perfection. The affect of joy (*affectum laetitiam*) which is related simultaneously to the mind and body I call pleasure (*titillationem*) or cheerfulness, and that of sadness, pain (*dolorem*) or melancholy (*melancholiam*)' (3p11s, C 500–1).
25. 'Love is nothing but joy accompanying the idea of an external cause (*Laetitia concomitante ideae causa externae*) and hate is nothing but sadness accompanying the idea of an external cause. We see, then, that one who loves necessarily strives to have present and preserve the thing he loves; on the other hand, one who hates strives to remove and destroy the thing he hates' (3p13s C, 502). Striving 'to have present' here can mean striving to imagine the thing loved (the thing imagined is always posited as present) or a desire to actually acquire it and keep it.
26. Cf. also 4app31.
27. 3p13: 'When the mind imagines those things that diminish or restrain the body's power of acting, it strives, as far as it can, to recollect things that exclude their existence'. It follows

'that the mind avoids imagining those things that diminish or restrain its or the body's power' (3p13c). Carriero reads the 'avoids [*aversatur*]' as a more or less mechanical reaction, as turning away, like a positive magnet does from another..., 'Conatus and Perfection', p. 81).

28. My recollections of how the dog passed away some eight years ago are still vivid enough to hinder me from keeping steady the happy thoughts of him playing around in his full form—thoughts I'd much rather dwell on.
29. 'For an imagination (*imaginatio*) is an idea that indicates the present disposition of the human body more than the nature of an external body, not indeed distinctly, but confusedly, whence it comes about that the mind is said to err' (4p1d).
30. Cf. Spinoza's explanation of error, which is a complication for his project of replacing confused ideas of affects with distinct cognition of their causes. A famous example is the image of the sun as it were at 200 feet distance from us, which is deceiving 'so long as we are ignorant of its true distance; but when its distance is known, the error is removed, not the imagination,... And so it is with the other imaginations by which the Mind is deceived, whether they indicate the natural constitution of the Body, or that its power of acting is increased or diminished: *they are not contrary to the true, and do not disappear on its presence*'. Only a stronger imagination can annihilate any of its ideas (4p1s, C, 548, my italics).
31. Cf. 3p9s, Curley 500. In the important proof of 4p8, Spinoza refers to 4d1 where good (*bonum*) is defined as 'what we certainly know to be useful to us'. Evil (*malum*) is defined as 'what we certainly know is an impediment to our attainment of some good' (4pd2). These are stipulative definitions. 4p8d explains the genesis of our ordinary ideas/beliefs/perceptions of good and bad. The cognition of good and evil *is* the idea of joy or sadness, idea which 'follows necessarily from the very affect of joy or sadness' by 2p22. The reference to 2p22 indicates that Spinoza here by consciousness or cognition of good and evil means the idea of the idea of the affect. Spinoza uses consciousness and cognition interchangeable, and I read this not as a matter of phenomenal consciousness but of noticing, or cognizing, that is, of cognitive awareness. He goes on to argue that this idea (idea of idea) is united to the (idea of the) affect in 'the same way as the mind is united to the body', so that, referring to 2p21s 'this idea is not really distinguished from the affect itself, or from the idea of the body's affection, only conceptually (*nisi solo conceptu*); therefore this cognition of good and evil is nothing else than the very affection, in so far as we are conscious of/take note of it' (4p8d, C 550–1). Like any affection, it involves some (inadequate) cognition of its cause, but just as to be conscious of one self in pride or sorrow is not to know one self adequately, so cognizing the good in desiring it is not knowledge of the good. Men, as Spinoza repeats, 'are conscious of their actions and appetites, but ignorant of the causes by which they are determined to want something' (4pref. C, 544–5).
32. 3p58s; II/189, C, 530, cf. 4pref; II/205, C. 543.
33. Spinoza seems to be working with two notions of essence. There is, on the one hand, an eternal unchanging idea of this individual essence or nature in the eternal intellect (idea that, presumably, is adequate and includes all its causes and effects). There is, on the other hand, this actual essence or striving of the presently existing body. See 2p11d, 2p13d,c,s, 2pp10–11 and the literature referred to in note 13 above.
34. 'Therefore, the power or conatus of anything, whereby it acts or strives to act in some ways alone or with other things (*potentia sive conatus, quo ipsa vel sola vel cum aliis quidcquam*

agit vel agere conatur), that is (by prop 6,III), its power or conatus, by which it strives to persevere in its being, is nothing but the given or actual essence of a thing' (3p7d).

35. Cf. note 22 above.
36. Posit and affirm are here used interchangeably (3p54d).
37. I do not take this as a striving to persist in temporal duration, and how it should spelled out is another tricky issue, but it has to do with an increase in degree of reality.
38. I owe thanks to John Carriero for pressing me to clarify my statement of the difficulty I see here.
39. Active affects cause virtuous dispositions or mindsets like strength of mind (fortitudo) that is subdivided into courage (*animositas*) and nobility (*generositas*). Courage or tenacity is the desire to preserve one's being according to the dictates of reason alone, and nobility is the desire to 'aid other men and join with them in friendship'—not from love or compassion, though, but from the dictates of reason alone (3p59s).
40. Spinoza may seem to fall back here on an Aristotelian line of thinking: this desire to understand is the very striving to persist in a being of a certain kind of complexity whose mind is powerful enough to form adequate ideas. The joy accompanying understanding would then have a natural explanation: the being, in understanding, exercises its essential capacity and experiences pleasure/rejoices when nothing impedes it and it does it well. Spinoza is also wedded to the ancient idea that there are degrees of reality and being corresponding to degrees of perfection. But Spinoza famously rejects teleology, and it is not clear how much help one can get from comparing his ethics to Aristotle's. For a helpful and fascinating account of the continuities and profound differences between Spinoza's ethical ideal and its medieval Aristotelian antecedents, see John Carriero, 'The Ethics in Spinoza's Ethics', in *Essays on Spinoza's Ethical Theory*, pp. 20–40.
41. With an analogy Spinoza uses elsewhere, in explaining affections, passive affects are like conclusions without premises (2p28), by opposition to adequate, self-explanatory, or self-evident ideas, which can be deduced from other adequate ideas, whose effects can be clearly and distinctly conceived through them (3def1).
42. Whatever we do, we do as the effect of external forces either concurring with or opposing our own striving to persist in being, and the transitions in power we undergo are at once physical and mental.
43. For 'actions of the mind', he stipulates, 'arise from adequate ideas alone; the passions depend on inadequate ideas alone' (3p3) so the Mind, in having inadequate ideas by 3p1, 'necessarily is acted on' (3p3d).
44. Differently from the case of joy which increases one's power and so always concurs with and strengthens one's own striving, the force with which pain or sorrow are affirmed depends wholly on the external cause and never on oneself. A confused idea of sorrow which affirms the present diminishing of my current power to act expresses a corresponding diminishing of power of clear and distinct thinking, hindering my capacity of reason from exercising itself in more constructive activities. For examples see my 'The Metaphysics of Affects and the Unbearable Reality of Confusion'.
45. Only self-generated active affects related to its innate striving to understand can strengthen it without threatening its independence, so truly perfect it. But see also Michael Le Buffe, 'The Anatomy of Passions' for an extensive discussion of the problem with passive joy first taken up by Paul Hoffman, 'Three Dualist Theories of Passions', *Philosophical Topics* 19 (1991): 153–200 (p. 177).

46. 'When the mind conceives (*concipit*) itself and its power of acting, it rejoices (by P53). But the mind necessarily considers itself (*se ipsam necessario contemplator*) when it conceives a true, *or* adequate idea (by 2p40s2). Therefore it also rejoices insofar as it conceives some adequate ideas, i.e., (by P1), insofar as it acts' (3p58d).
47. Earlier in Part Two Spinoza argued that the mind *conceives* itself, when 'it conceives a true, or adequate idea' (2p43), referring to what he takes to be self-evident, namely that whenever one has (or forms) a true idea, one knows that one has (conceives) a true idea (2p43d). A true idea is a norm of itself and of falsity—it makes itself known by itself just as light makes itself and darkness manifest (2p43s2). This is why one cannot have true beliefs without knowing that one has them, and one knows oneself only as one exercises adequate thinking, in understanding. Conception or forming concepts, as we saw before, involves genuine activity, which is defined as adequate causation in 3d1–d2 and 1ax4. Cf. 4app2. I reflect on what this tells us about the self that is the object (and subject?) of cognition in my 'Spinoza on Pride and Self-Knowledge'.
48. According to 2p40s2 we have adequate ideas of the common properties of things—e.g., properties of body that are equally in the part and the whole and that all bodies are said to share or 'agree in' (2L2), and which therefore can only be perceived adequately—clearly and distinctly. They are said to be 'common to all men' (2p38), meaning, presumably, that unlike universals formed by inadequate imagination depending on the constitution and affections of one's individual body, common notions are conceived in the same way by any mind endowed with a power of understanding. See also 2p45–7, 4p19, 2p27s. But how does one come by adequate ideas? Presumably, they are 'innate'—since they are shared or common they are everywhere, in whatever a mind–body experiences or senses and can be formed on the basis of comparing things. For discussion of common notions or axioms in the tradition known by Spinoza, e.g., Aristotle and Maimonides, see Harry A. Wolfson, *The Philosophy of Spinoza*, II, pp. 117–130. See also Donagan, *Spinoza*, pp.136–7.
49. 4app7 and 8 make it clear that Spinoza does not think such a life could depend on us as individuals but requires a community of individual's agreeing with each other in their rational nature. I will not discuss Spinoza's model of a free man here, and I am not quite clear about its role in the argument, or in the *Ethics* as a whole, a topic that lends itself to a wide variety of interpretations. For different recent takes on this see Andrew Youpa, 'Spinoza's Model of Human Nature', *Journal of the History of Philosophy* 48 (2010): 209–29; Matthew Kisner, *Spinoza on Human Freedom: Reason, Autonomy and the Good Life* (Cambridge: Cambridge University Press, 2011); Le Buffe, *From Bondage to Freedom*; and Huebner, 'Spinoza on Being Human and Human Perfection', pp. 124–42.
50. See in particular 4p2–p6.
51. 'So an affect cannot be either moderated or destroyed except by a contrary and stronger emotion' (4p7d). 'For the affect we are suffering (*patitur*) can neither be checked nor destroyed except... through the idea of an affection of the body stronger than and contrary to the affection we suffer (Gen Def of Passions)' (4p7c).
52. Cf. note 2 above.
53. This paper was presented at the UCLA Conference of Early Modern Philosophy, April 10–11, 2015. Earlier drafts were presented at a Department Colloquium at the Department of Philosophy; at the University of Toronto; at the Atlantic-Canada Seminar in Early Modern Philosophy held in Tel Aviv and Jerusalem in May 2013; at the First Finno-Hungarian

seminar in Early Modern Philosophy held at the Central European University, Budapest in November 2013; and at the Workshop on Psychology of Morality and Politics, University of Jyväskylä in June 2013. I am grateful both to the organizers of these meetings and to the participants for helpful discussions. I wish to thank most particularly John Carriero for his encouragement as much as for his hard questions in reading and commenting on the paper. I am much indebted also to Alix Cohen and Robert Stern for careful comments and for helping making the text more readable.

Bibliography

Alanen, Lilli. 'The Metaphysics of Affects and the Unbearable Reality of Confusion', in *The Oxford Handbook of Spinoza,* ed. Michael Della Rocca (Oxford: Oxford University Press, forthcoming).

Alanen, Lilli. *'Spinoza on Passions and Self-Knowledge: The Case of Pride', in Emotion & Cognitive Life in Medieval & Early Modern Philosophy*, ed. Martin Pickavé and Lisa Shapiro (Oxford: Oxford University Press, 2012), pp. 234–54.

Alanen, Lilli. 'Spinoza on the Human Mind', *Midwest Studies in Philosophy* 35 (2011): 4–25.

De Brabander, Firmin. 'Psychotherapy and Moral Perfection: Spinoza and the Stoics on the Prospect of Happiness', in *Stoicism: Tradition and Transformation*, ed. Steven K. Strange and Jack Zupko (Cambridge: Cambridge University Press, 2004), pp. 198–213.

Descartes, René. *The Passions of the Soul,* in *The Philosophical Writings of Descartes*, trans. John Cottingham, Robert Stoothoff and Dugald Murdoch, Vol. 1 (Cambridge: Cambridge University Press, 1985), pp. 328–404.

Carriero, John. 'Spinoza on Final Causality', in *Oxford Studies in Early Modern Philosophy*, ed. Daniel Garber and Steven Nadler (Oxford: Oxford University Press, 2005), Vol. 2, pp. 105–47.

Carriero, John. 'Conatus and Perfection in Spinoza', in *Early Modern Philosophy Reconsidered: Essays in Honor of Paul Hoffman*, ed. Peter A. French, Howard K. Wettstein and John Carriero, *Midwest Studies in Philosophy*, 35 (2011): 69–92.

Carriero, John. 'Spinoza on Three Kinds of Cognition: Imagination, Understanding and Essence', unpublished manuscript.

Carriero, John. 'The Ethics in Spinoza's Ethics', in *Essays on Spinoza's Ethical Theory*, ed. Matthew J. Kisner and Andrew Youpa (Oxford: Oxford University Press, 2014), pp. 20–40.

Damasio, Antonio. *Looking for Spinoza: Joy, Sorrow and the Feeling Brain* (New York: Harcourt, 2003).

Della Rocca, Michael. 'The Power of an Idea: Spinoza's Critique of a Pure Will', *Nous* 37 (2003): 200–31.

de Dijn, Herman. 'Spinoza's Theory of Emotions and its Relation to Therapy', in *Oxford Studies of Early Modern Philosophy*, ed. Daniel Garber and Steven Nadler (Oxford: Clarendon Press, 2010), pp. 71–90.

Donagan, Alan. *Spinoza* (Hertfordshire: Harvester Wheatsheaf, 1988).

Garrett, Don. 'Representation and Consciousness in Spinoza's Naturalistic Theory of the Imagination', in *Interpreting Spinoza: Critical Essays*, ed. Charlie Huenemann (Cambridge: Cambridge University Press, 2008), pp. 4–25.

Garrett, Don. 'Spinoza on the Essence of the Human Body and the Part of the Mind That Is Eternal', in *The Cambridge Companion to Spinoza's Ethics*, ed. Olli Koistinen (Cambridge: Cambridge University Press, 2009), pp. 284–302.

Hoffman, Paul. 'Three Dualist Theories of Passions', *Philosophical Topics* 19 (1991): 153–200.

Huebner, Karolina. 'Spinoza on Being Human and Human Perfection', in *Essays on Spinoza's Ethical Theory*, ed. Matthew J. Kisner and Andrew Youpa (Oxford: Oxford University Press, 2014), pp. 124–42.

Huebner, Karolina. 'Spinoza on Essences, Universals, and Beings of Reason,' *Pacific Philosophical Quarterly*, forthcoming.

Huebner, Karolina. 'Spinoza's Unorthodox Metaphysics of Will', in *The Oxford Handbook of Spinoza*, ed. Michael Della Rocca (Oxford, Oxford University Press, forthcoming).

LeBuffe, Michael. 'The Anatomy of Passions', in *The Cambridge Companion to Spinoza's Ethics*, ed. Olli Koistinen (Cambridge: Cambridge University Press, 2009), pp. 188–222.

LeBuffe, Michael. *From Bondage to Freedom: Spinoza on Human Excellence* (Oxford: Oxford University Press, 2010).

Long, Anthony A. 'Stoicism in the Philosophical tradition: Spinoza, Lipsius, Butler', in *The Cambridge Companion to the Stoics*, ed. Brad Inwood (Cambridge: Cambridge University Press, 2003), pp. 365–92.

Melamed, Yitzhak. 'Charitable Interpretations and the Political Domestication of Spinoza, or, Benedict in the Land of the Secular Imagination', in *The Methodology of the History of Philosophy*, ed. Eric Schlisser, Mogens Laerke and Justin Smith (Oxford: Oxford University Press, 2013), pp. 258–79.

Nadler, Steven. 'Spinoza on Consciousness', *Mind* 117 (2008): 575–601.

Neu, Jerome. *Emotion, Thought and Therapy: A Study of Hume and Spinoza and the Relationship of Philosophical Theories of the Emotions to Psychological Theories of Therapy* (Berkeley and Los Angeles: University of California Press, 1977).

Rutherford, Donald. 'Salvation as a State of Mind: The Place of *Acquiescentia* in Spinoza's Ethics', *British Journal for the History of Philosophy* 7 (1999): 447–73.

Schmalz, Tad. 'Spinoza and Descartes', in *The Oxford Handbook of Spinoza*, ed. Michael Della Rocca (Oxford: Oxford University Press, forthcoming).

Shapiro, Lisa. 'Spinoza on Imagination and the Affects', in *Emotional Minds: Passions and the Limits of Pure Enquiry II: The Seventeenth Century*, ed. Sabrina Ebbersmeyer (Berlin: De Gruyter, 2012), pp. 89–104.

Shapiro, Lisa. 'How We Experience the World: Passionate Perception in Descartes and Spinoza', in *Emotion & Cognitive Life in Medieval and Early Modern Philosophy*, ed. Martin Pickavé and Lisa Shapiro (Oxford: Oxford University Press, 2012), pp. 193–216.

de Spinoza, Benedict. *Spinoza Opera*, ed. Carl Gebhardt, four volumes (Heidelberg: Carl Winters, 1925).

de Spinoza, Benedict. *The Collected Works of Spinoza*, Vol. I, ed. and trans. Edwin Curley (Princeton: Princeton University Press, 1985).

Wilson, Margaret. 'Objects, Ideas and Minds: Comments on Spinoza's Theory of Mind', reprinted in *Ideas and Mechanism* (Princeton, NJ: Princeton University Press, 1999), pp. 126–40.

5

'I've Got a Little List'

Classification, Explanation, and the Focal Passions in Descartes and Hobbes

Amy Schmitter

5.1 Taxonomy and Methodology

Although my title might seem to promise a list of those who won't be missed,[1] this paper is, in part, a work in praise of taxonomies, classifications, and list-making in all their gloriously laborious varieties. Taxonomy may seem a dull and dusty business, a matter mostly of attaching tags to items arrayed under glass cases. Yet it thrived among seventeenth-century writers on the passions, from the famous names to the lesser lights. As evidence, let me offer Exhibit A: a short play, published in 1630, titled *Pathomachia, or the Battle of the Affections, Shadowed by a Feigned Siege of the City of Pathopolis*. The entire crux of its plot, such as it is, rests on the proper classification of the passions, or 'affections', each of which is personified as a character in a kind of palace-intrigue, with the overall taxonomy illustrated in terms of political affiliation.[2] It's a real oddity—as if one were to stage a musical comedy to celebrate the periodic table of the elements. But it's an oddity that shows just what boom years the European seventeenth century saw for passionate taxonomy.[3]

One reason for their proliferation is that taxonomies were often the workhorses for constructing philosophical psychologies both old and new. Most seventeenth-century philosophers simply adopted their psychologies and catalogues either piecemeal or wholesale from received accounts. But a handful self-consciously pursued innovative psychologies and re-categorized the passions accordingly. Section 5.2 surveys some of these revisionings, while subsequent sections concentrate on the classificatory schemes and individual passions found within those schemes in the work of Descartes and Hobbes. As we will see in Section 5.3, Descartes' taxonomy of the passions is particularly telling, since he directs an unusual degree of attention to his differences from his predecessors. In contrast, Hobbes devotes relatively little attention to principles of classification, and his enumerations seem less settled than Descartes'. But at least in one place he adopts a strikingly kinetic arrangement for the passions that I think is both unprecedented and powerful. Sections 5.4 and 5.5 of the chapter turn to concentrate on individual affects that occupy particularly prominent perches in the relevant inventories: 'wonder' for Descartes, and 'glory' for Hobbes. Each passion plays a central role in structuring the relevant classificatory scheme. Those roles are different, but we can consider both Cartesian wonder and Hobbesian glory as focal passions for their respective systems—points where many of the explanatory ambitions of their revisionary classifications converge.

Throughout, I hope to press (albeit surreptitiously) a broad methodological claim: that attention to both classificatory schemes (whether principled taxonomies or mere catalogues) and to the individual items they organize shows the deeply historical nature of diverse conceptions of the passions. That's worth pausing over, for it is pretty common to naturalize our emotions as raw, pre-social, and immediately natural subjective attitudes. But it is just as plausible that the concepts we apply to the passions and emotions are *not* neutral or inert to what they describe—that how we understand the passions affects what they *are*. If so, then we have reason to think that our emotions and passions are historically mediated, and open to some degree of cross-cultural and cross-historical variation. To be sure, determining the range and degree of variation to which our emotions are subject requires a great deal of hard empirical work, as well as reflective analysis on its significance. We seem *prima facie* to recognize something of our emotions, moods, etc., in seventeenth-century (and earlier) accounts. Identifying their objects by way of at least a few familiar features (either through projection or discovery) may well be a condition for translating earlier accounts into terms that are intelligible to us. So, we should not expect to find that emotions are historically variable in all respects; indeed, there would be little sense in labelling them 'emotions' were that so.

I do not want to underestimate the difficulties that any claim of such historical variability faces. Since my topic here is restricted to the philosophical theorizing available through texts, I can avoid the problems of epistemic access to the hearts and minds of the long-dead that social and psychological historians may encounter.[4] Nonetheless, there remains an obstacle of another kind, for it only makes sense to talk of variation if there is some basis for comparison. I propose that neither the schemes of classification, nor the passions given leading roles, nor even whether a taxonomy gives any passion a leading role, are fixed points. How, then, can we establish the degree of continuity that allows us to mark difference and change? One way is to trace historical lineages. Another is to look at the dialectic between broad classificatory schemes and the concrete items put up for classification, so that what may seem familiar and readily accessible can provide a context for what initially appears relatively exotic. Both strategies play a role in this paper. By narrowing the scope as discussion proceeds, I hope to place Descartes' and Hobbes's focal passions in an explanatory context that will make them appear both peculiar and intelligible.

Here it may also be helpful to distinguish between two issues that are often confused: first, the cultural variability to which some phenomenon is subject, and second, the degree to which that phenomenon is subject to molding by education, social practices and considered reflection. It is the latter issue that interests me most here, although *because* I take the emotions to be phenomena sensitive to education, social practices, and considered reflection, I suspect they will show variations over time and across cultures, as education, social practices and the resources for reflection vary. This second issue offers a plausible way to understand how emotions may be 'socially constructed', without suggesting that they are somehow fabricated from whole cloth. No matter how much our classifications might vary, we would have nothing to classify were humans not generally disposed to respond affectively to various features of their environment—just as we could not devise new social practices were we not able and disposed to adjust our behaviour to others. Allowing for social construction in this sense is not incompatible with considering the emotions to be biological phenomena selectively shaped by our evolutionary history. Nor is it incompatible with holding that we can consider emotion to be a natural kind, or divisible into natural kinds.[5] It only denies that a robust enumeration of natural kinds would exhaust all intelligible orderings applicable to philosophy, or to experience. Against such reductive demands, I hope here to take a few steps towards showing how our emotions, passions and affects—or at least the thinking about them—have a history, albeit a messy, discontinuous, and thoroughly non-whiggish one.

5.2 Lists, Lists and yet More Lists

One reason why inventories of the passions were an early modern growth industry is because ancient and medieval philosophy was rife with practised classifiers. Aristotle gives lists of what he knew as the '*pathē*', identifying eleven in the *Nicomachean Ethics* 2.5 (1105b19–1106a14) and fourteen in Book 2 of the *Rhetoric* (1377b15–1389b11); the Stoics notoriously reduced the number of *pathē* to four main ones;[6] Augustine reinterpreted these as different forms of love;[7] and Aquinas then brought the number back to eleven (*Summa Theologica*, II–1.23). Later, Francesco Suarez criticized most attempts at division as ill-founded, even as he experimented with a list of six contrasting passions.[8] Moreover, each major author introduced not just new enumerations, but new principles of classification: Aquinas's most lasting contribution was probably his split between 'concupiscible' and 'irascible' passions, which both Suarez and the sixteenth-century author Juan Luis Vives rejected.[9] Against this background, many early modern authors adopted a particular inventory as a simple and efficient way to declare allegiance to some philosophical school.[10] But more interesting than these reverent preservers of past classifications are the taxonomic rebels, such as Descartes, Hobbes, Malebranche, and Spinoza.

The latter two erected their new and improved models of the soul largely by reforming and deforming previous models. Spinoza offers perhaps the most readily recognizable example, for he directly appropriates the fourfold division of the passions practised by the Stoics. But even as he recognizes the Stoic passions, Spinoza rearranges the ordering and insists that there are only *three* primitive passions: desire, joy, and sadness.[11] He thereby collapses all the motivating passions into desire, or appetite, while using joy and sadness to mark the contrast between the kinetics of our appetite—a crucial move for his conception of finite modes and their states in general, and one that owes a great deal to Hobbes's account of 'endeavour'.

Malebranche gives the same list of three general passions, but subsumes them under the parent passions of love and aversion.[12] Even more basic to his account is the use he makes of Augustine's contrast between *caritas*, a properly ordered love, and *cupiditas*, viciously misdirected love. For Augustine, *caritas* and *cupiditas* are different species of love, distinguished by willing different objects. *Caritas* aspires to union with God, and loves other things only subordinately to this ultimate end. In contrast, *cupiditas* is directed to temporal things for their own sake, primarily as sources of corporeal gratification. In *The Search After Truth*, Malebranche adapts this Augustinian distinction to his own partition between our natural inclination towards the good and our postlapsarian passions. He does so by mapping it onto the contrast between a natural inclination that tends towards general good, i.e., God, and a disordered love that turns to the body in an attempt to satisfy self-love through the indulgence of particular sensible pleasures.[13] By wallowing in self-love and sensible pleasures without carrying through to the love of God, we become slaves to the body and our corrupted passions, grossly overvaluing the particular objects that appear to furnish sensible pleasure. Indeed, original sin has so altered the human body and imagination that we inherit a brain architecture that makes the passions unmanageable and gives them inexorable force in the face of particular objects.[14] Against the passions that seduce us to corporeality, we can oppose only our natural inclination towards God. This too is love, indeed the same love, but it lacks the sensible power and lure of passionate love. And so our love remains disordered and in need of divine grace.[15]

Even this brief sketch illustrates how Malebranche revamps the dualism he absorbed from Descartes, particularly the distinction between purely intellectual 'inner emotions' and body-based passions. Malebranche follows Descartes in insisting that the operations of bodies are purely mechanical. At the same time, he assimilates these Cartesian themes to his Augustinian picture of love and anti-Pelagianism. The result is an account that presents our passions as perversely *dys*functional, relying on bodily mechanisms so corrupted that our passions tend to overwhelm our natural inclinations and seduce the will to sensible pleasures. Malebranche's inclusion of the trio of desire, joy, and sadness as general passions can be seen in this context. Unlike Spinoza, Malebranche holds that these passions operate to determine love (or aversion), so that the 'three simple or basic passions that have the good as their object' are desiderative love, joyous love, and melancholy love.[16] This threefold division marks differences in the 'possession' of the loved object. While love remains basic to all our passions, such relations of possession are critical to Malebranche's understanding of our restless inclination towards the good and corruption as our attempt to arrest it.[17]

5.3 Ordering Cartesian Passions

Although Malebranche and Spinoza drew large parts of their taxonomies from ancient sources, they also tailored them to new forms of explanation championed by Descartes and Hobbes. Of these, the most important are the introduction of mechanical causation and the rejection of teleological explanation, at least in accounting for physical nature. Applying such revamped kinds of explanation to our psychologies disrupted the principles by which previous taxonomies had been constructed, and thus required new classifications of the passions. This is particularly marked in Descartes' last completed work, *The Passions of the Soul* (1649), where he emphasizes his novel definitions of the passions, his ingenious principles of classification, and the unfamiliar scope of his account. Just as important, I maintain, is his selection of a distinctive and peculiar passion to head off his taxonomy; this is the passion of 'wonder', which Descartes declares the first of all the passions. In contrast, Hobbes provides little by way of an ordered taxonomy. But he does offer long lists of passions, in which he gives a prominent place to 'glory'—a passion that had previously received a great deal of attention in political history and religious writings,[18] but never (as far as I know) made a crux of philosophical psychology. We will turn to these singular passions after considering how Descartes' new enumeration serves his explanatory goals.

In the second division of the *Passions of the Soul*, Descartes delves into the 'number and order of the passions'. There, he makes absolutely explicit his desire to break with the taxonomic past, devoting §68 to explaining why his 'enumeration of the passions [*dénombrement des passions*] is different from that commonly received'.[19] He particularly rejects the division of the sensitive part of the soul into the two concupiscible and irascible appetites on the ground that he recognizes no distinction of soul parts. Nor is he willing to divide our dispositions for the passions into desire [*concupiscence*] and anger. Such previous classifications, he claims, fail to be comprehensive, leaving out many of the principal passions.[20] Descartes instead identifies six principal passions, which he counts as 'simple and primitive:' wonder [*admiration*], love, hate, desire [*désir*], joy, and sadness.[21] Other passions are supposed to 'take their origin' from these six in various ways,[22] although Descartes does not trace their lineages systematically.

Part I of *The Passions* describes 'passions' in the broadest sense as simply those operations of the soul that are not actions: all perceptions are passions in this sense. Descartes then restricts the term to perceptions caused by, or at least 'based' in the body, thereby emphasizing that passions are receptive states. But in the strict sense, passions are defined as 'those perceptions, sensations or emotions of the soul which we refer particularly to it, and which are caused, maintained and strengthened by some movement of the spirits'.[23] This final gloss distinguishes passions from other body-based states, such as sense-perceptions and appetites. Such passions share a 'function' [*usage*], which Descartes declares 'consists solely in disposing the soul to will those things that nature declares to be useful to us, and to persist in this volition', at the same time initiating the bodily movements to execute our volitions.[24] Their function is thus to provide natural motivations, that is, to deliver the teachings of nature about how things in the world can affect us for good or ill, to push us to act on such teachings, and to prompt the body for the relevant actions. Ultimately, we should understand their functionality against the backdrop of Descartes' defence of our natural, God-given equipment in the Sixth Meditation: their functions explain why we are endowed with the disposition to experience passions in the first place, but not the means by which they perform those functions. In the performance of their functions, the passions harness the motions of the body; those motions, however, are simply the products of mechanical collisions that obey the laws of motion. Descartes thus endorses a form of 'functional explanation' in which purposes are served only by exploiting the effects of a non-purposive mechanism.[25]

With this description of the passions and their functions in hand, Descartes goes on to characterize particular passions by how they present their objects and the relation of those objects to us. But as he does for sense-perception more generally, Descartes also insists that the passions offer sometimes confused, and always highly selective, access to the external things that are their objects. That is because such objects act on our sensory-systems selectively: 'not according to all the diverse qualities in the objects, but just because of how they can hurt or profit us, or generally be important to us'.[26] The causes of the passions become part of their contents only insofar as they are, or appear, important to us.[27] This, in turn, provides the principle that generates Descartes' basic taxonomy of the passions: 'to enumerate the [passions], it is only necessary to examine, in order, in how many diverse ways that matter to us [*en combien de diverses façons qui nous importent*] our senses can be moved by their objects'.[28]

The initial result of his enumeration is the passion of *admiration*, now most commonly rendered 'wonder'. *Admiration*, Descartes declares, is 'the first of all the passions', one that has no contrary.[29] In part, this means that 'admiration' has a temporal priority: it can befall us before we recognize *how* the object we wonder at might be 'suitable' [*convenable*] for us.[30] But *admiration* is also basic to the structure of the other passions, which are characterized by adding relevant specifications to wonder. So, for instance, as soon as an object is represented as good to us, we experience love, if bad, then hate.[31] Descartes goes on to identify 'the same considerations of good and evil', viz., whether an object appears good or bad, as the birthplace of all the other passions,[32] adding temporal qualifications to generate the future-directed passion of 'desire' [*désir*]. Since Descartes assimilates aversion to desire (desire to avoid what is bad), his taxonomy posits no passion contrary to either *admiration* or *désir*.[33] But unlike desire, *admiration* had no particularly central place in previous taxonomies. So why does Descartes make it the *first* of his six primitive passions?

5.4 The 'Function' of Cartesian Wonder

The special place of wonder is not, I think, a matter simply of temporal or structural priority, but rather, of its function.[34] Descartes characterizes *admiration* and its causes as a

sudden surprise of the soul, which makes it come to consider attentively the objects that seem to it to be rare and extraordinary. As such, it is caused first by an impression one has in the brain, which represents the object as something rare and consequently worth close consideration; and then by the movement of the spirits, which are disposed by this impression to press with great force against the location of the brain where [the impression] is, to fortify and conserve it there; just as they are also disposed by [the impression] to pass from there into the muscles that serve to keep the organs of sense in the same situation ...[35]

On this basis, Descartes explains how *admiration* is functional [*utile*]: 'it makes us learn and retain in our memory things that we had previously ignored'.[36] At the same time, Descartes restates his view of what constitutes the functionality of any passion: to strengthen and maintain those 'thoughts in the soul that it is good that it conserve and which could easily be effaced from it without that passion'.[37] Strengthening and maintaining a thought through the comportment of muscles, spirits, and brain is precisely the effect of *admiration*, and so *admiration* enables the functionality of the other passions.

Descartes' account of *admiration* makes two explanatory moves that deserve remark. First, he describes how *admiration* performs its function by marshalling the movement of animal 'spirits', which like all bodies obey only the laws of mechanical causation. Second, he uses *admiration* to introduce considerations of intentionality into our body-based perceptions. Central to *admiration* is the mind's focus on an object, the way it directs attention. Yet all the passions are characterized as involving intentionality, that is, as having an object, which the the passion is said to 'represent'. Joy is an example: it is defined as an 'agreeable motion of the soul, in which consists the enjoyment it has of some good that the impressions of the brain represent to it as its own'.[38] Now, what Descartes means by 'represent' is, to put it mildly, a vexed issue. Even more puzzling is why Descartes here locates representation in a *brain* impression, especially since he also sometimes attributes the act of representing to the soul or to the passion itself.[39] Yet whatever we make of these difficulties, his introduction of representation signals that the objects of the various passions—objects of desire, or joy, or fear, or of course, wonder—are *intentional* objects. At the same time, the talk of how objects are represented by brain impressions, the senses, the passions, and body-based perceptions in general shows that Descartes is committed to some kind of *embodied* intentionality.

But Descartes' understanding of the nature of extension and its causality presents a real obstacle to understanding how perceptual intentionality could involve bodies in any significant way. For there is nothing in the Cartesian conception of bodies that could constitute anchors for intentional acts, much less intentional acts or entities themselves. The properties of bodies are only the modes of extension, e.g., motion, divisibility, shape, and a few general attributes. These modes allow us to trace the paths of mechanical transfers of motion readily enough, but the causal story is not the same as, and in fact, underdetermines what counts as the *objects* of perception. Ordinary middle-sized bodies do not have ontologically robust forms, or the intrinsic unities and boundaries that might furnish intentional focal points.[40] How, then, can we pick out various chunks of extension, even provisionally, as objects of perception? For reliable sense-perceptions, Descartes identifies the objects of perception with their causes. But such objects are embedded in causal chains that extend indefinitely (in both directions), and we pick out particular links as salient, as *the* causes, only because we have already identified them as the intentional objects of perception. In short, the nature of extension provides nothing on which to hang our common-sense maps of the external world, and so our folk-ontology seems unfounded, even inexplicable.

In contrast, Descartes' metaphysics of mind has ample room for intentionality: perception is typically, perhaps intrinsically, perception *of* some content, or object. Moreover, the *Passions of the Soul* may identify mental activity with intentionality even more closely than do earlier works, since Descartes here declares *volition*, not perception, to be the proper action of the soul; arguably, he thus conceives of willing as the activity by which the (created) mind directs itself, prior to any received perceptions, including perceptions of its own activity.[41] For the sake of present argument, I will assume that the mind's activity is sufficient to constitute some content as the target object of its perceiving and thereby endow mental states with intentionality.[42] Understood in this way, intentionality may be largely a matter of *attentive* activity. But even granting this assumption, Descartes still confronts a tricky problem in integrating the intentional character of perception with the inputs that come from the body so as to explain how sense-perception enables us to think about, attend to, and refer to bits of the external world. This is not a question of the correctness of our references to the world; it is the problem of how to embody intentionality in order to be oriented onto the external world at all. I propose that Descartes tackles it through *admiration*.

The problem of integrating the causal story about events in the extended world with the intentional character of the perceptions that result arises early in the *Passions of the Soul*. In teaching us how to distinguish the operations of the body from the operations of the mind, §§12–16 discuss how bodily members may be moved by the 'objects' of the senses alone. Here Descartes explains how bodies act on our body to stimulate a series of motions. Those motions are *causes* of our perceptions. To convey the information we perceive, they must be diversified in as many ways 'as they make us see diversities in the things'. These differentiated motions terminate in motions in the brain that 'represent these objects to the soul'. But then a gap appears in the account. Descartes says that the motions in the brain may create diverse 'sentiments' in the brain [*font avoir à notre âme divers sentiments*].[43] They may also push animal spirits towards the muscles of various members without the intervention of the soul at all, which Descartes illustrates by the reflex of flinching when a hand moves suddenly towards our eyes. So, following the motions that begin with sensible objects through the impacts on and in our bodies, we find that there they split into the proximate causes of what are vaguely referred to as *sentiments*[44] received by the mind and yet further motions that constitute the body's reflex movements. There are two causal chains of different kinds, but neither is sufficient for genuinely intentional perception and neither explains how the initial links in these chains become what the perceptions they stimulate are *about*.

It is the passion of wonder, I suggest, that brings the causal and the intentional accounts together. Consider how Descartes defines *admiration* in §70: it is a 'sudden surprise of the soul, that brings it to consider attentively the objects that seem to it rare and extraordinary'. Descartes then specifies the causes of the passion of *admiration* as an impression in the brain, which 'represents' the object [*l'impression qu'on a dans le cerveau, qui représente l'objet*] as rare and thus worthy of intense consideration.[45] This may seem doubly puzzling: not only does Descartes attribute some kind of intentionality to a bit of extension (albeit a bit that is the proximate cause of a mental perception), he has already emphasized that the impression in the brain is simply the effect of a sequence of motions. But because it is a structure in a particular location in the brain, it channels the animal spirits flowing through there in such a way as to fortify and conserve the brain impression. At the same time, it funnels animal spirits into the muscles that determine the orientation of the organs of sense, so that the impression is maintained by the similar flow of spirits by which it was formed. The impression in the brain is thus not only the proximate cause of a mental perception; it also sets up a feedback loop whereby the internal bodily motions that cause the impression rebound to sustain it and maintain the body in the same relation to outside things that initially set the causal chain in motion.

What we have here is an account of how in the passion of wonder, bodily operations work to produce a stable, mutually reinforcing, and durable set of causal conditions for a particular perception. Descartes particularly stresses the force of *admiration* in §72, which he attributes both to the novelty of the object and to how the internal bodily movement caused by such novel objects strikes the brain with full force from the start. There is a purely mechanical account for this effect, as well as for the entire feedback loop, that keeps the brain and senses directed at the novel object. But bodily comportment alone does not an intentional object make. Because of the condition of the sensory systems and the brain, the animal spirits flow at full force from the start of the perception. This translates into both a strong impact on the brain and a conspicuous, attention-getting perception in the mind. Although we can with effort disregard it, the perception disposes us to attend to it. Turning our attention to it is a volitional act, and like the volitional acts to move our feet to the beat, or to resist a feeling of fear, it causes brain events. Those events strengthen and maintain the motions that initially drew our attention. Thus, turning our attention to consider the information it carries strengthens the impression in the brain. The mind thus enters the feedback loop we have seen linking brain, senses and body; it turns the passion into a full-blown attentive act directed at the wonderful object that initially thrust itself on our attention.

To be sure, the passion of *admiration* does not explain how intentionality gets into the picture where there was no such thing before. Nor does it explain how specific motions in the brain are linked with specific perceptions in the mind, which is the work of 'natural institutions'. What it does explain is how the intentional object of a perception can be shaped by its bodily causes, so that we can talk about a genuinely body-based perception, not just a series of bodily motions that happen to give rise to a perception that coincidentally happens to be directed at some of its causes. *Admiration* makes sense of how our attention can be *drawn* by external things, while respecting both the freedom of our volitional acts and the mechanical operation of our bodies, sense organs, and brains. Wonder is supposed to make us learn and retain in our memories things of which we were previously ignorant.[46] One such thing it may enable us to learn is how to make perceptions caused by the external world also *refer* to it. That does not mean that wonder is always aroused whenever our sense-perceptions succeed in determining external intentional objects. But wonder may be how we first harness the mechanical operations of the body in order to get embodied intentionality off the ground. Children learn about the world by wondering at it, and in doing so, they learn that there is something independent for them to learn.

5.5 Leader of the Pack: Hobbesian Glory

I would now like to turn briefly to Hobbes to examine how his approach to the passions meets the demands of his preferred forms of explanation. By likewise adopting a mechanical conception of matter and motion, Hobbes faces all the same explanatory reformations and restrictions as did Descartes. For this reason, his *De corpore* (1655) declares 'a *final cause* has no place but in such things as have sense and will'.[47] But Hobbes goes further: *all* there is is matter in motion. Moreover, the causes and consequences of matter in motion have explanatory priority over almost all sciences, including the study of our passions.[48] So, as Hobbes conceives his materialism, it requires him to reject final causation for human actions and volitions, as well as for inanimate interactions. Indeed, Hobbes seems committed to the possibility of reducing the seeming purposefulness of our actions to their efficient causes. The efficient causes that push our actions are found in the 'motion or endeavour, which consisteth in appetite or aversion, to or from the object moving',[49] for which the 'object moving' provides the initial nudge by impacting our sense organs and transmitting motions to the heart.[50] So, we are not drawn by antecedently given objects or ends of good and evil: instead, we are pushed, as it were from behind: 'whatsoever is the object of any man's appetite or desire that is it which he for his part calleth good', and *mutatis mutandi* for 'evil'.[51] For this reason, even the hybrid form of functional explanation developed by Descartes, which combines purposes and intentions provided by the mind with the mechanical workings of the body, will not serve Hobbes's ultimate commitments. And that means that there is no independently available determination of how things 'matter to us' by which to classify the passions.

More generally, Hobbes cannot use anything like Descartes' notion of the passions of the soul to distinguish the passions from among the various motions we find in animals.[52] Such voluntary, 'animal' motion is the end of a circuit of motions that begins with the impact of external objects on our sense organs, is transmitted as the reverberations of 'decaying sense' to the imagination, and culminates in the movement of various limbs. In the *Elements of Law* (ms. 1640), Hobbes differentiates the passions from other motions mainly by their place in the body: whereas motions in the brain constitute sense and imagination, the continuation of those motions to the heart count as passions proper. Later, the *Leviathan* (1651) opts to locate the passions largely by their causal role: they are the 'interior beginnings of voluntary motions', which can generally be identified as endeavour, appetite, or desire, and its contrary, aversion,[53] and which manifest themselves in the diverse specific passions. When we deliberate, we alternate between competing passions, until we are left with a 'whole sum' that has motivating power, and constitutes the act of willing.[54] Thought and reasoning too are forms of animal motion, driven by the passions just as much as the movement of limbs is. 'Wit', for instance, is fuelled by desires for power, riches, knowledge or honour, all of which, Hobbes declares, 'may be reduced to... desire of power'.[55] By constituting motivations in both the psychological and kinetic sense, the passions provide the means for reducing voluntary action to the forward-driving motion of efficient causation.

Nonetheless, because motion circulates through the Hobbesian universe, continuous both within and without animal bodies, the passions cannot—and should not—be sharply distinguished from other animal motions. Even less clear are the classificatory principles by which Hobbes divides among kinds of passions. He has no problem generating long lists of passions: the *Elements of Law* offers about two dozen and the *Leviathan* about three dozen, neither of which pretend to completeness. Perhaps the most basic taxonomic division at work in these lists is that in the direction of the passions 'to or from the object moving', that is, between appetite or aversion. But Hobbes does not consistently group passions into pairs of contraries. The *Leviathan* also inserts a third term, 'contempt', between desire and aversion,[56] using it to describe such passions as magnanimity, impudence, and cruelty. Shortly thereafter, the work identifies six 'simple passions' of 'appetite, desire, love, aversion, hate, joy and grief'.[57] These passions figure in the descriptions of many subsequent ones, as befitting their status as 'simple', but not in several passions that are species of contempt alone, which Hobbes fails to list among the simples. Moreover, love collapses into appetite and desire, which he had earlier declared the same.[58] So, despite his fondness for enumerating the passions, Hobbes seems relatively uninterested in imposing the sort of taxonomic framework found in previous philosophers.

However, Hobbes does offer rather different means for organizing the passions. After identifying a long list of passions in Chapter 9 of the *Elements of Law*, he catalogues the main ones by way of their kinetic relations to each other and to our basic endeavour. These relations are arrayed as moments in a footrace:

> To endeavour is appetite
> To be remiss is sensuality.
> To consider them behind is glory.
> To consider them before is humility
> ...
> Continually to be out-gone is misery.
> Continually to out-go the next before is felicity.
> And to forsake the course is to die.[59]

The footrace metaphor does not offer principles of differentiation so much as causal-kinetic, or even governmental, associations among the passions. In somewhat similar fashion, Hobbes also organizes his accounts of the passions by honing in on the roles played by particular passions in larger schemes of human behaviour. Perhaps the most prominent example is the role of publicly sanctioned fear in governing unruly passions. Here, however, I want to focus on the somewhat exotic passion Hobbes calls 'glory', the first specific passion named after endeavour and appetite in the footrace catalogue. Chapter 9, in fact, starts out with a description of glory, putting it at the head of its list of passions. Glory is less conspicuous in the *Leviathan*, where it is described as a species of joy.[60] But it remains important, figuring as one of the three basic causes of war in the state of nature, that which makes us invade for reputation. Even in the commonwealth, glory requires a great deal of management, most obviously through the sovereign's diversion of the glory-seeking of its subjects to the pursuit of honors.[61] Moreover, despite refusing pride of taxonomic place to the passion of glory, the *Leviathan* leaves in place the explanatory demands that led to its prominence in the *Elements of Law*. To understand how the importance of this passion for Hobbes's explanatory ambitions, we need to look at the connection between desire (or general appetite), desire for power, and 'felicity'.

In dramatizing the various motive forms taken by our appetitive endeavour, the race metaphor links them closely to a distinctive account of felicity. Although the metaphor paints felicity in particularly competitive colours, what is important for our purposes is its location within the race. Throughout his works, Hobbes takes pains to stress that felicity is not an *end* for action, and registers his disagreement with the Epicureans and Stoics by insisting that it cannot be identified with 'the repose of a mind satisfied'. Instead he insists, there is 'no such *Finis ultimus* (utmost aim) nor *Summum Bonum* (greatest good)', since life itself is restless pursuing and procuring[62] and 'can never be without desire'.[63] For this reason, the *Elements of Law* declares 'felicity, therefore (by which we mean continual delight), consisteth not in having prospered, but in prospering'.[64] In this work, felicity is thus a passion. But *Leviathan* describes it in subtly different ways:

> Felicity is a continual progress of the desire from one object to another, the attaining of the former being still but the way to the latter. The cause whereof is that the object of man's desire is not to enjoy once only and for one instant of time, but to assure for ever the way of his future desire.[65]

Or more simply, felicity is a 'continual success', or 'continual prospering'.[66] Here, felicity does not appear so much a passion as the object of a kind of meta-desire: 'to assure forever the way of [our] future desire'.

However, this understanding of felicity poses a problem for Hobbes: unlike the simple satisfactions of non-human animals,[67] human felicity is future-directed. And it remains future-directed whether understood as a matter of a meta-desire for the future, or as a joy arising from the prospect of the future. Indeed, the *Elements of Law* makes all the passions, including the passion of felicity, 'consist in conception of the future'.[68] And therein lies the problem. Final causation can readily explain intentional relations to the future, for it can allow a not-yet-present-end to serve as an object and cause. But Hobbes has ruled out appeals to final causation. Instead, our ends are set by presently active desires that operate as efficient causes, pushing us from behind: the ends are simply byproducts of our desiring. How then is it possible that we can strive for felicity?

Hobbes tries to be true to his view that there is no final end, when he describes the 'general inclination of all mankind' for felicity as:

> a perpetual and restless desire of power after power, that ceaseth only in death.... because he cannot assure the power and means to live well which he hath present, without the acquisition of more [power].[69]

What makes for the prospect of success in satisfying our desires—that is, our passions—is power, and thus, the pursuit of happiness is a matter of striving for power. Still, this seems only to displace the problem from understanding what can drive the pursuit of felicity to the equally tricky task of explaining the mechanics involved in seeking power. However, Hobbes conceives of power as the way to link a present state of affairs with the future: 'there is something at the present that hath power to produce' anything that 'will be hereafter', and so 'all conception of future, is conception of power'.[70] For this move to work, we cannot understand the restless desire of power after power to be simply a desire for power that itself lies in the future. Rather, we must appreciate Hobbes's distinctive conception of power and our striving for power. Power is an ability that serves as means to an end. But the greatest part of an individual's power does not lie in individual abilities: it is socially constructed, either through the pooling of forces, or simply from the recognition of one's power by others. Thus, Hobbes insists that riches are power, honors are power, and 'reputation' is power.[71] These are concrete means towards ensuring the way of our future desire. And the passion that drives our pursuit of such means, particularly of honors and reputation, is glory.

Glory can explain the striving for power in a way that respects the rejection of final causation, because it is indeed a *passion* for Hobbes, an internal motion that we feel as an occurrent state and that initiates voluntary motions. As a first pass, we can understand glory as the desire for recognition of one's power, a manifestation of power striving after power. But glory cannot simply be identified as the *desire* for power, or ambition, for it is not a species of desire. In the *Elements of Law*, it is a special kind of passion, a form neither of love nor of joy,[72] but 'that passion which proceedeth from the imagination or conception of our own power'.[73] The *Leviathan*, in contrast, considers glory to be a kind of joy 'arising from imagination of a man's own power and ability'.[74] In both cases, glory arises from imagination; that is, it arises from a bodily (e.g., brain) state that constitutes an appearance of our own power.[75] Whether as a form of joy or something *sui generis*, the passion moves us to maintain and strengthen that imagined sense of our own power—to strive for continued recognition, particularly the kind of public recognition that is reputation. Glory is thus a particularly concentrated form of the striving after power, manifested in a present passion. But it is directed towards current reputation, a concrete and presently available means to future ends. It thus explains how we come to have power as an end. But it is not itself reducible to any ends, including power: for the passion of glory can, and often does, drive people to self-destructive behaviour—the ultimate loss of power. Even the most well-founded sense of glory can backfire, as Hobbes makes clear in treating the effects of acting on one's sense of glory in a situation of rough equality. Glory-hounds make life nasty, brutish, and short, both for themselves and others: one common cause of war-mongering are those people who would rather go out in a blaze of glory than enjoy the fruits of peace by submission. Thus, glory is also not the same as self-interest, or self-love. It might seem more closely related to pride and ambition, but unlike pride, it always involves the manifestation of and striving for more power through reputation. And unlike familiar kinds of ambition, it is not described primarily in terms of its ends, or even the calculated pursuit of its ends. For that reason, I think it is well-suited to Hobbes's attempt to account for human action without relying *irreducibly* on final causation. To be sure, by the time of the *Leviathan*, Hobbes no longer treats glory as a universal human motive. Nonetheless, the very possibility of glory illustrates how a passion can motivate the pursuit of ever more power, and thus the pursuit of a future-directed felicity, without requiring our animal motions to be directed by some distant end.

5.6 A Few Conclusions

I want to conclude by pressing the methodological point I touched on at the beginning: that looking to past taxonomies—or their absence—can show us how historically *and* theoretically mediated are many conceptions of the emotions, at least those that we find in philosophical treatises. Again, this is not the same claim as declaring the cultural variability of the emotions, for which one might find much better examples than early modern wonder or glory.[76] But the passions that head off Descartes' and Hobbes's different catalogues seem endemic to their native conceptual environments. Descartes' introduction of *admiration* as the lynchpin of his system was a genuine novelty, which we should not simply assimilate to familiar emotions of surprise or curiosity.[77] We do not usually think of 'wonder' as the most basic emotion of all basic emotions, nor do we tend to gloss self-esteem as a form of wonder at our own free will, as Descartes did in describing 'generosity'.[78] Hobbesian 'glory' may be yet more alien to us. Although we might encounter rudimentary forms among contemporary middle-school boys, publicity-seeking celebrities, and military dictators, Hobbes did not think of glory mainly as a quality of adolescent psychology.[79] 'Magnanimity' is glory 'well grounded upon certain experience of power sufficient to attain [one's] end in open manner',[80] while the nobility of those who keep their word for the sake of glory displays Hobbesian 'generosity'.[81] Here Hobbes conceives of generosity as the trait of those who bind themselves to their own previous promises out of a sense of their own power, whereas in Descartes' version, the generous are those who bind themselves to their promises out of a sense of their own freedom.[82] I hope this account has shown that both conceptions are intelligible in the appropriate context, particularly in the context of the taxonomies that delineate the web of passions, and the explanatory ambitions they serve. At the same time, I want to allow that their conceptions may be distant from our current affective experience. I suspect that we now find it hard to imagine a psychological environment in which Hobbesian glory would be, if not universal, at least *among* the more common motivations for human behaviour of diverse kinds. But even if his account offers a canny diagnosis of behaviour common in his own time, particularly among the Cavalier class, my interest here is not with the accuracy or applicability of either philosopher's conception of the emotions. Rather, I hope to have offered a bit of evidence that the nature of our passions and emotions is mediated by social and historical conditions, just as their conception is by the philosophical context in which they are embedded. The position that such conceptions occupy in taxonomies, lists, and other such differential schemes for explaining our passions offers a means both to access the intelligibility of historic accounts of particular emotions and to appreciate their unfamiliarity. The focal passions found in Descartes' and Hobbes's taxonomies simply offer vivid examples of such mediation at least for the philosophic conception of our emotions.[83]

Notes

1. With apologies to Gilbert & Sullivan, and lovers of the *Mikado*.
2. As Susanna Braund informs me, *Pathomachia* is surely modelled on the *Psychomachia* of Prudentius (4th Cent. C.E.). *Psychomachia* is essentially a battle-narrative, in which such virtues as Patientia, Mens Humilis, and Pudicitia face off against vices, including Ira, Superbia, and Libido. But the work does not conceive of these traits as passions.
3. For further discussion of publication in England, see Amy Schmitter, 'Passions and Affections in British Philosophy of the Seventeenth Century', in *The Oxford Handbook of British Philosophy in the Seventeenth Century*, ed. P. Anstley (Oxford: Oxford University Press, 2013), pp. 442–71.
4. For this reason, I won't try to decide how the theoretical concepts I trace might play a role in broad social history (although I doubt that they are inert). Distinguishing sharply between emotional experience and 'emotionology', the attitudes and standards taken towards

emotions, as do Peter and Carol Stearns, 'Emotionology: Clarifying the History of Emotions and Emotional Standards', *American Historical Review* 90 (1985): 813–36, and Peter Stearns in Jan Plamper, 'The History of Emotions: An Interview with William Reddy, Barbara Rosenwein, and Peter Stearns', *History and Theory* 49 (2010): 237–65 (pp. 262–3), may make philosophy seem doubly removed from experience. But explicit theories and taxonomies may offer the most readily accessible evidence for the historicity of the emotions. The importance of texts, even highly theoretical ones, for identifying the repertoire of 'emotional communities' is defended by Rosenwein in Plamper, 'The History of Emotions', pp. 253–4, 258–9.

5. For an example of current treatments of these issues, see Paul Griffiths, *What Emotions Really Are: The Problem of Psychological Categories* (Chicago: University of Chicago Press, 1997) and 'Is Emotion a Natural Kind?', in *Thinking About Feeling*, ed. Robert Solomon (Oxford: Oxford University Press, 2004), pp. 233–49.
6. See, e.g., Cicero, *Tusculan Disputations*, trans. J. E. King, Loeb Classical Library 141 (Cambridge, MA: Harvard University Press, 1927): Book 4.
7. See *CG* 14.7–9, pp. 286–319. References to Augustine are to *City of God*, Volume IV: Books 12–15, trans. P. Levine. Loeb Classical Library 414 (Cambridge, MA: Harvard University Press, 1966), cited as CG by book, chapter and pages.
8. See Tractatus quinque ad Primam Secundae D. Thomae Aquinatis 4.1.
9. See *The Passions of the Soul: The Third Book of 'De Anima et Vita'*, intro. & trans. G. Noreña (Lewiston, NY: E. Mellen Press, 1990), Introduction and Chapter 1 (pp. 1–9). There Vives proposed distinctions of his own, such as that between violent passions and gentle '*affectus*' or '*affectiones*'. The distinction may stem from authors such as Quintilian: see Lorenzo Casini, 'Aristotelianism and Anti-Stoicism in Juan Luis Vives's Conception of the Emotions', in *Moral Philosophy on the Threshold of Modernity*, ed. J. Kraye & R. Saarinen (Dordrect: Springer, 2006), pp. 291–3.
10. For instance, Thomas Wright (1601/4), Edward Reynolds (1640), and Jean-François Senault (1641) endorsed the canonical list of eleven passions found in Aquinas and derived from Aristotle: love, hate, desire (concupiscence, coveting), aversion (flight), joy (delight, pleasure), sadness (grief, pain), hope, despair, fear, daring (audacity), and anger (ire, indignation). Later philosophers such as John Norris and Mary Astell (1695), trumpet their Augustinian (and Malebranchean) sympathies by explaining the passions through the focal passion of love. See Schmitter, 'Passions and Affections' for further discussion.
11. *Ethics* 3P11s: 501; cf. *Ethics* 3P58–9: 529 for the two primitive active affects. References to Spinoza are to his *Ethics* in *Collected Works of Spinoza*, Vol. I., ed. & trans. E. Curley (Princeton: Princeton University Press, 1985), cited by part, proposition, component, and page.
12. ST 5.9: 391. References to Malebranche are to *The Search after Truth*, ed. & trans. T. Lennon & P. Olscamp (Cambridge: Cambridge University Press, 1997), cited as ST, followed by part, chapter and page.
13. ST 4.6: 287–8.
14. ST 2.1.7: 120.
15. Malebranche thinks of grace as providing a 'prevenient' pleasure, which rights the disorder in our love wrought by sin and strengthens our natural inclination towards God. This is because it is a *sensible* pleasure: a delight by which 'we sensibly perceive that God is our

good' (ST 5.7: 360). The result is that those gifted with grace gain what seems a genuinely *passionate* love for God.

16. ST 5.9: 391–3; see also ST 5.7: 375.
17. ST 4.2: 269–70.
18. Sources for Hobbes's notion of human glory may include Thucydides and Cicero, who describe political glory as one of the prime motivators and ends of human life (e.g., *Tusculan Disputations* 1.2.4), and Machiavelli. Augustine seems to identify the desire for glory with the love of praise and honour, even stating that the urge for glory [*libido gloriandi*] 'is called boasting' [*iactantia nuncupatur*], while distinguishing it from the urge to dominate [*libido dominandi*] (CG 14.15: 352–3). Although Augustine clearly thinks the search for human glory is largely vicious, since glory properly belongs only to God, he follows Cicero in attributing some political virtues to the desire for glory that outweighs self-interest and self-preservation; see *City of God*, Volume II: Books 4–7, trans. W. M. Green. Loeb Classical Library 412 (Cambridge, MA: Harvard University Press, 1963): 5.12 (pp. 200–1). In this respect, Hobbes may revere glory rather less than many of his predecessors.
19. PS 2.68: 379. All references to Descartes are to the *Passions of the Soul*, in *Oeuvres de Descartes*, Vol. XI, ed. C. Adam & P. Tannery (Paris, France: J. Vrin, 1996), cited as PS, followed by part, article, and page. (All translations are mine.)
20. PS 2.68: 379.
21. Descartes specifies that the passion is *désir*, not the scholastic *concupiscence* (PS 2.68: 379; cf. 2.69: 380).
22. PS 2.69: 380.
23. PS 1.27: 349.
24. PS 2.52: 372.
25. This usage is in accord with current philosophical custom, but Descartes' use of the French cognate '*fonction*' does not have this sense (cf. PS 1.2: 328). For more on this Cartesian kind of functionalism, see, e.g., Gary Hatfield, 'Animals', and Amy Schmitter, 'How to Engineer a Human Being: Passions and Functional Explanation in Descartes', in *A Companion to Descartes*, ed. J. Broughton & J. Carriero (Oxford: Blackwell Publishing, 2007), pp. 404–25 and pp. 426–44.
26. PS 2.52: 372.
27. This importance is usually a matter of whether the passion represents its object as *convenable* [apt, suitable, fitting, or convenient] or the opposite. But as we will see, wonder arises before we know if something is *convenable* or not. Thus what makes an object an object of wonder is only what makes it salient: its newness, or difference from what we have experienced or expect (PS 2.53: 373).
28. PS 2.52: 372.
29. PS 2.53: 373.
30. Moreover, the next article, PS 2.54: 373, clarifies that we may wonder at the greatness [*la grandeur*] or the smallness [*petitesse*] of the object, which joins either esteem or contempt [*le mépris*] to the *admiration*. What is crucial is that we are moved by the object somehow.
31. PS 2.56: 374.
32. PS 2.57: 374.
33. As Descartes remarks, refusing to pair desire with a contrary departs from the taxonomy of 'the Schools' (PS 2.87: 393). But because such desire aims only at bringing about what it

represents as '*convenable*' for us, he thinks it matters little whether we seek the presence of an absent good, or its conservation, or the absence of an evil. Spinoza adopts Descartes' approach, although Hobbes does not.

34. Although Malebranche adopts a similar picture of wonder, the features that give it a structural priority for Descartes simply make it an incomplete passion by Malebranche's reckoning (ST 5.7: 375).
35. PS 2.70: 380–1.
36. PS 2.75: 384.
37. PS 2.74: 383.
38. PS 2.91: 396.
39. PS 2.85–86: 391–2.
40. This is so even if Descartes thinks of microscopic divisions of extension as distinct substances.
41. See PS 1.17: 342, 1.19: 343.
42. This claim is neutral about the metaphysical status or epistemic accessibility of such objects.
43. PS 1.13: 338.
44. In seventeenth-century usage, *sentiment* is extremely ambiguous between cognition and mere feeling. See http://artflx.uchicago.edu/cgi-bin/dicos/pubdico1look.pl?strippedhw=sentiment.
45. PS 2.70: 380.
46. PS 2.75: 384.
47. Hobbes, *De Corpore*, in *The English Works of Thomas Hobbes of Malmesbury*, ed. W. Molesworth (London: J. Bohn, 1839), 10.7, p. 132.
48. L 9 table; 48. References are to *Leviathan*, ed. E. Curley (Indianapolis, IN: Hackett Publishing Co, 1994a), cited as L, followed by chapter, paragraph, and page.
49. L 6.9: 29.
50. Hobbes thereby seems to take the thing that causes sensations and subsequent actions to be their intentional object. However, the arguments that perceptual causes cannot determine an intentional object, which we saw for Descartes, also apply here. Hobbes might supplement his account by appeal to how the imagination forms internal pictures as its objects, but it seems unlikely that they will suffice to explain intentionality. However, I will not pursue the argument here.
51. L 6.7: 28.
52. For further discussion of these and related issues, see Schmitter, 'Passions and Affections', pp. 458–9, 462–3.
53. L 6.2: 28.
54. L 6. 49, 53: 33.
55. L 8.13–15: 40–1.
56. L 6.5: 28.
57. L 6.13: 30.
58. L 6.2–3: 28.
59. EL 9.21: 59–60. References to the *Elements of Law* are to *Human Nature and De Corpore Politico*, in *The Elements of Law*, ed. J. C. A. Gaskin (Oxford: Oxford University Press, 1994b), cited as EL, followed by chapter, paragraph, and page.
60. For a discussion of the changing fortunes of 'glory' over Hobbes's works, see Gabriella Slomp, 'From Genus to Species: The Unravelling of Hobbesian Glory', *History of Political*

Thought, XIX (1998): 552–69. In 'Hobbes on Glory and Civil Strife', in *The Cambridge Companion to Hobbes's Leviathan*, ed. P. Springborg (Cambridge: Cambridge University Press, 2007), pp. 129–47, Slomp argues for an even more prominent place for glory in the *Leviathan* than I do.

61. See L 10.18–52: 52–6.
62. L 11.1: 57.
63. L 6.58: 34–5.
64. EL 7.7: 45.
65. L 11.1: 57.
66. L 6.58: 34.
67. L 12.4: 63.
68. EL 8.3: 48.
69. L 11.2: 58.
70. EL 8.3: 48.
71. Knowledge, however, offers but 'small power'—largely because few others can *recognize* it as such (L 10.14: 51).
72. See, e.g., EL 9.16: 56.
73. EL 9.1: 50. In the *Elements of Law*, glory also appears to include the desire for the eclipse of others' power. The zero-sum, competitive element of glory is much reduced in *Leviathan* (but cf. Slomp, 'Hobbes on Glory and Civil Strife').
74. L 6.39: 31; the gloss I suggest here differs somewhat from Slomp, 'Hobbes on Glory and Civil Strife'.
75. In declaring that glory (like all passions) arises from an 'imagination', Hobbes does not mean that it rests on an illusion, but only that some state must hold in the faculty of 'imagination' (or *phantasia*) to provide the content of the passion. That imagination may be accurate, which is normal, or inaccurate, in which case the passion becomes 'vainglory'.
76. Martha Nussbaum offers a number of such examples, such as *fago* among the Ifaluk people: see *Upheavals of Thought: The Intelligence of Emotions* (Cambridge: Cambridge University Press, 2001), Chapter 3, p. 156.
77. I doubt that Cartesian wonder is the same as the surprise that figures prominently in, e.g., contemporary affect programme theory; see Griffiths, *What Emotions Really Are*, p. 15.
78. PS 3.150, 153: 444, 446.
79. Even less did previous authors who considered political glory, such as Cicero, or even Augustine (see n.18 above).
80. EL 9.20: 58–9.
81. L 14.31: 87.
82. PS 3.156, 203: 448, 481.
83. Thanks are due to the audiences at the conference 'Passions in Ancient and Modern Philosophy' (*Philosophy in Assos*, Turkey, 2012) and at a departmental colloquium at the University of Alberta (2012) for pressing me on the broad methodological claims here. Raffaella de Rosa commented on a version of this paper at a symposium at the Eastern Division of the American Philosophical Association (2012); both she and the audience there have my gratitude particularly for the discussion of wonder and embodied intentionality in Descartes. Lisa Shapiro helped a great deal in sorting out some of my thoughts about how Hobbes organizes his catalogues of passions, as did Alix Cohen and Bob Stern

with the structure of the paper. Two anonymous referees offered helpful comments. My able research assistants, Luke McNulty and Esther Rosario, caught a number of errors. Lastly, I am grateful to the participants in my winter 2014 seminar on seventeenth-century passions and affects for careful reading, excellent discussions, and a great deal of patience as the clock frequently ran out on us. Research and editing this paper was enabled by grant support from the Social Sciences and Humanities Council of Canada.

Bibliography

Anon, *Pathomachia: or, The battle of affections: Shadowed by a Feigned Siege of the City Pathopolis. Written some years since, and now first published by a friend of the deceased* author (London: Francis Constable, 1630).

Astell, Mary and John Norris. *Letters concerning the Love of God, between the Author of the Proposal to the Ladies and Mr. John Norris* (London: Samuel Manship and Richard Wilkin, 1695).

Augustine, *City of God, Volume IV: Books 12–15*, trans. P. Levine. Loeb Classical Library 414 (Cambridge, MA: Harvard University Press, 1966).

Casini, Lorenzo. 'Aristotelianism and Anti-Stoicism in Juan Luis Vives's Conception of the Emotions', in *Moral Philosophy on the Threshold of Modernity*, ed. J. Kraye and R. Saarinen (Dordrect: Springer, 2006), pp. 283–305.

Cicero, *Tusculan Disputations*, trans. J. E. King, Loeb Classical Library 141 (Cambridge, MA: Harvard University Press, 1927).

Descartes, René. 'Passions of the Soul', in *Oeuvres de Descartes*, Vol. XI, eds C. Adam and P. Tannery (Paris: J. Vrin, 1996). [cited as PS, followed by part, article, and page. All translations are mine.]

Dictionnaire de l'Académie française (1694), retrieved from http://artfl-project.uchicago.edu/content/dictionnaires-dautrefois.

Griffiths, Paul. *What Emotions Really Are: The Problem of Psychological Categories* (Chicago, IL: University of Chicago Press, 1997).

Griffiths, Paul. 'Is Emotion a Natural Kind?', in *Thinking about Feeling*, ed. Robert Solomon (Oxford: Oxford University Press, 2004), pp. 233–49.

Hatfield, Gary. 'Animals', in *A Companion to Descartes*, ed. Janet Broughton & John Carriero (Oxford: Blackwell Publishing, 2007), pp. 404–25.

Hobbes, Thomas. *De Corpore, The English Works of Thomas Hobbes of Malmesbury*, ed. William Molesworth (London: J. Bohn, 1839). [cited by chapter, paragraph, and page].

Hobbes, Thomas. *Leviathan*, ed. Edward Curley (Indianapolis, IN: Hackett Publishing Co., 1994). [cited as L, followed by chapter, paragraph, and page].

Hobbes, Thomas. *Human Nature and De Corpore Politico, The Elements of Law*, ed. J. C. A. Gaskin (Oxford: Oxford University Press, 1994b). [cited as EL, followed by chapter, paragraph, and page].

Malebranche, Nicolas. *The Search after Truth*, ed. & trans. T. Lennon & P. Olscamp (Cambridge: Cambridge University Press, 1997). [cited as ST, followed by part, chapter, and page].

Nussbaum, Martha. *Upheavals of Thought: The Intelligence of Emotions* (Cambridge: Cambridge University Press, 2001).

Plamper, Jan. 'The History of Emotions: An Interview with William Reddy, Barbara Rosenwein, and Peter Stearns', *History and Theory* 49 (2001): 237–65.

Reynolds, Edward. *A Treatise of the Passions and Faculties of the Soul of Man, with the Several Dignities and Corruptions thereunto belonging* (London: Robert Bostock, 1640).

Schmitter, Amy. 'How to Engineer a Human Being: Passions and Functional Explanation in Descartes', in *A Companion to Descartes*, ed. Janet Broughton and John Carriero (Oxford: Blackwell Publishing, 2007), pp. 426–44.

Schmitter, Amy. 'Passions and Affections in British Philosophy of the Seventeenth Century', in *The Oxford Handbook of British Philosophy in the Seventeenth Century*, ed. Peter R. Anstley (Oxford: Oxford University Press, 2013), pp. 442–71.

Senault, Jean-François. *De l'usage des Passions* (Paris: Vve J. Camusat, 1641).

Slomp, Gabriella. 'From Genus to Species: The Unravelling of Hobbesian Glory', *History of Political Thought* 19 (1998): 552–69.

Slomp, Gabriella. 'Hobbes on Glory and Civil Strife', in *The Cambridge Companion to Hobbes's Leviathan*, ed. Patricia Springborg (Cambridge: Cambridge University Press, 2007), pp. 129–47.

Spinoza, Benedictus de. 'Ethics', in *Collected Works of Spinoza*, Vol. I, ed. & trans. Edward Curley (Princeton: Princeton University Press, 1985). [cited as E, followed by part, proposition, component, and page].

Stearns, Peter and Carol Stearns. 'Emotionology: Clarifying the History of Emotions and Emotional Standards', *American Historical Review* 90 (1985): 813–36.

Vives, Juan Luis. *The Passions of the Soul: The Third Book of De Anima et Vita*, intro. and trans. Carlos G. Noreña (Lewiston, NY: E. Mellen Press, 1990).

Wright, Thomas. *The Passions of the Mind in General* (London: Walter Burre, 1601/1604).

6

The Passions and Actions of Laughter in Shaftesbury and Hutcheson

Laurent Jaffro

> 'Strange! that none of our Hobbists banish all Canary birds and squirrels, and lap-dogs and pugs, and cats out of their houses, and substitute in their places asses, and owls, and snails, and oysters, to be merry upon.' Francis Hutcheson[1]

Laughter may be considered as more than the facial expression of various emotions: it may also be considered a moral emotion in its full right, at least in some of its varieties, from two different angles. One angle is that of its object, i.e. of the answers to the following questions: What kind of situations, attitudes, events, actions, speeches, typically make us laugh? Laughter in particular circumstances may be considered as an appropriate response, but to what? In what do the laughable and the ridiculous consist? Some early modern moralists claimed that laughter, like other emotions, has a formal object: since people do not spontaneously laugh at anything—although they might perhaps decide to make a laugh out of anything—they tried to give a general picture of what is typically laughable. They insisted upon the obvious social dimension of laughter and the way in which it plays with moral or aesthetic values in a context of interpersonal comparison, thus suggesting that there is some affinity between laughter and passions such as shame, admiration, respect, envy, or resentment. By contrast, another angle is that of the function of laughter. It is a moral emotion, not only because its object consists in values or is relative to values, but also because, as a practice, it has ethical effects, which may be more or less controlled or encouraged. For instance, the way we laugh, in the long run, may make us morally better or morally worse, collectively or individually. The impact, good or bad, of our use of laughter is social as well as individual. Thus, laughter itself is also an object of moral evaluation and, as social manners, of aesthetic evaluation as well.

In a post-Hobbesian context, Shaftesbury and Hutcheson are among the few philosophers to deal with laughter exclusively from a moral perspective. They do not pay much attention to the linguistic and stylistic aspects of wit and humour, or to the physiological dimension of the question, and treat of laughter only as an object for moral psychology and as a tool of social criticism. Although Hutcheson generally thinks that he agrees with Shaftesbury—indeed he defends him against Mandeville's attack on several topics—there are interesting differences in their approaches to the normative question of the use of laughter. The main difference between Shaftesbury's and Hutcheson's accounts is that the latter puts the emphasis on laughter as a response to a value, whereas the former focuses on laughter as a social action. Shaftesburian 'ridicule' (the term has a subjective as well as objective sense) or 'raillery', or 'wit', is the name of the social activity that consists in laughing at what deserves to be laughed at. Both philosophers recognize the importance of both aspects, but the way they tackle the question of laughter leads them to give priority to one over the other.

Let us reverse the historical order and start with Hutcheson's *Reflections upon Laughter*. For we need first to sketch out the account of laughter as a response to a value in order to highlight certain aspects of laughter, as depicted by Hutcheson, that do not fit his account well and thus require another kind of approach. Then we will shift from a theory of the perception of values to an account of what Robert Solomon calls a 'politics of emotions', in his eponymous 1998 paper, that 'takes as the framework of describing emotions neither the mind nor the body but the social situation, in all of its elaborate ethical and interpersonal complexity'.[2]

Beginning with laughter as a passion, we will also stress the importance of laughter as an action, and eventually we will concentrate on the dispositional dimension of laughter, what Shaftesbury terms 'good humour': the disposition to laugh appropriately, which is induced by, and induces in turn, a proper use of laughter, both as an action and as a passion. 'Good humour', which is a normative as well as psychological notion, provides the answer to a major problem, that of the regulation of laughter. For Shaftesbury and Hutcheson, the problem of how to control laughter appears most urgent when we consider laughter as an action, since in that case we might (to some extent) decide to laugh at anything, including what deserves not to be laughed at. The problem is also relevant to laughter as a passion, but in a different way. Here regulating the passion of laughter does not mean voluntarily limiting our use of laughter, but rather becoming more sensitive to the values to which laughter responds.

6.1 Laughter as a Passion

Hutcheson's *Reflections upon Laughter* consists in three papers, which were first published in the *Dublin Weekly Journal* in 1725–1726. The *pars destruens* is that reducing laughter to an expression of self-love and a kind of contempt for others' defects does not provide a good account of laughter. Hutcheson offers several arguments against Hobbes' s view on laughter and puts forward an alternative account. For the author of *The Elements of Law* (I, ix, 13), laughter involves an evaluative comparison between others and ourselves: we laugh at someone because we suddenly become aware or think that we are superior to that person:

> The passion of laughter is nothing else but a sudden glory arising from sudden conception of some eminency in ourselves, by comparison with the infirmities of others, or with our own formerly: for men laugh at the follies of themselves past, when they come suddenly to remembrance, except they bring with them any present dishonour.[3]

This has an interesting consequence: Since we cannot be superior to our present selves (although, without breaching the principle of identity, we can be superior to our former self, as Hobbes insists), we cannot laugh at ourselves. The reduction of laughter to a manifestation of self-love, which extreme Augustinian divines share with Hobbes, entails that the object of laughter cannot be oneself. As a French Protestant divine, Jacques Abbadie, writes in his 1692 treatise *The Art of Knowing Oneself*, 'men never laugh at themselves'.[4] The reason for this alleged fact, in Abbadie's argument, is that human beings are unable to imagine that they are not eminent. On the contrary,

> men don't only value themselves upon Qualities which would make 'em Ridiculous, could they but duely weigh and consider 'em, but also seek to gain a Reputation by Crimes and Villanies.[5]

Because of the immense gap between our being worthy of admiration, our 'natural dignity' as creatures of God, on the one hand, and, on the other hand, our 'ridiculous vanity', we certainly deserve to be laughed at, but at the same time we are unable to respond through laughter to our objective 'universal ridiculousness'.[6]

Contrary to Augustinian and Hobbesian diagnoses, according to which laughter cannot be reflexive because, in the present condition of mankind, self-love prevails in every one, some British moralists stress the moral significance of reflexive laughter in creatures capable of being aware of their own infirmities and of acknowledging the value of others.[7] In order to make room for a use of laughter as a means of self-criticism, which Shaftesbury calls 'good humour', we must give up the theory of dominant self-love and accept instead the view that human beings, although often blind, have a true sense of their own frailty.

According to Hutcheson, the problem with Hobbes' s theory of laughter is that it takes a part for the whole, conflating laughter with mockery and ridicule only.[8] As a description of one species of laughter—ridicule—Hobbes's picture might be acceptable. Hutcheson contrasts Hobbes' s definition with Aristotle's remark in his *Poetics*: what is risible is 'some mistake, or some turpitude, without grievous pain, and not very pernicious or destructive' (1149a31–5, as quoted by Hutcheson[9]). The difference between Hobbes and Aristotle on this topic lies not in the content of the description, but, according to Hutcheson, in the scope they give to it. Aristotle did not intend to give a general account of laughter; he 'has justly explained the nature of one species of laughter, viz. the ridiculing of persons', whereas Hobbes has reduced *all* species of laughter to this one.[10]

What matters most is the 'nothing else but' element in the definition from *The Elements of Law* quoted above. Hutcheson responds, first, that 'there are innumerable Instances of Laughter, where no person is ridiculed'[11] and, second, that in the case of ridicule, the belief that we are superior is not sufficient to trigger laughter.

If Mr. Hobbes's notion be just, then, first, there can be no Laughter on any occasion where we make no comparison of ourselves to others, or of our present state to a worse state, or where we do not observe some superiority of ourselves above some other thing: and again, it must follow, that every sudden appearance of superiority over another must excite Laughter, when we attend to it. If both these conclusions be false, the notion from whence they are drawn must be so too.[12]

So the argument in the *Reflections upon Laughter* is a double *modus tollens* against the Hobbesian claim that our feeling superior is both a necessary and a sufficient condition of laughter. Hutcheson needs to show not only that laughter cannot be reduced to 'ridicule' proper (that is, laughing at people for their defects), but that ridicule proper cannot be explained by the passion of sudden glory, but requires more on the side of the object: 'Even in ridicule itself there must be something other than bare opinion to raise it.'[13]

Is the sudden awareness of one's superiority a *necessary* condition of laughter? It is not, as several counter-examples show. Hutcheson mentions the laughter induced by literary parodies 'in those who may have the highest veneration for the writing alluded to, and also admire the wit of the person who makes the allusion'.[14] He also points out that we laugh at the 'ingenuity in dogs and monkeys, and not at their duller actions, in which they are much below us'.[15]

Is the sudden awareness of one's superiority a *sufficient* condition of laughter? Hutcheson argues that, in cases where the belief that we are superior plays a role in our mirth, this belief is always complemented by something that is laughable in the situation. One of his counter-examples is that we well know that what is funny about someone's behaviour, when we observe it, is not so funny when we just hear about it: 'We shall not be disposed to Laughter by bare narration.'[16] Hutcheson claims, it seems, that laughter demands direct acquaintance with the laughable. We might object to Hutcheson that academics who prefer not to attend departmental meetings are nevertheless keen to hear them reported upon. Hutcheson would respond that the reason for this must be that there is a funny quality in the report. For he applies to the case of ridicule (I take the word here in a general sense, that of the risible or laughable, not in the specific sense, that is, the ludicrous in people) his general scheme that any kind of perception should be analysed into two components, a quality on the side of the object, that plays a causal role and thus has to be somehow directly present to the observer, and an affective response on the side of the observer, which supposes also that the observer has the disposition to thus respond.

The case of ridicule is not different from that of beauty or of moral goodness. The source of laughter is not to be found in the belief that we are superior, but in some quality present to the laugher, and which the philosopher tries to identify. The laugher does not necessarily have a cognitive access to the quality, or to put it the other way round, laughter often provides the only access to that quality, exactly as we sometimes come to know about a danger only through our instinctive fear of it. To sum up, we laugh at *x* not because *x* gives us the opportunity of thinking of our own eminence, but because there is something funny about *x*. For Hutcheson as for Wiggins, the quality of being funny and our amusement are 'made for one another'.[17] Thus Hutcheson is a realist about the laughable, but of the indirect kind: when laughter is appropriate, there is something really laughable out there, but, although it plays a major causal role in the generation of the relevant belief, it is not necessarily an object of that belief. This kind of realism is compatible with a non-cognitivist bent. On the contrary, Hobbes seems to be a cognitivist about laughter, since he claims that it depends on a cognitive state, the belief that others are inferior to us. Laughter does not give any access to a laughable that would cause it. For the cause of laughter is psychological and lies in a passion, 'sudden glory', which has no real basis beyond the belief in our superiority. So Hobbes' s cognitivism is combined with an anti-realist claim about the laughable.[18]

To be sensitive to the risible requires a distinct internal sense, the 'sense of ridicule'. Hutcheson employs this expression in a passage of his *Short Introduction* (I, 14), in which, commenting on Aristotle's definition of the risible, he sums up the views set out in his *Reflections upon Laughter*:

> When by means of these senses, some objects must appear beautiful, graceful, honourable, or venerable, and others mean and shameful; should it happen that in any object there appeared a mixture of these opposite forms or qualities, there would appear also another sense, of the *ridiculous*. And whereas there's a general presumption of some dignity, prudence and wisdom in the human species; such conduct of theirs will raise laughter as shews 'some mean error or mistake, which yet is not attended with grievous pain or destruction to the person': for all such events would rather move pity.[19]

In the second part of his *Reflections*, Hutcheson, drawing on Joseph Addison,[20] identifies what he calls the 'ground' of laughter. It is less a quality in its own right than a contrast or discrepancy between moral or aesthetic qualities, and especially between ideas of dignity and ideas of meanness.[21] Thus Hutcheson subscribes to an incongruity theory of the comic, against the Hobbesian version of the superiority theory.[22] The qualities we sense through laughter are a 'mixture' of moral or aesthetic qualities, or, more precisely, consist in the tension between opposite values. Moreover, the 'sense of ridicule' is not only a power to sense, but also a power to act in so far as it allows us to practise moral criticism as well as to entertain the laughers:

> Laughter is a grateful commotion of the mind; but to be the object of laughter or mockery is universally disagreeable, and what men from their natural desire of esteem carefully avoid. Hence arises the importance of this sense or disposition, in refining the manners of mankind, and correcting their faults. Things too of a quite different nature from any human action may occasion laughter, by exhibiting at once some venerable appearance, along with

something mean and despicable. From this sense there arise agreeable and sometimes useful entertainments, grateful seasoning to conversation, and innocent amusements amidst the graver business of life.[23]

What matters to my argument is that laughter is primarily considered as a response to a value, whether the value is a quality that basically plays a causal role (Hutcheson) or is the object of an evaluative judgement (Shaftesbury). In both cases laughter itself is a passion in so far as it is a response to a value and not merely the physical effect of another passion. This view of laughter as being a passion and not the manifestation or product of a passion is very different from what we find in Hobbes and Descartes.

In *The Elements of Law* (I, ix, 13), Hobbes somewhat misleadingly spoke of 'the passion of laughter';[24] in *Leviathan* (I, 6) he does not consider laughter as a passion, but as the facial expression or effect of the passion which he calls sudden glory: 'Sudden glory is the passion which maketh those grimaces called laughter.'[25] This is consistent with his reductivist view. In Descartes' *Passions of the Soul*, there is also a reluctance to consider laughter as a passion rather than a bodily expression that 'accompanies' a passion.[26] What we call *laughter*, Descartes maintains, is only the facial expression.[27] Laughter, is an external sign (established by nature) through which we 'read' the joy of the laugher.[28] It would be incorrect to say that laughter, thus understood, has an object. It is a sign, which more or less confusedly signifies its cause.

Hutcheson interestingly resists calling laughter a passion. The reason is not that he would consider it, like Descartes or Hobbes, as the bodily expression of a passion, but only that laughter exists as an action as well as a passion. With a hesitation from which there is much to learn, he says that laughter may be called a 'sensation, action, passion, or affection'; he adds: 'I know not which of them a philosopher would call it.'[29] Far from being what Hobbes terms in *The Elements of Law* a 'distortion of the countenance',[30] laughter has the same psychological status as pleasure in the aesthetic experience and it is one of the affections.[31] But the disjunctive characterization 'sensation, action, passion, or affection' also suggests that laughter may function as an 'action'.

How can we make sense of this thesis? On the surface, there is an analogy between laughing and blushing. Laughing seems to be to Hobbesian 'sudden glory' what blushing is to shame (and perhaps to other various passions, such as embarrassment, anger, or pride). But this is wrong. Laughter does not consist only in the bodily sign or effect of another passion, although vocal and facial manifestations are obviously essential to it. We must pay attention to the fact that we may react to someone's mistake by getting angry, or feeling pity, or laughing. Here, laughter is one of several possible responses in a repertoire of passions. It is on the same footing as, say, contempt. In order to laugh, we do not have to go through the passion that 'has no name' in common language,[32] and which the philosopher describes in his technical language as 'sudden glory'. What leads Shaftesbury and Hutcheson to consider laughter as a passion is simply that they view it as an immediate response to a situation. When we react to some situation by laughing, the emotional response consists in laughing and nothing suggests that we should construe laughter as the expression or effect of yet another emotional response.

Ronald de Sousa has claimed that laughter is the expression of the passion of 'mirth', although he is aware that 'laughter [...] is still not a single species but a class of responses of which some formal objects are the funny, the comical, and the ridiculous'.[33] However, if we take seriously the diversity of formal objects, then, perforce, we should accept the diversity of the emotions de Sousa lumps together as 'mirth'; now, if we accept that diversity, and if we consider laughter as an expression of emotions, then we should consider that there is one very ambiguous expression of a variety of emotions. But this is not the case. Although there are indeed situations in which laughter is ambiguous—is it gentle or not?—usually we are sensitive to the variety of unequivocal laughters, which accords with the variety of formal objects. Instead of considering one generic laughter as an expression of 'mirth' understood as a conglomerate of different emotional responses, we should stress the variety of specific laughters. As we shall see, this is precisely what Shaftesbury has done in his *Pathologia*, and, more generally, what early modern British moralists were doing when paying attention to the distinction between wit and humour, ridicule, and amiable laughter.[34] The fact that we may refer one laughter to hate, another laughter to love, does not imply that both laughters *express* hate or love, but rather that they are species of these passions.

In a short piece in Latin, *Pathologia*, written in 1706, which remained unpublished till 2013, Shaftesbury intends to clarify Horace's philosophical evolution and for that he draws on Cicero's *Tusculan Disputations*, for he is convinced that to correctly read Horace we need to understand the Stoic conception of passions. The Stoics consider passions as implicit judgements that ascribe value to an event, a person, a situation, etc. These evaluative beliefs, in which passions consist, are all erroneous, because events, persons, situations, cannot have the kind of value passions ascribe to them. In all our passions, the good or the bad is not appropriately represented, simply because there is no real good but the agent's virtue, and there is no real bad but the agent's vice. Correct evaluative beliefs are responses to a true good or bad. They are not passions or perturbations, but constant dispositions or virtues.

Let us apply this account of passions to the case of laughter. The evaluative belief implicitly at work in laughter is, so to say, that there is something laughable, or ludicrous, or ridiculous here. What is interesting in the following passage is that all kinds of laughter are related to an imagined (*opinatum*), not to a true, good or bad:

> As to that mockery, if one wonders Horace had mounted a guard of virtue so severe that he would not allow him even that joy; we must respond that according to our Stoic theory of the passions, that mocking and laughing joy is a kind of malice. For we must distinguish between mockery [*jocositas*] and mirth [*hilaritas*]. Mirth, i.e. moderate and controllable laughter is a species of admiration; i.e. a kind of overwhelming pleasure in view of or upon the examination of an external thing fancied beautiful. For if it is seen as internal, either by acquisition or as inherent to us, it becomes immediately a boasting pleasure, i.e. a form of pride as mentioned above. As to mockery, i.e. immoderate, uncontrollable, loud laughter, it is pleasure about some ugliness in external things and other people, as if it was a good for us. For there is no joy or

pleasure that is not about a good or beauty, true or fancied so. And since this laughter is neither desire nor aversion nor pain, but joy or pleasure, it follows necessarily that its object (i.e. that ridicule and ill in other people) is considered as if it was a good or beauty in ourselves. And therefore this laughter arises from malevolence and is a species of malice or malignity. Since we consider every ridicule as if it was something ugly in itself and an odious illness, hence one can easily infer that nothing is more offending than being pointed at and stigmatised because of a ridicule.[35]

Hilaritas, which is here translated mirth, is a kind of laughter that deeply differs from ridicule (*jocositas*), and signifies that something highly pleasant is occurring, as when people laugh because they are especially happy with a situation or feel at ease. The distinction between *jocositas* and *hilaritas* looks similar to the distinction between ridicule and good humour that we find throughout the first volume of *Characteristicks of Men, Manners, Opinions, Times* (1711). But there are important differences. Good humour in *A Letter concerning Enthusiasm* and in *Sensus Communis* is a disposition rather than a response, nay, a good disposition, a virtue, whereas *hilaritas* remains a passion in the *Pathologia*.[36] According to *A Letter concerning Enthusiasm*, good humour is a disposition that allows us to control the action of ridicule and the excesses of wit. So, in this tentative classification, we would need a third category, beyond laughter as an action and laughter as a passion: laughter as a disposition. Thus we would have (1) the action of ridiculing, (2) the passion that responds to the risible, (3) the disposition to laugh.

In the *Pathologia*, where Shaftesbury endorses Stoic moral psychology, laughter, in all its occurrences, is a passion or rather a set of passions in a normative, pejorative sense. For there are several very different passions under the name of laughter: it may be a kind of pride, or of contempt, or of 'admiration' (this word is always pejorative in the *Pathologia*).[37] Therefore, we should speak of the passions of laughter, in the plural.

To sum up, Hobbes's definition of laughter corresponds to what Shaftesbury calls *jocositas* in his *Pathologia*, and to what both Shaftesbury and Hutcheson call 'ridicule'. In the *Pathologia* Shaftesbury rejects the use of ridicule, or rather explains that the Stoics reject it; in his published works he recommends the use of ridicule as a pacific weapon, compatible with toleration, against enthusiasm. In the Latin manuscript, ridicule is a passion and the disposition to laugh at people for their defects is also a vice. In *Characteristicks*, the picture is quite different: ridicule is a legitimate strategy. The main target of ridicule is religious fanaticism.

6.2 Laughter as an Action

For the British moralists, laughter, especially ridicule (in the subjective sense), is also an action in a social context.[38] As an action, it must be voluntary. To some extent, we can decide to laugh at *x*. Since laughter is usually considered as involuntary, is this identical with deciding to simulate laughter? When we speak of 'deciding to laugh', for instance as a manner of confronting adversity, what we have in mind is different from either simulating laughter or of laughing at will: we decide to have recourse to laughter; the decision opens up a way of sensing the laughable aspect in the situation, and this does not entail that laughter is under full and direct control. It is also well known that we have the ability to contain laughter, or on the contrary to indulge in it, which implies a voluntary dimension in the use of laughter, if not in laughter itself.

Shaftesbury's and Hutcheson's strategy of laughter may be considered as part of what Robert Solomon calls a politics of emotions. Solomon's view of emotions as actions in a social context aptly fit the case of laughter. I will not discuss his general (Sartrean) claim that 'emotions do not just happen to us... they are, with some contentious stretching of the term, activities that we "do", stratagems that work for us, both individually and collectively'.[39] Whether this is true or not of all emotions, it is certainly true of laughter and early modern philosophers were well aware of that.

How should we construe the relations between laughter as a passion and laughter as an action? Should we consider that one and the same emotion may be seen as more or less active or more or less passive? Or are there active emotions on the one hand, and passive emotions on the other hand, that differ in nature? There are also more general questions about what early modern philosophers call the use of passions: because of the voluntary dimension in the use of passions, we might be tempted to view it as a kind of action. Many philosophers consider that only another passion can counteract a passion. But how can we voluntarily use a passion, if having a passion is not voluntary, in so far as passions are affective responses?

A way out of this difficulty might be found if we envisage that having a passion may be more or less voluntary or involuntary. One possible way of giving sense to this claim is to pay attention both to our direct, albeit partial, control on our body and to the close connections between bodily movements and passions of the soul. We well know that, to some extent, we are able to control some of our facial expressions. No doubt, there are facial expressions that are almost impossible to control, such as blushing in some cases, perhaps because the emotions involved are almost impossible to control; however, there are other facial expressions that are easy to control, such as smiling or laughing, or screaming when angry. In any case, when we control our expressions, we thus control also to some extent our passions, because facial expressions are intimately connected with our emotions. Our experience of some degree of control over some of the facial expressions of many emotions, combined with the claim that those expressions are constitutive parts of the emotion and not only its effects or signs, suggests that the claim that emotions may be more or less active or passive is plausible.

To get back to the main point, about how we move from an account of laughter as a passion (a response in the passive sense) to an account of laughter as an action (a response in a different sense, when we decide to respond), although Solomon does not discuss laughter in his book, I would like to apply to laughter his idea of a

> shift from thinking about emotions and emotional responses as mere products and think of them instead as strategies for dealing with others and strategies for dealing with ourselves.[40]

Laughter under the guise of ridicule might be viewed as a strategy for dealing with others. Under the guise of humour, or as Shaftesbury says 'good humour', it is clearly a strategy for dealing with oneself. Shaftesbury gives centre stage to the politics of laughter in his *Characteristicks*. There is a similar move, from emotional response to strategy, in Hutcheson, but in a very limited form, with only a few remarks tending to suggest he may have held that kind of view. Other eighteenth-century philosophers stress that at least one species of laughter, ridicule, has not only a political or practical dimension, but also a motivational aspect, since it can deter us from acting in this or that way. Thus, laughter may aim at influencing the will, whether the laugher's will or that of the target.[41]

In the third section of Hutcheson's *Reflections*, we find several although admittedly weak echoes from Shaftesbury on the topic of ridicule. Ridicule should be applied in some cases to enthusiastic imagination. It is a corrective to the false sublime. As Hutcheson says, 'it is well known, that our passions of every kind lead us into wild enthusiastic apprehensions of their several objects'.[42] Ridicule helps us in deflating the imposture:

> When any object either good or evil is aggravated and increased by the violence of our passions, or an enthusiastic admiration, or fear, the application of ridicule is the readiest way to bring down our high imaginations to a conformity to the real moment or importance of the affair.[43]

We should pay attention to Hutcheson's use of the term 'application', which suggests that there is a decision here, that it is a voluntary action.

Ridicule may be used against several kinds of defects. Hutcheson has interesting conceptions about ridicule as a response to guilt. When guilt is not serious at all, when it is a matter of trifles, ridicule might be the appropriate response. Drawing on analogies with moral justifications of punishment, we might say that this is a reform theory of ridicule: what justifies the recourse to ridicule is the perspective of helping people to rectify their small defects:

> If smaller faults, such as are not inconsistent with a character in the main amiable, be set in a ridiculous light, the guilty are apt to be made sensible of their folly, more than by a bare grave admonition.[44]

Here Hutcheson is close to Shaftesbury's quite optimistic claim that laughter is a better substitute for punishment in the case of religious enthusiasts, and is lenient enough to be compatible with the requirements of toleration. Ridicule, not resentment, is the politics of emotions we should adopt against fanaticism.

However, Hutcheson does not go farther than those few remarks on the possible use of ridicule. He was not keen on using ridicule as a cure for enthusiasm, whereas Shaftesbury is a kind of enthusiast about the use of wit and humour against enthusiasts. One question to Hutcheson would be: why the reluctant stance towards a critical use of laughter? There are contextual answers to that question—perhaps Hutcheson's commitment to some version of Christianity—but I will confine myself to reasons that lie within Hutcheson's concepts and arguments. Let us get back first to Shaftesbury's view about laughter as a cure of enthusiasm.

Shaftesbury tackles the question of laughter in the first two pieces of the first volume of *Characteristicks of Men, Manners, Opinions, Times*, that is, *A Letter Concerning Enthusiasm* (first published in 1708), and its follow-up *Sensus Communis, or an Essay on Wit and Humour* (first published in 1709). The *Letter* is a discussion about how to understand the strange behaviour of enthusiasts and especially of the London 'French prophets'[45]—whom the Shakers will later emulate—who threaten the Church by Law established, and about how to respond to it. The correct reaction, according to Shaftesbury, is not to punish, but to laugh. Wit and raillery are the 'remedy' 'against extravagances and splenetick humour', and for this we need 'freedom of raillery'.[46] Moreover, laughing instead of punishing is compatible with toleration. Laughter is the adequate response to enthusiasm, because the fanatical 'crime' that deserves retribution lies in the effects of a melancholy temper, which fosters gloomy images of the divinity. Persecution would increase melancholy and inflame fanaticism.

Now we must raise an objection: How will we know that laughter is the appropriate response? Shall we become buffoons, and make fun of anything and everything? We need a regulation of laughter. We must learn to use laughter in a proper way, that is as a response only to what deserves to be laughed at:

> 'Tis in reality a serious Study, to learn to temper and regulate that Humour which Nature has given us, as a more lenitive Remedy against Vice, and a kind of Specifick against Superstition and melancholy Delusion. There is a great difference between seeking how to raise a Laugh from every thing; and seeking, in every thing, what justly may be laugh'd at. For nothing is ridiculous except what is deform'd: Nor is any thing proof against Raillery, except what is handsom and just. And therefore 'tis the hardest thing in the World, to deny fair Honesty the use of this Weapon, which can never bear an Edge against her-self, and bears against every thing contrary.[47]

Shaftesbury's answer is not fully satisfactory. If ridicule is an action, as such under our control, then we may decide to 'raise a laugh from anything', unless something hinders us from applying it to some cases. Thus, the problem has been identified, but not the solution.

Shaftesbury thinks that the solution lies in the free market of social criticism. He has good reasons to be unhappy with external constraints on criticism, mainly because there is no reason why any authority should be a priori protected against criticism. But he concludes that the practice of criticism suffices to regulate itself. This is a fallacy. The fact that a critique has reasons to resist any external limitation of the right to criticize does not entail that a critique is able by itself to correct itself when it is unfair. These are two different issues. Moreover, unfair criticism is obviously the price we have to pay if we favour an unlimited freedom to criticize.

Leibniz, in his 'Remarks in the Letter concerning Enthusiasm', raises a different objection. He was shocked by passages like this one:

> The Vulgar, indeed, may swallow any sordid Jest, any mere Drollery or Buffoonery; but it must be a finer and truer Wit which takes with the Men of Sense and Breeding. How comes it to pass then, that we appear such Cowards in reasoning, and are so afraid to stand the Test of Ridicule?[48]

What I call the free market claim about laughter (that laughter is self-regulating), Leibniz says, 'would be true if men would prefer reasoning to laughing'. Moreover, Leibniz points out that Shaftesbury's defence of the freedom to criticize by the aristocratic view of a liberty of the club, distinct from the vulgar, seems very dangerous. For 'many polite people are vulgar in so far as reasoning is concerned'.[49] In a sense, Shaftesbury himself raises that objection, when he notices in *Sensus Communis*: 'Everyone thinks himself well-bred.'[50] However, raising the objection and responding to it are two very different things.

In the passage quoted above, Shaftesbury employs the expression 'test of ridicule', which might be misleading. There must be some difference between the 'test of ridicule' and ridicule as a 'test of truth', a view that has been ascribed to Shaftesbury, from Berkeley's *Alciphron* to John Brown's *Essays on the Characteristicks* (1751). In Berkeley's *Alciphron*, III, 15, Shaftesbury's spokesman claims that 'ridicule is the sure test of truth'.[51] This rests on a misunderstanding of Shaftesbury's project, as several commentators have shown.[52] Ridicule is not an epistemic tool in the sense that it could act as a substitute for reason or intuition in the discovery of truth, although it does have an epistemic scope, in so far as the detection of the ludicrous is concerned.

However, there is at least one passage in *Sensus Communis* in which ridicule is presented as a 'manner of proof' in the context of the recognition of truth:

> That which can be shewn only in a certain Light, is questionable. Truth, 'tis suppos'd, may bear all Lights: and one of those principal Lights or natural Mediums, by which Things are to be view'd, in order to a thorow Recognition, is Ridicule it-self, or that Manner of Proof by which we discern whatever is liable to just Raillery in any Subject.[53]

In fact, in the immediate context of this passage the question is whether we should tolerate Baconian idols or false appearances 'in some dark corner of our own minds', or whether we should question them through self-criticism. What is tested is not truth, but our own convictions and prejudices.

Thus the free market claim applies also to the dark corner of our minds. We should not exempt ourselves from critique: We ought to 'make as free with our own opinions as with those of other people'.[54] Laughter as an action is intimately connected with the Stoic practice of self-discourse, a technique of mental control of our 'imaginations'. Laughing at oneself is a way of practising what Shaftesbury terms 'soliloquy' in his eponymous essay.

In a sense, Shaftesbury tries to give to laughter the status of a self-centred emotion such as shame. We might object to Shaftesbury that laughter is primarily other-directed, and that being self-centred is a potential that may be developed or not, whereas shame is primarily self-centred, although we may also be ashamed of other people especially when they are closely related to us. 'Wit', 'raillery', 'ridicule', 'good humour', are words that Shaftesbury uses to designate both dimensions of laughter, although 'humour' tends to be self-centred in his account.

In his essay on self-discourse as a means of moral improvement, *Soliloquy or Advice to an Author*, Shaftesbury says that those who laugh at the revival of Stoic asceticism are themselves ridiculous, 'which is a Specimen of that very Art or Science we are about to illustrate'.[55] It is explicit here that laughter and self-discourse are interwoven one with the other.

6.3 Laughter as a Disposition

One way to answer the objection that laughter, as an action, might degenerate into arbitrary scorn is to appeal to the virtue of the good laugher. Hutcheson has an interesting comment on the happy disposition to laugh, which seems to be close to Shaftesbury's good humour:

> Every one is conscious that a state of Laughter is an easy and agreeable state, that the recurring or suggestion of ludicrous images tends to dispel fretfulness, anxiety, or sorrow, and to reduce the mind to an easy happy state; as on the other hand, an easy and happy state is that in which we are most lively and acute in perceiving the ludicrous in objects.[56]

There is a kind of feedback of the feeling of the ludicrous on the disposition to feel it. However, although there are passages like this one in Hutcheson, good humour is not for him the ultimate answer to the problem of how to discipline laughter. On the contrary, he maintains that we need restrictive rules to prevent laughter from running astray. Although Hutcheson admits that a good disposition to laughter may be cultivated, which would help us in laughing properly, he prefers the security of rules as far as ridicule in the strict sense is concerned, for it may easily degenerate into contempt:

> The rules to avoid abuse of this kind of ridicule are, first, 'either never to attempt ridicule upon what is every way great, whether it be any great being, character, or sentiments'; or, if our wit must sometime run into allusions, on low occasions, to the expressions of great sentiments, 'let it not be in weak company, who have not a just discernment of true grandeur'. And, secondly, concerning objects of a mixed nature, partly great, and partly mean, 'let us never turn the meanness into ridicule, without acknowledging what is truly great, and paying a just veneration to it'. In this sort of jesting we ought to be cautious of our company.[57]

Now we understand why Hutcheson is so reluctant in his comments on the use of ridicule against enthusiasm. He does not believe that laughter can regulate itself. We need restrictive rules to do that. Here Hutcheson is doing something that Shaftesbury, in *Sensus Communis*, calls 'laying an embargo':

> Wit is its own Remedy. Liberty and Commerce bring it to its true Standard. The only danger is, the laying an Embargo. The same thing happens here, as in the Case of Trade. Impositions and Restrictions reduce it to a low Ebb: Nothing is so advantageous to it as a Free-Port.[58]

Hutcheson thinks on the contrary that restrictions are necessary. If we know that *x* is truly grand, then we ought not to mock *x*. For what is grand deserves not to be mocked but to be respected. In mixed cases, we should both laugh and pay respects at the same time—a psychological tour de force! Far from accepting such a prohibition or restriction, Shaftesbury writes: 'Gravity is of the very essence of imposture. It does not only make us mistake other things, but is apt perpetually almost to mistake it-self'.[59] Gravity is not only the ideal target for wit and humour; it is also that which is utterly devoid of wit and humour. It is clear here that Shaftesburian humour is a power of self-distancing.

Shaftesbury would have rejected Hutcheson's conception about restrictive rules; for he explicitly identifies the rules of laughter with an immanent self-regulation. These rules consist in nothing else but the habitual use of laughter:

> Now what Rule or Measure is there in the World, except in the considering of the real Temper of Things, to find which are truly serious, and which ridiculous? And how can this be done, unless by applying the Ridicule, to see whether it will bear? But if we fear to apply this Rule in any thing, what Security can we have against the Imposture of Formality in all things? We have allow'd our-selves to be Formalists in one Point; and the same Formality may rule us as it pleases in all other. 'Tis not in every Disposition that we are capacitated to judg of things. We must beforehand judg of our own Temper, and accordingly of other things which fall under our Judgment. But we must never more pretend to judg of things, or of our own Temper in judging them, when we have given up our preliminary Right of Judgment, and under a presumption of Gravity, have allow'd ourselves to be most ridiculous, and to admire profoundly the most ridiculous things in nature, at least for ought we know.[60]

Is deciding to apply the test of ridicule to anything deciding to laugh at anything? That would not be fair and appropriate. But what does deciding to apply the test of ridicule consist in if not in deciding to laugh? In deciding not to refrain from laughing? More than that. Shaftesbury apparently thinks that we should decide to cultivate a critical disposition, so that we would not miss the chance of laughing at what deserves to be laughed at and also we would diminish the risk of laughing at what does not deserve to be laughed at. Good humour is the disposition that is required for the practice of laughter, to regulate the politics of ridicule. This is a self-centred critical disposition: we learn to laugh at ourselves, so that when we persist in applying the test of ridicule to what is not ridiculous at all, we detect that we are ridiculous in doing this.

In short, Shaftesbury's ethics of laughter is a virtue ethics, which puts stress on the quality of the laugher, whereas Hutcheson, at least in his *Reflections*, emphasizes the dependence of the value of laughter on the quality of the target, thus justifying restrictive rules and defining a list of objectively laughable and non-laughable things, which Shaftesbury would not accept.[61] On the other hand, we might object to Shaftesbury's free market view that it is not sufficient to account for the cultivating of the correct hilarious disposition, at least if we stick to the traditional, Aristotelian, understanding of practical dispositions, according to which their value depends on the value of the corresponding actions. For we need some normative background to ensure that the agents are initially trained in the correct practice. Are the free market view and the virtue view consistent without further constraints? It is not clear why the market of laughter, without a visible hand, would produce wise mockers, nor why wise mockers would try their wit on everything that has an air of gravity. Market self-regulation is taken for granted by Shaftesbury, whose motto is, so to speak, let us see... We cannot know in advance whether our critique is excessive and will fall back on us, or not. Even though it is a plausible claim that when our laughter is ill grounded, we may *deserve* to be laughed at, and that the retribution of laughter, in those cases, ought to be targeted at the laugher, it is quite optimistic to expect this regulation to happen smoothly in a free market of laughter.

Therefore Hutcheson's and Shaftesbury's liberal ethics of laughter, although similar on a number of aspects, go in opposite directions: Hutcheson favours a regulation of laughter by action restricting rules, while Shaftesbury thinks that laughter is self-regulating and thus construes good humour as a virtue obtained through unrestricted commerce.

6.4 Conclusion

Contrary to some, I have tried to make sense of Hutcheson's disjunctive characterization of laughter as a 'sensation, action, passion, or affection'.[62] Analogous to a sensory response to the causal impact of certain qualities in the object, laughter is a passion. It may also be, under the guise of ridicule, a voluntary action. Should we then speak of a voluntary use of passions, or rather of an ambivalence of emotions between action and passion? When I feel depressed by a situation that looks scandalous to me, I can decide, to some extent, to be angry rather than giving up and becoming more depressed—at least disciples of Sartre believe we can do that. Should we say that I use the passion of anger against another passion, or rather that anger is an action rather than a passion in that case? Is the voluntary aspect in the *use* of passions or is it already present in what we call 'passions', which may in some contexts be actions? Hutcheson interestingly views the same affection, laughter, as a passion and as an action.

In his own Stoic way, Shaftesbury considers that passions are to some extent voluntary, in so far as they involve an assent to what they represent—for, following Epictetus, he believes assent to be within the agent's control. Indeed, Shaftesbury had to deeply revise the Stoic account of laughter we find in his *Pathologia*, in order to envisage a politics of laughter against what in his time was called enthusiasm; but there again in *Characteristicks* the active dimension of laughter surfaced, through the strategy of ridicule.

So both moralists agree not to confine laughter—and other 'passions' as well, the term being misleading—to a passive dimension. Another lesson is about the question whether laughter ought to be regulated, and how. Shaftesbury and Hutcheson agree that uncontrolled laughter might degenerate into buffoonery or coarse mockery. However, the former entrusts laughter with the responsibility of controlling laughter, whereas the latter does not. There is a significant difference between Hutcheson's somewhat awkward conception of 'rules to avoid abuse' of ridicule, intended to shelter grave subjects from hilarious attacks, and the interesting but unconvincing idea in Shaftesbury of a normative control immanent to the practice of critical laughter. What is unconvincing is not the view that laughter is liable to significant adjustments without external constraints, by the sole play of laughing interactions, but the claim that the process of laughter revision in the free market will end up with the kind of polished laughter people of taste would expect.

In any case, one essential resource in the revision of laughter is its reflexivity. Shaftesbury gives much importance to laughing at one's laughter, and at one's own limits or failures. This was precisely ruled out by the Augustinian and Hobbesian accounts, which left no room for anything else than self-deception or lucid depression in relation to one's own defects. Reflexivity takes centre stage in Shaftesbury under the name of 'good humour'. Opening up the possibility of a kind of silent laughter about oneself is a fruitful consequence of the rejection of Hobbesian and Augustinian views about dominant self-love.[63]

Notes

1. Francis Hutcheson, *Reflections upon Laughter, and Remarks upon The Fable of the Bees* (Glasgow: R. Urie, 1750), p. 12.
2. Robert C. Solomon, *Not Passion's Slave: Emotions and Choice* (Oxford: Oxford University Press, 2003), p. 144.
3. Thomas Hobbes, *The Elements of Law Natural and Politic*, ed. F. Tönnies (London: Frank Cass & Co, 1969), p. 42.
4. Jacques Abbadie, *The Art of Knowing Oneself, or, An Enquiry into the Sources of Morality Written Originally in French* (Oxford: L. Lichfield, 1695), p. 249.
5. Ibid.
6. Abbadie, *The Art of Knowing Oneself*, p. 248.
7. What is wrong in Hobbes's egoistic account of laughter is not its normative, but its theoretical aspect. In *Leviathan*, I, 6, Hobbes says that 'much laughter at the defects of others is a sign of pusillanimity' (Thomas Hobbes, *Leviathan*, ed. Richard Tuck (Cambridge: Cambridge University Press, 1996), p. 43). Hutcheson and Shaftesbury have nothing against the normative claim that such an expression of self-love is bad. What they reject is the theoretical claim that laughter amounts to an expression or effect of self-love. So I do not understand why R.E. Ewin thinks that the fact that Hobbes views laughter 'as something not to be encouraged' should constitute a qualification of the view that Hobbes is a psychological egoist (Robert E. Ewin, 'Hobbes on Laughter', *The Philosophical Quarterly*, 51 (2001): 29–40 (p. 31)). The French

Protestant refugee is also a psychological egoist and this does not prevent him from writing: 'Men think their laughing is always innocent, and indeed it is always criminal and blamable' (Abbadie, *The Art of Knowing Oneself*, p. 267).

8. In passing, we should notice that we find a similar defect in Bergson's approach to laughter: he too, at least in his eponymous book, is one of the authors 'who have never distinguished between the words Laughter and Ridicule' (Hutcheson, *Reflections upon Laughter*, p. 13). For a survey of the philosophy of humour and ridicule from Hobbes to Bergson and Freud, see Michael Billig, *Laughter and Ridicule: Towards a Social Critique of Humour* (London: Sage, 2005).
9. Hutcheson, *Reflections upon Laughter*, p. 5.
10. Ibid.
11. Hutcheson, *Reflections upon Laughter*, p. 13.
12. Hutcheson, *Reflections upon Laughter*, p. 7.
13. Hutcheson, *Reflections upon Laughter*, p. 13.
14. Hutcheson, *Reflections upon Laughter*, p. 8.
15. Hutcheson, *Reflections upon Laughter*, p. 11.
16. Hutcheson, *Reflections upon Laughter*, p. 14.
17. David Wiggins, *Needs, Values, Truth: Essays in the Philosophy of Value* (Oxford: Oxford University Press, 1998), pp. 107–8.
18. Thomas Reid gives an account of laughter and specifically of 'ridicule' that combines realism and cognitivism about the laughable. See Giovanni Grandi's 'Reid on Ridicule and Common Sense', *The Journal of Scottish Philosophy*, 6 (2008): 71–90. Grandi also discusses Hutcheson's and Shaftesbury's views on ridicule and what later Scottish philosophical rhetoric says about the topic. Reid tends to identify the quality that is responsible for the ridicule as the absurd. It triggers laughter but is also the object of an accompanying judgement.
19. Hutcheson, *A Short Introduction to Moral Philosophy, in Three Books. Containing the Elements of Ethicks and the Law of Nature*, Second Edition (Glasgow: R. & A. Foulis, 1753), p. 26.
20. Joseph Addison & Richard Steele, *The Spectator*, vol. II, ed. Donald F. Bond (Oxford: Clarendon Press, 1965), No. 249, December 15, 1711, pp. 465–9.
21. Hutcheson, *Reflections upon Laughter*, p. 21.
22. Elizabeth Telfer, 'Hutcheson's Reflections on Laughter', *The Journal of Aesthetics and Art Criticism*, 53 (1995: 359–69.
23. Hutcheson, *A Short Introduction*, pp. 26–7.
24. However, the use of the expression 'the passion of laughter' (Hobbes, *The Elements of Law*, p. 42) does not commit Hobbes to the view that laughter is a passion. It means the passion signified by laughter as a facial expression.
25. Hobbes, *Leviathan*, p. 43.
26. René Descartes, *The Passions of the Soul*, in Descartes, *Philosophical Writings*, ed. John Cottingham, Robert Stoothof, Dugald Murdoch (Cambridge: Cambridge University Press: 1985), vol. 1., art. 62, p. 351.
27. Descartes, *The Passions of the Soul*, art. 124, p. 371.
28. René Descartes, *Treatise on Light*, chapter 1, in Descartes, *The World and Other Writings*, ed. Stephen Gaukroger (Cambridge: Cambridge University Press, 1998), p. 4; see also, on laughter as an 'external sign', *The Passions of the Soul*, art. 112, p. 367.
29. Hutcheson, *Reflections upon Laughter*, p. 16.

30. Hobbes, *The Elements of Law*, p. 41.
31. Hutcheson, *Reflections upon Laughter*, p. 27.
32. Hobbes, *The Elements of Law*, p. 41.
33. Ronald de Sousa, *The Rationality of Emotion* (Cambridge Mass.: MIT Press, 1987), p. 277.
34. On this topic in a literary context, see Stuart M. Tave, *The Amiable Humorist: A Study in the Comic Theory and Criticism of the Eighteenth and Early Nineteenth Centuries* (Chicago: University of Chicago Press, 1960).
35. Shaftesbury, 'Pathologia', edited and translated by Laurent Jaffro, Christian Maurer & Alain Petit, 'Part II: Pathologia, A Theory of the Passions', *History of European Ideas* 39 (2013): 221–40 (p. 240).
36. Christian Maurer & Laurent Jaffro, 'Part. I: Reading Shaftesbury's Pathologia: An Illustration and Defence of the Stoic Account of the Emotions', *History of European Ideas* 39 (2013): 207–20 (pp. 217–18).
37. Maurer & Jaffro, 'Part. I: Reading Shaftesbury's Pathologia', pp. 217–19.
38. Billig, *Laughter and Ridicule*, p. 74.
39. Solomon, *Not Passion's Slave*, p. 147.
40. Solomon, *Not Passion's Slave*, p. 148.
41. See for instance George Campbell's understanding of the connections between ridicule and the will; the purpose of ridicule is to influence conduct (Grandi, 'Reid on Ridicule and Common Sense', p. 80).
42. Hutcheson, *Reflections upon Laughter*, p. 31.
43. Hutcheson, *Reflections upon Laughter*, p. 29.
44. Hutcheson, *Reflections upon Laughter*, p. 31.
45. On the historical context of 'enthusiasm', see Michael Heyd, *'Be Sober and Reasonable'. The Critique of Enthusiasm in the Seventeenth and Early Eighteenth Centuries* (Leiden: Brill, 1995).
46. Shaftesbury, *Characteristicks of Men, Manners, Opinions, Times*, ed. Douglas Den Uyl (Indianapolis: Liberty Fund, 2001), vol. I, p. 13.
47. Shaftesbury, *Characteristicks*, vol. I, p. 80.
48. Shaftesbury, *Characteristicks*, vol. I, p. 8.
49. 'Remarques sur un petit livre traduit de l'anglois, intitulé *Lettre sur l'enthousiasme*', in *Recueil de diverses pièces sur la philosophie, la religion naturelle, l'histoire, les mathématiques, etc., par Mrs Leibniz, Clarke, Newton, et autres autheurs célèbres*, ed. P. Desmaizeaux (Amsterdam: H. du Sauzet, 1720), vol. II, pp. 245–68 (p. 247), my translation. The argument deserves to be quoted in full: 'Il y a encore moins de sujet de vouloir, qu'il soit permis de tourner tout en ridicule; le ridicule, dit-on, ne peut tenir contre la Raison. Cela seroit vrai si les hommes aimoient plus à raisonner qu'à rire; mais le faux ridicule, ajoute-t-on, n'éblouira que le Vulgaire. Je réponds que le Vulgaire a plus d'étendue qu'on ne pense; il y a quantité de gens polis qui sont peuple par rapport au raisonnement. Souvent même les plus raisonnables se laissent aller au plaisir de rire plus qu'il ne faut.'
50. Shaftesbury, *Characteristicks*, vol. I, p. 42.
51. George Berkeley, *Berkeley's 'Alciphron': Text and Essays in Interpretation*, ed. Laurent Jaffro, Geneviève Brykman, Claire Schwartz (Hildesheim: Georg Olms Verlag, 2010), p. 111.
52. As Alfred Owen Aldridge correctly puts it: 'Ridicule decides whether a doctrine deserves a sober hearing rather than whether the doctrine is true' ('Shaftesbury and the Test of Truth', *Publications of the Modern Language Association* 60 (1945): 129–56 (pp. 131–2)). Beside

the main protagonists, Aldridge discusses many other figures who took part in the controversy on ridicule as a test of truth: Anthony Collins, Mark Akenside, Lord Kames, Allan Ramsay, William Warburton, et al.

53. Shaftesbury, *Characteristicks*, vol. I, p. 40.
54. Ibid.
55. Shaftesbury, *Characteristicks*, vol. I, p. 99.
56. Hutcheson, *Reflections upon Laughter*, pp. 26–7.
57. Hutcheson, *Reflections upon Laughter*, p. 35.
58. Shaftesbury, *Characteristicks*, vol. I, p. 42.
59. Shaftesbury, *Characteristicks*, vol. I, p. 8. Leibniz replies to Shaftesbury: 'We have reason to say that gravity suits imposture; however, I would not say that it is essential to it; for jest (*la badinerie*) suits it as well. All that amuses and diverts from the point under discussion is susceptible of deceiving' (Leibniz, 'Remarques sur un petit livre traduit de l'anglois', p. 248, my translation).
60. Shaftesbury, *Characteristicks*, vol. I, pp. 8–9.
61. However, in *A System of Moral Philosophy* (I, I, chap. 7, §10), Hutcheson also speaks the Shaftesburian language of the good disposition to laugh: 'Whatever value we put on mirth and gayety it must be cast into the side of virtue: since that mind is always best disposed for the reception of all chearfulness and pleasantry where all is kind and easy; free from anger, ill-will, envy, or remorse. These pleasures are always social, and fly solitude' (Francis Hutcheson, *A System of Moral Philosophy, in Three Books* (Glasgow: R. & A. Foulis, 1755), pp. 135–6).
62. Elizabeth Telfer does not see anything intelligible here: 'The first problem is to work out what the theory is a theory of. He says that laughter is a "sensation, action, passion, or affection, I know not which of them a philosopher would call it". This list runs together laughter the observable phenomenon and what produces it; laughter itself is not a sensation, passion, or affection. But neither is it usually an action, something deliberately performed for a reason' (Telfer, 'Hutcheson's Reflections on Laughter, p. 359).
63. I thank David Leech and Christian Maurer for their help on this paper.

Bibliography

Abbadie, Jacques. *The Art of Knowing Oneself, Or, An Enquiry into the Sources of Morality Written Originally in French* (Oxford: L. Lichfield, 1695).

Addison, Joseph & Richard Steele. *The Spectator*, vol. II, ed. Donald F. Bond (Oxford: Clarendon Press, 1965), No. 249, December 15, 1711: 465–9.

Aldridge, Alfred Owen. 'Shaftesbury and the Test of Truth', *Publications of the Modern Language Association* 60 (1945): 129–56.

Berkeley, George. *Berkeley's 'Alciphron': Text and Essays in Interpretation*, ed. Laurent Jaffro, Geneviève Brykman, Claire Schwartz (Hildesheim: Georg Olms Verlag, 2010).

Billig, Michael. *Laughter and Ridicule: Towards a Social Critique of Humour* (London: Sage, 2005).

Ewin, Robert. E. 'Hobbes on Laughter', *The Philosophical Quarterly* 51 (2001): 29–40.

Grandi, Giovanni B. 'Reid on Ridicule and Common Sense', *The Journal of Scottish Philosophy* 6 (2008): 71–90.

Descartes, René. *Philosophical Writings*, ed. John Cottingham, Robert Stoothof, Dugald Murdoch (Cambridge: Cambridge University Press: 1985), vol. 1.

Descartes, René. *The World and Other Writings*, ed. Stephen Gaukroger (Cambridge: Cambridge University Press, 1998).

De Sousa, Ronald. *The Rationality of Emotion* (Cambridge Mass.: MIT Press, 1987).

Heyd, Michael. *'Be Sober and Reasonable': The Critique of Enthusiasm in the Seventeenth and Early Eighteenth Centuries* (Leiden: Brill, 1995).

Hobbes, Thomas. *The Elements of Law Natural and Politic*, ed. F. Tönnies (London: Frank Cass & Co, 1969).

Hobbes, Thomas. *Leviathan*, ed. Richard Tuck (Cambridge: Cambridge University Press, 1996).

Hutcheson, Francis. *Reflections upon Laughter, and Remarks upon the Fable of the Bees* (Glasgow: R. Urie, 1750).

Hutcheson, Francis. *A Short Introduction to Moral Philosophy, in Three Books. Containing the Elements of Ethicks and the Law of Nature*, Second Edition (Glasgow: R. & A. Foulis, 1753).

Hutcheson, Francis. *A System of Moral Philosophy, in Three Books* (Glasgow: R. & A. Foulis, 1755).

Jaffro, Laurent, Christian Maurer & Alain Petit, 'Part II: Pathologia, a Theory of the Passions', *History of European Ideas* 39 (2013): 221–40.

Jaffro, Laurent & Christian Maurer, 'Part. I: Reading Shaftesbury's Pathologia: An Illustration and Defence of the Stoic Account of the Emotions', *History of European Ideas* 39 (2013): 207–20.

Leibniz, Gottfried W., 'Remarques sur un petit livre traduit de l'anglois, intitulé *Lettre sur l'enthousiasme*', in *Recueil de diverses pièces sur la philosophie, la religion naturelle, l'histoire, les mathématiques, etc., par Mrs Leibniz, Clarke, Newton, et autres autheurs célèbres*, ed. P. Desmaizeaux (Amsterdam: H. du Sauzet, 1720), vol. II, pp. 245–68.

Shaftesbury, Third Earl of, *Characteristicks of Men, Manners, Opinions, Times*, ed. Douglas Den Uyl (Indianapolis: Liberty Fund, 2001).

Solomon, Robert C. *Not Passion's Slave: Emotions and Choice* (Oxford: Oxford University Press, 2003).

Tave, Stuart M. *The Amiable Humorist: A Study in the Comic Theory and Criticism of the Eighteenth and Early Nineteenth Centuries* (Chicago: University of Chicago Press, 1960).

Telfer, Elizabeth. 'Hutcheson's Reflections on Laughter', *The Journal of Aesthetics and Art Criticism* 53 (1995): 359–69.

Wiggins, David. *Needs, Values, Truth: Essays in the Philosophy of Value* (Oxford: Oxford University Press, 1998).

7

Alcali and Acid, Oil and Vinegar

Hume on Contrary Passions

Elizabeth S. Radcliffe

In his discussion of the passions in Book 2 of *A Treatise of Human Nature*, Hume writes,

> If the objects of the contrary passions ... be intimately connected, the passions are like an *alcali* and an *acid*, which, being mingled, destroy each other. If the relation be more imperfect, and consists in the contradictory views of the same object, the passions are like oil and vinegar, which, however mingled, never perfectly unite and incorporate.[1]

Hume discusses several psychological principles that explain how the affections identified as emotions and passions develop, motivate our actions, and affect each other. Among the principles he invokes are ones that explain the relation between 'contrary' passions, passions that are opposed in various ways, most importantly in their motivational direction. Hume's portrait of our passionate psychology reveals many sources of conflict endemic to human nature. Annette Baier remarks that Hume depicts the conflicting tendencies between self-concerned and other-concerned passions as alternating, 'wheeling us about from love of undeserved praise to contempt for our flatterers, from disinterested benevolent love to a "great partiality in our own favor" '.[2]

The solution to conflict for many of the philosophers and theologians writing prior to Hume's time was to invoke reason as referee of the passions and the guide to action. For instance, the French philosopher Jean-François Senault thought that the passions are useful, but only when moderated. He thought it dangerous for one passion to moderate another by its opposition (e.g. opposing hope to fear), 'fortifying one enemy to destroy another'. Moderation instead requires reason, which is 'king over Passions ... their government is one of her chief Employments'.[3] Samuel Clarke, writing in the eighteenth century, thought it a person's duty to govern the passions with reason, because when left alone, the passions would hurry a person on to 'exorbitant and unreasonable' things. Clarke maintained that the passions are useful when properly directed and make us diligent in pursuit of 'those Actions of Life which Reason *directs* and the Passions *execute*'.[4] Hume rejects the rationalist answer to the governance of the passions, arguing that reason is not the sort of faculty that can control passions or recommend action.

He proposes instead the very view eschewed by Clarke, namely, that the passions govern themselves. In this essay, I present a close study of Hume's treatment of the psychology of emotional difference and opposition and of the means at our disposal, on his theory, for moderating our passions and dealing with upheaval and emotional conflict.

Although it is not quite clear in Hume's discussion what counts as contrary passions (he seems to countenance contrary passions even when their objects differ), it seems right to say that contrary passions are opposed in their production (by pleasure or by pain), in the favourable or unfavourable attitudes they produce towards the same object, or in their motivational effects (urging us in opposite directions). This essay will commence with an overview of Hume's anatomy of the passions in Section 7.1, followed in Section 7.2 by a treatment of two opposed psychological functions that Hume imputes to human beings and that produce many contrary passions: sympathy and comparison. Sympathy is the mechanism by which we share others' feelings, and comparison is the function by which we find ourselves feeling passions opposed to others' feelings. Sympathy can lead me to feel pleased at your good fortune, while comparison can lead me to feel resentment or envy. Then in Section 7.3, I consider another way in which passions become opposed and create upheaval: by an increase in the feeling of their 'violence', which is produced in various ways on Hume's theory. In Section 7.4, I consider the effects of conflicting passions on our psychological state, and in Section 7.5, I investigate the ways in which the passions might regulate each other, on Hume's theory, given the various psychological principles he identifies. I argue that, even though reason cannot control the passions, and despite all the sources of conflict endemic to our emotional psychology, there are resources in Hume for establishing some degree of order, harmony, and psychological health.

7.1 Hume's Anatomy of the Passions

In the opening paragraph of Book 2, Hume divides impressions, or experiences, into those of sensation (original impressions) and those of reflection, or 'reflexion' (secondary impressions).[5] Impressions of sensation arise from external objects' affecting the organs, from the constitution of the body, and from the 'animal spirits.'[6] These include ordinary sensations, like feelings of warmth and coldness, color, tastes, feelings of pleasure and pain, and so on. Impressions of reflection arise from those original sensations or from the ideas of those sensations and include the passions and 'other emotions resembling them'.[7] While Hume does not often write about the 'emotions', the term seems to designate impressions of reflection that are not felt with the violence of a passion. His most frequent concern is with the passions, many of which are motives to action. These passions originate by a reflexive operation, whereby a perception recurs to the mind and causes a new impression. In Book 1 of the *Treatise*, Hume says that we perceive 'heat or cold, thirst or hunger, pleasure or pain of some kind', and the mind makes a copy of the impression, which is an idea. That idea returns to mind and produces new impressions of 'desire and aversion, hope and fear' (and other passions). These secondary impressions can also be copied and give rise to other impressions and ideas.[8]

At the beginning of Book 2, Hume describes passions as arising *either* from ideas of sensations *or* immediately from the sensations. He says, for instance, 'A fit of gout produces a long train of passions, as grief, hope, fear; but is not deriv'd immediately from any affection or idea.'[9] So, a physical malaise, which is not dependent on an impression or idea, can give rise directly to passions without the intervention of ideas. On Hume's theory, it is our perceiving objects as sources of pleasure or pain that originates these derived passions, so any perception that returns and produces a passion does so in virtue of its being pleasurable or painful. I call these 'derived' passions, because the set of passions includes not only those derived from sensations or their ideas, but also natural instincts, which are not acquired. They are productive of pleasure and pain, rather than being produced by those sensations. Among the instincts are benevolence, love of life, kindness to children, the inclination to natural good and away from evil, desire of punishment to enemies and happiness to friends, and bodily appetites.[10]

Hume divides impressions of reflection into the calm and the violent, perhaps borrowing an idea originating in the Stoics, who regarded passions as perturbations that cause emotional upheaval. The characterization of the passions as tumultuous and as detrimental to practical reasoning was promulgated by many of the seventeenth- and eighteenth-century philosophers and theologians.[11] Hume intends to combat this view by showing that passions are sometimes calm. His distinction between calm and violent passions is not an exact one, since it is a phenomenological one, and a passion can change from one into the other.[12] Calm passions are those felt with little inner turmoil, are known more by their effects than by their feeling, and are often mistaken for reason. Among the calm passions are typically the sentiments of morality and beauty, benevolence, resentment, love of life, kindness to children, and the appetite for natural good and aversion to evil. The violent passions are experienced with greater forcefulness than the calm passions and cause more disorder in a person's temper; they generally include love and hatred, grief and joy, pride and humility.[13] Hume writes that 'the raptures of poetry and beauty frequently rise to the greatest height', while other passions 'may decay into so soft an emotion, as to become, in a manner imperceptible', illustrating the fluidity of the passions.[14] Hume's calm–violent distinction turns out to be crucial to his theory of motivation, as I later explain.

Hume also divides the passions into direct and indirect. Direct passions arise immediately from pleasure or pain (natural good or evil), and the indirect arise from pleasure and pain in conjunction with other qualities (including reference to the self or to others). For instance, pride, an indirect passion, has as its cause a person's thought of a subject that has a pleasing quality and is related to the self, the object of pride. Indirect passions include 'pride, humility, ambition, vanity, love, hatred, envy, pity, malice, generosity, with their dependents'. Direct passions include 'desire, aversion, grief, joy, hope, fear, despair, and security'.[15] Louis Loeb argues that none of the passions, direct or indirect, could ever be calm, given the psychological mechanism by which each is produced.[16] The manner in which a passion is produced largely determines whether it is forceful and tumultuous or calm and reason-like. Since the indirect passions are produced by what Hume calls 'a double relation of impressions and ideas', the resulting passion is felt with force and violence. The direct passions, which play a role in the production of the indirect, are reinforced by the indirect passions they resemble and help produce, and so tend to be violent just as the indirect are. So, I am pleased at my fine painting, pleasure that is the direct passion of joy. Since the painting is mine, I associate it with an idea of my self, and since joy is agreeable, it resembles the impression of pride. This double relation of ideas and impressions thus causes the indirect impression of pride. Hume says that this indirect passion in turn gives 'new force', or 'additional force', to the initial joy.[17] So, both the direct passion of joy and the indirect passion of pride are experienced with violence.

On the other hand, many of the instinctual passions are generally calm, but not all. Hume writes in his discussion of motivation, 'Now 'tis certain, there are certain calm desires and tendencies, which, tho' they be real passions, produce little emotion in the mind.'[18] Then he names some of the instincts I've mentioned (benevolence and resentment, the love of life, kindness to children and the general appetite to good, and aversion to evil). There are violent versions of at least some of these instincts, and resentment is one: '[w]hen I receive any injury from another, I often feel a violent passion of resentment, which makes me desire his evil and punishment, independent of all considerations of pleasure and advantage to myself'.[19] Among the other instincts are surely some that are generally calm and some that are generally violent (desire of punishment to our enemies and of happiness to our friends, hunger, lust, and a few other bodily appetites).

Since Hume offers three major divisions of the passions—instincts ('primary') versus derived ('secondary') passions, calm versus violent passions, and direct versus indirect passions—there is disagreement among the commentators about how these categories work with one another.[20] I believe that the best way to understand Hume's scheme is to first divide the passions into primary (instincts) and secondary (derived). The secondary are derived either from pleasures and pains or from the primary, by interposition of an idea (which copies the primary impression). The secondary include both direct and indirect passions. Any passion can be either calm or violent, but the generally calm primary passions include at least the moral and aesthetic senses (which encompass certain calm pleasures and pains) and other instincts I've noted. All the secondary passions are *initially* violent, I think, due to their manner of derivation, but Hume makes it clear that even if they originate with some violence, these passions can change. He writes, 'when a passion has once become a settled principle of action, and is the predominant inclination of the soul, it commonly produces no longer any sensible agitation'.[21]

After Hume's classification of the passions, the calm–violent distinction is raised again in the discussion of motivation in *Treatise* Book 2, Part 3, Section 3, 'Of the influencing motives of the will', and in the subsequent section in which Hume explains the causes of violent passions. Its role is very important there, for several reasons. First, the existence of the calm passions is called upon to explain why it appears that reason can oppose passion over the determination of action, and the doctrine is offered as his substitute for rationalist theories of motivation. Any mental activity that operates with calmness and tranquility is confused with reason; so in fact, passions are opposing other passions.[22] Hume allows, then, that contrary to the views of many early modern rationalists, the passions can regulate themselves without the guidance of reason.[23] In persons of certain character, the opposition of one passion to another will result in the practical success of the healthy or virtuous passion, which is often calm, over its competitors. Second, the calm and violent passions doctrine reconciles Hume's causal theory of motivation with an important feature of conventional motivational psychology. Since Hume distinguishes a violent passion and a causally strong one, and a calm passion and a causally weak one, he allows that we can act on passions that, in a phenomenal sense, we hardly feel, even when having an intense experience of a contrary passion. Thus, he can make sense of our feeling of doing something we really don't want to do.[24] Calm passions can have greater causal strength than violent ones and be effective in action, even though felt much less powerfully than the violent, a point which has implications for the causal strength of prudential or moral motives, which are typically calm. Third, even though causal force and violence are distinct features of the passions, Hume indicates his belief that persons more frequently act on violent passions over calm ones by writing that it is 'certain' that if we want to push someone to action, ''twill commonly be better policy to work upon the violent than the calm passions, and rather take him by his inclination, than what is vulgarly call'd his *reason*'.[25] Hume's advice is that we employ strategies that increase the violence of the passion, which is then more likely to increase its motivational strength. Jane McIntyre has argued that Hume has a problem validating the strength–violence distinction because he offers very little commentary on how to increase the causal strength of a passion without working on increasing its violence.[26] I will say more about this later, but for now, my point is that the violence of a passion is crucial to Hume's treatment of the dynamic of the passions and to the phenomenon of motivational conflict.

7.2 The Contrary Principles of Sympathy and Comparison

Hume draws on two principles of the human mind to explain the varied effects of other people's feelings and situations on our passions. Sympathy is connected to passions oriented towards the good of others—passions like pity and compassion (some readers add benevolence).[27] The principle of comparison, on the other hand, is the source of the asocial traits, such as contempt, malice, and envy, which incline us away from others' well-being. So, Hume's theory identifies two capacities fundamental to human nature that produce passions often at odds with each other. I begin with sympathy.

Hume introduces the mechanism of sympathy, which plays a crucial role in his moral philosophy, when discussing the passions of pride and humility. Hume remarks that our character, reputation, beauty, and riches are causes of pride, but would have little effect on us if not 'seconded' by the opinions and sentiments of others. Sympathy accounts for the influence on us of others' feelings and views. Hume notes that we feel hatred, resentment, esteem, love, courage, mirth, and melancholy more from communication by others' behaviour than from our own natural temperaments.[28] He comes close to defining sympathy when he writes,

> When any affection is infus'd by sympathy, it is at first known only by its effects, and by those external signs in the countenance and conversation, which convey an idea of it. This idea is presently converted into an impression, and acquires such a degree of force and vivacity, as to become the very passion itself, and produce an equal emotion, as any original affection.[29]

I notice another's laughter, which gives me an idea of that person's cheer, and when I sympathize, that idea is converted into a jovial feeling of my own. Hume attributes national character and citizens' uniformity of thinking to sympathy. Sympathy is affected by the same associative tendencies that facilitate the passions, and Hume remarks that among people, 'where, beside the general resemblance of our natures, there is any peculiar similarity in our manners, or character, or country, or language, it facilitates the sympathy'.[30]

Hume does not explicitly argue that sympathy gives rise to benevolence, a view that would be inconsistent with his view of benevolence as an instinct. Hume writes that the desire of happiness or misery for another, which is 'an arbitrary and original instinct', may be 'counterfeited' on certain occasions and so arise from 'secondary principles'. Then he goes on to explain how pity, concern for the misery of others, and malice, joy in others' misery (without friendship, on the one hand, or enmity, on the other) are derived from other affections.[31] So, he seems to indicate that the passion with which he is concerned is not benevolence, but pity, which he says imitates the effects of love. Love, Hume argues in an earlier discussion, is not a motive, but is causally connected to a motive, namely, benevolence for the beloved. (And hatred is not a motive but connected to the motive of anger for the one hated.) So, in this sense, pity is counterfeited benevolence. In his classic study of Hume on sympathy, Páll Árdal asks, 'But why, even if I am affected through the process of communication, should I be concerned about the other person's suffering or sorrow?' Why don't we hate the person who makes us feel uncomfortable, or why don't we just turn our attention away?[32] I address this question after examining Hume's account of the origin of pity in sympathy and of malice in comparison.

Others' 'affliction and sorrow' strike us in a livelier manner than any enjoyment does, and they produce in us an analogous feeling, which is pity. This must happen by sympathy, Hume thinks, since spectators to tragic plays experience a train of passions—grief, terror, indignation, and even joy as the characters undergo reversals of fortune. It makes most sense to think that these passions are felt by the spectator, not each originating by a distinct cause, but through a general principle, sympathy. And the fact that our feelings of pity depend on contiguity to or distance from the object (person) is further corroboration that the imagination, which is an integral part of sympathy, is at work in producing pity.[33] Then Hume recognizes 'a pretty remarkable phaenomenon of this passion', that pity (and some other passions conveyed by sympathy) are sometimes stronger when the feeling in the subject is weaker, or even non-existent.

> ...when a person...inherits a great fortune, we are always the more rejoic'd for his prosperity, the less sense he seems to have of it, and the greater equanimity and indifference he shews in its enjoyment. In like manner a man, who is not dejected by misfortunes, is the more lamented on account of his patience; and if that virtue extends so far as utterly to remove all sense of uneasiness, it still farther encreases our compassion.[34]

Few commentators have discussed the principle of comparison, the complement to the principle of sympathy, whereby we experience certain passions, notably contempt, malice, and envy, upon comparison of our situations with others. Gerald Postema writes,

> Hume, like Montaigne and Mandeville, thought the dark passions to which we are susceptible are deeply rooted in human nature, as deeply in fact as the fellow-feeling and sociality championed by Shaftesbury....The key to unlocking the mystery of human passions, according to Hume, lay in the interaction between two fundamental psychological mechanisms or principles: sympathy and comparison. Both our sociality and our asociality find their psychic origins in the complex interaction between them.[35]

Malice, for Hume, imitates the effects of hatred. Hatred, he argues earlier, is followed by anger; so, malice is a sort of imitation anger, as pity is an imitation of benevolence (although Hume doesn't put it that way). The general principle at work here, according to Hume, is that objects appear greater or less by comparison with others. A sizable object looks greater next to a tiny object; an ugly one even uglier when put next to a beautiful object. So,

> as we observe a greater or less share of happiness or misery in others, we must make an estimate of our own, and feel a consequent pain or pleasure. The misery of another gives us a more lively idea of our happiness, and his happiness of our misery. The former, therefore, produces delight; and the latter uneasiness.[36]

Hume calls this 'a kind of pity reverst, or contrary sensations arising in the beholder, from those which are felt by the person, whom he considers'.[37]

Hume's notion of comparison is indebted to Malebranche, who explains how the passions of esteem and its relatives and contempt and its relatives depend on our dispositions to compare ourselves to others.[38] Postema argues that there are actually three principles of comparison in Hume's discussion. First, the 'contrast' principle enhances the features of objects when the items around them are sharply different, which is illustrated in the examples above of size and beauty. Second, on reversal comparison, we sympathize with others, but instead of acquiring feelings like theirs, we experience feelings that are contrary to theirs, taking pleasure in their pain or pain in their pleasure. Thus, as already noted, such feelings can take the form of envy or malice when the other person experiences advantages to which we react by comparison.[39] However, I don't see these as independent principles, since in Hume's analysis, reversal requires contrast: Hume's explanation why one experiences displeasure at another's good fortune has to do with one's perception of one's own fortune as small in comparison to the other person's. Third, in 'context' comparison, we evaluate and measure objects in context by comparison to things around them. Hume suggests that we are deeply influenced by the opinions of others in social contexts, so social referencing plays a large part in the formation of our attitudes, views, and desires.

Some points about reversal comparison, my main interest here, are unexpected. Hume thinks we can experience malice towards *ourselves* in the sense that the thought of past pain is agreeable when we find our present condition satisfying, and the thought of past pleasure make us uneasy when we find ourselves presently in disadvantageous circumstances by comparison. While it sounds odd to think of these feelings as malice, '[t]he comparison being the same, as when we reflect on the sentiments of others, must be attended with the same effects'.[40] Moreover, the distress of a friend can actually move us to seek displeasure through reversal comparison. The contrast with my friend's circumstances might have made me feel even more pleased at my good fortune, however, Hume says, 'But as grief is here suppos'd to be the predominant passion, every addition falls to that side, and is swallow'd up in it, without operating in the least upon the contrary affection.'[41] The same phenomenon accounts for remorse and its effect.

> When a criminal reflects on the punishment he deserves, the idea of it is magnify'd by a comparison with his present ease and satisfaction; which forces him, in a manner, to seek uneasiness, in order to avoid so disagreeable a contrast.[42]

Furthermore, envy, for Hume, is explained by the same principles as malice. Envy is excited by some present enjoyment of another, which by comparison diminishes our idea of our own enjoyment and malice is an unprovoked desire of evil for another, in order to gain pleasure from the contrast with ourselves.[43] Finally, in the cases of envy of our inferiors who are approaching or superseding our happiness or status, the effects of comparison are twice repeated:

> A man, who compares himself to his inferior, receives a pleasure from the comparison: And when the inferiority decreases by the elevation of the inferior, what shou'd only have been a decrease of pleasure, becomes a real pain, by a new comparison with its preceding condition.[44]

Now I return to the question how sympathy with someone's bad situation gives rise to pity, a form of benevolence, when we might actually despise a person for making us feel uncomfortable (or we might simply turn away to avoid the sympathetic feeling). Hume recognizes the issue himself:

For as pity is an uneasiness, and malice a joy, arising from the misery of others, pity shou'd naturally, as in all other cases, produce hatred; and malice, love. This contradiction I endeavour to reconcile, after the following manner.[45]

He begins with the crucial point that it is not 'the present sensation alone or momentary pain or pleasure, which determines the character of any passion, but the whole bent or tendency of it from the beginning to the end'.[46] An impression can resemble another in its sensation (pleasurable or painful) but also in the direction each imparts to action, which is the bent or tendency. So, there are two causes from which a transition of passions may arise; one is the double relations of ideas and impressions already explained, and another is a conformity in the tendency and direction of two desires that arise from difference causes. Hume's view is that when sympathy with another's uneasiness is weak it actually *does* produce hatred or contempt, through the double association. (The idea of another person's uneasy situation makes me uneasy and so makes me feel displeasure or hatred towards that person, so there are two impressions of displeasure and two associated ideas of the other person.) But when sympathy is stronger, it will produce 'love or tenderness' by the conformity in direction of two passions, the sympathetic response and benevolence.[47] Pity, as we have seen, resembles benevolence, the effect of love, but we feel it when the object is a stranger, rather than someone close to us. Postema makes the best sense of how Hume draws on 'the whole bent' of benevolence to explain the effect of sympathy in producing pity:

The whole bent of benevolence, which one feels towards a family member, loved-one, friend, or partner, consists not merely of unconnected momentary sensations, but also of an extensive pattern of emotionally charged links tracking the fortunes and misfortunes of the beloved as she goes through life.[48]

Of course, with strangers we have no such history and connections, so we would expect our momentary engagement with them to result in antagonistic passions. But sympathy can originate pity, for Hume, when the sympathizer has been able to use her imagination to cast a wider net and experience vividly the person's past, present, and future situation. Hume writes,

'*Tis* certain, that sympathy is not always limited to the present moment, but that we often feel by communication the pains and pleasures of others, which are not in being, and which we only anticipate by the force of imagination. For supposing I saw a person perfectly unknown to me, who, while asleep in the fields, was in danger of being trod under foot by horses, I shou'd immediately run to his assistance; and in this I shou'd be actuated by the same principle of sympathy, which makes me concern'd for the present sorrows of a stranger. . . . '[T]is evident, that, in considering the future possible or probable condition of any person, we may enter into it with so vivid a conception as to make it our own concern; and by that means be sensible of pains and pleasures, which neither belong to ourselves, nor at the present instant have any real existence.[49]

When sympathy is extended in this way, the bent or motive force of benevolence is transferred to the sympathetic person, who thereby feels pity and is moved to give assistance.[50] One crucial feature in determining that pity rather than hatred or aversion is evoked is the liveliness and vivacity of the initial sympathetic response.

When the present misery of another has any strong influence upon me, the vivacity of the conception... gives me a lively notion of all the circumstances of that person, whether past, present, or future; possible, probable or certain. By means of this lively notion I... feel a sympathetic motion in my breast, conformable to whatever I imagine in his.[51]

If the vivacity of the first idea is diminished, on the other hand, so is the vivacity of the ideas related to it ('pipes can convey no more water than what arises at the fountain'), and I will not be interested in the well-being of the other person. Thus, whether we experience extended or limited sympathy—and thus whether we experience love or benevolence, on the one hand, or hatred and contempt, on the other—depends upon the vivacity of the sympathetic impression: a great degree of misery or strong sympathy towards it causes benevolence, while a small misery or weak sympathy towards it produces contempt.

7.3 Violence and Contrary Passions

Hume calls upon several basic principles of associationist psychology in order to explain how passions are generated, intensified, and transformed into other passions. He argues in Book 1 of the *Treatise* that we naturally associate ideas by their resemblance, contiguity, and cause and effect. These tendencies are carried into the passions. Hume writes in his discussion of the passions that resembling impressions (of which passions are a subset) follow the same principles of association:

All resembling impressions are connected together, and no sooner one arises than the rest immediately follow. Grief and disappointment give rise to anger, anger to envy, envy to malice, and malice to grief again, till the whole circle be completed.... Changeableness is essential to... [the human mind].[52]

Hume avers that the association of ideas and of impressions 'assist and forward each other', so that the intensity of a passion is increased when that passion involves both an association of ideas and impressions, as is the case with an indirect passion. Contiguity comes into play when Hume suggests that the situation of an object affects the intensity of passion, so that '[t]he same good, when near, will cause a violent passion, which when remote, produces only a calm one'.[53]

Hume's discussion of how the violence and forcefulness of passions is increased occurs in the part of Book 2 of the *Treatise* that deals with the will and the direct passions. While some indirect passions are motives, the direct passions seem to have the closest connection with action, since they arise immediately from the perception of pleasurable or painful objects. One principle at work in magnifying the violence of the passions is what I call 'conversion'. When two passions are produced by separate causes, they 'mingle and unite' even if they have no relation to one another. 'The predominant passion swallows up the inferior, and converts it into itself', with the prevailing passion determining the direction of action.[54] The prevalence mentioned here is in terms of violence (the phenomenal dimension), rather than in terms of causal strength (its motivational dimension). Hume's examples verify this point. A man's love for his mistress is intensified by the jealousy and quarrelsome affections her faults give rise to; a politician raises a question that he delays in answering in order to heighten curiosity on the part of the public. In the former case, jealousy intensifies love, and in the latter anxiety intensifies curiosity. Even when two passions pull in contrary directions, the connection between them is more intimate than the connection between a passion and indifference.

Contrary passions, according to Hume, will have a similar stimulating effect on a person, as will uncertainty. If the same object excites contrary passions, then the agent will experience internal upheaval or disorder, which will increase the violence of whichever passion is dominant. So, Hume thinks this explains why we naturally desire what is forbidden and are sometimes more desirous of doing what it wrong just because it is contrary to duty.[55] The dominant passion turns out to be more violent than it would have been had it met with no opposition at all, and the effect is the same whether the opposition is internal or external. Our reactions to fictional tragedies illustrate this principle as well. The sorrow, indignation, and compassion we feel increase our appreciation of the beauty of the performance.[56] Furthermore, when we are uncertain about the outcome of an event or an action, the mind jumps from one reaction to another (hope, fear, etc.), which has the overall effect of increasing the vivacity of the dominant passion. The same happens when there is uncertainty about the nature of an object:

> 'Tis certain nothing more powerfully animates any affection, than to conceal some part of its object by throwing it into a kind of shade...; the effort, which the fancy makes to compleat the idea, rouzes the spirits, and gives an additional force to the passion.[57]

Furthermore, absence can increase or diminish passions depending on the circumstances: 'absence destroys weak passions, but encreases strong; as the wind extinguishes a candle, but blows up a fire'.[58] This point is illustrated by the familiar experience of missing a beloved who must be away. The imagination, with which we bring ideas of sources of pleasure and pain before the mind, also intensifies the passions, and the more specific the goods or evils we imagine, the more violent the responses we experience.

7.4 The Effects of Contrary Passions on Our Psychology and Motivation

Hume's account of the psychology of the passions reveals that we are subject to many forms of contrariety in our emotions and passions. Annette Baier writes, 'The sorts of "contrariety", opposition, and hostile coexistence that human passions exhibit is one of Book Two's recurrent themes.'[59] Contrariety can increase the force or violence of the predominant passion, but it can have other effects as well. Hume's treatment of the direct passions includes his discussion of contrariety, and he names the contrary pairs of direct passions: desire and aversion, grief and joy, hope and fear. He spends a good deal of space on the effects of probability, which not only increases vivacity, but also determines the particular passion one experiences, depending on the degree of certainty or uncertainty of good or evil. Desire arises from simple consideration of prospective good and aversion from evil. When good is certain or probable, it produces joy; when evil is certain or probable, it produces grief or sorrow. Uncertain good or evil gives rise to fear or hope, according to the degrees of uncertainty on the one side or the other.[60]

When there is uncertainty about the existence of an object, the understanding fluctuates between two opposites views. Thus, if the object is an object of desire, the mind fluctuates between joy and grief as it considers the contrary points of view.[61] Then Hume adds:

> Now if we consider the human mind, we shall find, that with regard to the passions, 'tis not of the nature of a wind-instrument of music, which in running over all the notes immediately loses the sound after the breath ceases; but rather resembles a string-instrument, where after each stroke the vibrations still retain some sound, which gradually and insensibly decays.[62]

The imagination can quickly change its views, but the passions are slower to change and so they are mixed with each other.

> According as the probability inclines to good or evil, the passion of joy or sorrow predominates in the composition... [T]he grief and joy being intermingled with each other, by means of the contrary views of the imagination, produce by their union the passions of hope and fear.[63]

Although Hume has earlier emphasized that contrary passions increase the violence of the dominant passions, which happens when they first clash, he observes other possible effects of contrariety. First, both the passions exist successively by short intervals; sometimes, that they destroy each other, so that we feel neither of them; and sometimes both remain united in the mind. Consistent with his aim of finding the ultimate tenets in human psychology, he asks to what basic principles the other effects can be attributed. The first happens when the contrary passions arise from completely different objects, with no relation to one another. Hence, they can neither mingle nor be opposed to one another. 'If the objects of the contrary passions be totally different, the passions are like two opposite liquors in different bottles, which have no influence on each other.' Thus a man distressed for the loss of a law-suit and joyful for the birth of a son will feel one, then the other affection, and neither can provoke or moderate the other. The second situation, where the passions cancel each other and leave the mind in a state of tranquility, happens when a single object, because of its mixed character, provokes two reactions. So, if a play is both funny and sad, the spectator leaves in a state of equanimity. 'If the objects be intimately connected, the passions are like an *alcali* and an *acid*, which, being mingled, destroy each other.' In the third instance, when an object, either good or evil, is uncertain, then contrary passions will occur together, but neither destroys nor neutralizes the other, but instead, the two unite and produce a new affection. Hume thinks this is so because the opposition between passions in the case of probabilities is not a constant and perfect opposition in terms of sensation and direction. The imagination must alternate between two views, each of which produces a passion that 'vibrates' as it fades by degrees into the other. 'If the relation be . . . imperfect, and consist in the contradictory views of the same object, the passions are like oil and vinegar, which, however mingled, never perfectly unite and incorporate.'[64] This last situation is illustrated by the examples of grief and joy and hope and fear, discussed above. When the existence of good and evil is uncertain, there is both grief and joy, with hope for good and fear of evil. As the preponderance of evidence grows on the side of evil, fear increases and hope and joy diminish. Fear becomes grief when evil is certain. On the other hand, if the probabilities favour the existence of good, hope increases, as fear and grief decline. Hope eventually becomes joy when good is certain.[65]

7.5 Moderating the Passions with the Passions

All these sources of violence and contrariety may indicate that Hume depicts our emotional life as one dominated by disorder and conflict. Rationalist thinkers appeal to reason as the regulator of the passions, bringing them under its judgments of propriety and directing actions accordingly. Hume argues, however, that reason cannot motivate action and cannot oppose passion in its direction of the will. Rather, sustaining and strengthening the effects of the calm passions is one of the chief remedies to our situation—which implies that motivation cannot be a function only of the violence of a passion. But the reader may wonder whether Hume believes that we have any control over our passions, in light of reflections like the following:

> Both the *causes* and *effects* of these violent and calm passions are pretty variable, and depend, in a great measure, on the peculiar temper and disposition of every individual. Generally speaking, the violent passions have a more powerful influence on the will; tho' 'tis often found, that the calm ones, when corroborated by reflection, and seconded by resolution, are able to controul them in their most furious movements. What makes this whole affair more uncertain, is, that a calm passion may easily be chang'd into a violent one, either by a change of temper, or of the circumstances and situation of the object, as by the borrowing of force from any attendant passion, by custom, or by exciting the imagination. Upon the whole, this struggle of passion and of reason, as it is call'd, diversifies human life, and makes men so different not only from each other, but also from themselves in different times.[66]

I want to suggest that, while temperaments and dispositions are original to persons, the particular affections, emotions, and passions they experience are a function of their dispositions in conjunction with other factors. Manipulating these factors, I think, allows for passions to moderate the effects of other passions. Here I want to highlight the elements in Hume's account that permit this reading. At least three features of Hume's theory of emotional conflict imply that regulation of the passions is possible. The first lies in his discussion of custom and calm passions. The second is a key point in his treatment of conflicting passions, the fact that one passion can neutralize another just as an alkaline neutralizes an acid. The third lies in Hume's treatment of a virtue called 'greatness of mind', which is connected in an unobvious way to his discussion of the principles of sympathy and comparison.

(1) *Custom and calm passions.* Hume suggests that those for whom the calm passions are motivationally stronger than the violent passions possess a virtue he calls strength of mind.[67] He introduces this virtue in the context of a conflict between concern for long-term self-interest and a violent passion (say, a desire for something immediately appealing, but unhealthy in the long run). He notes that some people are not influenced by the notion of their greatest possible good, while others can counter the influence of the violent passions and be undetermined by present uneasiness.

> In general we may observe, that both these principles operate on the will; and where they are contrary, that either of them prevails, according to the *general* character or *present* disposition of the person. What we call strength of mind, implies the prevalence of the calm passions above the violent...[68]

In the *Enquiry Concerning the Principles of Morals*, Hume connects strength of mind with happiness, and the lack of strength of mind with misery. Then he remarks that it is our calm passions that specify the priority of objects and give us resolutions for action, but sometimes our resolve is derailed by violent passions provoked by imaginative portrayals of immediate pleasure.[69] Only the person of resolute temper who can keep distant pursuits in focus has a chance at happiness and honor.

How can we cultivate strength of mind? Hume has earlier made the point that the easiest way to motivate a person is by augmenting the violence of the relevant passion or desire, but he also implies that the motivational force of calm passions can be increased by the impact of habit. The more accustomed we become to acting for a long-term good over a short-term one or to acting from calm benevolence over disgust, etc., the more strongly we are inclined to act on the relevant passion again. Hume writes that custom bestows 'a *facility* in the performance of any action or the conception of any object; and afterwards a *tendency or inclination* towards it'.[70] When we initiate action towards a new object, the effort is difficult but also exciting, and enlivens the mind, producing surprise. Hume thinks that surprise augments both agreeable and disagreeable feelings. But when the motivating passions returns and we act on it repeatedly, the novelty wears off and the passion is calmed. Likewise, the facility with which we so act is increased and becomes a source of quiet pleasure.

> The pleasure of facility does not so much consist in any ferment of the spirits, as in their orderly motion; which will sometimes be so powerful as even to convert pain into pleasure, and give us a relish in time for what at first was most harsh and disagreeable.[71]

So, if the desire for a distant good can be made lively or violent, perhaps by imagining its consequences and benefits and bringing them in picturesque ways before the mind, then it is more likely to have a causal force strong enough to motivate even in the face of competing desires. If I can envision the healthy and pleasant consequences of having a regular exercise programme, I might be able to overcome the desire to relax on my sofa for the next hour instead of getting out to the gym. If an agent succeeds at this mental maneuver frequently, then this way of behaving will become habitual, and the desire or passion from which she acts will become calm, but effective.

(2) *Neutralizing certain passions.* Hume's account of the principles at play in the mind's reaction to conflicting passions suggests a strategy for cancelling certain passions or their effects. (a) Sometimes a more violent passion will absorb a less violent one and increase the former's forcefulness (violence) even more. So, if we can bring a good vividly to mind, we might provoke a passion that incorporates another passion we think is noxious for us. So, if I feel envy at my colleague's good fortune, I might focus on the value of her contributions to the university and profession so that I feel gratitude or admiration. If that gratitude or admiration is experienced vividly or forcefully enough, it might consume envy and perhaps intensify the feeling of admiration. (b) When we have conflicting passions resulting from alternate views of an object, Hume observes that the two will neutralize one another, leaving the mind in a state of equanimity. So, if I want to minimize the distress I feel from the prospect of a medical treatment, I might try imagining the beneficial effects of the procedure in order to produce a reaction that annuls the painful one. Of course, the difficulty lies in achieving a reaction forceful and lively enough to counter the fear, but Hume's view leaves open the possibility that we can neutralize negative passions by what we attend to. (c) If the conflict of passions is due to uncertainty about the nature of an object, the passions of joy and sadness will alternate, with their intensity heightened by the insecurity. They eventually blend into a new passion of hope or fear. These observations suggest that we might push the mix towards hope by concentrating on the possibility that the good will result. Since understanding probabilities is a crucial factor in how and to what degree the passions of joy and sadness alternate, attending closely to the odds of one outcome over another can affect whether the emotion of hope or fear is predominant as well.

(3) *Greatness of mind.* In a section of the *Treatise* close to the end of Book 3 (Of Morals), Hume discusses a virtue he calls 'greatness of mind' and connects it to the principles of sympathy and comparison. Hume calls greatness of mind 'heroic virtue', the sort of trait that prompts acts of courageousness and magnanimity, and says it essentially partakes of proper pride and well-established self-esteem.[72] To introduce the topic, Hume returns to the principles of sympathy and comparison, which he detailed in Book 2, and comments that since sympathy and comparison are directly contrary, 'it may be worth while to consider, what general rules can be form'd, beside the particular temper of the person, for the prevalence of the one or

the other'.[73] Once again, he refers to temperament as a factor in the passions we commonly experience, but implies that there is more at work than simply natural dispositions. He uses an example to draw out the principles underlying the use of sympathy and comparison. If I'm safely on land, I might think of people miserable at sea in a storm, but this idea increases my own happiness by comparison only when the idea of those people suffering out on the ocean is very forceful and lively. The effects, however, of my imagination will never equal that of my actually witnessing (from my safe position on land) the ship at a distance being tossed by the waves and in danger of sinking. Then Hume asks us to suppose 'the ship to be driven so near me, that I can perceive distinctly the horror, painted on the countenance of the seamen and passengers, hear their lamentable cries, see the dearest friends give their last adieu, or embrace with a resolution to perish in each other's arms'. In this case, sympathy is activated and comparison is muted: 'No man has so savage a heart as to reap any pleasure from such a spectacle, or withstand the motions of the tenderest compassion and sympathy.'[74] The general principle at work, he concludes, is that the liveliness of an idea of another's situation determines whether our conception has a sympathetic or comparative effect on us. When too dull, it has no effect. Comparison requires some degree of vivacity, but sympathy, being the conversion of an idea of another's feeling into our own, requires a very lively and striking idea. In fact, his example shows that not only does sympathy require lively ideas of others' conditions, but that such ideas forces us to feel sympathetic responses over comparative ones.

In applying these principles to the case of pride, Hume observes that the presence of 'a great man' can sometimes cause envy and hatred in us, as we shrink by comparison, but it can sometimes cause respect and esteem through sympathy with his pride. Simply imaging a person of superior qualities doesn't much affect us. However, when a person

> whom we are really persuaded to be of inferior merit, is presented to us; if we observe in him any extraordinary degree of pride and self-conceit; the firm persuasion he has of his own merit, takes hold of the imagination, and diminishes us in our own eyes, in the same manner, as if he were really possess'd of all the good qualities which he so liberally attributes to himself.[75]

Here the conditions are right for comparison to take hold, since the ideas are forceful enough to make us experience resentment. If, on the other hand, we were convinced that the person actually possesses the merit he or she purports to have, the idea is strong enough for sympathy, and we feel admiration. Hume concludes that 'an overweaning conceit' of our merits is vicious, because it makes others uncomfortable, while a justified sense of our talents and accomplishments is a virtue. '... nothing is more useful to us in the conduct of life, than a due degree of pride, which makes us sensible of our own merit, and gives us a confidence and assurance in all our projects and enterprizes'.[76]

There are a couple of ways in which the lessons from Hume's analysis of greatness of mind can be used to minimize conflict and the experience of stressful passions. First, if we can fasten onto a firm but lively idea of another's condition, we might cause ourselves to experience unwavering sympathetic reactions that result in our feeling benevolence, love, or pity rather than resentment, hatred, or malice by comparison. Of course, sympathetic feelings with others in distress are not pleasurable and we might prefer to avoid them. However, all things considered, they seem superior to the team of emotions associated with hatred, given that the former are more likely to procure the admiration of others than the latter. Furthermore, we will have a much better life if we surround ourselves with those who have a genuine sense of their own merits than if we spend time around those with inflated opinion of their own worth. Then, we will find ourselves frequently sharing in the joy of others and admiring them, rather than feeling resentment and jealously of others who constantly make us feel less accomplished than we otherwise might feel. More importantly, in order to be productive, ambitious, courageous, or magnanimous, we need to make a fair assessment of our own contributions and take pride in our talents and accomplishments. 'Whatever capacity any one may be endow'd with, 'tis entirely useless to him, if he be not acquainted with it, and form not designs suitable to it.' Hume thinks that we should know our own strengths, and if we err on one side or the other, we should overate our merit. 'Fortune commonly favours the bold and enterprizing; and nothing inspires us with more boldness than a good opinion of ourselves.'[77]

7.6 But Is Not Reason Really Doing the Work?

Since the strategies Hume suggests for moderation of passionate conflicts frequently involve bringing ideas to mind with forcefulness, a natural question is whether the work of regulation is actually being done by reason after all. Of course, the practice of moderation requires the use of the understanding and imagination to bring to mind the ideas that provoke the passions we aim to cultivate, but this does not mean that reason works alone. First, reason is not deciding what passions are best. As Hume emphasizes, it is our own calm passions that determine our priorities, by reflective approval of various passionate motivations, based on their generally agreeable effects. Second, whether we engage in moderation at all is a function of emotional constitution. While some people may simply lack the psychological constitution to develop strength of mind, or to arouse ideas vivacious enough to experience regularly sympathetic feelings over comparative ones, or to feel the proper pride definitive of greatness of mind, many of us are able to affect our own passions and practise a useful regulation of some passions by others. Since many of the generally calm passions are instinctual, we all experience them to some degree. Third, the impetus to control some passions by other passions depends on to what degree we can tolerate conflict and upheaval, which varies from person to person, depending not on reason, but again on affective constitution. Finally, it's worth noting that the success of the attempt to moderate the passions depends on other background passions inherent in one's nature. That is to say, the outcome is never a product of reason alone; bringing to mind the image of a cliff overlooking an open vista may make you feel exhilarated and make me feel nauseous. Reason, then, for Hume works in service of the passions in the process of self-governance, which allows that our lives are not necessarily dominated by emotional chaos and contrariety. When we do run up against our own limits, government steps in, but that's another story.

Notes

1. David Hume, *A Treatise of Human Nature* (1739–40), ed. David Fate Norton and Mary Norton (Oxford: Oxford Clarendon Press, 2007), Book 2, Part 3, Section 9, paragraph 17. Citations to Hume's *A Treatise of Human Nature* are hereafter 'T', followed by Book, Part, Section, and paragraph number.
2. Annette Baier, *A Progress of Sentiments* (Cambridge: Harvard University Press), pp. 145–6. The Hume quote is from T 2.1.11.9.
3. Jean-François Senault, *The Use of the Passions*, trans. Henry, Earl of Monmouth (London: Printed for J. L. and Humphrey Moseley, 1641), Third Treatise, pp. 117–19. He adds that reason is not sufficient without the grace of God.
4. Samuel Clarke, *The Government of Passion*, A Sermon Preach'd before the Queen, at St James Chapel, on Sunday the 7th of January, 1710–11, in *XVII Sermons on Several Occasions* [Eleven of which Never Before Printed] (London: printed by William Botham, for James Knapton, 1724), p. 145.
5. Hume's original term 'reflexion' has been changed to 'reflection' in the standard Norton and Norton Oxford edition. But 'reflexion' captures the fact that impressions of 'reflection' do not depend on reflection, or reasoning, but on the mind's reflex, turning back to a previous experience. Nonetheless, for consistency, I follow the Norton edition's spelling.
6. T 2.1.1.1. 'Animal spirits' refers to seventeenth-century theories of the production of sensation, such as that found in Descartes. The nerves are filled with animal spirits, which move like a wind through them, and serve to explain how the sense organs produce perceptions.
7. T 2.1.1.1.
8. T 1.1.2.1.
9. T 2.1.1.2.
10. T 2.3.3.8 and 2.3.9.8. I also think that the instincts are the source of other derived passions. Benevolence, for instance, can originate generosity, when the circumstances for its manifestation present themselves. See also, Rachel Cohon, 'Hume's Indirect Passions', in *A Companion to Hume*, ed. Elizabeth S. Radcliffe (Malden, MA: Wiley-Blackwell, 2008), pp. 159–200 (p. 164). She argues that the instincts are not actually passions, but give rise to passions. Hume, however, does call them passions and treats them as among the passions.
11. Edward Reynolds, *A Treatise of the Passions and Faculties of the Soul of Man* (London: Printed by R.H. for Robert Bostock, 1640); Jean-François Senault, *The Use of the Passions*; Nicolas Malebranche, *The Search after Truth* (1674–75), trans. and ed. Thomas M. Lennon and Paul J. Olscamp (Columbus: Ohio State University Press, 1980); William Ayloffe, *The Government of the Passions according to the Rules of Reason and Religion* (London: Printed

for Knapton, 1700); M. Burghope, *The Government of the* Passions, A sermon preach'd in the Temple Church, on Midlent Sunday, March the 30th (London, 1701); Francis Bragge, *A Practical Treatise of the Regulation of the Passions* (London: Printed by J.M. for John Wyat, 1708); Samuel Clarke, *The Government of Passion.*

12. In the eighteenth century, Francis Hutcheson highlights the calm–violent distinction as well and maintains that 'affections' are calm because they are felt within the soul, and passions are violent because they involve the body. See Francis Hutcheson, *An Essay on the Nature and Conduct of the Passions and Affections with Illustrations on the Moral Sense* (1742), ed. Aaron Garrett (Indianapolis: Liberty Fund, 2002), pp. 30–1, 42–4.
13. T 2.1.1.3 and T 2.3.3.8.
14. T 2.1.1.3.
15. T 2.1.1.4.
16. Louis Loeb, 'Hume's Moral Sentiments and the Structure of the Treatise', *Journal of the History of Philosophy* 15 (1977): 395–403 (p. 398).
17. T 2.3.9.2–4; Loeb, 'Hume's Moral Sentiments', p. 398.
18. T 2.3.3.8.
19. T 2.3.3.9.
20. Norman Kemp Smith interprets Hume's scheme as dividing all passions into two classes: instincts (primary passions) and those derived from pleasure and pain (secondary passions). The derived or secondary passions then divide into direct and indirect, with direct passions being further divided into calm and violent (Norman Kemp Smith, *The Philosophy of David Hume* (London: Macmillan and Co., 1941), pp. 164–8). But, as Pall Árdal notes, the indirect passions of pride, humility, love, and hatred are (generally) violent passions for Hume; hence, Kemp Smith's interpretation cannot be correct. Árdal suggests instead that every class of passions should be further subdivided into calm and violent: primary, secondary, direct, and indirect passions (Pall S. Árdal, *Passion and Value in Hume's Treatise* (Edinburgh: Edinburgh University Press, 1966), pp. 10–11). Penelhum agrees with Árdal (Terence Penelhum, *Hume* (London and Basingstoke: Macmillan Press Ltd., 1975), pp. 89–97). Loeb suggests that the proper interpretation divides all passions into the 'generally calm' and the 'generally violent', with the former constituted by the moral sentiments, and the latter constituted by the other passions, which are either direct or indirect (Loeb, 'Hume's Moral Sentiments', pp. 395–6). James Fieser notes that Loeb's account forgets the instincts (James Fieser, 'Hume's Classification of the Passions and its Precursors', *Hume Studies* 18, April 1992, pp. 1–17 (pp. 10–11)).
21. T 2.3.4.1.
22. T 2.3.3.8.
23. See James A. Harris, 'The Government of the Passions', in *The Oxford Handbook of British Philosophy in the Eighteenth Century*, ed. James A. Harris (Oxford: Oxford University Press, 2013), pp. 270–88.
24. T 2.3.4.1.
25. T 2.3.4.1.
26. Jane McIntyre, 'Strength of Mind: Problems and Prospects for a Humean Account', *Synthese* 152 (2006): 393–401 (p. 397).
27. Philip Mercer argues that Hume's view of sympathy is egocentric and doesn't leave room for concern for others, but this seems clearly false to me (Philip Mercer, *Sympathy and Ethics* (Oxford: Clarendon Press, 1972), p. 44). I agree with Jacqueline Taylor, who argues

that the self is not the object of passions derived from sympathy (Jacqueline Taylor, 'Sympathy, Self, and Others', in *The Cambridge Companion to Hume's* Treatise, ed. Donald Ainslie and Annemarie Butler (Cambridge: Cambridge University Press, 2015), pp. 188–205 [p. 191]). It's just that, as Hume says, others' sentiments 'can never affect us, but by becoming, in some measure, our own... as if they had been originally deriv'd from our own temper and disposition' (T 3.3.2.3).

28. T 2.1.11.1–2.
29. T 2.1.11.3.
30. T 2.1.11.5.
31. Desire of ill-will for another that comes from injury of us would instead produce revenge (T 2.2.7.1).
32. Árdal, *Passion and Value in Hume's* Treatise, pp. 51–2.
33. T 2.2.7.3–4.
34. T 2.2.7.5.
35. Gerald Postema, '"Cemented with Diseased Qualities": Sympathy and Comparison in Hume's Moral Psychology', *Hume Studies* 31(2005): 249–98 (p. 251).
36. T 2.2.8.8–9.
37. T 2.2.8.8–9.
38. In comparing Hume with Malebranche, Susan James argues that the principle of sympathy, which is not part of Malebranche's theory, downplays the 'more corrosive effects of comparison' for Hume. Hume moderates the destructive effects of passions like contempt 'with the more benign role of sympathy in our passionate responses' (Susan James, 'Sympathy and Comparison: Two Principles of Human Nature', in *Impressions of Hume*, ed. Marina Frasca-Spada and Peter Kail (Oxford: Oxford University Press, 2005), pp. 107–24 (pp. 119–20)).
39. Postema, '"Cemented with Diseased Qualities"', pp. 264–8.
40. T 2.2.8.10.
41. T 2.2.8.11.
42. T 2.2.8.11.
43. T 2.2.8.12.
44. T 2.2.8.12.
45. T 2.2.9.1.
46. T 2.2.9.2.
47. T 2.2.9.12.
48. Postema, '"Cemented with Diseased Qualities"', p. 271.
49. T 2.2.9.13.
50. See also Postema, '"Cemented with Diseased Qualities"', p. 271.
51. T 2.2.9.14.
52. T 2.1.4.3.
53. T 2.3.4.1.
54. T 2.3.4.2.
55. T 2.3.4.5.
56. David Hume, 'Of Tragedy', in *Essays, Moral, Political, and Literary* (1777), ed. Eugene F. Miller (Indianapolis: Liberty Fund, 1987), paragraphs 9–10.
57. T 2.3.4.9.
58. T 1.2.4.10.
59. Baier, *A Progress of Sentiments*, p. 145.

60. T 2.3.9.5–7.
61. T 2.3.9.11.
62. T 2.3.9.12.
63. T 2.3.9.12.
64. All quotes in the paragraph are from T 2.3.9.17.
65. T 2.3.9.10–19. These points about the contrary passions are repeated in section 1 of Hume's *Dissertation on the Passions* in *A Dissertation on the Passions and the Natural History of Religion* (1757), ed. Tom L. Beauchamp (Oxford: Clarendon Press, 2007).
66. T 2.3.8.13.
67. I have argued that strength of mind for Hume is not simply the motivational dominance of any calm over violent passion—for instance, someone motivated by calm pursuit of evil does not possess it. It is instead the motivational prevalence of certain calm passions over violent ones and is defined, I think, in terms of a general disposition to be motivated by any of a set of traits (which are also instinctive): benevolence, resentment, love of life (self-love), kindness to children, and the moral and aesthetic sentiments. See Elizabeth S. Radcliffe, 'Strength of Mind and the Calm and Violent Passions', *Res Philosophica* 92 (2015): 1–21.
68. T 2.3.3.10.
69. David Hume, *Enquiry concerning the Principles of Morals* (1751), ed. Tom L. Beauchamp (Oxford: Clarendon Press, 1998), section 6, paragraph 15.
70. T 2.3.5.1.
71. T 2.3.5.3.
72. T 3.3.2.13.
73. T 3.3.2.5.
74. T 3.3.2.5.
75. T 3.3.2.6.
76. T 3.3.2.8.
77. T 3.3.2.8.

Bibliography

Árdal, Páll. *Passion and Value in Hume's 'Treatise'* (Edinburgh: Edinburgh University Press, 1966).

Ayloffe, William. *The Government of the Passions according to the Rules of Reason and Religion* (London: Printed for Knapton, 1700).

Baier, Annette. *A Progress of Sentiments: Reflections on Hume's 'Treatise'* (Cambridge, MA: Harvard University Press, 1991).

Bragge, Francis. *A Practical Treatise of the Regulation of the Passions* (London: Printed by J.M. for John Wyat, 1708).

Burghope, M. *The Government of the* Passions, A sermon preach'd in the Temple Church, on Midlent Sunday, March the 30th (London, 1701).

Clarke, Samuel. *The Government of Passion*, A Sermon Preach'd before the Queen, at St. James Chapel, on Sunday the 7th of January, 1710–11, in *XVII Sermons on Several Occasions* [Eleven of which Never Before Printed] (London: printed by William Botham, for James Knapton, 1724).

Cohon, Rachel. 'Hume's Indirect Passions', in *A Companion to Hume*, ed. Elizabeth S. Radcliffe (Malden, MA: Wiley-Blackwell, 2008), pp. 159–200.

Fieser, James. 'Hume's Classification of the Passions and Its Precursors', *Hume Studies* 18 (1992): 1–17.

Harris, James A. 'The Government of the Passions', in *The Oxford Handbook of British Philosophy in the Eighteenth Century*, ed. James A. Harris (Oxford: Oxford University Press, 2013), pp. 270–88.

Hume, David. 'Of Tragedy', in *Essays, Moral, Political, and Literary* (1777), ed. Eugene F. Miller (Indianapolis: Liberty Fund, 1987).

Hume, David. *An Enquiry Concerning the Principles of Morals* (1751), ed. Tom L. Beauchamp (Oxford: Clarendon Press, 1998).

Hume, David. *A Dissertation on the Passions and the Natural History of Religion* (1757), ed. Tom L. Beauchamp (Oxford: Clarendon Press, 2007).

Hume, David. *A Treatise of Human Nature* (1739–40), ed. David Fate Norton and Mary J. Norton (Oxford: Oxford Clarendon Press, 2007).

Hutcheson, Francis. *An Essay on the Nature and Conduct of the Passions and Affections with Illustrations on the Moral Sense* (1742), ed. Aaron Garrett (Indianapolis: Liberty Fund, 2002).

James, Susan. 'Sympathy and Comparison: Two Principles of Human Nature', *Impressions of Hume*, ed. Marina Frasca-Spada and P.G.E. Kail (Oxford: Oxford University Press, 2005), pp. 107–24.

Kemp Smith, Norman. *The Philosophy of David Hume* (London: Macmillan and Co., 1941).

Loeb, Louis. 'Hume's Moral Sentiments and the Structure of the *Treatise*', *Journal of the History of Philosophy* 15 (1977): 395–403.

Malebranche, Nicolas. *The Search after Truth* (1674–75), trans. and ed. T. M. Lennon and P. J. Olscamp (Columbus: OH State University Press, 1980).

McIntyre, Jane. 'Strength of Mind: Problems and Prospects for a Humean Account', *Synthese* 152 (2006): 393–401.

Mercer, Philip. *Sympathy and Ethics* (Oxford: Clarendon Press, 1972).

Penelhum, Terence. *Hume* (London and Basingstoke: Macmillan Press Ltd., 1975).

Postema, Gerald. '"Cemented with Diseased Qualities": Sympathy and Comparison in Hume's Moral Psychology', *Hume Studies* 31 (2005): 249–98.

Radcliffe, Elizabeth. 'Strength of Mind and the Calm and Violent Passions', *Res Philosophica* 92 (2015): 547–67.

Reynolds, Edward. *A Treatise of the Passions and Faculties of the Soul of Man* (London: Printed by R.H. for Robert Bostock, 1740).

Senault, Jean-François. *The Use of the Passions*, trans. Henry, Earl of Monmouth (London: Printed for J. L. and Humphrey Moseley, 1641).

Taylor, Jacqueline. 'Sympathy, Self, and Others', in *The Cambridge Companion to Hume's 'Treatise'*, ed. Donald C. Ainslie and Annemarie Butler (Cambridge: Cambridge University Press, 2015), pp. 188–205.

8

Kant on the Moral Cultivation of Feelings

Alix Cohen

Kant's ethics is traditionally portrayed as unequivocal on one issue: affective states, including feelings, emotions, and inclinations, are intrinsically at odds with morality. From the *Groundwork* to the *Critique of Practical Reason* and the *Metaphysics of Morals*, his works seem to warrant this view:

'[T]he inclinations themselves, as sources of needs, are so far from having an absolute worth, so as to make one wish to have them, that it must instead be the universal wish of every rational being to be altogether free from them'[1]

'[Inclinations] are always *burdensome* to a rational being, and though he cannot lay them aside, they wrest from him the wish to be rid of them.'[2]

'virtue necessarily presupposes *apathy*'; it 'forbid[s] him to let himself be governed by his feelings and inclinations (the duty *of apathy);* for unless reason holds the reins of government in its own hands, his feelings and inclinations play the master over him'.[3]

The passage from the *Groundwork* is read as claiming that grudgingly obeying one's duty is morally preferable to doing one's duty with pleasure; the passage from the *Critique of Practical Reason* as claiming that emotions need to be annihilated and that the ideal will is a holy will, a purely rational creature entirely devoid of feelings and always solely governed by reason, in contrast with impure human wills; and the passage from the *Metaphysics of Morals* as claiming we have a duty of apathy, a duty to strive to be without feelings.

However, these passages do not entail that there is no role for affectivity in Kant's ethics. For instance, Kant seems to suggest that the feeling of sympathy is one noteworthy exception to his supposed emotionless ideal: 'while it is not in itself a duty to share the sufferings (as well the joys) of others, it is a duty to sympathize actively in their fate'.[4] This statement is not only in conflict with traditional portrayals of his ethics, but more importantly it may seem surprising for Kantian morality to endorse the claim that we have duties, albeit indirect, to cultivate feelings of sympathy in order to use them as means to moral ends. The aim of this paper is to spell out and defend the claim that the cultivation of certain feelings is one of our moral duties.

To do so, I will first argue that, far from always being hindrances to the realization of duty, feelings can be crucial helps to it insofar as their cultivation makes agents more morally efficacious. It is in this respect that we have an indirect duty to cultivate them. Second, I will question the sense in which their cultivation is in fact a moral duty. For the fact that feelings are means for promoting the performance of duty could be interpreted as suggesting that they are more akin to rules of skills than indirect duties. If so, they would not be duties in any meaningful sense of the term: they would be neither morally obligatory, nor necessary for the realization of our direct duties, and cultivating them would not be morally required. Yet as I will argue, although indirect duties are not entailed by the moral law, they can be said to be necessary given certain features of human nature. For what is ultimately at stake is our understanding of their function for embodied human agents. And far from being in conflict with Kant's account of freedom, I show in Section 8.3 that making the cultivation of our feelings a part of our moral lives points to the way we have to think about the exercise of autonomy at the empirical level, as free embodied rational beings. On this basis, I will conclude that we have a duty to cultivate our feelings because doing so promotes and facilitates the exercise of virtue from the standpoint of worldly action, thus making human agents more morally efficacious.

8.1 Feelings as Help to Moral Efficacy

Throughout his work, Kant maintains that feelings, not even moral ones, cannot play the role of moral compass: 'we no more have a special *sense* for what is (morally) good and evil than for *truth*'.[5] They cannot guide our moral deliberations by telling us what is right or what we ought to do. They neither ground nor spell out our duties; the moral law and practical reason do that.[6] For, feelings, emotions, and inclinations, 'can lead only contingently to what is good and can very often also lead to what is evil'.[7] For instance, sympathetic feelings are contingent and unreliable: they can misfire; we may not feel them when faced with distress; they need to be trained, cultivated, kept in check by practical reason and so on. And more importantly, although they give us an affective access to others and their needs, they fall short of providing us with a *moral* interest in them:

> [T]he *receptivity*, given by nature itself, to the feeling of joy and sadness in common with others [...] is *unfree* [...] the compassionate natural (aesthetic) feelings in us [...] is still one of the impulses that nature has implanted in us.[8]

As a psychological feeling agents have the capacity for, sympathy is just something they may or may not happen to feel empirically.[9]

Yet in spite of all these shortcomings, Kant argues that we have the indirect duty to cultivate our capacity to feel sympathy:

> [T]o use this [sympathetic feelings] as a means to promoting active and rational benevolence is still a particular, though only a conditional duty. [...] But while it is not in itself a duty to share

the sufferings (as well the joys) of others, it is a duty to sympathize actively in their fate; and to this end it is therefore an indirect duty to cultivate the compassionate natural (aesthetic) feelings in us, and to make use of them as so many means to sympathy based on moral principles and the feelings appropriate to them.[10]

To avoid misunderstandings, note that this duty does not command having sympathetic feelings since it would be impossible to act on such a command, just as it is not possible 'to love someone merely on command'.[11] Rather, the duty is to cultivate the capacity for having sympathetic feelings and to strengthen the feelings one already has. This duty can take a number of forms and shapes that are relative to our nature and our circumstances. Some of them are negative ('refrain from') and others are positive ('cultivate'). For instance, some activities are forbidden because they harm our capacity for sympathy—in particular, the maltreatment of animals:

With regard to the animate but nonrational part of creation, violent and cruel treatment of animals is [...] opposed to a human being's duty to himself, and he has a duty to refrain from this; for it dulls his shared feeling of their suffering and so weakens and gradually uproots a natural predisposition that is very serviceable to morality in one's relations with other people.[12]

Prescribing that we refrain from the maltreatment of animals is intended to hinder the hindrances to duty and thereby empower our capacity to sympathize. Thus, what makes this duty indirect is that it is prescribed as a means to the realization of a direct duty, namely the duty that commands the pursuit of one's own perfection.

According to Kant, this duty is twofold: it prescribes the cultivation of both our natural and our moral perfection. The former is expressed in the maxim 'Cultivate your powers of mind and body so that they are fit to realise any ends you might encounter.' The latter is expressed in the maxim 'strive with all one's might that the thought of duty for its own sake is the sufficient incentive of every action conforming to duty'.[13] Of course, these duties of perfection are wide duties—they can be realized in many different ways, and it is up to the agent to choose the form that the realization of these duties should take:

[I]f the law can prescribe only the maxim of actions, not actions themselves, this is a sign that it leaves a playroom (*latitudo*) for free choice in following (complying with) the law.[14]

In other words, there is latitude in the way in which we can comply with wide duties generally.

Yet as already noted, in the case of wide duties to the self, in spite of this latitude, a set of indirect duties points towards particular ways of complying with them. And crucially for my argument, these ways have to do with our emotional capacities—the indirect duty to cultivate our capacity for sympathy being a case in point. The thought seems to be that we ought to attend to our emotional capacities because some feelings impact our moral agency. How? By being helpful or harmful to it. More precisely as I will suggest, there are two essential ways in which our affective states bear upon the realization of our duty. I will spell this out using the example of Kant's account of human temperaments.

In his *Anthropology*, Kant distinguishes between four temperaments: the choleric, the phlegmatic, the melancholic, and the sanguine. Whilst it is unnecessary to discuss the detail of these temperaments here, what is crucial for my present purpose is that each temperament has particular natural tendencies, and in particular tendencies that favour certain moods, emotions, and inclinations. For instance, the sanguine, 'is carefree and of good cheer; he attributes a great importance to each thing for the moment, and the next moment may not give it another thought'; the melancholic who 'attributes a great importance to all things that concern himself'; the choleric who 'is hot-tempered, flares up quickly like straw-fire'; and finally, the phlegmatic, has 'the propensity to inactivity'.[15] In other words, each temperament has its own emotional profile, and this profile is directly relevant to an agent's moral activity. For depending on whether it is in conformity with what duty demands, it makes our acting from duty either easier or harder, and either clearer or more uncertain. Let me spell this out.

First, our emotional profile is relevant epistemically because with it come potential moral pitfalls.[16] For instance, our emotional tendencies can point in the same direction as duty (for instance, the sanguine and the duty of benevolence, since he is naturally generous), or conversely they can point away from duty (for instance, the melancholic and the duty to keep promises, since he doesn't naturally keep his word). It follows that in coinciding situations (when emotional tendencies and duty converge), I should discriminate between the moral and the non-moral motive so as to isolate the dutiful one. Conversely, in conflicting situations (when emotional tendencies and duty diverge), I should exercise control over the non-moral motive so as to facilitate action from the moral one. For instance, the melancholic should be wary of making promises unless he is certain he can keep them; or in situations when the duty of benevolence applies, the sanguine should question his seemingly benevolent motives whilst the choleric should temper his selfish motives. In other words, our feelings can make moral deliberation, and thus the realization of our moral goals, more efficient.

Second, our emotional profile is relevant motivationally because with it comes the tendency to weaken the use of certain capacities—or rather, to pose stronger obstacles to the use of certain capacities for moral purposes. For instance, choleric temperaments are more prone to passions than others. Since passions hinder the ability to choose rationally, cholerics ought to refine, and if possible overcome, their passions in order to strengthen their capacity for self-control. Although taming their inclinations is not a virtue, it eases the realization of their duty by facilitating self-control. In a similar way, each temperament has particular weaknesses that it ought to address. Sanguine temperaments ought to attend to their capacity for self-mastery by refining their feelings. Phlegmatic temperaments on the other hand are not prone to feeling sympathy. They are naturally insensitive to human distress, and thus unable to detect situations where they ought to exercise their duty of benevolence.[17] As a result, it is more important for them to attend to their capacity for sympathy by ensuring acquaintance with other people's painful feelings. The melancholic, by 'attributing a great importance to all things that concern himself', is naturally selfish. Thus it will be important for him to attend to his capacity for disinterested love by cultivating his appreciation of natural beauty. Of course, the affective capacities thereby cultivated have no intrinsic moral worth. For one could just as well use them for immoral purposes. A melancholic who develops his sympathetic feelings, or a choleric who learns to control his emotions, is not a morally improved agent; his moral character is not better than if he had not cultivated these capacities. Rather, first, he is a more efficient moral agent in the sense that he will be better armed to carry out his purposes; and second, one could say that this agent will be more confident (though never certain) that he is as committed as possible to the realization of duty; or at least that he will be more warranted in feeling confident than agents who do not cultivate these capacities.

8.2 Are Indirect Duties 'Duties'?

Whilst what I have argued so far is sufficient to account for the indirectness of the duty to cultivate certain feelings, their nature as actual duties remains to be accounted for. For, the fact that they merely point to the means of promoting the performance of our direct duties suggests that they are not morally required, but more importantly that acting from them has no moral colour, however faded. For instance, having sympathetic feelings is not a moral quality unless it is connected with a good will, in which case it carries an indirect moral worth:

> Some qualities are even conducive to this good will itself and can make it much easier; despite this, however, they have no inner unconditional worth but always presuppose a good will, which limits the esteem one otherwise rightly has for them and does not permit their being taken as absolutely good.[18]

Thus, it seems that the role of indirect duties is akin to that of rules of skills: they are 'necessary for attaining some possible purpose to be brought about by it [...] Whether the end is rational and good is not at all the question here, but only what one must do in order to attain it.'[19] If this is the case, then it follows that indirect duties are not in fact duties in any meaningful sense of the term: they are neither morally obligatory, nor necessary for the realization of our direct duties. They do not have any duty-making features; rather, they are mere optional and contingent means.[20] The idea that indirect duties should be relegated to the status of mere rules of skill is supported by the fact that their contribution to moral agency is limited to the role of making agents better prepared for realizing their goals, moral or otherwise—just as being more informed about technical imperatives about the world helps them improve their efficiency. If so, they would be mere pseudo-duties.

However, I believe that there is a crucial difference between rules of skill and indirect duties: namely, indirect duties have to do specifically with the self and the means to the improvement of its capacities (or to the hindrance of what hinders their functioning). In this sense, the means identified by indirect duties are means that define human beings as agents: they define the conditions of agency. This has two implications for their status as duties. First, as already noted, improving the means to realize our duty entails that we are thereby improving ourselves *qua* agents, which is certainly part of realizing the duty towards our own perfection. However, this point alone is not sufficient to differentiate between indirect duties and rules of skills. For one could also say that by improving one's skills, one is also improving oneself *qua* agent. But second, and more importantly, I want to argue that we could not actually maintain our moral standing whilst not performing the actions that fall under indirect duties. If so, this would imply that indirect duties are in fact proper duties.

To support this claim, it is necessary to go back to yet another imperative, namely the one that commands the use of all the means necessary to the realization of the ends that we are committed to: 'Whoever wills the end also wills [...] the indispensable necessary means to it that are within his power'.[21] From this imperative, it follows that if we are committed to the improvement of the capacities necessary to the actualization of our moral commitments (which we ought to be through direct duties), we are thereby committed to the means necessary to its realization (through indirect duties). Or put the other way round, if we are not actually committed to the means necessary to the improvement of our ability to actualize our moral commitments, we are in fact at least inconsistent *vis-à-vis* our moral commitments, at worst violating them. As Kant suggests,

> [W]ith respect to contingent (meritorious) duty to oneself, it is not enough that the action does not conflict with humanity in our person as an end in itself; it must also *harmonize with it*. Now there are in humanity predispositions to greater perfection, which belong to the end of nature with respect to humanity in our subject; to neglect these might admittedly be consistent with the *preservation* of humanity as an end in itself but not with the *furtherance* of this end.[22]

Thus, by being committed to the improvement of the capacities necessary to the actualization of our moral commitments, we are thereby committed to the means necessary to its realization.

Of course, one could object that in the case of indirect duties, these means are not strictly speaking necessary. For we could, in principle, act from duty without actively cultivating these capacities, and thus without cultivating what helps the improvement of these capacities. In this sense, from the perspective of the moral law, the link between the end (direct duties) and the means (indirect duties) remains contingent. The latter are not in fact duties.

Yet I believe that whilst this is true for rational beings in general, it is not the case for embodied human agents whose actions take place in the empirical world we know. Although indirect 'duties' are not entailed by the moral law, the fact that they are directed to an embodied human agent suggests that they can be said to be necessary given certain features of human nature. For the opacity of human motivation and the human propensity for deception (including self-deception) entail not only that we can never be certain of having ever acted from duty, but also that we can be mistaken about our moral strength: 'Very often he mistakes his own weakness, which counsels him against the venture of a misdeed, for virtue.'[23] So what is at stake here is not so much a matter of determining whether indirect 'duties' are proper duties (the answer to which is negative from the perspective of pure ethics). Rather it is a matter of understanding their function for embodied human agents. For it is the epistemic and moral opacity of human beings that creates the 'necessary' resort to the cultivation of their emotional capacities—what I could improperly call a "human necessity" or perhaps more accurately a human need.[24] If human beings could be certain of their motives and their moral strength, they would not need the emotional backup provided in the form of indirect duties. But insofar as they cannot be certain of it, they would be letting themselves down if they were not adopting indirect 'duties' as means to further their moral efficacy *and yet* claiming to be fully committed to realizing their moral ends. It is in this respect that indirect duties are not morally neutral, or at least they are not morally neutral in the same way as rules of skills.[25]

8.3 Indirect Duties, Freedom, and Feelings

Whilst what I have argued so far is sufficient to account for the moral nature of the duty to cultivate our emotions, it seems to create further conflicts with Kant's account of freedom. The indirect duties to cultivate certain capacities for feelings take the form of recommendations such as 'If you have a choleric temperament, you ought to learn to control your emotions so that it is easier for you to respect others.' There is no doubt that this claim is action-guiding: it is a recommendation that takes place from the practical standpoint and thus under the presupposition of freedom. However, it also seems to presuppose that feelings (which are part of the empirical dimension of the self) have an impact on our choices, and thus that we are not (or at least not fully) free. That is to say, it presupposes that our actions are in some sense determined or at least affected by empirical states and in particular our affective states. In other words, either feelings do affect our choices, in which case we are not working under the presupposition of freedom; or we are completely free from any empirical determination, in which case feelings become irrelevant to our moral choices.[26] Whichever way we go, it seems that we have to give up one of Kant's claims—either freedom or the moral relevance of feelings. Given Kant's transcendental framework, we seem to be stuck with the impossibility of any type of influence of the sensible on the intelligible. The implication of this claim takes the form of a dilemma. Theoretically, there can be no causal influence of the empirical on the intelligible and the only possible causal connection between the agent and his environment operates from the latter to his empirical character. Yet practically, our affective states seem to have a moral relevance that cannot be accounted for. As a result, either we should abandon the theoretical impossibility of an empirical influence on the intelligible, or we have to accept the moral irrelevance of these states, including feelings, emotions, and inclinations.

However, I believe that this dilemma is in fact based on a misunderstanding of the kind of claims that can be made from the practical standpoint. When I deliberate under the assumption of freedom, it certainly does feel like I am nevertheless affected by my desires, passions, feelings, and so on—in other words, the empirical world. So even from a practical standpoint, I have to take into account the naturalistic dimension of my self. But the crucial point is that doing so does not amount to presupposing that I am not free; it does not entail that empirical elements do in fact affect my choice. Rather, it amounts to seeing myself as an empirical being who is nonetheless free. Acting under the idea of freedom requires me to understand my experience of deliberation (which includes my feelings, my desires, my emotions, etc.) as compatible with the possibility of freedom, although I can neither know nor understand how I can be both empirically affected and yet free. As Kant writes,

> it is impossible to explain the phenomenon that at this parting of the ways (where the beautiful fable places Hercules between virtue and sensual pleasure) the human being shows more propensity to listen to his inclinations than to the law. For we can explain what happens only by deriving it from a cause in accordance with the laws of nature, and in so doing we would not be thinking of choice as free. —But it is this self-constraint in opposite directions and its unavoidability that makes known the inexplicable property of freedom itself.[27]

This is precisely the locus of the fundamental and necessary mystery of freedom: it cannot be known, but adopting the practical standpoint is nothing but presupposing that when I act, I can be affected by my affective states whilst being ultimately free to choose against them. Insofar as I have to assume that these elements affect me but do not determine my choice, I have to presuppose that I could always have acted otherwise, despite the fact that it is necessarily incomprehensible to me.

However, this still leaves our problem untouched, for if the two-standpoint interpretation is effective in making sense of the relevance of the empirical dimension of the self whilst preserving the possibility of freedom, it does not account for the moral relevance of emotions. Rather, it defines empirical claims about our emotional states on a par with other facts about the empirical world: for instance, that 'I am a body that acts in space and time', 'this person is my father', 'if I hit the ball, it will have these effects', and so on. There is no doubt that all these facts are relevant to my decision-making process insofar as they inform me about the world in which my actions take place. But the difficulty is precisely that certain facts about the world, namely facts about my emotional states, seem to have a special status *vis-à-vis* my decision-making process—which is why they are the object of indirect duties rather than mere rules of skill. Can this special status be accounted for?

I believe that on the basis of what I have argued so far, we can conclude that whilst claims about feelings are not morally relevant from the standpoint of the *rational* deliberating agent, from the standpoint of the *human* deliberating agent, an embodied agent who acts in the empirical world, feelings are morally relevant because they interfere with the realization of autonomy at the empirical level. Because of the opacity of motivation already mentioned in Section 8.2, we can never know whether we have ever met moral demands: we 'can never, even by the most strenuous self-examination, get entirely behind our covert incentives'.[28] Thus we do not know, and can never know, what an autonomous choice or a virtuous act looks like from an empirical perspective. Empirically, all actions appear the same insofar we have no insight into maxims and motives, whether our own or those of others. On my interpretation, indirect duties compensate for this opacity: their moral relevance consists in teaching us a certain way of thinking about how we, free beings, should act in the empirical world. Insofar as they are forward-looking, prescriptive duties, they instruct us that we should choose to control our emotions, cultivate our sympathetic feelings, and develop our self-mastery since these actions support the exercise of autonomy in the empirical world.

In this sense, our affective states are morally relevant to our exercise of freedom because exercising self-control, mastering all the elements that constitute our empirical selves, is nothing but how we must understand the practice of autonomy at the empirical level. This is why indirect duties about our emotional states can be prescriptive and action-guiding without threatening the presupposition of freedom. They are addressed to agents who are embodied, who 'feel nature's push' whilst they deliberate, despite the fact that they deliberate under the idea of freedom. In other words, for Kant, from the practical standpoint, the exercise of our rational and moral capacities is experienced 'as empirically embodied' (i.e., as taking place together with the experience of nature's push) rather than happening in some timeless inaccessible world. Since we must see ourselves as empirical beings who act freely, our emotional capacities can be morally relevant without threatening either our autonomy or our capacity for agency.

8.4 Conclusion

As is well known, Kant is often described in less than flattering terms as an abstract, moralizing, formalist philosopher. As the French poet Charles Péguy said, Kant has clean hands but he has no hands. What Péguy expresses is a very common criticism against what is often seen as Kant's lack of concern for some crucial dimensions of human life, and in particular the empirical, contingent, and messy features of worldly action.[29] What this chapter has tried to show is that Kant does have hands. Of course, a lot more needs to be said about how these hands actually relate to the rest of the Kantian body, but what I have argued is that, contrary to traditional portrayals of Kant's ethics, feelings not only play an important role in making us more efficient moral agents, their cultivation is part and parcel of our moral duties and thus a crucial part of our moral lives.[30]

Acknowledgements

An earlier version of this paper was presented at a workshop on Eighteenth-Century Anthropology at the University of St Andrews and the UK Kant Society at the University of Lancaster. I would like to thank all the participants for their helpful comments, and in particular Jens Timmermann and Alice Pinheiro Walla.

Notes

1. Immanuel Kant, 'Groundwork', in *Practical Philosophy*, ed. Mary J. Gregor (Cambridge: Cambridge University Press, 1999), pp. 37–108 (p. 79 [4:428]). In all reference to Kant's texts, I have included a citation to the English translation in parentheses, followed by a citation to the German text of the Prussian Academy edition (volume and page reference) in brackets.
2. Immanuel Kant, 'Critique of Practical Reason', in *Practical Philosophy*, ed. Mary J. Gregor (Cambridge: Cambridge University Press, 1999), pp. 133–271 (p. 235 [5:118]).
3. Immanuel Kant, 'Metaphysics of Morals', in *Practical Philosophy*, ed. Mary J. Gregor (Cambridge: Cambridge University Press, 1999), pp. 353–603 (p. 536 [6:408]).
4. Kant, *Metaphysics of Morals*, p. 575 [6:456–7].
5. Kant, *Metaphysics of Morals*, p. 529 [6:400].
6. '[C]ommon human reason, with this compass in hand [the moral law], knows very well how to distinguish in every case that comes up what is good and what is evil, what is in conformity with duty or contrary to duty' (Kant, *Groundwork*, p. 58 [4:404]).
7. Kant, *Groundwork*, p. 65 [4:411]. As Sherman puts it, they 'serve poorly both as norms and as motives' (Nancy Sherman, *Making a Necessity of Virtue: Aristotle and Kant on Virtue* (Cambridge: Cambridge University Press, 1997), p. 128).
8. Kant, *Metaphysics of Morals*, p. 575–6 [6:456–7].
9. Think of the misanthrope of the *Groundwork* who happens to feel indifferent towards others (Kant, *Groundwork*, p. 54 [4:398–9]).
10. Kant, *Metaphysics of Morals*, p. 575 [6:456–7].
11. Kant, *Critique of Practical Reason*, p. 207 [5:83].
12. Kant, *Metaphysics of Morals*, p. 564 [6:443]. Kant makes a similar claim against the mal-treatment of animals: 'A propensity to wanton destruction of what is *beautiful* in inanimate nature (*spiritus destructionis*) is opposed to a human being's duty to himself; for it weakens or uproots that feeling in him which, though not of itself moral, is still a disposition of sensibility that greatly promotes morality or at least prepares the way for it: the disposition, namely, to love something [...] even apart from any intention to use it.' (Kant, *Metaphysics of Morals*, p. 564 [6:443]).
13. Kant, *Metaphysics of Morals*, 523 [6:392–3].
14. Kant, *Metaphysics of Morals*, p. 521 [6:390].
15. Immanuel Kant, 'Anthropology from a Pragmatic Point of View', in *Anthropology, History and Education*, ed. Gunter Zöller and Robert B. Louden (Cambridge: Cambridge University Press, 2007), pp. 227–429 (pp. 386–8 [7:288–90]).

See also Immanuel Kant, *Observations on the Feeling of the Beautiful and Sublime* in *Anthropology, History and Education*, ed. Gunter Zöller and Robert B. Louden (Cambridge: Cambridge University Press, 2007), pp. 18–62 (pp. 33–6 [2:220–4]).

16. Knowledge of one's temperament is also a crucial help to moral deliberation. For knowing one's temperament points to potential moral pitfalls, and thus makes one's deliberation more effective. However, since this chapter is focused on the cultivation of emotions, I will not discuss it here. See Cohen, *Kant and the Human Sciences*, ch. 4.
17. Kant, *Anthropology*, p. 386 [7:288].
18. Kant, *Groundwork*, pp. 49–50 [4:393–4].
19. Kant, *Groundwork*, p. 68 [4:415].
20. This is what Timmermann argues: '"indirect" duty is not even a lesser kind of duty: it is not a species of duty at all. [...] Any of these actions [commanded by indirect duties] are *per se* morally neutral acts because they are not immediately made *necessary* by the moral law' (Jens Timmermann, 'Kant on Conscience, "Indirect" Duty, and Moral Error', *International Philosophical Quarterly*, 46 (2006): 293–308 (pp. 298–9).
21. Kant, *Groundwork*, p. 70 [4:417]. As O'Neill comments, '[t]his amounts to saying that to will some end without willing whatever means are indispensable for that end, insofar as they are available, is, even when the end itself involves no conceptual inconsistency, to involve oneself in a volitional inconsistency. It is to embrace at least one specific intention that, far from being guided by the underlying intention or principle, is inconsistent with that intention or principle' (Onora O'Neill, *Constructions of Reason* (Cambridge: Cambridge University Press, 1989), p. 91.
22. Kant, *Groundwork*, pp. 80–1 [4:430]. See also 'Imperfect duties alone are, accordingly, *duties of virtue*. Fulfilment of them is *merit* (*meritum*) = – a: but failure to fulfil them is not in itself *culpability* (*demeritum*) = – a) but rather mere *deficiency in moral worth* = o [...] It is only the strength of one's resolution, in the first case, that is properly called *virtue* (*virtus*); one's weakness, in the second case, is not so much *vice* (*vitium*) as rather mere *want of virtue*, lack of moral strength (*defectus moralis*).' (Kant, *Metaphysics of Morals*, p. 521 [6:390]).
23. Kant, *Metaphysics of Morals*, p. 523 [6:392–3].
24. See for instance the end of the passage I have already referred to: 'The depths of the human heart are unfathomable. [...] our cognition of ourselves can never adequately tell us whether [a sum of virtues] is complete or deficient' (Kant, *Metaphysics of Morals*, p. 567 [6:447]).
25. So in contrast with Timmermann, I believe that taking one's clothes off in order to save a drowning child is not a rule of skill of the same kind as taming one's inclinations or pursuing one's own happiness (Timmermann, 'Kant on Conscience', p. 299). The analogy between indirect duties and the various ways of rescuing someone is misleading because it overlooks the fact that the former are concerned with improving the self's capacities and thus its *moral* efficaciousness rather than its general efficaciousness (Timmermann, 'Kant on Conscience', p. 308).
26. For another formulation of this problem, see Patrick Frierson, 'Two Standpoints and the Problem of Moral Anthropology', in *Kant's Moral Metaphysics*, ed. James Krueger & Benjamin Bruxvoort Lipscomb (Berlin: Walter De Gruyter, 2010).
27. Kant, *Metaphysics of Morals*, p. 512fn [6:380].
28. Kant, *Groundwork*, p. 53 [4:397].

29. For similar criticisms, see for instance Bernard Williams's denunciation of Kant's 'purist view of morality' (Bernard Williams, 'Evolution, Ethics, and the Representation Problem', in *Making Sense of Humanity* (New York: Cambridge University Press, 1995), p. 104), Annette Baier's denunciation of Kant as a 'misamorist' (Annette Baier, *Moral Prejudices* (Cambridge, MA: Harvard University Press, 1994), p. 48), Simon Blackburn's mocking reference to the 'Kantian captain' (Simon Blackburn, *Ruling Passions* (Oxford: Oxford University Press, 1998), p. 252), and Susan Wolf's denigration of Kant as the 'Rational Saint' (Susan Wolf, 'Moral Saints', *The Journal of Philosophy* 79 (1982): 430–2).
30. For recent works that go in the same direction, see for instance Alix Cohen (ed.), *Kant on Emotion and Value* (London: Palgrave, 2014), and more generally the works of Barbara Herman, Nancy Sherman, Marcia Baron, Patrick Frierson, Robert Louden, and Allen Wood.

Bibliography

Cohen, Alix. *Kant and the Human Sciences: Biology, Anthropology and History* (London: Palgrave Macmillan, 2009).

Frierson, Patrick. 'Two Standpoints and the Problem of Moral Anthropology', in *Kant's Moral Metaphysics*, ed. James Krueger and Benjamin Bruxvoort Lipscomb (Berlin: Walter De Gruyter, 2010), pp. 83–110.

Kant, Immanuel. *Lectures on Ethics* (Cambridge: Cambridge University Press, 1997).

Kant, Immanuel. *Practical Philosophy* (Cambridge: Cambridge University Press, 1999).

Kant, Immanuel. *Religion and Rational Theology* (Cambridge: Cambridge University Press, 2001).

Kant, Immanuel. *Anthropology, History and Education* (Cambridge: Cambridge University Press, 2007).

Kant, Immanuel. *Lectures on Anthropology* (Cambridge: Cambridge University Press, 2014).

Louden, Robert B. *Kant's Impure Ethics: From Rational Beings to Human Beings* (New York, Oxford: Oxford University Press, 2000).

Louden, Robert B. 'The Second Part of Morals', in *Essays on Kant's Anthropology*, ed. Patrick Kain and Brian Jacobs (Cambridge: Cambridge University Press, 2003).

O'Neill, Onora. *Constructions of Reason* (Cambridge: Cambridge University Press, 1989).

Schmidt, Claudia. 'The Anthropological Dimension of Kant's Metaphysics of Morals', *Kant-Studien* 96 (2005): 66–84.

Sherman, Nancy. *Making a Necessity of Virtue: Aristotle and Kant on Virtue.* (Cambridge: Cambridge University Press, 1997).

Sullivan, Roger. *Immanuel Kant's Moral Theory* (Cambridge: Cambridge University Press, 1989).

Timmermann, Jens. 'Kant on Conscience, "Indirect" Duty, and Moral Error', *International Philosophical Quarterly* 46 (2006): 293–308.

9

Grace, Freedom, and the Expression of Emotion

Schiller and the Critique of Kant

Christopher Bennett

In this chapter I ask what Schiller can tell us about expressive action, specifically the expression of emotion. Schiller's discussion of the expression of emotion takes place in the context of his arguments for the importance of *grace*, a value he thinks neglected by Kant's writings on ethics. Grace is sometimes thought of as moral beauty, and its interest specifically aesthetic as opposed to ethical.[1] For this reason Schiller's concerns are sometimes regarded as peripheral to the main business of moral and political philosophy. However, I will argue that what is at stake in Schiller's discussion of grace is rather the nature of freedom and the development of a distinctive model of human perfection.

The expressions of emotion that help to constitute grace, on Schiller's view, are not merely physiological changes that accompany emotion; neither are we to understand 'expression of emotion' in the way that later philosophers and artists would see this as relating to the nature of art—at least not in the first instance (there will be a connection with the nature of art to be explored further on).[2] Rather, we are concerned here with expressions of emotion that are *gestures*. We can think of these as being like the 'arational actions' discussed by Rosalind Hursthouse, for instance, jumping for joy, hitting the table in anger, ruffling a child's hair out of affection, hugging a dead beloved's clothes in grief—in other words the gamut of what we call 'action out of emotion'.[3] The characteristic of such action, we might say, is that it is voluntary, intentional action (unlike blushing or crying) through which the presence of the emotion is manifested; where the intention, however, is not to express the emotion; but where the fact that the emotion is manifested has some formative influence on the resultant action. Another way of putting the point, close to Hursthouse's characterization, is that the action is voluntary, but does not seem to be directed at a further end (even an end such as displaying or communicating or venting the emotion)—rather, the action is expressive. That is why it seems appropriate to explain it as having been done 'out of emotion' rather than with some further end in mind.

I will argue that Schiller notices that actions like this pose a problem for what he takes to be an attractive, Kantian conception of freedom. I don't think that he solves the problem. But his wrestling with it is instructive. We could put the point like this. Either we act freely when acting out of emotion, or we do not. If we do not act freely, it looks as though we must take ourselves to be literally overpowered by emotion. But this does not seem to be correct—many actions out of emotion, as Hursthouse points out, are controlled and intentional actions. Therefore, we might be pushed to view action out of emotion as free action. But if free then, on the Kantian view, this can only be because action out of emotion is responsive to laws of reason that govern the action in question. So, how can we see action out of emotion as governed by rational laws? Two possibilities suggest themselves. Either action out of emotion is subsumed under the already-accepted Kantian principles of practical reason—so, for instance, the way we act when we act out of emotion is governed by principles such as universalizability and nothing more—or else we have to admit further principles of practical reason governing the expression of emotion in particular. Kantians may be tempted to take the first line—but this may simply add to the impression that they cannot explain the rationality of action from emotion. The second response, by contrast, will lead us to a kind of rationalist phenomenology of the emotions, on which emotions bear a strong relation to judgements and other cognitive attitudes, and which we might see as running through Franz Brentano and Max Scheler, to Charles Taylor and Martha Nussbaum via Anthony Kenny's *Action, Emotion and Will*.[4] The key claims of this view would be something like this: that justificatory reasons do, in principle, govern emotions and emotional behaviour; that this is in part because emotions are complex states with rich intentional content, and emotional behaviour bears some intelligible relation to that content; that these reasons may, indeed, be central to morality; and that, because these reasons are specific to the realm of the emotions, the emotions would be our medium for discovering such reasons.

Schiller does not take this second path. But he does stand at a pivotal point in its history. For he accepts that action out of emotion cannot be explained simply mechanistically, and accepts the Kantian conception of freedom as spontaneity; but he breaks new ground in asking how that view—of spontaneous action as action responsive to principles of practical reason—is to be reconciled with the fact that sometimes we act expressively, out of emotion. The ideal of grace is an ideal where we act expressively yet freely. If grace requires something of us in regards to the emotions we feel and the way we express them then, from Schiller's point of view, this means that only with certain expressive tendencies can we be truly free.

The central topic of the paper, then, is the expression of emotion, but in order to explain the distinctiveness of Schiller's view we must first explain what is at stake in it. Thus in Section 9.1 I give an introduction to Schiller's moral psychology, emphasizing his concern with freedom and, because of that, the distinctive model of human perfection that he introduces. This model of freedom and perfection is examined in more detail in Section 9.2; and Schiller's theory of beauty in art is introduced to help explain it in Section 9.3. In Section 9.4 I look at the range of theoretical possibilities for analyzing Schiller's model. In Section 9.5, I defend the view that Schiller's model is a model of expressive action; and Section 9.6 asks what we can learn from Schiller about the study of emotion and its expression. Section 9.7 concludes.

9.1 An Introduction to Schiller's Moral Psychology

In this chapter I will concentrate on Schiller's views as expressed in the *Kallias Letters*, his essay *On Grace and Dignity*, and his *Letters on the Aesthetic Education of Man* (*Aesthetic Letters*).[5] Schiller's philosophical writings reveal a concern with a number of related themes. In this section I give a survey of some of Schiller's characteristic concerns and positions.

First of all, Schiller is concerned with the nature of freedom. He takes it that freedom is both, on the one hand, a key value to be realized in a person's life and in political society, and on the other a basic and defining feature of human agency. In a letter to his friend Körner he says: 'Certainly, no greater words have ever been spoken by a mortal human being than these Kantian ones, which at the same time are the content of his whole philosophy: determine yourself!'[6] Thus Schiller seems to agree with the Kantian belief in the possibility of spontaneity, as much as he agrees with Kant's attachment to the nobility of the life in which we gives laws to ourselves rather than receiving them passively from outside. Schiller's conception of freedom appears to change through his life[7]—for instance, there is a conception of freedom as liberation from social rules celebrated in his early play *The Robbers*, which it might be thought that the older Schiller came to reject. But the attempt to define and capture the importance of freedom, particularly in opposition to Kant, seems to have been an abiding concern.

Secondly, Schiller follows Kant in accepting an important link between our freedom and our capacity for rational thought and agency. He recognizes that this implies a distinction between those aspects of the self that are capable of rational thought and directly controllable by it, and those that are not. This explains his recognition of some distinction or split between reason and materiality.

However, and this is the third general theme, Schiller rejects what he sees as the Kantian approach of treating these distinctions in too rigid a way. He is concerned, on the one hand, with a range of issues to do with the emotions, taste, the non-arbitrariness of sensible and not merely rational or intellectual responses to the world, and the nature and appreciation of art: the very possibility of such 'educated' or 'fine' sensibility; and its role in the good human life and society. And on the other hand, he is concerned about the effect on the quality of human life of seeing ourselves as definitively split in such a way. We can briefly point to two aspects of this concern. Firstly, Schiller is concerned about the very fact of fragmentation within the individual psyche—as displayed for instance in his concerns about the effects of specialization in modern society in the famous seventh of the *Aesthetic Letters*.[8] And secondly, he is worried, as we will see, that where there are two intractably distinct faculties, the only way forward is for one to dominate the other. This suggests that Schiller is concerned, not just with harmonious integration of the elements of the psyche, but also that each should have space to develop in its own way, undominated by force external to itself. Only thus, Schiller will suggest, can the human being as a whole be free.

Schiller, therefore, is interested in the way in which the apparent split between reason and sensibility, which we seem forced to accept if we are to explain how and to what extent human beings can subject their behaviour to standards that they could endorse on reflection, can be overcome in certain respects in order to allow for the possibility of harmonious and all-round human development and adequate sensible responses to morality and the arts. His way of thinking about this tends to emphasize, not that the Kantian dichotomies are illusory, or that it is only at a superficial initial level of analysis that reason and sensibility are truly distinct (as later thinkers in the Idealist or Romantic traditions would claim),[9] but rather that there is greater scope for cooperation between the two sides than Kant recognizes. But whether or not we regard that solution as sufficient, it is clear that Schiller is responsible for raising important questions that those following him have also wanted to ask about Kantian ethics. For one thing we can see innovations such as his conception of the 'play-drive' in the *Aesthetic Letters*, which consists in a proper balance between reason and sensibility, as an early version of the concept of unity-in-difference (or the unity of unity and multiplicity) that would play such an important role in the later history of German philosophy.[10] We can also see his thinking as playing an important role in the development of ideas of freedom and perfection, perhaps making Schiller the first to attempt to develop what Douglas Moggach has called a 'post-Kantian perfectionism'.[11]

9.2 Schiller's Model of Freedom

As I have mentioned, Schiller's attempt to overcome the opposition between reason and sensibility involves a commitment to the possibility of unity-in-difference (or the 'unity of unity and multiplicity'); and his way of thinking about this possibility involves thinking of the differentiated elements as having a certain nature that causes them to behave in potentially conflicting ways, but where this nature is in some way malleable rather than fixed and intractable, and hence open to creative transformation.[12] Frederick Beiser has pointed out that Schiller's ambition for this reconciliation of opposites in unity is exhibited, not just in his moral psychology, but also in his thinking about political arrangements, and in his thinking about the nature of beauty in the work of art.[13] Beiser thinks that there is continuity between Schiller's views on these topics, and that some apparently peculiar claims that Schiller put forward can be made more intelligible when seen in the light of his early writings.

In 'Grace and Dignity', the psychological reconciliation is illustrated by means of a political analogy. One type of political arrangement comes about when a ruler imposes his will on his subjects in opposition to their inclinations. Another type comes about when the subjects impose their will on the ruler. Both of these are unsatisfactory: the one dictatorial; the other disordered and anarchic. The latter is formless; the former has form but it is harsh and imposed against the will of the populace. But a third possibility is that type of liberal government under which, although ruled over by the will of some particular ruler, each citizen 'can still persuade himself that he is living according to his own lights and simply following his inclinations'.[14] Here, the idea is, there is form that does not do violence to its material, but rather appears to arise spontaneously. On the 'republican' reading of Schiller, this in turn requires that citizens have acquired certain virtues.[15] This is Schiller's model for the rule of reason over sensibility: it is at its best where sensibility appears to be following its own course yet nevertheless does the bidding of reason:

> Humans either suppress the demands of their sensuous nature in order to have a proper relation to the higher demands of their rational nature; or they reverse this and subjugate the rational part of their being to the sensuous . . . ; or the impulses of the sensuous settle into harmony with the rules of the rational and human beings are at one with themselves.[16]

It is perhaps hard to know how to unpack this metaphor. But the basic idea is that, not only our rational nature, but also the matter/particular/content side of things, has a claim that has to be respected; that in some way things are better for a human being, or perhaps the human being herself is better, when this claim is respected; and that the highest form of being is therefore one in which harmony between the two sides of human nature is achieved.[17]

Now this is not just Schiller's view of beauty or human perfection, or the fulfilment of human nature; it is also his view of freedom, properly conceived. His idea is that freedom must be freedom of the whole person; and therefore that a being whose rational nature must coerce and suppress its sensible side cannot be fully free. Schiller is therefore offering an internal critique of Kant's approach to ethics. Kant's conception of autonomy, he takes it, requires only that reason should be unimpeded by sensibility in its determination of the will; specific states of sensibility are at best irrelevant to autonomy.[18] Schiller's claim, by contrast, is that we are not truly *free* if our rational will is simply imposed on sensibility; it is only when sensibility is somehow respected and integrated that we are free. Since the human being as a whole combines reason and sensibility, the mere imposition of the demands of reason on sensibility must be experienced as brute constraint by some aspect of one's being.[19] But freedom, Schiller reasons, must be increased when one's being is under less constraint. Therefore freedom must be greater when two conditions are met: firstly, one's action and character are such that one behaves rationally without one's sensibility stopping one from doing so; and secondly, at the same time in behaving as reason requires one does not leave sensibility unsatisfied. For genuine freedom to arise some integration is necessary whereby an agent can satisfy sensibility *through*, or at least concurrently with, following the demands of reason. The problem of fragmentation is not simply the aesthetic one that we fail to be beautiful when there is no harmony. And neither is it (simply) that when we fail to achieve harmony we fall short of human perfection. Rather, Schiller is concerned with the ways in which internal fragmentation and division make us unfree by restricting the free development of one or other central aspect of the self.

However, Schiller is concerned not only with the internal psychological structure of freedom, but also its external appearance. It is for this reason that Schiller's choice of the term 'grace' is not arbitrary, and neither does it imply a concern with the purely aesthetic intruding into his account of moral behaviour.[20] Schiller takes it that there is a deep connection between freedom, beauty, and perfection.[21] As we will see in more detail further on, he thinks that when one behaves in such a way as to be truly free—in the sense that one's sensibility is unconstrained and appears to satisfy its own demands yet conforms to morality—one appears as beautiful. One will appear as graceful, or beautiful in a specific respect, when one's actions effortlessly rather than unwillingly comply with morality.

Furthermore, although I have argued that Schiller is concerned with freedom rather than perfection, a more adequate way of putting it might be that, for Schiller, true freedom *requires* a certain kind of perfection. For Schiller, freedom requires that neither side of human nature should impose constraint on the other; it involves, in other words, an arrangement in which each side should be allowed space for the full development of its demands, while at the same time, the integration of these demands with those of the other side. This is a version of the thought that human perfection involves the full development but also the integration of a human being's faculties and powers: in this case, there are basically two powers, each with its own developmental potential or trajectory; the two powers are potentially conflicting; but when both fully realize themselves yet also cohere, there is the perfection of what, in the *Aesthetic Letters*, Schiller calls 'play'. And that can be thought of as a distinctive conception of perfection.[22] It is not a view of human perfection on the model of a pre-existing blueprint that appropriately trained inquirers can cognize, apply to their own case, and hence realize in their own person. Rather, the Schillerian model makes central a certain type of internal relation between the different parts according to which unity can be achieved, a unity that does not require us to posit a pre-existing model of perfection accessible to cognition. However, the model cannot be wholly formal either. This is because both reason and sensibility must be understood as having a certain content or developmental trajectory, such that certain forms of imposition by the other side of the person will amount to a distortion or unfulfilment or transgression of the demands of the oppressed side. In other words, for Schiller to be able to claim that the Kantian model of autonomy is compatible with sensibility being merely coerced or (less metaphorically) frustrated it must be the case that sensibility has an inner tendency towards certain determinate kinds of satisfactions. Thus Schiller's perfectionism emphasizes a formal arrangement of parts, but it requires that these parts have a content of their own in order to make meaningful his requirement that the other side should not interfere with the development of that content.

9.3 Beauty as the Appearance of Freedom

We can get a better idea of what this model of freedom involves by looking at Schiller's early writings on the nature of the beautiful work of art. In these early writings similar concerns about the relation between freedom, perfection (or beauty), form, and content are in evidence. And this will also give us a chance to address a concern that might have arisen about the model as explained so far. The concern comes in the form of a dilemma. Certainly, it might be said, it can be understood that practical reason has its requirements, and that sensibility has its own inner tendencies. But the most plausible way in which the tendencies of sensibility should be understood makes it hard to see how the two sides can be reconciled. Desires and emotions have natural ends—food, sex, warmth, reputation, perhaps—but unconstrained by reason and will they lead away from morality and impartial concern for others. The only way out of this is to build moral motivation into sensibility in the first place. But then it is unclear whether we can really talk about sensibility having these motivations as an inner tendency. Schiller's response to this dilemma is complex, and we will look at it in more detail as we go through. Indeed, there is a question whether he has a satisfying response to this dilemma. But as mentioned above, his response has to be to see the content of both reason and sensibility as not fixed and intractable but capable of mutual adjustment. This is what is suggested in his model of freedom in the artwork.

Let us turn, then to Schiller's crucial claim that freedom is not just autonomy but 'heautonomy', as this idea is developed in relation to artworks in the *Kallias Letters*. Heautonomy, Schiller claims, is the 'inner principle of the existence of a thing, which can be at the same time seen as the ground of its form: *the inner necessity of form*'.[23] The idea, as we will develop it below, is that the principles of form relevant for a certain being are not merely laws stemming from the nature of that thing, as (he thinks) they would be in autonomy; rather, they are at the same time freely given, such that the being is freely complying with the demands of its own nature.[24] Let us explore this complex idea in more detail.

First of all, it will come as a surprise to many readers that we look to artworks to discover what Schiller thinks about freedom; so this requires some initial explanation. In this early set of letters to his friend Körner, Schiller aims to provide an 'objective criterion of beauty'. For Schiller, this criterion is 'freedom in appearance': what is beautiful is such because it appears (as it happens, illusorily) to be free or, crucially, self-determining.[25] Furthermore, the structure of self-determination that Schiller ascribes to the artwork is similar in some respects to that exhibited by the self-determining human agent, particularly in the aspect of reconciling two apparently irreconcilable opposites: form and matter (or reason and sensibility).

In brief paraphrase, Schiller's argument seems to go something like this. An artifact is such that it normally draws attention to the purpose for which it is made. In Schiller's terms, this means that it appears to us as having been determined 'from the outside'—that is, according to a purpose or rule extrinsic to itself. This is not to say that it cannot exhibit a kind of perfection. A house or a chair may be perfectly suited to its function. In this case, it perfectly complies with the rule for a thing of that type. But it is not beautiful by virtue of that perfection. Schiller's diagnosis of this is that beauty only arises when the object appears, not merely to have had a certain form given to it (from outside, by a maker, according to a certain further end), however perfectly, but rather to somehow be *freely adapting* itself to that form.[26] Beauty is 'the inner necessity of form' and arises when the object not only perfectly obeys or conforms to a rule, but appears to have *given the rule to itself*.[27] As with his account of freedom in human nature, the material of which the artwork is made has its own tendencies and claims that have to be respected. Nevertheless, in the case of the artwork, the freedom in question is only a matter of effect or appearance: the artwork is not free even in the noumenal realm. An artwork is always created 'from the outside' by a maker who has certain motivations and is abiding by a more or less determinate conception of the thing being made.[28] Thus, although in some sense we always know the artwork's origins, beauty is achieved when it is created in such a way that we do not attend to those origins, and thus it compellingly appears self-determining: 'thus a form appears as free as soon as we are neither able nor inclined to search for its ground outside it'.[29]

This might all seem hopelessly metaphorical, but an example might help to illustrate the point:

> A landscape is beautifully composed if all of the particular parts out of which it is constituted play along together so well that they set their own limitations, and the whole becomes the result of the freedom of the particular parts. Everything in a landscape must refer to the whole and yet the particular should only be constrained by its own rule, should only seem to follow its own will. But it is impossible that the process of cohering to a whole should not require some sacrifices on the part of the particular, since a collision of freedoms is unavoidable ... Freedom comes about because each restricts its inner freedom such as to allow every other to express its freedom. A tree in the foreground might cover a nice spot in the background; to require of the tree that it not do this would come to close to its freedom and would reveal dilettantism. What does the able artist do? He allows that branch of the tree which threatened to cover the background to sink down under its own weight and thus freely make place for the view behind it; thus the tree fulfils the will of the artist by following its own.[30]

Thus a successful artwork must achieve some arrangement of the whole, an arrangement that will be determined in part by the nature of the medium, the rules of the genre, etc. Furthermore, when we look at the individual components of the work, such as the tree, again there is a sense in which they are as they are to serve the overall purposes of the work. But to be successful these rules should not constrain the work of art; rather the work in its very nature should seem to need precisely those rules and precisely that medium. Thus the tree which needs to allow the view behind it to be seen must be portrayed as sinking down *under its own weight.*

However we judge its success as an aesthetic theory,[31] Schiller's view is intriguing. It is presumably this view that is in the background of Schiller's claim (or rather assumption) that the appearance of genuine freedom in human behaviour—as grace—will necessarily appear beautiful to us. One of the theoretical attractions of the view as a theory of beauty is perhaps that it is in large part a formal conception of beauty. Though, as discussed above in relation to human perfection, it requires the parts to have some content of their own, this substantive aspect is small. For Schiller's model dictates nothing about what the content or claims of the individual elements should be; it simply requires that there should be such content, and that perfection in life and art arises when the claims associated with such content can be made compossible.

I will argue that Schiller's most direct and promising account of what such reconciliation between form and matter would look like when applied to human psychology comes in the case of the expression of emotion. The category of emotion is itself hard to disentangle into cognitive and non-cognitive elements, and rather seems to be a synthesis of the two. Schiller is aware of this, and argues that it is in emotion and its expression that reason and sensibility can be seen as cooperating. Indeed, as I suggested at the outset, we can see Schiller as looking at the phenomenon of the expression of emotion and arguing that this phenomenon is hard to do justice to on the Kantian assumption that reason and sensibility are radically at odds. But a corollary of this, on Schiller's view, is that it is in and through our capacity for emotion that we are enabled to achieve the balance between reason and sensibility without which the two sides of our nature would merely be at war. Emotion is therefore a crucial mediating category, on Schiller's account. The question, however, is what sort of mediation this represents. Before we look at his analysis in detail, we will look in Section 9.4 at the range of theoretical possibilities.

9.4 On Reconciling Reason and Sensibility: Some Possibilities

> When the mind expresses itself in the sensuous nature that depends on it [*in der von ihm abhängenden sinnlichen Natur*] in such a way that nature faithfully carries out the will of the mind and expresses its sentiments clearly, without contravening the demands that the senses make on them as appearances, then there will arise what we call grace. However, one would be equally far from calling it grace if either the mind were to reveal itself forcibly in the sensuous or if the expression of the mind were missing from the free effect of the sensuous. For in the first case there would be no beauty present and in the second it would not be the beauty of play.[32]

Schiller's view here seems to be that there can be expressions of the mind that take place in the 'free play of the sensuous'. Before we look at this view in more detail in Section 9.5, it will be useful to put it in the context of a range of competing views of how reason and sensibility might interact and harmonize.

The central axis on which these views differ is the extent to which, and the means by which, sensibility can be responsive to reason. The first would be a conception of instrumental reason: here sensibility is unresponsive to reason, but reason can harmonize with desire because the only job reason has is to seek means to the satisfaction of desires. In an expansive view, instrumental reason might also have the job of ordering less fundamental desires according to more fundamental desires, however 'fundamental' is to be understood. This might end up, as some have argued, giving a close approximation to a more rationalistic account of the will. But however plausible this line might be, we will not pursue it here, since it is clear that Schiller subscribes to a more substantial account of the authority of reason.

Secondly, then, we might instead have a view on which reason and desire harmonize because reason can understand the ends proper to a human being, and can approve of the extent to which desires have been trained to pursue those ends. On the (Aristotelian) view I am imagining,[33] the desires and emotions themselves are non-cognitive as on the instrumental conception, but are more malleable and trainable, and there are rational standards that they have to meet such as some objective standards of flourishing or appropriateness. Reason can recognize these standards and hence approve of the desires which have been brought indirectly into line with those standards, for instance through their cultivation in a good upbringing.

A third form of harmonization would come about where there is a desire to do as reason demands. This interpretation is suggested by Schiller's claim, in 'Grace and Dignity', which virtue consists in an 'inclination for duty'.[34] In other words, the virtuous person is in a state of harmony because or insofar as her desires cohere with her most fundamental desire, and her most fundamental desire is to do her duty, whatever that turns out to be. Some may think that such an inclination would be a strange one to have. The claim has been put forward by Bernard Williams and Michael Smith that moral desires tend to be for particular ends, such as the welfare of this particular person, rather than for 'what is right, because it is right'.[35] On the other hand, however, perhaps it does not seem so implausible that a person might have a desire to act rightly on the basis of some recognition of the importance of right. But putting the matter this way leads us to see that there are two ways of thinking about this position. The way I just put it is that the desire arises *as a result of* some rational apprehension of desirability. Otherwise put, the inclination is responsive to reason or intellectual apprehension. That is one way of thinking about the possibility of harmony between reason and sensibility: that at least some aspects of sensibility are as they are because of our grasp of considerations that are accessible to reason.[36] On the other hand, the second way of understanding this view would be to think of the inclination for duty as simply a desire that is hardwired into us alongside desires for food, warmth, sex, and so on. This position would perhaps look strange; one might be drawn to it if, however, one thinks that reason and sensibility are quite distinct faculties and that sensibility cannot properly be said to be capable of being informed by reason.

Therefore one might have the view that there are forms of sensibility like an inclination for duty, and then think either that the inclinations themselves are cognitive, and responsive to the authority or majesty of duty, or one might have the view that they are non-cognitive and merely coincide with duty.

The view quoted at the start of this section, with its talk of the 'expression of the mind in the sensuous nature that depends on it', seems to envisage a more intimate connection between reason and sensibility than any of those views that see sensibility as non-cognitive. However, it also seems to gesture towards something more than just an 'inclination for duty', however that should be understood. Indeed, if one accepts that reason can inform, shape, and perhaps initiate forms of sensibility such as an inclination for duty then perhaps there is no principled reason why one should not accept other forms of interaction between reason and sensibility. At any rate one would need to make controversial meta-ethical assumptions to explain why only duty can be the object of those cognitive emotions whose existence one has accepted. Otherwise, by allowing at least one inclination that depends for its nature on existence on the way its object is cognized, one has opened the doors to a wide range of cognitive emotions and desires in which sensibility is responsive to and capable of being directly shaped by cognitive considerations—that is, considerations that can come up in a subject's deliberations, and may continue to appear authoritative on reflection. Hence, if this is Schiller's view then perhaps we could see him as an early proponent of something like that cognitivist tradition of the emotions, mentioned earlier, that runs through Brentano to Nussbaum.

That this possibility is envisaged by Schiller is, however, denied by Stephen Houlgate in a recent paper.[37] Houlgate argues that, for Schiller:

> Human actions are beautiful when our sensible nature is not under the direct control of our free reason, but when it accords independently and autonomously with the demands of our free reason. Beauty in human action thus consists in the harmonious coordination and cooperation of two quite distinct autonomies: the autonomy of our sensuous nature and the autonomy of our free, moral reason. Neither directs the other, but each follows (or appears to follow) its own law. Yet the two fit together harmoniously as in an arabesquely composed English dance.[38]

And Houlgate quotes Schiller's view, from the *Kallias Letters*, that the image of the dance captures most aptly his image of the cooperation of the two faculties in action:

> Everything has been arranged such that the first has already made room for the second before he arrives, everything comes together so skillfully and yet so artlessly that both seem merely to be following their own mind and still never get in the way of the other. Thus is the most fitting picture of maintained person freedom and the spared freedom of the other.[39]

On this picture of their relationship, reason and sensibility interact with one another to the limited extent of setting limits to one another, and cooperate freely with one another in producing action (though how exactly this process is envisaged is pretty mysterious). But what is not taken as a possibility here is that sensibility might actually be directly responsive to the demands of reason. 'What is never considered', Houlgate claims, is precisely what I want to say that Schiller does recognize and go some way to developing: 'that free reason might actually *manifest*, *express* or *embody* itself directly in the realm of the senses'.[40] This passage is quoted, as Houlgate acknowledges, from an early work. But although he recognizes that later works may be more complex and subtle, Houlgate thinks that Schiller could never significantly assent to this genuinely expressive view. The culprit, he thinks, is that, 'for all his subtlety, Schiller's thought remain in thrall to Kant's distinction between reason and sensibility', implausibly seeing the two sides as autonomous parties that must learn to cooperate rather than two aspects of a higher unity. However, as we will now see, I think that we can find precisely that expressive view in 'On Grace and Dignity'.

9.5 Schiller on Emotion and Expression

We are now ready to look in more detail at Schiller's claims about emotion and its role in the reconciliation of opposites in moral psychology. The reason I would like to look at 'Grace and Dignity' in particular is that here we find a detailed model of how reason and sensibility might cooperate rather than merely dominate one another in human behaviour. The model is 'drawn from life' or given in examples, rather than based on the sometimes ponderous metaphysical psychology unveiled in the *Aesthetic Letters*. I will suggest that the account given here shows that Schiller clearly envisages genuinely expressive action. However, it is also true that many aspects of Schiller's view do seem premised on taking the Kantian dichotomy for granted while at the same time criticizing it.[41] Perhaps we can say that Schiller at least glimpsed the possibility of a psychology that would definitively surpass the Kantian dichotomy, though its full theoretical elaboration would have to wait for a later generation of thinkers.[42]

Schiller begins his analysis by identifying grace as a type of beauty. This seems plausible: graceful action is to be pleasing to the eye. Is it all beauty, or all personal beauty? No, Schiller says, for there are many sorts of beauty. In particular, we need to distinguish grace from what he calls *architectonic* beauty, which is the beauty of a person considered as a natural being: sheer beauty. Grace (or gracefulness?), on the other hand, is beauty associated with a certain sort of movement. However, grace is not associated with purely natural, instinctive, or compulsive movements, Schiller says: it is associated with movements that are voluntary or chosen, hence intentional. It is not associated with movement that is purely intentional or calculated, though: there must be some mixture of sentiment in the cause of the action. Schiller seems therefore to have in mind that category of movements that are on the one hand under our voluntary control in the way that mere reflexes are not, but on the other hand are caused by emotion, and are spontaneous in the sense of not being the result of cold calculation—what we have called expressive actions. However, now Schiller draws a crucial distinction, arguing that grace is associated with emotional expression in which it is the rational and not merely the natural being that acts:

Grace, then, can only be attributed to [voluntary] movements and only to those that are an expression of *moral* sentiments. Movements that have no other source than sensuality, despite their [voluntariness], still only belong to nature, which cannot of its own accord ever arrive at grace. If desire or instinct could be expressed as grace, then grace would no longer be capable or worthy of human expression.[43]

Such movements are therefore either, on the one hand, voluntary, intentional, and purposive; or on the other hand they can occur:

without the person's willing, following a law of necessity—but at the behest of a sentiment [*Empfindung*]; these I call *sympathetic* movements. Although the latter are instinctive [*unwillkührlich*] and based in sentiment [*Empfindung*], one ought not to confuse them with those determined by feelings [*sinnliche Gefühlvermögen*] and natural instinct [*Naturtrieb*], since natural instinct is not a free principle, and what it brings about is not an action by the person.[44]

Grace is therefore a property of 'sympathetic movements'. Sympathetic movements can be understood as expressions of sentiments or attitudes, but this is distinct from the outpouring of natural drives. Rather, expressive actions are genuinely free actions, but are not directed at a purpose in the way that most free actions are.[45] Hence Schiller's view is that grace is specifically associated with the expression of emotion that is also a product of free rationality, presumably acting under conditions of spontaneity: 'Grace is always only beauty of the physique that *freedom sets in motion*, and movements that *simply belong to nature* are not worthy of the name.'[46]

The result of this is that some emotions and the behaviour that expresses them can be thought of as the product of free agency. An agent need not be thought of as merely determined by nature in performing the actions that constitute such expression. Yet actions that constitute free, spontaneous, unimpeded expressions of emotion also seem to be actions in which sensibility is given free play. Therefore, the fact that Schiller chooses this category of action suggests that he has a view of emotion as a good example of the interaction between reason and sensibility.

This seems to show that for Schiller, expressive action is more than just the *cooperation* or *coincidence* of reason and sensibility. The claim that non-natural sentiments are *expressed* in such action would appear to give at least a *causal* role to reason, on the reading of 'expression' on which something's being expressed is a sign of its presence. On a more ambitious reading of 'expression', furthermore, the mind's expressing itself in sensuous nature would involve the mind, not merely causing, but actively shaping, giving form to, the sensuous matter of expressive activity. Schiller here clearly seems to want to go beyond the view represented in the passage on the English dance. In this passage from 'Grace and Dignity', for instance, the mind is visible in the expression of emotion:

When people speak, we see their gaze, their facial features, their hands, often their whole body *speaking at the same time* and the mimetic part of the conversation is frequently considered the most eloquent.[47]

This passage seems precisely to envisage the mind being present or embodied in the sensuous. We might, to be sure, question whether Schiller has the theoretical wherewithal to articulate or develop the idea that reason or cognitive states can be embodied in expressive behaviour. For instance, he lacks the idea that expressive behaviour can have meaning, that it can symbolize or refer to the content of cognitive states; and he lacks the idea that behaviour might form a symbolic system in which such reference could take place. Perhaps it takes these elements to be in place before we can fully understand how reason and sensibility might satisfactorily be related. But despite this, I would argue that Schiller's conception can be seen as a pivotal point in the development of the idea of expressive behaviour as free behaviour.[48]

9.6 What Does Schiller Teach Us about the Expression of Emotion?

If we now return to the question that opens this paper—what Schiller can tell us about expressive action, and in particular the expression of emotion—we are now in a position to provide some answers. First of all, Schiller provides a defence of the emotional life. His defence seems to be conditional, in the respect that it takes as its starting point the fact that we are embodied, sensible beings. Given this starting point, however, Schiller argues that the only way to be free is to endorse one's emotional side and to cultivate it. Otherwise one will achieve rationality only at the cost of frustration. In the *Aesthetic Letters*, he takes this further, arguing that lack of emotionality also leads to a loss of contact with the world. There are two ways in which the human being might 'miss his destiny', Schiller claims there: one through a preponderance of immediate sense, the other through a preponderance of universal rationality. (In this latter discussion, Schiller talks of sensibility as the faculty of receptivity more generally.) While human beings can never do away with receptivity altogether, they can develop or repress it; and Schiller argues that an insufficiency of such receptivity or openness leads an agent to respond to the world with rationalistic prejudice rather than open-hearted honesty and generosity. The cultivation of sensibility—as well as its subjection to rational thought—emerges as an attractive ideal for human nature:

The more facets his Receptivity develops [*ausbildet*], the more labile it is, and the more surface it presents to phenomena, so much more world does man apprehend, and all the more potentialities does he develop in himself. The more power and depth the Personality achieves, and the more freedom reason attains, so much more world does man comprehend, and all the more form does he create outside of himself. His education will therefore consist, firstly, in procuring for the receptive faculty the most manifold contacts with the world, and within the purview of feeling, intensifying passivity to the utmost; secondly, in securing for the determining faculty the highest degree of independence from the receptive, and, within the purview of reason, intensifying activity to the utmost. Where both these aptitudes are conjoined, man will combine the greatest fullness of existence with the highest autonomy [*Selbständigkeit*] and freedom, and instead of losing himself to the world, will rather draw the latter into himself in all its infinitude of phenomena, and subject it to the unity of his reason.[49]

Secondly, through thinking about the possibility of expressive action as free action, Schiller begins to make a distinction between emotions that are merely instinctive natural feelings, and emotions in the experience of which we are present as free, thinking beings. When it comes to the latter, emotions are not simply brute sensations triggered by events but intelligent responses to those events. With this move, Schiller takes us into the realm of the adequacy or appropriateness of such responses. One way to talk about the fittingness or appropriateness of emotional responses is to see emotions as reflecting a pre-existing normative structure in reality. Schiller, however, provides a sketch of an alternative. For him, appropriateness in emotion would not consist in representing the normative features already present in the situation; rather, appropriateness would be a formal feature. Emotion would be appropriate (or perhaps warranted) where a non-alienated harmony between the claims of sensibility and the claims of reason could be achieved: where one's intellectual grasp of the situation and one's emotional *Gestalt* or sense of rightness support and reinforce one another.[50] This criterion of appropriateness, to be plausible, would have to be fairly robust—for instance, it would have to be the case, for an emotion to be appropriate or warranted, that one could not easily be led into a state of disharmony or alienation by the presentation of new evidence, or a change of mood. But there is a distinctive position here that is worth thinking through.

Thirdly, the claim that reason and sensibility are perfectly balanced only in appropriate emotion makes sense of Schiller's otherwise confusing approach to the notion of grace. As those already familiar with Schiller will have noted, his essay is concerned not just with 'grace' but with 'dignity'. A thorny question for Schiller interpretation has been what to make of the relation between the two: this is thorny because, having attacked Kant in no uncertain terms for overlooking the possibility of grace, Schiller follows his discussion of grace with a much more Kantian-sounding discussion of dignity, where dignity is 'peace in suffering', specifically the suffering born of inappropriate natural desires and emotions.[51] 'Control of impulses through moral strength is spiritual freedom, and its expression in appearance is called dignity.'[52] This has confused many readers, since it appears that Schiller's emphasis on grace is precisely to suggest that human beings can have an attitude to their inclination that goes beyond mere self-control; whereas in the second half of his essay he seems to revert to the Kantian view that such self-control is precisely the best that we can realistically hope for.

However, the interpretation presented here of Schiller's purposes in highlighting the graceful expression of emotion can, I think, be made compatible with this. Schiller's view seems to be that, with respect to (perhaps many, even most) individual instances of emotion and its expression, human beings are capable of grace, where emotion is experienced as free and appropriate. However, he can also recognize that the nature of emotion is such that human beings will be highly unlikely ever to perfectly align emotion and reason, and hence will always also stand prey to impulses that are experienced as rationally ungovernable and uncultivable. The only thing to do when those impulses fail to align with morality is to have dignity: to suppress them and endure them with equanimity as far as possible. Hence both grace and dignity are fundamental virtues of the embodied but imperfect human condition.

On this interpretation, Schiller leaves it open to what extent our nature can be cultivated and brought within the realm of reason; his talk of the 'beautiful soul', whose temperament is a perfect harmony of reason and sensibility, captures the structure of *episodes* of human existence rather than a providing an attainable model for life as a whole. However, from the point of view of Schiller's argument with Kant, even the existence of episodes of action where cognitive attitudes are expressed in sensibility is enough to show that Kantian psychology is in trouble. Human beings are *capable* of appropriate emotion, emotion that will express itself in grace; and this fact needs to be accounted for in our moral psychology, something that Kant's account cannot do. But the idea of a life in which all one's emotions are appropriate is something human beings, because of the ungovernable nature of parts of their embodiment, cannot expect to achieve. '[T]his beauty of character [grace], the ripest fruit of humanity, is only an idea that they can vigilantly strive to live up to, yet, despite all efforts, can never fully attain.'[53] This interpretation accounts for the fact that Schiller, in discussing grace, writes as though he is pointing out a basic and familiar fact of human existence—albeit one that has not been sufficiently acknowledged in theory—namely that reason and sensibility align in at least some expressive behaviour, while in discussing dignity seems to treat the life of grace as an unattainable ideal.

Fourthly, Schiller raises an interesting question about the 'claims of sensibility' that need to be satisfied at the same time as the claims of reason if we are to be fully free. Schiller's point seems to be to recognize that, as embodied agents with susceptibility to pleasure and pain and other feelings, we are subject to felt states that have satisfaction-conditions, and where satisfaction brings a kind of pleasure and dissatisfaction a cost of some felt pain. Earlier I considered a dilemma for Schiller, which stated that the more plausible one's account of the satisfaction of such embodied states, the more difficult it would be to see that satisfaction being responsive to morality. As I said, Schiller's response is to take the view that sensibility is more malleable than the criticism allows. In Section 9.4 we saw that Schiller seems to have the view that sensible states are responsive to the demands of reason; it is not simply that they happen to coincide with the demands of reason, but that they have the satisfaction-conditions they do because of the shaping influence of reason. With the brief discussion of dignity, we have now seen that Schiller is doubtful whether all states of sensibility can be so shaped. But perhaps that is a plausible position, and recognizes the extent to which the supposed dilemma does get at something important.

9.7 Conclusion

In this paper I have investigated Schiller's concern with freedom and its bearing on his contribution to our thinking about emotion and its expression. I have claimed that Schiller thinks of freedom as requiring a kind of internal structural perfection that mirrors his conception of the interaction between form and matter in the beautiful work of art. And I have argued that it is in grace, or the fitting expression of emotion, that he gives the most convincing picture of what the joint freedom of reason and sensibility might look like at the level of human psychology. I have also considered some criticisms of Schiller's project, and shown how, although that project is avowedly incomplete, it may have the resources to answer them.

In closing, I would like to offer what I think is a more telling criticism of Schiller's programme. The malleability of sensibility is not the only way to reach reconciliation between reason and sensibility. One might think that reason would also have to be malleable, and not present itself as an intractable opposite to sensibility. However, if this is right then it seems that a limiting criterion for the validity or rational appropriateness of some moral standard, for Schiller, would have to be its possibility of being the object of appropriate emotion for a human being. If this limiting criterion were not in place then it would be at least possible, depending on the content of morality, that there could be moral standards our compliance with which could never be achieved by someone possessing perfect grace. However, if on the other hand this limiting criterion were in place then it would mean that moral standards were hostage to the contingencies of the psychology of human agents: the content of moral standards would be constrained by the extent to which acting in that way can 'feel right' to us given our emotional make-up. This is something accepted, for instance, by David Wiggins in his 'sensible subjectivism;'[54] but it conflicts with Schiller's Kantian claim that the demands of the sensuous are 'completely rejected in the sphere of pure reason and moral legislation' and that 'the part played by inclination demonstrates nothing about the purely dutiful nature of the action'.[55] Alternatively, then, perhaps Schiller does intend to argue that dignity is necessary, not only because of the ungovernable nature of our natural inclinations, but also because of the inhuman nature of some moral obligations, the binding nature of which is unaffected by the fact that no human being could comply with them gracefully. Which view is more Schillerian is not something we can resolve in this paper. But if the claims of this paper are correct, it does raise a central issue for Schiller interpretation.[56]

Notes

1. Though it has also been argued that Schiller was part of a tradition that collapses this distinction by arguing that 'moral beauty' is a literal description, and that physical beauty is tied to wisdom and virtue. This tradition goes back at least to Plato's Symposium, and its appropriation by Plotinus, but there is also a wider discussion about the Ancient Greek

notion of *kalokagathia*, a notion that seems to have pre-dated Plato. This is picked up by, amongst others, Shaftesbury, by whom we know Schiller was influenced, at least indirectly. For some discussion, see R. E. Norton, *The Beautiful Soul: Aesthetic Morality in the Eighteenth Century* (Ithaca, NY: Cornell University Press, 1995).

2. See e.g. Wordsworth's preface to the *Lyrical Ballads* (1798); and for a more developed view, R. G. Collingwood, *Principles of Art* (Oxford: Oxford University Press, 1938).
3. Rosalind Hursthouse, 'Arational Actions', *Journal of Philosophy* 88 (1991): 57–68.
4. For Brentano, see e.g., *The Origin of the Knowledge of Right and Wrong*, trans. Roderick M. Chisholm and Elizabeth H. Schneewind (London: Routledge, 1969). For Scheler, see e.g. 'Repentance and Rebirth', in Scheler, *On the Eternal in Man*, trans. B. Noble (New Brunswick, NJ: Transaction, 2010), pp. 33–65. For Charles Taylor, see e.g. the opening Part of C. Taylor, *Sources of the Self: The Making of the Modern Identity* (Cambridge: Cambridge University Press, 1989). See Martha Nussbaum, *Upheavals of Thought: The Intelligence of Emotions* (Cambridge: Cambridge University Press, 2001) and Anthony Kenny, *Action, Emotion and Will* (London: Routledge and Kegan Paul, 1963).
5. Friedrich Schiller, 'Kallias or Concerning Beauty: Letters to Gottfried Körner', trans. Stefan Bird-Pollan, in J. M. Bernstein (ed.), *Classic and Romantic German Aesthetics* (Cambridge: Cambridge University Press, 2003), pp. 145–83; 'On Grace and Dignity/Ueber Anmuth und Würde', trans. Jane V. Curran, in Jane V. Curran and Christophe Fricker (eds), *Schiller's 'On Grace and Dignity' in Its Cultural Context: Essays and a New Translation* (Woodbridge: Camden House, 2005), pp. 123–70 (references to GD in the text are to this work); *On the Aesthetic Education of Man*, ed. and trans. E. M. Wilkinson and L. A. Willoughby (Oxford: Clarendon Press, 1982).
6. Quoted in Frederick Beiser, *Schiller as Philosopher: A Re-Examination* (Cambridge: Cambridge University Press, 2008), p. 214.
7. For an overview, see Beiser, *Schiller as Philosopher*, Ch. 7; also, Sabine Roehr, 'Freedom and Autonomy in Schiller', *Journal of the History of Ideas* 64 (2003): 119–34.
8. For discussion, see Patrick J. Kain, *Schiller, Hegel and Marx: State, Society and the Aesthetic Ideal of Ancient Greece* (Montreal: McGill-Queen's University Press, 1982), ch. 1; L. P. Wessell, Jr., 'The Aesthetics of Living Form in Hegel and Marx', *Journal of Aesthetics and Art Criticism* 37 (1978): 189–201.
9. Though see: 'Human nature is a more coherent whole in reality than a philosopher, who can only achieve results through separation [*der nur durch Trennen was vermag*], is permitted to reveal' (GD, p. 152; NA 286).
10. Beiser, *Schiller as Philosopher*, p. 216.
11. Douglas Moggach, 'Post-Kantian Perfectionism', in *Politics, Religion and Art: Hegelian Debates*, ed. Douglas Moggach (Evanston IL: Northwestern University Press, 2011), pp. 179–200.
12. Douglas Moggach, 'Schiller, Scots and Germans: Freedom and Diversity in *The Aesthetic Education of Man*', *Inquiry* 51 (2008): 16–36.
13. Beiser, *Schiller as Philosopher*, pp. 143–4, 150–3.
14. Schiller, GD, p. 146.
15. Beiser, *Schiller as Philosopher*, pp. 123–9.
16. Schiller, GD, p. 147.
17. See Robert Stern, *Understanding Moral Obligation: Kant, Hegel, Kierkegaard* (Cambridge: Cambridge University Press, 2014), ch. 4.

18. See Schiller's criticisms of Kant at GD pp. 148–51 (NA 282–6). Whether this view of Kant is adequate is of course a matter of controversy. For a good recent discussion, see Carla Bagnoli, 'Emotions and the Categorical Authority of Moral Reason', in *Morality and the Emotions*, ed. Carla Bagnoli (Oxford: Oxford University Press, 2011), pp. 62–81. For a Kantian response to Schiller's criticisms in 'On Grace and Dignity', see Paul Guyer, 'The Ideal of Beauty and the Necessity of Grace: Kant and Schiller on Ethics and Aesthetics', in *Friedrich Schiller und der Weg in die Moderne*, ed. W. Hinderer (Würzburg: Könighausen & Neumann, 2006), pp. 187–204.
19. Cf. Beiser, *Schiller as Philosopher*, p. 217.
20. Anne Margaret Baxley, 'Pleasure, Freedom and Grace: Schiller's "Completion" of Kant's Ethics,' *Inquiry* 51 (2008): 1–15 (p. 6).
21. For a good background to the conception of 'moral beauty' that informs Schiller's view, and its development through Kant and Schiller to Hegel and Goethe, see Norton, *The Beautiful Soul*.
22. I am grateful to Robert Stern for this way of categorizing models of perfection. See his 'The Ethics of the British Idealists: Perfectionism after Kant', in his *Kantian Ethics: Value, Agency and Obligation* (Oxford: Oxford University Press, 2015), pp. 190–201.
23. Schiller, 'Kallias Letters', p. 166.
24. See Beiser, *Schiller as Philosopher*, pp. 67–8; Roehr, 'Freedom and Autonomy in Schiller', pp. 120–1.
25. Schiller accepts the Kantian view that freedom cannot actually appear in the realm of causality. On the ambiguity in the term 'appearance of freedom'—depending on whether to give 'appearance' a veridical or non-veridical reading—and the correct way to read it within Schiller's theory, see Beiser, *Schiller as Philosopher*, p. 64.
26. It might be said that this is Schiller's interpretation of Kant's idea in the *Critique of Judgement* that beauty involves 'purposiveness without purpose'.
27. Schiller, 'Kallias Letters', p. 166.
28. Having said this, artists do sometimes say that they are unable to get the artwork right until it begins to take on a life of its own and dictate its own terms: for instance, the common novelistic conceit that the characters spring off the page and the writer is only following them rather than creating them. This might also be a theme worth exploring in relation to Schiller's view and its effect on later thinkers.
29. Schiller, 'Kallias Letters', p. 155.
30. Schiller, 'Kallias Letters', pp. 171–2. The most helpful discussion I have found of Schiller's view on this point is Stephen Houlgate, 'Schiller and the Dance of Beauty', *Inquiry* 51 (2008): 37–49.
31. For some sympathetic scepticism about its ultimate value, see Eva Schaper, 'Friedrich Schiller: Adventures of a Kantian', *British Journal of Aesthetics* 4 (1964): 348–62.
32. Schiller, GD, p. 146.
33. See for instance Myles Burnyeat, 'Aristotle on Learning to be Good', in *Essays on Aristotle's Ethics*, ed. A. O. Rorty (Berkeley: University of California Press, 1980), pp. 69–92.
34. Schiller, GD, p. 149. For discussion, see Stern, *Understanding Moral Obligation*, ch. 4.
35. This is the notorious 'one thought too many' criticism. See Bernard Williams, 'Persons, Character and Morality', in *Moral Luck* (Cambridge: Cambridge University Press, 1979), pp. 20–39; Michael Smith, *The Moral Problem* (Oxford: Blackwell, 1994), pp. 71–6.

36. In other words, they are what Thomas Nagel calls 'motivated desires'. See his *The Possibility of Altruism* (Princeton NJ: Princeton University Press, 1970).
37. Houlgate, 'Schiller and the Dance of Beauty'.
38. Houlgate, 'Schiller and the Dance of Beauty', p. 46.
39. Schiller, 'Kallias Letters', p. 174. Quoted by Houlgate, 'Schiller and the Dance of Beauty', p. 46.
40. Houlgate, 'Schiller and the Dance of Beauty', p. 47.
41. As Schaper puts it in the context of the Aesthetic Letters, Schiller 'plays fast and loose with the Kantian view he ostensibly defended but could not but drastically modify in the process' (Eva Schaper, 'Towards the Aesthetic: A Journey with Friedrich Schiller', *British Journal of Aesthetics* 25 (1985): 153–68 (p. 162)).
42. A full assessment of Schiller's view would also have to pay attention to the suggestive discussion of the 'aesthetic condition' and the 'play-drive' in the *Aesthetic Letters* in the light of what I will go on to say here—though that would require another paper. For some discussion, see the sensitive reading of the aesthetic condition and the play-drive in Jeffrey Barnouw, '"Aesthetic" for Schiller and Peirce: A Neglected Origin of Pragmatism', *Journal of the History of Ideas* 49 (1988): 607–32.
43. Schiller, GD, p. 126. I have altered the translation slightly here. Schiller uses '*willkuerlich*' to signify both 'intentional' in the sense of the property of being not-a-mere-reflex and 'intentional' in the sense of 'serving some end, or being done for the sake of some further end'; the Curran translation solves this problem by reserving 'intentional' for 'serving some end' and using 'arbitrary' for merely 'not a reflex', but the latter term, though presumably meant to conjure up the idea of being subject to choice rather than natural necessity, hardly seems appropriate; as a result I have replaced it with 'intentional'.
44. Schiller, GD, p. 135.
45. Cf. the view taken in Hursthouse, 'Arational Actions', and discussed earlier.
46. Schiller, GD, p. 134
47. Schiller, GD, p. 136.
48. It is perhaps a final irony to close on that, in order to further the inquiry that has been launched in this paper, one would have to look at the development of the tradition of thinking about symbols in this sense that Kant begins with his discussion of the human being as a symbol in the third Critique. I am grateful to Chris Janaway for helping me to draw this connection.
49. Schiller, *Aesthetic Letters*, pp. 88–9.
50. See the remarks on the epistemological role of 'spontaneity of feeling', with a long footnote referring to Schiller, in John Skorupski, 'Propositions about Reasons', *European Journal of Philosophy* 14 (2006): 26–48 (p. 37 and n. 23). See also John Skorupski, *The Domain of Reasons* (Oxford: Oxford University Press, 2010), pp. 416–17.
51. Schiller, GD, p. 160.
52. Schiller, GD, p. 158.
53. Schiller, GD, p. 154.
54. David Wiggins, 'A Sensible Subjectivism?', in his *Needs, Values, Truth*, 3rd ed. (Oxford: Oxford University Press, 1998), pp. 185–214.
55. Schiller, GD, p. 149. For this point, see also Katerina Deligiorgi, 'Grace as a Guide to Morals? Schiller's Aesthetic Turn in Ethics', *History of Philosophy Quarterly* 23 (2006): 1–20 (p. 6).

56. An ancestor of this paper was given at the inaugural conference of the White Rose Centre for the History of Philosophy at the University of York in 2011. I presented a more recent version to an audience in Sheffield in 2013. I am grateful to those who attended these events for comments that have been helpful in strengthening the paper, particularly Bob Stern, Christopher Janaway, Simon Blackburn, Gerald Lang, Alix Cohen, and Jan Kandiyali; and also to two anonymous readers for this volume.

Bibliography

Bagnoli, Carla. 'Emotions and the Categorical Authority of Moral Reason', in *Morality and the Emotions*, ed. Carla Bagnoli (Oxford: Oxford University Press, 2011), pp. 62–81.

Barnouw, Jeffrey. '"Aesthetic" for Schiller and Peirce: A Neglected Origin of Pragmatism', *Journal of the History of Ideas* 49 (1988): 607–32.

Baxley, Anne Marie. 'Pleasure, Freedom and Grace: Schiller's 'Completion' of Kant's Ethics', *Inquiry* 51 (2008): 1–15.

Beiser, Frederick. *Schiller as Philosopher: A Re-Examination* (Cambridge: Cambridge University Press, 2008).

Brentano, Franz. *The Origin of the Knowledge of Right and Wrong*, trans. Roderick M. Chisholm and Elizabeth H. Schneewind (London: Routledge, 1969).

Burnyeat, Myles. 'Aristotle on Learning to be Good', in *Essays on Aristotle's Ethics*, ed. Amélie O. Rorty (Berkeley: University of California Press, 1980), pp. 69–92.

Collingwood, Robin G. *Principles of Art* (Oxford: Oxford University Press, 1938).

Deligiorgi, Katerina. 'Grace as a Guide to Morals? Schiller's Aesthetic Turn in Ethics', *History of Philosophy Quarterly* 23 (2006): 1–20.

Guyer, Paul. 'The Ideal of Beauty and the Necessity of Grace: Kant and Schiller on Ethics and Aesthetics', in *Friedrich Schiller und der Weg in die Moderne*, ed. W. Hinderer (Würzburg: Könighausen & Neumann, 2006), pp. 187–204.

Houlgate, Stephen. 'Schiller and the Dance of Beauty', *Inquiry* 51 (2008): 37–49.

Hursthouse, Rosalind. 'Arational Actions', *Journal of Philosophy* 88 (1991): 57–68.

Kain, Patrick J. *Schiller, Hegel and Marx: State, Society and the Aesthetic Ideal of Ancient Greece* (Montreal: McGill-Queen's University Press, 1982).

Kenny, Anthony. *Action, Emotion and Will* (London: Routledge and Kegan Paul, 1963).

Douglas, Moggach. 'Schiller, Scots and Germans: Freedom and Diversity in *The Aesthetic Education of Man*', *Inquiry* 51 (2008): 16–36.

Douglas, Moggach. 'Post-Kantian Perfectionism', *Politics, Religion and Art: Hegelian Debates*, ed. Douglas Moggach (Evanston IL: Northwestern University Press, 2011), pp. 179–200.

Nagel, Thomas. *The Possibility of Altruism* (Princeton, NJ: Princeton University Press, 1970).

Norton, Robert E. *The Beautiful Soul: Aesthetic Morality in the Eighteenth Century* (Ithaca, NY: Cornell University Press, 1995).

Nussbaum, Martha. *Upheavals of Thought: The Intelligence of Emotions* (Cambridge: Cambridge University Press, 2001).

Roehr, Sabine. 'Freedom and Autonomy in Schiller', *Journal of the History of Ideas* 64 (2003): 119–34.

Schaper, Eva. 'Friedrich Schiller: Adventures of a Kantian', *British Journal of Aesthetics* 4 (1964): 348–62.

Schaper, Eva. 'Towards the Aesthetic: A Journey with Friedrich Schiller', *British Journal of Aesthetics* 25 (1985): 153–68.

Scheler, Max. *On the Eternal in Man*, trans. B. Noble (New Brunswick, NJ: Transaction, 2010).

Schiller, Friedrich. *On the Aesthetic Education of Man*, ed. and trans. E. M. Wilkinson and L. A. Willoughby (Oxford: Clarendon Press, 1982).

Schiller, Friedrich. 'Kallias or Concerning Beauty: Letters to Gottfried Körner', *Classic and Romantic German Aesthetics*, ed. J. M. Bernstein, trans. Stefan Bird-Pollan (Cambridge: Cambridge University Press, 2003), pp. 145–83.

Schiller, Friedrich. 'On Grace and Dignity/Ueber Anmuth und Würde', *Schiller's 'On Grace and Dignity' in Its Cultural Context: Essays and a New Translation*, ed. Jane V. Curran and Christophe Fricker, trans. Jane V. Curran (Woodbridge: Camden House, 2005), pp. 123–70.

Skorupski, John. 'Propositions about Reasons', *European Journal of Philosophy* 14 (2006): 26–48.

Skorupski, John. *The Domain of Reasons* (Oxford: Oxford University Press, 2010).

Smith, Michael. *The Moral Problem* (Oxford: Blackwell, 1994).

Stern, Robert. *Understanding Moral Obligation: Kant, Hegel, Kierkegaard* (Cambridge: Cambridge University Press, 2014).

Stern, Robert. 'The Ethics of the British Idealists: Perfectionism after Kant', *The Cambridge History of Ethics*, ed. Sacha Golob and Jens Timmerman (Cambridge: Cambridge University Press, forthcoming).

Taylor, Charles. *Sources of the Self: The Making of the Modern Identity* (Cambridge: Cambridge University Press, 1989).

Wessell,Jr., Leonard P. 'The Aesthetics of Living Form in Hegel and Marx', *Journal of Aesthetics and Art Criticism* 37 (1978): 189–201.

Wiggins, David. 'A Sensible Subjectivism?', in *Needs, Values, Truth*, 3rd ed. (Oxford: Oxford University Press, 1998), pp. 185–214.

Williams, Bernard. 'Persons, Character and Morality', *Moral Luck* (Cambridge: Cambridge University Press, 1979).

Wordsworth, William. *Lyrical Ballads* (1798).

10

Affect and Cognition in Schopenhauer and Nietzsche

Christopher Janaway

In this chapter I examine two nineteenth-century thinkers who are concerned with the 'affects and passions' and who disagree pointedly concerning their influence on cognition. Schopenhauer defends the view that emotions impair cognition, while Nietzsche apparently replies that they are ineliminable from cognition, and that they enhance it. The overall shape of the essay is as follows. Schopenhauer argues that human individuals are naturally disposed to comprehend their environment in affective terms. Affects and passions are for him 'movements of the will', and for any human individual, cognition is essentially in the service of the will that constitutes our ineliminable common essence. This is Schopenhauer's *descriptive* account of the relation between cognition and affective states: as ordinary human individuals we cannot naturally have the one without the other. At the same time, his *evaluative* position concerning this relation is negative: cognition is spoiled, warped, or tainted by its inability to shake off the emotions, desires, or drives that belong to human nature. Hence we have an instance of the characteristically pessimistic pattern that permeates Schopenhauer's thought. What we are by nature, what we are in essence, is something we would be better not being. Cognition proper would be *objective*, in the sense that it would mirror the world purely, with no intervening influence from the needs, desires, interests, or feelings of the individual. But, alas, human individuals are not cut out for cognition proper, unless one of two extraordinary things happens, propelling the human individual away from his or her human nature into a state in which, as Schopenhauer says, he or she 'becomes pure subject of cognition'. This can occur in aesthetic experience, a rare oasis of peace in which all willing abates temporarily, and which Schopenhauer explicitly claims is a cognitively superior state. It can also occur in the total self-negation of the will to life in the face of suffering, the extreme state that he regards as the necessary condition of 'true salvation, redemption from life and from suffering' (*WWR* 1, p. 424). But in the absence of these two relatively abnormal cases, ordinary empirical cognition is doomed to be the slave of will and affect, and hence imperfect.

Nietzsche, I suggest, accepts something analogous to Schopenhauer's descriptive position on the relation between cognition and the affects. For Nietzsche the self is a complex of drives and it is primarily these drives and their associated affects that interpret the world.[1] But he firmly rejects Schopenhauer's evaluative stance. He denies the possibility of a pure, objective, affect-free cognition, and identifies the philosophical aspiration towards such a form of cognition as a target for criticism. Further, he seeks to use the descriptive account of the relation between cognition and the affects to give an undermining explanation, a genealogical explanation, of this aspiration. The would-be 'pure' cognition is merely theoretical, it is a myth, but the drives and affects of the theorizer can, thinks Nietzsche, explain why the myth has been so compelling for philosophers, and most notably for Schopenhauer. Secondly, Nietzsche argues for a reversal of Schopenhauer's evaluative stance: that is to say, he seeks to reveal the influence of the affects on human cognition not only as necessary, but as beneficial. Cognition is improved by affect, and by multiplying affects. This is a key point in Nietzsche's so-called perspectivism, or, as I have previously argued,[2] this really is what he means with the famous statement, 'There is . . . only a perspectival "knowing"; and *the more* affects we allow to speak about a matter . . . that much more complete will our "concept" of this matter, our "objectivity" be' (*GM* III, 12).

How could Nietzsche so much as think that affects can be cognitively beneficial? In the final part I consider some objections along these lines. In dealing with such objections, it is important to free ourselves of certain assumptions which may be thought to characterize 'traditional epistemology'. In one recent account, given by the editors of a volume on epistemology and emotion, 'emotions did not play a significant role in traditional epistemology and if they were paid any attention at all, they were mainly thought of as impairing cognition'.[3] This conception, they continue, can be characterized in the following terms: a concentration on context of justification rather than context of discovery, a fixation upon propositional knowledge, and an assumption that knowledge requires infallible foundations.[4] If, for example, the dominant question for epistemology concerns how a belief that *p* is justified, and justified in such a way as to ensure certainty, then emotional or affective responses, which are variable, subjective, and fallible, can seem at best irrelevant, at worst detrimental to the task of understanding the nature of knowledge. Similarly, under this 'traditional assumption' little attention may be paid to the many roles that emotions or affects may play in motivating, guiding and enabling the *activities* of seeking and gaining knowledge. Examples of the latter are the doubt and disappointment that may spark investigation, the satisfaction of discovery (Moritz Schlick's 'sense of fulfilment' or 'joy in knowledge . . . the exaltation of having guessed correctly'[5]), the ability to focus attention on objects that emotions make salient, and, perhaps more contentiously, the discerning of features of an environment that are themselves response-dependent (e.g. 'Seeing the utterly specific ways in which a situation, animal or person is *appealing* or *repellent*'[6]).

Neither Schopenhauer nor Nietzsche can be regarded as adherents of 'traditional epistemology' in the sense we have outlined. When Nietzsche speaks of what we often translate as 'knowledge' or 'knowing' (*Erkenntnis*, *Erkennen*), or of 'we knowers' (*wir Erkennenden*[7]), he tends to have in mind a complex and protracted *project of investigation* for someone whose concern is, for example, the value of morality:

> Whoever sticks here...and *learns* to ask questions here, will fare as I have fared:—an immense new vista opens up to him, a possibility takes hold of him like a dizziness, every sort of mistrust, suspicion, fear springs forth, the belief in morality, in all morality totters... [W]e need a *critique* of moral values...and for this we need a knowledge [*Kenntnis*] of the conditions and circumstances out of which they have grown, under which they have developed and shifted,...knowledge of a kind that has neither existed up until now nor even been desired. (*GM*, Preface, 6)

Nietzsche, I shall argue, claims that the affects are necessary to 'knowing'. That claim can seem implausible if we relate it to the narrow concerns of 'traditional epistemology'. But, I shall contend, it becomes a more plausible and interesting claim if we focus on the kind of cognitive enterprise Nietzsche is predominantly concerned with.

Schopenhauer, to whom Nietzsche expressly responds, recognizes propositional knowledge as a distinctive form of cognition: within *Erkenntnis* ('cognition') he discerns a subspecies, which he calls *Wissen* ('knowledge' or 'knowing').[8] While all animals have some form of cognition, *Wissen* depends on the ability to form concepts and is possessed only by human beings. It amounts to propositional knowledge which is adequately justified either by relation to further propositions or direct perception.[9] However, the species of affect-free cognition that Schopenhauer privileges is wholly different from this. It is exemplified by the aesthetic experience in which conceptual thought is an abeyance, and in which

> we devote the entire power of the our mind to intuition [*Anschauung*]...we *lose* ourselves in the object completely, and continue to exist only as pure subject, the clear mirror of the object.... [T]hen what we thus cognize is no longer the individual thing, but rather the *Idea*, the eternal Form. (*WWR* 1, p. 201)

In Schopenhauer's conception, eliminating affects enables a superior cognitive encounter with a timelessly existing reality. He goes even further in the same direction when discussing the kind of cognition or knowledge that characterizes the morally good, compassionate person. This is a kind of knowledge which he finds prefigured in the Upanishads and Neo-Platonism: 'the same knowledge that makes up the essence of all true mysticism', a state in which someone 'recognizes [*erkennt*] his own essence in itself in someone else's appearance' (*BM*, p. 255).

Finally, a word on the range of affective states that our two thinkers recognize. For both Schopenhauer and Nietzsche *Affekt* (affect) is readily coupled with *Leidenschaft* (passion) and encompasses but is not exhausted by what we tend to call emotions. For Schopenhauer all instances of affect are categorized as movements of the will. 'Willing' (*Wollen*) is an immensely comprehensive notion for him, which explicitly includes

> all desiring, striving, wishing, longing, yearning, hoping, loving, enjoying, rejoicing and the like, no less than not-willing or resisting, and detesting, fleeing, fearing, being angry, hating, grieving,

suffering pain, in short all affects and passions [*Affekte und Leidenschaften*]. For these affects and passions are simply movements, more or less weak or strong, now violent and stormy, now gentle and calm, of one's own will that is either restrained or released, satisfied or unsatisfied, and they all relate in multiple variations to the attainment or non-attainment of what is willed, and to enduring or overcoming what is detested; thus they are decided affections of the same will that is in operation in decisions and actions. (*FW*, p. 38)

It seems that for Nietzsche too all affects are at bottom inclinations or aversions, or some kind of positive and negative stirrings of the will. He talks at times simply of 'inclinations and aversions', 'pro and contra', or 'for and against'. But the range of affects is even more extensive for him. In the *Genealogy* and *Beyond Good and Evil* alone Nietzsche applies the term *Affekt* to all of the following: anger, fear, love, hatred, hope, envy, revenge, lust, jealousy, irascibility, exuberance, calmness, self-satisfaction, self-humiliation, self-crucifixion, power-lust, greed, suspicion, malice, cruelty, contempt, despair, triumph, feeling of looking down on, feeling of a superior glance towards others, desire to justify oneself in the eyes of others, demand for respect, feelings of laziness, feeling of a command, and brooding over bad deeds.[10] So when we inquire about the relation of cognition to affects, we have to deal with a broad range of felt states with some positive or negative tone.

10.1 Schopenhauer: Cognition Naturally Influenced by Affects

Schopenhauer presents a strong and rounded conception of what is natural to any living being—namely willing: striving towards ends, individual self-affirmation, and striving towards living and reproducing life. Will to life, in his phrase, is the essence of a human being; he or she is an individual expression of will to life. Much can be unfolded out of this essence for Schopenhauer. Individual living beings are active by nature: they strive for ends and do so insatiably. Their striving frequently fails of fulfilment, and that guarantees suffering. Life is a perpetual flux of striving, suffering, temporary satiation, and more striving, located in a body, a living organism, which is akin in essence to the whole of nature. The human being is not the rational intellect or immaterial soul of some dominant parts of the philosophical tradition. Schopenhauer, by contrast, seeks to translate the human being back into nature—to use Nietzsche's well-known phrase (*BGE* 230). Human beings naturally affirm the will to life, or, as Schopenhauer declares we might as well say, affirm the body. It is because willing is the primary characteristic of human beings that emotion-related cognition belongs to our natural condition.

When it comes to our ordinary cognition of the world we find it permeated by will, and the panoply of affective states that fall under the category of 'willing'. Here are some samples from *The World as Will and Representation*:

Cognition in general, rational as well as merely intuitive, proceeds originally from the will itself and... [is] a mere mechanism, a means for the preservation of the individual and the species as much as any organ of the body. Originally in the service of the will and determined by the accomplishment of its aim, cognition remains almost entirely in its service throughout: this is the case in all animals and in almost all human beings. (*WWR* 1, p. 177)

In the immediate intuition of the world and of life, we consider things as a rule merely in their relations.... For example, we regard houses, ships, machines, and the like with the idea of their purpose and the suitability to it; human beings with the idea of their relation to us, if they have any, and then in their relation to one another... In most cases and as a rule, everyone is abandoned to this mode of consideration; I believe even that most people are incapable of any other. (*WWR* 2, p. 372)

Here are some of his examples (some of them liable to cause offence) of the way things are perceived with an inescapable affective aspect:

Even an inanimate object, which is yet to become the instrument for some event we abhor, appears to have a hideous physiognomy; for example the scaffold, the surgeon's case of instruments, the travelling coach of loved ones, and so on; indeed, numbers, letters, seals can grin at us horribly and affect us like fearful monsters. On the other hand, the instruments for fulfilling our wishes immediately look pleasant and agreeable; for example, the old woman with a hump who carries a love letter, the Jew with the *louis-d'ors*, the rope-ladder for escape.... [And this effect] is present in a lesser degree in the case of every object that has only some remote relation to our will, in other words, to our inclination or aversion [*Neigung oder Abneigung*]. (*WWR* 2, p. 373)

Still, natural and common though this effect apparently is, Schopenhauer regards it as spoiling and falsifying cognition:

In order to see that a purely objective, and therefore correct, apprehension of things is possible only when we consider them without any personal participation in them, and thus under the complete silence of the will, let us picture to ourselves how much every affect [*Affekt*] or passion [*Leidenschaft*] obscures and falsifies knowledge, in fact how every inclination or aversion [*Neigung oder Abneigung*] twists, colours, and distorts not merely the judgement, but even the original perception of things. (*WWR* 2, p. 373)

the intellect can fulfil its function quite properly and correctly only so long as the will is silent and pauses. On the other hand, the function of the intellect is disturbed by every observable excitement of the will, and its result is falsified by the will's interference. (*WWR* 2, p. 215)

Schopenhauer gives numerous examples of such interference, citing a range of emotions: 'A great fright deprives us of our senses to such an extent that we become petrified, or do the most preposterous things'; 'Anger makes us no longer know what we do, still less what we say'; 'Fear prevents us from seeing and seizing the resources that still exist, and are often close at hand'; 'Love and hatred entirely falsify our judgement; in our enemies we see nothing but shortcomings, in our favourites nothing but merits and good points, and even their defects seem amiable to us' (all from *WWR* 2, pp. 215–17). Hope provides an interesting case: it 'magnifies its object', making 'what we desire appear probable and near':

Here the intellect is bound to do violence to its own nature, which is aimed at truth, since it is compelled, contrary to its own laws, to regard as true things that are neither true nor probable, and often scarcely possible, merely in order to pacify, soothe, and send to sleep for a while the restless and unmanageable *will*. We clearly see here who is master and who is servant. (*WWR* 2, pp. 216–17)

There is an apparent peculiarity here. On the one hand the intellect is a mere instrument towards the will's ends; on the other hand the intellect's peculiar function, aiming at truth, is hindered by the very will to which it is the servant. However, there is, I suppose, no contradiction in Schopenhauer's position. The *origin* of intellect is explained by its fulfilling ends for the organism; but not all the ends of the organism are best served by the intellect's fulfilling its peculiar function to the optimum degree. It is intelligible to think that we may not always live best by grasping reality with the least degree of intervention from the affects and passions. But Schopenhauer's point is that the intellect would do better at attaining the ends peculiar to it without its subjection to the will's mastery.

Schopenhauer also anticipates Freud's notion of repression, as Freud himself noted.[11] The will can assert its hegemony over the intellect, Schopenhauer says,

by prohibiting the intellect from having certain representations, by absolutely preventing certain trains of thought from arising, because it knows, or in other words experiences from the self-same intellect, that they would arouse in it any one of the emotions previously described. It then curbs and restrains the intellect, and forces it to turn to other things. (*WWR* 2, p. 208)

Note that the more primitive will has the power of absolutely preventing certain trains of thought from arising in the intellect. That is to say, although such thoughts are in some sense present as ours, we never consciously entertain them. The process of prevention must therefore be an unconscious one. Schopenhauer gives many examples from everyday life—the sort of thing that 'anyone who is attentive can observe in himself' (*WWR* 2, p. 210)—in which the will makes decisions or plans as it were 'in secret', decisions from which the intellect remains excluded and 'can only get to know them, like those of a stranger, by spying out and taking unawares; and it must surprise the will in the act of expressing itself, in order merely to discover its real intentions' (*WWR* 2, p. 209). A conscious judgement as to the desirability or undesirability of acting thus-and-so is swept away 'to my own astonishment' by a 'jubilant, irresistible gladness' (ibid.) that reveals the true orientation of my underlying will. But Schopenhauer in general regrets that matters are thus—the will has a 'direct, unconscious, and *disadvantageous* influence on knowledge' (*WWR* 2, p. 219, my emphasis).

10.2 Pure Cognition

What, then of the other term in the contrast that Schopenhauer makes between cognition as servant of will, and those rarer states of cognition in which it becomes purified of willing? To grasp the depth of this contrast we have to look at the dialectical shape of Schopenhauer's philosophy as a whole. *The World as Will and Representation* presents a struggle between the natural, embodied, willing self and the pure, non-individuated subject: a tension that is there from the start, and remains till the end. 'Subject' is introduced on the first page of the book, and immediately in §2 we encounter this:

> The *subject* is the seat of all cognition but is itself not cognized by anything.... We all find ourselves as this subject, although only in so far as we have cognition of things, not in so far as we are objects of cognition. But the body is already an object among objects... [I]t is situated within the forms of all cognition, in space and time (by means of which there is multiplicity). The subject, on the other hand, having cognition, but never cognized, is not situated within these forms. (*WWR* 1, p. 25)

The body that each of us experiences as our own is an object in space and time. But the subject is not an item in the world. We 'find ourselves as' the subject in whose consciousness all objects are present, but this subject cannot itself be conceived as existing among the objects. So 'subject' does not mean the same for Schopenhauer as 'person' or 'human individual'. These latter terms refer to items in the world of objects. As person or embodied human individual each of us is in and of the world, something existing as an object among objects. But we are not simply individuals, for Schopenhauer, because we each find ourselves as subject—though not (note) as *subjects*, because 'subject' is not a count noun.

Behind Schopenhauer's picture of the subject lies a familiar Kantian thought about the 'I' of self-consciousness: 'I cannot cognize as object itself that which I must presuppose in order to cognize an object at all'.[12] The awareness one has of oneself as a centre of consciousness is not sufficient to identify the self that one finds oneself as with any object, body, person, or individual thing in the world. In that case, there will potentially be a genuine tension in our sense of self for Schopenhauer to exploit. Our sense of self may shift according to whether we view ourselves as naturally embodied human individual or as pure subject. *The World as Will and Representation* can be seen as structured around this opposition, with different forms of self-identification becoming available to us as our sense of self shifts from one pole to another. As active, willing beings our consciousness is that of a bodily individual, but in aesthetic experience, as Schopenhauer conceives it, we become the '*pure*, will-less, painless, timeless *subject of cognition*' (*WWR* 1, p. 201), and he thinks that, if the will within us negates itself, we reach a redemptive state of consciousness in which we do not regard ourselves as individuated, separated from everything else, at all.

When Schopenhauer calls this state of consciousness (like that of aesthetic contemplation) a state of 'peace' or 'rest' (*Ruhe*), the crucial point he is urging upon us is that the subject feels no affect or passion, because consciousness is void of willing. He describes the will-less aesthetic state as one in which 'happiness and unhappiness disappear' (*WWR* 1, p. 221); and the same must apply to the supposed saintly state in which the will to life negates itself—except that happiness and unhappiness must constantly threaten to intrude because the human essence, will to life, can only be dissociated from consciousness, though not, of course (being an *essence*), lost altogether. Schopenhauer conceives of this pure, will-less cognition as objective precisely because it escapes the influence of the individual human being's desires and affects. The purely cognitive subject is 'not capable of any willing or affect at all [*überhaupt keines Wollens oder Affektes*]' (*WWR* 2, p. 498; translation modified), and so can become an indifferent, detached spectator, which 'cannot take part or interest [*Antheil oder Interesse*] in anything' (*WWR* 2, p. 499). Schopenhauer takes this indifference or disinterestedness to be sufficient for objectivity.

10.3 Nietzsche: No Affect-Free Knowing

Nietzsche's most potent response to Schopenhauer comes in one of his most famous and most discussed passages, *Genealogy* III, 12 (which is often considered the definitive published text that presents Nietzsche's 'perspectivism'). When Nietzsche announces that 'there is *only* a perspectival seeing, *only* a perspectival "knowing"', he is opposing the conception of 'objectivity' championed by Schopenhauer in his aesthetic theory, the objectivity allegedly attained by a 'pure, will-less, painless, timeless subject of knowledge' (or again 'cognition'). In Schopenhauer's view, as we saw, ordinary consciousness is in thrall to the will, with its host of 'passions and affects', which are constantly ebbing and flowing pro- and con-attitudes, or movements of the will; but in the consciousness of the artistic genius, and to a lesser extent in all of us, a purer kind of cognition is attainable, according to Schopenhauer, in which all affects and passions are switched off or suspended and the subject comes as close as it can to being a passive mirror of what is objectively there. In *Genealogy* III, 12 Nietzsche takes this account of 'objectivity' beyond its aesthetic context, and portrays it as emblematic of a wider temptation for philosophers, that of positing an ideal cognitive state in which we may attain true knowledge, unpolluted by emotions, desires, and personal or bodily attachments.

The passage reaches its climax as follows:

> Finally let us, particularly as knowers, not be ungrateful toward such resolute reversals of the familiar perspectives and valuations with which the spirit has raged against itself all too long now, apparently wantonly and futilely: to see differently in this way for once, to *want* to see differently, is no small discipline and preparation of the intellect for its future 'objectivity'—the latter understood not as 'disinterested contemplation [*interesselose Anschauung*]' (which is a non-concept and absurdity), but as the capacity to have one's pro and contra *in one's power*, and to shift them in and out: so that one knows how to make precisely the *difference* in perspectives and affective interpretations useful for knowledge. For let us guard ourselves better from now on, gentlemen philosophers, against the dangerous old conceptual fabrication that posited a 'pure, will-less, painless, timeless subject of knowledge [cognition]'; let us guard ourselves against the tentacles of such contradictory concepts as 'pure reason', 'absolute spirituality', 'knowledge in itself': here it is always demanded that we think an eye that that cannot possibly be thought, an eye that must not have any direction, in which the active and interpretive forces through which seeing first becomes seeing-something, are to be shut off, are to be absent; thus

what is demanded here is always an absurdity and non-concept of an eye. There is *only* a perspectival seeing, only a perspectival 'knowing'; and *the more* affects we allow to speak about a matter, *the more* eyes, different eyes, we know how to bring to bear on one and the same matter, that much more complete will our 'concept' of this matter, our 'objectivity' be. But to eliminate the will altogether, to disconnect the affects one and all, supposing that we were capable of this—what? would that not be to *castrate* the intellect? ...

Nietzsche doesn't always 'do argument', but here there is one:

(1) all cognition is active interpretation rather than passive reception of data
(2) all active interpretation is in the service of the will
so (3) all cognition is in the service of the will.

So the idea of a cognition wholly free of the will, of positive and negative motivation, and of all affect, is the idea of something impossible. But the assumptions of this argument are Schopenhauer's own. And if we restrict ourselves to Schopenhauer's conception of *empirical* cognition, ordinary cognition that an individual human being with an unreformed consciousness can attain, Schopenhauer will agree that such cognition is always in the service of the will.

Nietzsche then turns Schopenhauer against himself, by explaining Schopenhauer's positing of a will-less objective cognition as itself driven by hidden affects of Schopenhauer's own—despair over the life of willing, torment from his own desires, hope of redemption from ordinary existence. The very idea of a will-less cognition here gives evidence, in other words, of a particular 'will' at work. When Nietzsche, at the end of the same essay, famously diagnoses a 'will to nothingness' as lying behind the all-pervading ascetic ideal, Schopenhauerian ideas are again to the fore. The very expression 'will to nothingness' is a verbal play on 'will to life'. And Schopenhauer is clearly among those targeted here:

this hatred of the human, still more of the animal, still more of the material, this abhorrence of the senses, of reason itself, this fear of happiness and of beauty, this longing away from all appearance, change, becoming, death, wish, longing itself—all of this means—let us dare to grasp this—a will to nothingness, an aversion to life, a rebellion against the most fundamental presuppositions of life; but it is and remains a *will*! (*GM* III, 28)

If we are still thinking of Schopenhauer when we reach this culmination in the diagnosis of the ascetic ideal (as I think we must), then we should note the Schopenhauerian pattern being turned against Schopenhauer. The explanations Nietzsche hints at for Schopenhauer's ascetic theorizing of disinterested aesthetic objectivity and the negation of will all cite affective states: hatred, abhorrence, fear, aversion, longing, will. He diagnoses a longing to escape from longing, a will to will-lessness. Nietzsche's view elsewhere is that philosophers in general 'take some fervent wish that they have sifted through and through and made properly abstract—and they defend it with rationalizations after the fact' (*BGE*, 5). Schopenhauer's theory of an altered sense of self in which one enters a state of pure cognition, and identifies oneself with an arena of consciousness purged of all affect (other than the blissfulness of not having to feel affects) is constructed in the service of a will or wish whose aversions and longings shape his attempts to understand reality. But that is just what we would expect according to Schopenhauer's own theory of the primacy of the will and its dominant influence over cognition. In other words, Nietzsche seeks to undermine Schopenhauer's theorizing about affect-free cognition by applying a version of Schopenhauer's own theory that affects and passions are always liable to drive our conceptual thinking.

10.4 Perspectivism, Affects, and Nietzsche's Cognitive Enterprise

Beyond claiming that Schopenhauer's ideal of pure cognition is a myth, what does Nietzsche mean when he says 'There is ... only a perspectival "knowing" '? And what does he mean when he says '*the more* affects we allow to speak about a matter ... that much more complete will our "concept" of this matter, our "objectivity" be'? He is not only at odds with Schopenhauer, but would appear to call for a reassessment of any view that regards the affects as merely liable to impair cognition. But precisely what that reassessment should involve is a matter of some dispute. In a previous discussion,[13] I offered the following interpretation of the chief claims contained in this part of Nietzsche's text:

(1) that there is only knowledge that is guided or facilitated by our feelings,
(2) that the more different feelings we allow to guide our knowledge, the better our knowledge will be.

However, this reading has been subjected to a number of objections. First, that in the relevant passage Nietzsche need not be read as primarily concerned with proposing a general thesis about knowledge, a view put forward by Ken Gemes:

> we should think of perspectivism primarily as ... the injunction to let as many drives as possible be expressed.... Schopenhauer is clearly not simply describing knowledge as involving the quieting of the will, what Nietzsche in GM derides as 'the passions cooled', but is actually thereby advocating a withdrawal from the world of passions and more generally willing. By interpreting perspectivism not primarily as a thesis about the nature of knowledge and objectivity but as a normative injunction to a certain ideal of health we more directly connect with the issue of primary importance to Nietzsche.[14]

We can agree that Nietzsche's attack on Schopenhauer's conception of 'pure knowledge' is part of his wider campaign against the unhealthy 'ascetic ideal'—indeed we have said so above—and that the unhealthiness Nietzsche is concerned with is a matter of some debilitation of our drives. But the injunction in the perspectivism passage is addressed specifically to *philosophers*. And it is plausible to think that if we are to identify a healthy, life-affirming way of being a philosopher, we will require a revised conception of the philosopher's characteristic enterprise of 'knowing', as Nietzsche explicitly states.

Drives are in action when we do philosophy, for Nietzsche. He characterizes the philosopher in terms of a particular complex of drives: 'his doubting drive, his negating drive, his wait-and-see ("ephectic") drive, his analytical drive, his exploring, searching, venturing drive, his comparing, balancing drive' (*GM* III, 9). Elsewhere he says of the philosopher that 'the order of rank [in which] the innermost drives of his nature stand to one another' constitutes 'who he is' and that all the 'basic drives', rather than any fundamental 'drive for knowledge', have practised philosophy (*BGE*, 6). Philosophy is a way of giving expression to one's drives. Hence, one way of giving healthy expression to one's drives may well be to philosophize in a healthy way. But a precondition for attaining that healthy way of approaching the philosopher's activity is, as Nietzsche says, to resist the yearning for the mythical state of 'pure', affect-free cognition. That Nietzsche issues the injunction that Gemes identifies is therefore compatible with his proposing a claim about knowledge.

Paul Katsafanas[15] takes issue with claim (2) on two grounds: (a) that the text does not license the idea that knowing is 'better' the more feelings one brings to bear on the object of knowledge; (b) for anyone to make such a claim would be 'incredible'. (The two points are independent, unless one believes Nietzsche could not have claimed something incredible, a belief it would be hard to justify.) How we should read the text may in the end hinge on nuance and impression, as much in Nietzsche's writings does. But it looks as though, having warned philosophers against the conception of 'knowing' as a wholly disinterested, affect-free state, Nietzsche next gives them a *reason* to avoid that conception. The reason is that 'knowing' is more complete with more affects, less complete with fewer affects, so to think of a knower from whom *all* affect is absent is to think of someone who succeeds less as a 'knower'. To succeed less as a knower is to be worse as a knower, and so to have more affects brought to bear on the object of one's knowledge is to be better as a knower. The text at least bears that construal without undue distortion.

If we find (2) an odd thing to say, we should at least consider whether it is an odd thing for *Nietzsche* to be saying. And, to the contrary, we find that it harmonizes with a number of utterances he makes elsewhere. For example, he insists that for his book *Thus Spoke Zarathustra* to be properly intelligible to an interpreter, he or she must have been 'at sometime deeply wounded and at sometime deeply delighted by each of its words' (*GM*, Preface, 8). Again he pronounces that

> 'Selflessness' has no value in heaven or on earth; all great problems demand *great* love.... It makes the most telling difference whether a thinker has a personal relationship to his problems and finds in them his destiny, his distress, and his greatest happiness, or an 'impersonal' one, meaning he is only able to touch and grasp them with the antennae of cold, curious thought. In the latter case nothing will come of it, that much can be promised (*GS*, 345).

It is undeniable here that the 'cold' and 'impersonal' approach is one that seeks to eliminate affects (love, distress, happiness), and that Nietzsche proclaims it an unfruitful approach to the thinker's task.

So Nietzsche's texts at least lend some credence to his making claim (2). Is it in itself a credible claim, though? Katsafanas confronts the claim with the following example:

> I am serving on a jury and must assess the case against an individual charged with murder. Following... claim (2), I attempt to cultivate feelings of rage, indignation, sympathy, desire for revenge, desire for forgiveness, and so forth. Is this emotional tangle really going to help me to adjudicate the merits of the case, weigh the evidence, and achieve 'better' knowledge of the arguments on each side? That seems incredible.[16]

But, in reply, how relevant is such an example to Nietzsche? Nietzsche is concerned with enhancing knowledge by bringing multiple affects to bear on 'one and the same matter [*Sache*]', but we should pause to ask what that might embrace. It is unlikely that he means 'one and the same proposition'. So his claim is unlikely to be that I have better knowledge of whether X murdered Y, the more affects I bring to bear on that question. In his *Genealogy*, as we saw, Nietzsche is seeking knowledge *of moral values*—'a knowledge of the conditions and circumstances out of which they have grown, under which they have shifted and developed... knowledge of a kind that has neither existed up until now nor even been desired' (*GM*, Preface, 6). This kind of 'knowing' is an investigative project that for Nietzsche must involve the investigator in doubt, insecurity, anxiety, and distress. If Nietzsche's question is how a philosopher should best go about the task of exploring, analysing, understanding, and reacting to the pervasive and complex aspect of human life that is 'morality', repeatedly challenging his or her own secure preconceptions and values in the process, then to take 'knowing' as if it meant satisfying conditions for having knowledge of a single proposition—what we earlier saw referred to as the concern of 'traditional epistemology'—is clearly misplaced.

Gemes provides another objection: that both (1) and (2) are either trivial causal claims or implausible constitutive claims, neither of which Nietzsche is likely to be making. Here is Gemes again:

> The worry with the causal reading is that this may be seen as a fairly banal reading of the alleged affect-dependence of knowledge according to which what affects we have will, to some degree, determine the knowledge we have. For instance, one whose affects are aroused by cricket is more likely to have knowledge of Bradman's test average than one who has no affects aroused by cricket. The claim that the more affects we have the more knowledge we (are likely to) have has the implication, for instance, that one whose only affects concerning London are wholly focused on London's tourist attractions is likely to have less knowledge of London than one who has an affective response to multiple facets of London (tourist attractions, history, politics, transport network, etc). All this makes perspectivism a fairly trivial thesis.[17]

Perhaps these are 'trivial' claims. But even if they are, it should not need stating that we cannot infer from their triviality to the conclusion that Nietzsche does not make them. And if we are afraid of diminishing Nietzsche's contribution here, we should reflect that in the dialectical context in which he is working, arguing against an opponent who holds the theory that 'every affect or passion obscures and falsifies knowledge', it would serve Nietzsche well to advert to some uncontroversial truths that conflict with the opponent's view. Therefore, there is no obvious reason to conclude that Nietzsche does not advance the kinds of causal claim Gemes cites.

The example of 'knowledge of London' provides a much better model for understanding Nietzsche's concerns than 'knowing whether X murdered Y'. The former is a complex, varied, and potentially inexhaustible kind of knowledge, which cannot be assimilated to the weighing of evidence for believing a single proposition, or even a conjunction of propositions. And it seems plausible to say that multiplying affects plays a role in this kind of knowledge. To elaborate the example, the more I can enjoy springtime in a central London square, feel at home in some parts and uneasy in others, confident about how to traverse the city but frustrated by the bus service, disappointed by some of the changes in architecture, excited by the choice of music performances, admiring of the cultural diversity and tolerance, envious of the super-rich, sympathetic to beggars, but also apprehensive and annoyed about their presence on the streets, and so on, the better I know the city. Nietzsche's project of gaining 'knowledge' about the origins and value of morality is more plausibly analogous to our example of progressively coming to know London than it is to someone's weighing evidence for believing that X murdered Y.

The other horn of Gemes' dilemma was that if Nietzsche claims not merely a causal, but a constitutive connection between cognition and affect, then he says something implausible. The textual evidence for Nietzsche's making a constitutive claim of this kind is admittedly far from conclusive. He states that a cognizing mind that is not actively interpretative is 'an absurdity and non-concept [*ein Widersinn und Unbegriff*]'. That could be interpreted as saying that it would be contradictory to think of such a mind. And since the only forms of active interpretation mentioned explicitly in the context are 'affective interpretations [*Affekt-Interpretationen*]', we may think that what is contradictory is the conception of a cognitive mind that does not make affective interpretations; in other words, that making affective interpretations is constitutive of a cognizing mind. This is perhaps to labour the text. But if Nietzsche did mean this, would it be so implausible a claim? On the one hand, it might be that the kind of strenuous investigative project of 'knowing' that a *Nietzschean philosopher* would undertake has 'great love', 'deep delight', 'suspicion', and 'fear' as ineliminable components—that you could not engage your intellectual conscience and probe deeply enough into your philosophical prejudices unless you underwent such emotions in the process. Nietzsche straightforwardly says as much about the ideal 'Nietzschean knower'. But one might also argue that even more sober, non-Nietzschean processes of investigation in search of knowledge belong to a type of activity of which some affects—feeling uncertain, feeling disappointed, feeling confident, empowered or satisfied—are constitutive. Similar ideas can be found among Nietzsche's pragmatist contemporaries. William James writes that 'the transition from a state of puzzle and perplexity to rational comprehension is full of lively relief and pleasure',[18] and Peirce that 'Doubt is an uneasy and dissatisfied state from which we struggle to free ourselves and pass into the state of belief'.[19] A case might be made for saying that the process of human investigation—the sort of activity engaged in by all *Erkennenden*—essentially involves affects at various stages. If so, then it will be only from within a narrow 'traditional epistemological' assumption about the relation of affects to cognition (which may anyway turn out to be a rather recent orthodoxy) that it can so automatically seem odd that Nietzsche takes the view he appears to in his remarks about perspectival 'knowing'.

10.5 Conclusion

To see the import of the point at issue between Schopenhauer and Nietzsche—whether affects spoil or enhance knowledge or cognition—we must beware of imposing on either thinker a particular epistemological paradigm, which we have here labelled that of 'traditional epistemology'. Neither philosopher is principally seeking an analysis of 'S knows that p'. Schopenhauer thinks of *Erkenntnis* in a broadly Platonic manner as a cognitive state of mind in which the subject achieves some degree of access to reality. In this model, access to reality is increased by the absence of subjective desires and affects, but also by the replacement of conceptual thought by a higher form of intuitive insight. For Nietzsche, *Erkennen* is primarily an activity, a protracted and demanding search for knowledge and understanding of a novel kind. One thing that Schopenhauer and Nietzsche have in common, as we have seen, is the belief that affective states play a pervasive role in guiding and shaping human cognition as they conceive it. Schopenhauer combines this view with the claim that cognition is consequently imperfect, and for him there is also the potential for a 'pure' cognitive access to reality, which tends towards objectivity precisely to the extent that affective states of the subject are in abeyance. Nietzsche criticizes Schopenhauer's position by making the following claims: (a) there is no possibility of a 'pure', objective, affect-free cognition, (b) cognition is not rendered imperfect through its being guided and shaped by affects, and (c) the belief that there is an absolutely 'pure' objective form of cognition is itself an instance of theoretical thinking's being motivated by underlying affective states, such as a longing to be free of desires, a hatred of the human, or an aversion to life. This third critical point shows that for Nietzsche it is possible to *go wrong* because one's understanding is driven by affects. Engagement of the affects is not sufficient for gaining knowledge. But in his view, cognition is improved not by eliminating affects, which he holds to be impossible, but rather by opening oneself to a wider range of differing affects. Nietzsche's position can seem hyperbolic, as when he suggests that the activity of inquiry can succeed only in the presence of great love, highest elation, and deepest despair. Nonetheless, we have suggested that, when thinking of cognition or 'knowing' as an investigative activity, we should recognize it as having typical affective contours, such as a transition from calmness into doubt and dissatisfaction, and from these states into the joy of discovery. But in particular it is arguable that the kind of self-critical investigative activity Nietzsche envisages, his opening up of 'immense new vistas', in which all one's previous attitudes towards morality must be called into question, could not be undertaken effectively by someone who was not prepared to experience and confront some anxieties and ambivalences of feeling. In *Beyond Good and Evil* he suggests that somebody who 'considers even the affects of hatred, envy, greed, and power-lust as the conditioning affects of life... will suffer from such a train of thought as if from sea-sickness' and will enter a realm of 'dangerous knowledge' (*BGE*, 23). Such knowledge as this, at any rate, is not to be gained, in Nietzsche's view, without undergoing deeply unsettling feelings.[20]

Notes

1. See *BGE* 6, 12; *WLN* pp. 96, 139. I refer to the following works of Nietzsche by abbreviation: *Beyond Good and Evil* (*BGE*); *On the Genealogy of Morality* (*GM*); *The Gay Science* (*GS*); *Writings from the Late Notebooks* (*WLN*). Citations of *WLN* are to page numbers. Citations of Nietzsche's published works are to section numbers. I refer to the following works of Schopenhauer by abbreviation: *On the Fourfold Root of the Principle of Sufficient Reason* (*FR*); *Prize Essay on the Basis of Morals* (*BM*); *Prize Essay on the Freedom of the Will* (*FW*); *The World as Will and Representation* vol. 1 (*WWR* 1); *The World as Will and Representation*, vol. 2 (*WWR* 2).
2. Christopher Janaway, *Beyond Selflessness: Reading Nietzsche's Genealogy* (Oxford: Oxford University Press, 2007), pp. 202–16.
3. Georg Brun and Dominique Kuenzle, 'Introduction: A New Role for Emotions in Epistemology?', in *Epistemology and Emotions*, ed. Brun, Kuenzle and Ulvi Doguoglu (Abingdon: Ashgate, 2008), pp. 1–31 (p. 1).
4. See Brun and Kuenzle, 'Introduction', pp. 3–4.
5. Moritz Schlick, 'On the Foundation of Knowledge', in *Moritz Schlick: Philosophical Papers*, ed. Henk Mulder and Barbara van de Velde-Schlick, vol. 2. (Dordrecht: Reidel, 1971), pp. 370–87 (p. 382). (Cited in Brun and Kuenzle, 'Introduction', p. 2).
6. Mark Johnston, 'The Authority of Affect', *Philosophy and Phenomenological Research* 43 (2001): 181–214 (p. 181).
7. As at *GM*, Preface, 1.
8. See *WWR* 1, pp. 57–76 (§§ 8–10); and Christopher Janaway, 'Schopenhauer on Cognition (Erkenntnis) (W 1 §§ 8–16)', in *Arthur Schopenhauer: Die Welt als Wille und Vorstellung*, ed. Oliver Hallich and Matthias Koßler (Berlin: De Gruyter, 2014), pp. 35–50.
9. See *FR*, pp. 100–4 (§§ 29–33).
10. See Janaway, *Beyond Selflessness*, pp. 205–6. Sources are *BGE* 19, 23, 187, 192, 260; *GM* I, 10, 13; *GM* II, 11, 15; *GM* III, 20.
11. See Christopher Janaway, 'The Real Essence of Human Beings: Schopenhauer and the Unconscious Will', in *Thinking the Unconscious: Nineteenth-Century German Thought*, ed. Angus Nicholls and Martin Liebscher (Cambridge: Cambridge University Press, 2012), pp. 140–55 (pp. 142–3).
12. *Critique of Pure Reason*, A402. Schopenhauer compares his view to Kant's at *WWR* 2, p. 277.
13. Janaway, *Beyond Selflessness*, p. 206.
14. Ken Gemes, 'Janaway on Perspectivism', *European Journal of Philosophy* 17 (2009): 101–12 (pp. 106–7).

15. Paul Katsafanas, 'Review of Christopher Janaway, *Beyond Selflessness: Reading Nietzsche's* Genealogy', *Mind* 122 (2013): 553–60 (pp. 557–8).
16. Katsafanas, 'Review of Janaway', p. 557.
17. Gemes, 'Janaway on Perspectivism', p. 105.
18. 'The Sentiment of Rationality', in *The Will to Believe and Other Essays in Popular Philosophy* (New York: Longmans, 1897), p. 63.
19. 'The Fixation of Belief', in *The Essential Peirce: Selected Philosophical Writings*, vol. 1 (1867–1893), ed. Nathan Houser and Christian Kloesel (Bloomington/Indianapolis: Indiana University Press, 1992), p. 114. For further discussion see Christopher Hookway, 'Doubt: Affective States and the Regulation of Inquiry', in Hookway, *Truth, Rationality and Pragmatism: Themes from Peirce* (Oxford: Oxford University Press, 2002), pp. 246–64.
20. Earlier versions were delivered at the inaugural conference of the Centre for the History of Philosophy at the University of York, and at research seminars at the University of Southampton and Birkbeck, University of London. I am grateful for comments from the audiences on these occasions, and specific thanks to Ken Gemes, Marie Guillot, Aaron Ridley, the editors of the present volume, and an anonymous referee.

Bibliography

Works by Schopenhauer

On the Fourfold Root of the Principle of Sufficient Reason (*FR*), trans. David E. Cartwright, Edward E. Erdmann, and Christopher Janaway (Cambridge: Cambridge University Press, 2012).

Prize Essay on the Basis of Morals, in *The Two Fundamental Problems of Ethics* (*BM*), trans. and ed. Christopher Janaway (Cambridge: Cambridge University Press, 2009).

Prize Essay on the Freedom of the Will, in *The Two Fundamental Problems of Ethics* (*FW*), trans. and ed. Christopher Janaway (Cambridge: Cambridge University Press, 2009).

The World as Will and Representation, vol. 1 (*W1*), trans. and ed. Judith Norman, Alistair Welchman, and Christopher Janaway (Cambridge: Cambridge University Press, 2010).

The World as Will and Representation, vol. 2 (*W2*), trans. E.F.J. Payne (New York: Dover, 1958).

Works by Nietzsche

Beyond Good and Evil, ed. Rolf-Peter Horstmann and Judith Norman, trans. Judith Norman (Cambridge: Cambridge University Press, 2002).

On the Genealogy of Morality, trans. Maudemarie Clark and Alan J. Swensen (Indianapolis: Hackett, 1998).

The Gay Science, ed. Bernard Williams, trans. Josephine Nauckhoff and Adrian del Caro (Cambridge: Cambridge University Press, 2001).

Thus Spoke Zarathustra, trans. R. J. Hollingdale (Harmondsworth: Penguin, 1969).

Writings from the Late Notebooks, ed. Rüdiger Bittner, trans. Kate Sturge (Cambridge: Cambridge University Press, 2003).

Other works

Brun, Georg and Dominique Kuenzle. 'Introduction: A New Role for Emotions in Epistemology?', in *Epistemology and Emotions*, ed. Georg Brun, Ulvi Doguoglu, and Dominique Kuenzle (Abingdon: Ashgate, 2008).

Gemes, Ken. 'Janaway on Perspectivism', *European Journal of Philosophy* 17 (2009): 101–12.

Hookway, Christopher, 'Doubt: Affective States and the Regulation of Inquiry', in Hookway, *Truth, Rationality and Pragmatism: Themes from Peirce* (Oxford: Oxford University Press, 2002), pp. 246–64.

James, William, 'The Sentiment of Rationality', in *The Will to Believe and Other Essays in Popular Philosophy* (New York: Longmans, 1897), pp. 63–110.

Janaway, Christopher. *Beyond Selflessness: Reading Nietzsche's* Genealogy (Oxford: Oxford University Press, 2007).

Janaway, Christopher. 'The Real Essence of Human Beings: Schopenhauer and the Unconscious Will', in *Thinking the Unconscious: Nineteenth-Century German Thought*, ed. Angus Nicholls and Martin Liebscher (Cambridge: Cambridge University Press, 2012).

Janaway, Christopher. 'Schopenhauer on Cognition (*Erkenntnis*) (W1 §§ 8–16)', in *Arthur Schopenhauer: Die Welt als Wille und Vorstellung*, ed. Oliver Hallich and Matthias Koßler (Berlin: De Gruyter, 2014), pp. 8–16.

Johnston, Mark. 'The Authority of Affect', *Philosophy and Phenomenological Research* 43 (2001): 181–214.

Johnston, Mark. *Surviving Death* (Princeton: Princeton University Press, 2010).

Kant, Immanuel. *Critique of Pure Reason*, trans. Paul Guyer and A. W. Wood (Cambridge: Cambridge University Press, 1997).

Katsafanas, Paul. 'Review of Christopher Janaway, *Beyond Selflessness: Reading Nietzsche's* Genealogy', *Mind* 122 (2013): 553–60.

Pierce, Charles S. 'The Fixation of Belief', in *The Essential Peirce: Selected Philosophical Writings*, vol. 1 (1867–1893), ed. Nathan Houser and Christian Kloesel (Bloomington/Indianapolis: Indiana University Press, 1992), pp. 109–123.

Schlick, Moritz. 'On the Foundation of Knowledge', in *Moritz Schlick: Philosophical Papers*, vol. 2, ed. H. Mulder and B. van de Velde-Schlick (Dordrecht: Reidel, 1971).

11

Thrills, Orgasms, Sadness, and Hysteria

Austro-German Criticisms of William James

Kevin Mulligan

11.1 Introduction

Is there anything 'in' the mind which is not 'about' something? Ever since the end of the nineteenth century, philosophers of mind have disagreed about whether mental or psychological states or experiences are, as Brentano argued, always directed towards something, whether they enjoy what he called the property of intentionality. Four of the favourite candidates for the role of mental or psychological items which lack intentionality are visual sensations, bodily pains, bodily sensations such as thrills, and moods. The disagreement spans the two most important traditions in the philosophy of mind: that inspired by Brentano, and analytic philosophy of mind. Thus Husserl argues that visual sensations and bodily pains lack intentionality. Sartre and other phenomenologists argue that there are no visual sensations but that pain lacks intentionality, Broad that there are objectless feelings, and Searle that pain and what are often called moods lack intentionality.

One of the most influential sources of these disagreements is the reaction by Brentano's student, Carl Stumpf, in 1899, 1907, and 1916, to James's account of emotions. James, Stumpf argues, is wrong to identify emotions and bodily feelings, since the former unlike the latter enjoy intentionality. Accounts of the structure of emotions and bodily feelings like Stumpf's are also defended by another student of Brentano's, Husserl, and by the phenomenologist Max Scheler. The three accounts rely on an unfamiliar philosophy of the mind which is not only thoroughly mentalistic but attributes to mental phenomena quite distinctive types of complexity.

Many aspects of James's philosophy were taken very seriously indeed by Brentano's students, Anton Marty and the already mentioned Carl Stumpf and Edmund Husserl, who knew just how much Brentanian descriptive psychology James had absorbed and how much he had rejected. Husserl's remarks about James in his *Logical Investigations* are a good indication of the high esteem he enjoyed amongst Brentano's heirs:

> How little James's genius for observation in the field of descriptive psychology entails psychologism, can be seen from the present work. For the advances in descriptive analysis that I owe to this distinguished thinker have only facilitated my release from the psychologistic standpoint.[1]

And in a very early (1892) review of James's *Principles of Psychology*, Marty takes over fifty pages to nail what are presented as James's mistakes and carelessness amid much praise for the liveliness and accuracy of many of his descriptions. James's views about emotions are discussed in detail in the Brentanian tradition not only by Stumpf, Marty, and Scheler (in his very detailed account of the emotions),[2] but also by Brentano[3] himself and by Stumpf's student, the essayist, philosopher, and novelist, Robert Musil,[4] in his account of emotions as *Gestalten*.[5] And in the last important phenomenological account of the emotions, Sartre also criticizes James.[6]

James was familiar with some of the discussion by Brentano's heirs of his views on the emotions and psychology, as his correspondence with his friend, Stumpf, shows. Thus he writes in a letter to Stumpf of Marty's review (very generously, since the review does not always avoid the tone of the professorial pedant):

> Many indeed most of his objections hit the mark, some of the things he says are based on misunderstandings. But he proceeds in too microscopic a fashion, he takes too little account of the general pedagogical approach of such a book. Who apart from myself will even read such a long report? But I feel honoured and touched that someone has studied the book so thoroughly. Only Germans are capable of such devotion.[7]

In what follows I first (§11.2) identify the central thesis defended by James about emotions which will be the focus of part of the subsequent discussion. I then (§§11.3–6) consider some Austro-German accounts of sensations and emotions and their relations to James's views. *Emotions* (§11.5), according to many of Brentano's heirs, are essentially spontaneous attitudes which enjoy two distinct kinds of intentionality. They are directed towards the objects and situations presented or represented by the perceptual and intellectual acts or states they depend on. But they are also directed towards values. The distinction between the two types of intentionality is rooted in a further distinction, which is supposed to be found in all cases of intentionality, between mental 'modes' and contents. *Bodily feelings*, such as pain, on the other hand, are not attitudes, lack intentionality, and, according to Stumpf, Husserl, and Scheler, are in fact a type of sensation (§11.3), which they call affective sensations (*Gefühlsempfindung*).[8] It follows, they argue, that emotions and sensations differ in many ways (§11.5). Some of these differences are not unfamiliar to the contemporary philosopher since they are discussed by Wittgenstein. But, as we shall see, Wittgenstein's apparent agreement with Brentano's heirs does not go very far. For what the latter say about emotions and affective sensations is rooted in an essentialist, mentalist account of mental complexity and structure and in naïve realism about values—all of which is very foreign to Wittgenstein. Finally (§11.6), I consider some aspects of Scheler's critique of James and his claim that there is nevertheless a grain of truth in the American philosopher's account of emotions.

11.2 James's Emotions

James's *identity thesis* is that 'bodily changes follow directly the perception of the exciting fact, and that our feeling of the same changes as they occur *is* the emotion'.[9]

There are many questions which can and have been raised about this formulation and other things James says. Is it a scientific hypothesis?[10] What is the relation between *feeling* bodily changes and *feeling* an emotion? James sometimes suggests that the link between feelings of bodily changes and (felt) emotions, although very intimate, is not identity—'our emotions probably owe their pungent quality to the bodily sensations which they involve'; in his discussion of one type of emotion he says 'the bodily condition takes the lead, and... the mental emotion follows'.[11] In one of its later and most charming formulations James sums up his account thus:

> According to [the Lange-James[12]] theory, our emotions are mainly due to those organic stirrings that are aroused in us in a reflex way by the stimulus of the exciting object or situation. An emotion of fear, for example, or surprise, is not a direct effect of the object's presence on the mind, but an effect of that still earlier effect, the bodily commotion which the object suddenly excites; so that, were this bodily commotion suppressed, we should not so much *feel* fear as call the situation fearful; we should not feel surprise, but coldly recognize that the object was indeed astonishing. One enthusiast has even gone so far as to say that when we feel sorry it is because we weep, when we feel afraid it is because we run away, and not conversely... Now, whatever exaggeration may possibly lurk in this account of our emotions (and I doubt myself whether the exaggeration be very great), it is certain that the main core of it is true, and that the mere giving way to tears, for example, or to the outward expression of an anger-fit, will result for the moment in making the inner grief or anger more acutely felt... Action seems to follow feeling, but really action and feeling go together; and by regulating the action, which is under the more direct control of the will, we can indirectly regulate the feeling, which is not.[13]

If emotions are 'mainly due' to organic stirrings, one may wonder what else they are due to. And this passage raises many questions about just what it means to say that action, that is to say, expressive action such as weeping, and feeling 'go together'. If giving way to tears makes inner grief more intensely felt, are we to assume that the grief was already felt, albeit less intensely, before the weeping? But then why claim that we feel grief because we weep rather than that we feel more intensely because we weep? Nevertheless James here clearly identifies many of the different pieces of the jigsaw puzzle which psychologists and philosophers of emotions endlessly reassemble in order to provide an account of emotions: organic stirrings and feelings thereof, emotions and felt emotions, the presence to the mind of objects and situations, expressive behaviour, and even such properties as the fearfulness of a situation.[14]

If episodic emotions and felt bodily commotions are the very same thing, then whatever is true of the one must be true of the other—they must have the same 'multiplicity', to use a term popular with Brentano's heirs and Wittgenstein. Karl Bühler notes that consideration of the relevant multiplicities is at the heart of the two great criticisms of James's theory which ask whether his 'affect formula' can be 'reversed', the criticisms of Cannon and of Stumpf in his 'classic treatise' of 1899:

> If anger is identical with certain sensations (*Sensationen*), then these sensations must be identical with anger. And it must be possible to find again in the bodily processes mentioned and their 'being felt' the subjectively graspable multiplicity of affects.[15]

11.3 Sensations—Affective, Organic, and Perceptual

Stumpf, Husserl, and Scheler all endorse distinct versions of the extreme view that not only such 'sensory feelings' (*sinnliche Gefühle*) as localized, bodily pains but many other sensory feelings are just sensations, affective sensations. Stumpf's version of this view, the earliest version to be published, grows directly out of his *Auseinandersetzung* with James's account of emotions.[16]

In 1899 Stumpf objects to James's subtraction argument in support of what Stumpf calls his 'sensualist' account of emotions, that although it is quite true that we cannot *think* of someone who is frightened without thinking of her as flinching, of someone who is angry without thinking of his red or pale face, the fact that one thing cannot be thought of without thinking of something else by no means shows that the two things are identical. James's subtraction argument lacks all 'logically compelling force'. The question is whether a person's emotion would in fact disappear if all organic sensations disappeared whilst the intellectual state of the person remained the same. James, Stumpf argues, overlooks the fact that the disappearance of organic sensations necessarily disturbs and modifies the intellectual functions.[17]

But, Stumpf says, the only way to reply to what, thanks to James and Lange, has become a 'burning question', the question about 'the features common to the extraordinary multiplicity' of affective states and about 'what distinguishes them from other psychic states', is to provide a philosophical account of the phenomena with which, according to James and Lange, emotions are to be identified and of related phenomena.[18] James, he says, has proposed a revision of the 'older view' according to which what was always taken to be mere accompaniments of emotions are the emotions themselves. Stumpf proposes to defend the older view. But in order to do so he is driven to defend a radical version of part of the old view, the claim that sensory feelings are just sensations and that bodily pain is only one of many such sensations. In 1899 he says of 'the purely sensory feelings of pleasantness and unpleasantness' that they are produced by sense impressions—the 'sensory pleasantness of a colour, of a taste...is directly called forth by the sensory impression'.[19] In 1907 he identifies sensory feelings as affective sensations, which include

> purely bodily pains (i.e. pains which occur without the concomitant participation of intellectual functions); secondly, the feeling of bodily well-being in its more general and in its more special forms, the latter including the pleasure-component in tickle, the feeling produced by itch, and the sexual feelings; and lastly the pleasantness and unpleasantness that may be connected, in the most various degrees of gradation, with the sensations of all or nearly all the 'special' senses, with temperatures, odours, tastes, tones, colours.[20]

Stumpf distinguishes two alternatives to his view. First, the view that sensory feelings are properties or dimensions of perceptual sensations, 'emotional tones' of these. Secondly, the view that sensory feelings are a new species of psychological elements or states. Against the first view, he argues (following Külpe) that although we may distinguish in a visual sensation its quality and strength, no emotional tone could be an aspect of a visual sensation in this sense. For sensory feelings display, just like visual sensations, a variety of properties such as qualitative differences, differences of strength and duration. Furthermore, perceptual sensations can occur without any affective element. In order to show that it is less plausible to take sensory feelings to be a new type of psychological element than to assign them to the category of sensations, Stumpf argues that the properties of sensory feelings are all exhibited by one or another type of perceptual sensation. In this connection he puts forward what is perhaps his single most important claim about sensory feelings: they are given as possessing spatial properties, such as extent, localization, and diffuseness: 'the pointedness of a pricking pain, the diffuseness of general discomfort is... due mainly to an immanent spatiality of pain itself as a content of consciousness'.[21] In this respect, they resemble, Stumpf argues, colour sensations which, according to a view he made famous, are inseparably connected with sensations of spatial extension.

Does this account of affective sensations yield an objection to James's account? Stumpf says that the core of the account is that the essence of emotions consists in the 'peripheral, bodily processes, which are usually taken to be expressions, reactions, accompaniments of emotions', but that a 'more exact' formulation of the account is that the essence of emotions lies in the feelings which we have of these peripheral, bodily processes *and* of the sensory feelings bound up with these. Stumpf thinks that the sensations referred to by James include both organic sensations and their 'affective tone', bodily commotions and their (un)pleasantness, and that James thinks that affective tone is 'decisive' for the nature of emotions.[22] But Stumpf here seems to have misunderstood James. For James, on at least one occasion, clearly asserts that the 'general seizure of excitement', which is, he says, what he means by an emotion is not to be confused with the 'tone of feeling', the 'pleasantness or painfulness' of content.[23] What Stumpf calls a more exact formulation of James's view is not the formulation given by James. But something like the 'more exact formulation' is often employed in contemporary accounts of emotions which incorporate aspects of James's theory. These accounts often differ from James in including in the class of felt bodily modifications essential to emotions not just James's organic sensations but whatever is responsible for the valence or polarity of affective phenomena. One candidate for the latter role is precisely affective sensations of pleasure, pain, and unpleasure.[24]

Husserl's 1901 account of sensory feelings also asserts these to be affective sensations. Sensory pains and pleasures, such as 'the pleasant taste of a dish, the pleasant fragrance of a rose', are not only typically fused with visual (auditive, tactile etc.) sensations; they also behave in all respects like perceptual sensations. Visual and affective sensations are 'interpreted' or 'grasped' as relating to objects: a red sensation to the property of redness, and a sensation of pain to a part of the body.[25] Although affective sensations have no directedness in and of themselves, they are essential to emotions, which are directed. Similarly, visual sensations enjoy no intentionality but are essential to seeing, which does. The 'act-character' of being pleased by an object is not any pleasure sensation.[26] Husserl repeats this claim in later writings: 'Sensations play a role in . . . intentional experiences in the sphere of emotions which is analogous to the role played by primary sensations in intentional experiences in the sphere of experience'; each type of sensation provides intentional experiences with their 'stuff'.[27]

In 1913–16 Scheler endorses the claims made by Stumpf and Husserl about affective sensations: 'unlike all other feelings, they are given as *extended* and *localised* in particular parts of the living body (*Leib*)'.[28] Amongst his examples of affective sensations are sensory pains and pleasures, feelings of the pleasantness and unpleasantness of food and drink, of touch and tickling sensations, and sensual, for example, sexual, pleasures. The tickle (*Kitzel*) of sexual feelings, he thinks, is 'the concentration of positive sensory feelings'.[29] He makes three further claims. First, an affective sensation 'is as a matter of essential necessity given as a *state*'.[30] Secondly, pleasantness and unpleasantness are value-properties, sensory or hedonic values.[31] Finally, Scheler attaches no importance to the analogy drawn by Husserl between visual sensations and affective sensations; visual sensations are a philosophical invention and the category of sensations should be restricted, as ordinary language suggests, to organic sensations, affective sensations, and their ilk.[32]

Affective sensations and organic sensations lack intentionality, according to Stumpf, Husserl, and Scheler. According to Husserl, affective sensations are 'non-intentional experiences'.[33] 'Even the most primitive form of intentionality', says Scheler, 'is missing in the pure sensory feelings';[34] 'being directed (*Gerichtetsein*) is not immanent' to affective sensation. From this feature of affective sensations Scheler draws the conclusion that they cannot be 'motivated'. Emotions, on the other hand, according to all heirs of Brentano, enjoy intentionality and can be motivated. As we shall now see, their account of these two properties of emotions is unusual, subtle, and baroque.

11.4 Emotions—Attitudes, Modes, Correctness, and Values

The unusual and subtle features of the account of emotions given by Brentano's heirs emerge clearly if we take, as an object of comparison, Wittgenstein's views about emotions, views which, like those of Stumpf, often take the form of reactions to James.[35]

Like Brentano's heirs, Wittgenstein distinguishes between directed and undirected emotions, between 'fear *at* something, joy *over* something', on the one hand, and anxiety (*Angst*), when it takes the form of 'undirected fear'.[36] Both Heidegger and Freud distinguish in a similar way between fear, which is directed, and *Angst*, which is not. *Angst* belongs to the category of 'objectless emotions or moods (*Stimmungen*)' described by Pfänder, one of the founders of the phenomenological movement, in 1904.[37] Similarly, Scheler describes both bliss and despair as affective states which, like affective sensations, have no objects, unlike the love and hate which may give rise to bliss and despair.[38] Within the category of directed experiences, there is a distinction, noted by Husserl, between experiences which have a determinate direction and those which have an indeterminate direction:

> [There are] intentional experiences, which are characterised by indeterminateness of objective direction, an indeterminateness which does not amount to a privation, but which stands for a descriptive character of one's presentation. The idea we have when 'something' stirs, when there is a rustling, a ring at the door, etc., . . . has indeterminateness of direction, and this indeterminateness is of the intention's essence, and is determined as presenting an indeterminate 'something'.

As he points out in the same passage, presentations which present what they present in an indeterminate way, as a particular rather than a singular state of affairs, may provide the basis for emotion and for desires.[39]

Like many early phenomenologists, Wittgenstein classifies directed emotions as attitudes (*Stellungnahme*). Wittgenstein's examples are surprise, fright, admiration, and enjoyment.[40] 'Attitude' in contemporary philosophy of mind is typically employed to refer to so-called 'propositional attitudes' such as belief-that and desire-that and is often combined with the view that an attitude is an attitude towards propositions. But Wittgenstein and phenomenologists such as Adolph Reinach, Moritz Geiger, Edith Stein, and Dietrich von Hildebrand[41] think that both regret *that* one behaved in a certain way and admiration *of* or being pleased *by* someone, propositional and non-propositional emotions, are attitudes. This is the first difference between the contemporary account of attitudes and the earlier account.[42] Thus in 1916 von Hildebrand writes:

> If we consider joy about something, enthusiasm, longing... then all these experiences (*Erlebnisse*) display a common character. In spite of their qualitative differences they are all attitudes of mine towards the world of objects.[43]

Attitudes which are emotions, he goes on to argue, are *responses*: 'indignation (*Empörung*)... is a response (*Antwort*) to certain qualities, an attitude'.[44] And they are *spontaneous*:

> An attitude is a spontaneous experience, for every attitude (position-taking) is taken towards an object and thus has an intention towards something objective. Its content (*Gehalt*) has an ideal direction (*Richtung*) towards the object.[45]

This view is a development of Reinach's account of attitudes, intellectual and non-intellectual, as typically characterized by polar opposition and degrees: belief is opposed to disbelief, positive striving to negative striving, and love to hate. Knowledge and perception, on the other hand, are not attitudes.[46] This is a further difference between the view of attitudes now popular and the earlier view.[47] As we shall see, the phenomenologists thought that knowledge and perception cannot be attitudes *because* attitudes are responses and knowledge is not any sort of response.

Von Hildebrand's claim that emotions are not only attitudes but spontaneous attitudes marks a sharp break with earlier accounts of emotions; Stumpf, for example, following a long tradition, thinks of emotions, in contrast to, for example, desires, as passive phenomena.[48] The view that emotions are spontaneous emerges much later in an extreme form in Sartre's 1938 phenomenology of emotions.

The distinction between reactive, affective attitudes and pleasures and pains drawn by the early phenomenologists had been anticipated by one of James's early critics. Irons distinguishes reactive 'feeling-attitudes', of which emotions are one species, in which there is a 'feeling towards' something, on the one hand, and pleasure and pain, on the other hand. In the latter 'the line of direction is from the object to the self', in the former 'from the self outwards'.[49] In his reply to Irons, James 'fully agrees' with Irons' distinction between feeling-attitudes and pleasures and pains but suggests that 'visceral and muscular sensibility' can 'give the direction from the self outwards, if the higher senses (taken broadly, with their ideational sequelae) give the direction from the object to the self'.[50] James himself employs the category of attitudes and indeed anticipates the view that belief is an attitude towards a proposition. In his discussion of the views of Brentano and Marty on judging he distinguishes between the object of belief and 'the psychic attitude in which our mind stands towards the proposition taken as a whole'; this attitude is 'the belief itself'.[51] We shall return to James's views about attitudes in §11.6 in order to compare them to the views of the phenomenologists.

According to the early phenomenologists and Wittgenstein, then, directed emotions are both experiences and attitudes. According to the former, emotions are also spontaneous responses to something. *What, then, is it for an emotion to be directed towards something? And what are emotions responses to?*

The very sketchy answers given by the phenomenologists and Wittgenstein to the first question have some features in common. The answer given by the phenomenologists to the second question, which has no counterpart in Wittgenstein's reflections, is that what an emotion is a response to is not what it is about or directed towards. To anticipate, fear of a dog is directed towards a dog but is a response to its (apparent) danger, indignation that *p* is a response to the (apparent) injustice of the fact that *p*.

The answer given by the phenomenologists to the first of our two questions employs a distinctive account of mental complexity. According to Husserl's version of this account, we may distinguish within every mental act or state which enjoys intentionality, its 'mode' ('act-quality', 'act character') and its content. The three mental episodes of judging that *p*, supposing that *p* and seeing that *p* have the same content and object but differ in their mode, as do seeing and remembering *x*. Similarly, willing that *p* and hoping that *p* differ in their modes, as do admiring *x* and being displeased by *x*. A mode is what is often called a particularized property (Husserl's term is '*Moment*'); it is as particular and non-repeatable as the act or state of which it is a 'part'. So, too, is a content. So understood, contents are what are often called token contents, not to be confused with the abstract propositions which, on Husserl's account, some token contents instantiate, such as the content of a particular act of judging that *p*. Modes and contents are mutually dependent within the unity of a mental act or state. Modes come in two kinds: some may be independent of all other modes, some are dependent. The modes of seeing, conjecturing and judging are independent modes. The modes of emotions, desires, and willing are dependent modes; they depend one-sidedly (are founded) on thoughts, beliefs, perceptions, memories, anticipations etc. Dependent modes, like all modes, are inseparable from contents. But dependent modes inherit their content from the modes they depend on. Thus emotions inherit their 'directedness' from underlying seeings, rememberings, judgings, expectings. An emotion, then, consists of an affective mode—it is an admiring, a fear, a regret—and an intellectual or perceptual episode, which itself has a mode—it is a seeing, a remembering, a judging—and a content, and, as we have seen, affective and perhaps other sensations.[52] To say that an emotional mode depends on the mode of an intellectual or perceptual episode is to say that the former cannot exist without the latter and also that this modal claim is grounded in the nature or essence of episodes which enjoy the property of intentionality. Thus Husserl says of emotions such as 'being pleased by a melody', 'being displeased by a shrill whistle', 'joy' or its opposite that they are 'about something',[53] are 'intentional' and

> ...'owe' their intentional relation to certain presentations on which they are based.—But it belongs correctly to the meaning of talk about owing that they now have what they owe to these presentations.[54]

> Joy about some future event presupposes belief in the future event, expectation of the future event is the basis of the joy.[55]

Husserl's view is an application of his views about essence and modality:

It seems to belong to the essence of emotional acts (*Gemütsakte*) to be founded acts, indeed to be founded in intellective acts. Every emotional act is grounded in some presented or represented object, in some object which is taken to exist, in some state of affairs, in some assumption, certainty, conjecture etc., and this necessarily.[56]

Wittgenstein seems to accept all Husserl's negative modal claims:

If I say 'Every time I thought about it I was afraid'—did fear *accompany* my thoughts?—How is one to conceive of separating what does the accompanying from what is accompanied?

We could ask: How does fear pervade (*durchdringt*) a thought? For the former does not seem to be merely concurrent with the latter.... One also says: 'Thinking about it takes my breath away', and means not only that, as a matter of experience, this or that sensation or reaction accompanies this thought.[57]

Fear does not merely contingently coexist with or pervade thoughts. Emotions do not merely accompany or pervade thoughts. As Husserl puts it:

Whether we turn with pleasure to something, or whether its unpleasantness repels us, an object is presented. But we do not merely have a presentation with an added emotion (*Gefühl*) associatively tacked on to it.... [Rather], pleasure or distaste direct (*richten sich auf*) themselves to the presented object, and could not exist without such a direction.[58]

But although Wittgenstein accepts all Husserl's negative claims, he stops short of Husserl's positive claim, that emotions are dependent items, that 'joy is not an act on its own and the judgment an act standing beside it, the judgment is the act which founds the joy'.[59]

Wittgenstein cannot accept Husserl's positive claim because he rejects the view that there is the type of complexity peculiar to mental and psychological phenomena of which Brentano's heirs are so fond—dependent modes and interdependent modes and contents[60]—and because of his view that to describe the nature of mental phenomena is to describe the ways words are and ought to be used.[61] The rejection of such complexity is also to be found in James. This is one of Marty's chief complaints in his review of James's *Principles*. James's account of fringes and transitive states claims that such phenomena cannot be analysed into parts or aspects, dependent and independent. Here and elsewhere, argues Marty, James rejects the tradition of psychological analysis because he confuses real unity and simplicity.[62]

Wittgenstein offers us instead a metaphor. 'Emotions (*Gemütsbewegungen*)', he says, 'colour (*färben*) thoughts'.[63] One of his pupils unpacks this sort of claim as follows:

Imagine a great book in which a man's successive thoughts are written down in the form of sentences: the content of the thought (what it is a thought about) would be represented by the words that were printed; the emotional or desiring attitude with which the thought came would be represented by the colour of ink in which the words were printed, and plain black ink would be used if the thought had no emotional colouring.[64]

Jealous thoughts would then be expressed in green ink, ashamed thoughts in bright scarlet ink, depressed thoughts in grey or blue, and so on.[65]

Another claim made by Husserl about the relation of directedness or intentionality, which is due to the content of a mental act or state, is that it is no causal relation:

> We say that the object arouses our pleasure just as we say in other cases that some state of affairs inspires doubt, compels agreement, provokes desire etc. But the result of such apparent causation, the pleasure, doubt or agreement provoked, is itself through and through intentional…[I]t is absurd in principle, here or in like cases, to treat an intentional as a causal relation.[66]

Wittgenstein makes a related negative claim: 'a face which inspires fear or delight (the object of fear or delight), is not on that account its cause, but—one might say—its target (*Richtung*)'.[67] Since he also says that 'I hate Smith' is not equivalent to 'I hate + Smith is the cause of my hatred'[68] he seems to accept that the relation of hating Smith is not any causal relation between Smith and hatred or a hater rather than the claim that the object of an emotion is never its cause.[69]

In order to better understand the relation between the category of mental modes and its determinate, the category of attitudes, it is useful to consider an alternative to Reinach's view that emotions and belief are attitudes and so can vary in degrees, an alternative which has been advanced by some phenomenologists and other philosophers. Husserl formulates without quite endorsing a very radical way of distinguishing between emotions and affective sensations: differences of intensity between emotions belong 'primarily and properly' to the affective sensations emotions contain rather than to the emotions themselves; the mode of an emotion is degreeless.[70] Scheler defends an analogous view of belief: although there are no degrees of belief, all belief is bound up with certainty, which does admit of degrees; similarly, one may be more or less loath to give up a belief.[71] The view that affective and doxastic modes are themselves degreeless might be called, using Jamesian language, the spiritualist view of platonistic psychologists.

What, according to the phenomenologists, are spontaneous, affective attitudes responses to? Their answer to this question provides the second part of their account of the intentionality of emotions. As already indicated, their unanimous reply is: value. Husserl's version of this view involves supplementing the account already sketched of modes, contents, and objects by distinguishing between the *proper* and *improper* objects of acts and states. In fear of a dog the dog is the proper object of the fear and its danger the improper object of the fear. Husserl also distinguishes in a very similar way between 'the full intentional correlate' of an emotion and a less than full correlate, between a 'valuable thing' and a 'mere thing'.[72] The distinction is by no means restricted to emotions. It holds of non-affective attitudes and of some non-attitudes. Thus the proper object of judging that Sam is sad is Sam, its improper object is the obtaining of the state of affairs that Sam is sad. The improper object of the conjecture that Sam will be at the party is its being probable that Sam will be at the party. And the proper objects of preference for *x* over *y* are *x*, *y* whereas its improper object is the betterness of *x* with respect to *y*.

With the help of the distinction between proper and improper objects Husserl defends two further claims. First, that the exemplification of value by the proper object of an emotion or a preference constitutes the correctness condition for the emotion or preference. An attitude may be more or less reasonable or unreasonable. In particular, it is correct or incorrect. To ask the *Vernunftfrage* about an emotion is to ask whether an attitude of 'valuing' (*werten*, a term which Husserl uses for all emoting) 'is correct valuing, whether the intended value really is a value' of the proper object of the emotion.[73] Fear of a dog, we may say, is correct iff the dog is dangerous; shame about some past act is correct iff the act was shameful; the preference for *x* over *y* is correct iff *x* is better than *y*. Husserl notes that the correctness of an emotion should not be confused with the correctness of its basis: 'a joy is not yet correct if its doxastic basis is in the right'.[74] Thus, unlike many philosophers of emotions who reject Jamesian views, he does not say of joy that it must be based on an evaluative belief. For the proper object of joy, for example, the arrival of a friend (which may be the object of perception or of a non-evaluative belief) is not its improper object, the positive value of this event. His second claim is that if an emotion is correct, it is correct *because* the correctness condition holds, *because* value is exemplified; the emotion is not only correct but 'grounded' and it is correct because it is grounded or has a correctness maker.[75]

The idea that emotions, desires, and choices and not merely beliefs and assertions have correctness conditions goes all the way back to Plato and Aristotle. But although the correctness of non-intellectual states and acts reappears in, for example, Anselm and Aquinas, it seems to have been Husserl's teacher, Brentano, who revived the idea. Since Brentano was no naïve realist about value he rejected very forcefully Husserl's second claim in favour of an early version of what has been called a buck-passing (Scanlon) or recessive (Meinong) theory: for things to exemplify value is for certain attitudes towards those things to be correct, fitting, appropriate or reasonable. (And, Brentano adds, for this to be knowable).[76] Another difference between Brentano and Husserl is that the former typically concentrates on giving an account of non-contingent exemplification of value (love is intrinsically good, that is to say, love of love is correct) whereas Husserl also gives examples of contingent predications of value.

If Husserl is right, the modes of affective attitudes do not present or represent value or anything else, since only content can present or represent. Rather, the internal relation of intentionality between different emotions and values is given by the correctness conditions for the different emotions and by the principle that satisfaction of correctness conditions makes emotions correct. And an emotion has the correctness condition it has in virtue of its mode and the affective sensations it contains. But Husserl also sometimes says, perhaps inconsistently with the foregoing, that value 'appears' in emotions as do states of affairs in judging.

Something like Husserl's account of modes and values is shared by the early phenomenologists. But the account, as sketched so far, is neutral about one difficult question: how, in the most basic cases, do we become acquainted with the exemplification of values? The early phenomenologists give two, rival answers to this question. The first has it that emotions, if correct, are what reveal that value is exemplified. The second answer has it that correct emotions are responses to acquaintance with value and that emotions themselves cannot constitute such knowledge. The first answer is often endorsed by Husserl (and by late Meinong) and is still popular. The second answer is given by Reinach, Scheler, von Hildebrand, and Edith Stein. These four philosophers rely on the claim, already introduced, that acquaintance, like other forms of knowledge, is not itself any sort of attitude. As we have seen, they argue that attitudes are responses and are responses to what we know or seem to know. This, they think, is true of both beliefs and emotions. The second answer comes in two versions, an uninformative and a slightly more informative version. Scheler and others often simply assert that the exemplification of value is felt, and add that feeling value is not any sort of emoting. Edith Stein attempts to go further and, as we shall see, introduces a distinctively neo-Jamesian dimension into her answer. Non-intentional affective sensations and related phenomena, she argues, play two distinct rôles. Like Husserl, she thinks they are essential to emotions. But they also occur independently of emotions as components of direct acquaintance with the exemplification of value, acquaintance which may precede or occur simultaneously with emotional responses and which motivates such responses. Affective sensations and related phenomena 'have a double constitutive function: they are the material on the basis of which values come to be given to us and they also furnish the stuff of the corresponding affective attitudes'.[77] What is it exactly which plays these two roles?

First, sensory pleasure, pain, and unpleasure: non-intentional sensory pleasure is 'the stuff on which my grasp of the beauty of a colour is based, and simultaneously founds my joy in this value'.[78] Secondly, she distinguishes a variety of impressions which arise in interpersonal contexts, different non-intentional ways of being affected (*berührt*) by others, of which the most important are the different forms of attraction and repulsion: an impression of this sort 'is the foundation for the grasp of specifically personal values' and of attitudes towards the person exemplifying such values.[79] Finally, she argues that uneasiness (*Unbehagen*), disquiet (*Beklommenheit*), exaltation, and relief play the same sort of double role: 'the uneasiness, on the basis of which the disvalue of my envy discloses itself to me is also constitutive of my shame or remorse'; similarly, the states of disquiet, exaltation, and relief may reveal the values to which fear, hope, and confidence are the responses, and 'enter into' these emotions, 'the correlates of which are not absolute values but what is of importance for the subject'.[80] Unlike sensory pain and pleasure, attraction, repulsion, and disquiet are not given as located; they 'fill' the subject. But nor, she thinks, are they emotions.

Uneasiness, disquiet, exaltation, and relief are, I suggest, simply examples of James's organic or visceral sensations, felt bodily commotions. And it may be the case that attraction and repulsion essentially involve sensations of the same kind. Stein does not say as much, although she knows and explicitly rejects James's theory of emotions.

James himself had noted that grasp of value or normative properties triggers bodily commotions: 'we thrill at the case of justice, or tingle at the act of magnanimity':

> [In] every art, every science, there is the keen perception of certain relations being *right* or not, and there is the emotional flush and thrill consequent thereupon.[81]

Similarly, contemporary accounts of emotions which take seriously parts of James's account argue that bodily sensations or affective sensations may (re)present or help to (re)present value or importance.[82] In this respect, they follow in James's footsteps. For, as we have noted, James suggests that 'visceral and muscular sensibility' can 'give the direction from the self outwards'. But if the phenomenologists are right, no causal or other external relation, such as co-variation or signalling, whether selected by evolution or not, can be or constitute a relation of intentionality. On the other hand, the most detailed proposal by a phenomenologist, that given by Stein, unfortunately does not tell us just how affective and organic sensations and their ilk are supposed to turn perception of value-bearers and their non-axiological properties into value-perception (*Wertnehmen*).

11.5 Emotions vs Sensations

If Husserl is right, then, sensations, whether affective or organic, are not emotions. They are not and do not contain contents and so neither present nor represent anything. They are not and do not contain modes and so they have no correctness conditions. As Scheler puts it: 'sensory feelings, unlike all other feelings, are without all "Intention"', although they may of course become the objects of enjoying and suffering.[83] Because sensations do not enjoy intentionality, they cannot be motivated or justified. They

> lack all continuity of sense since there are no connexions of fulfilment between them, no essential connexions and incompatibilities between them... [A] purely sensory feeling 'requires' nothing; at best, it 'fulfils' a striving for it, but it never fulfils another emotional function. It 'points' to nothing in the past and to nothing in the past.[84]

Emotions, on the other hand, are the responses which the exemplification of value requires:

> there are synthetic relations of requirement (*Forderungsverhältnisse*) between value-situations and emotional responses, a value situation, e.g. 'that a friend has arrived' 'requires' (*fordert*) a 'rejoicing', another value situation requires sadness...[85]

Reasons for fear, admiration, regret, or indignation come in two kinds according to the phenomenologists. There are, as here, non-defeasible reasons—the fact that a situation is unjust makes indignation correct, the injustice of the situation requires or merits indignation. And there are defeasible reasons—the fact that the reliable owner of a dog has told me it is dangerous is a defeasible reason to fear the dog.[86]

Another difference between emotions and sensations has to with their different relations to time:

> Sensations of pleasure and pain can endure after the act-characters based on them have disappeared. When the facts which arouse pleasure recede into the background the pleasurable excitement (*Lusterregung*) may continue for a long time.[87]

Wittgenstein arrives at some apparently similar conclusions without the help of any essentialist philosophy of modes, contents, and value. Emotions, he says, have no place, are neither localized nor diffuse.[88] They are 'experiences' but not the experiences Wittgenstein calls 'undergoings' (*Erfahrungen*). The latter seem to comprise both localized pain[89] and localized organic and muscular sensations.[90] Of an emotion such as fear we may say that there is no reason for it. But we cannot say this of pain[91] nor presumably of organic sensations. Unlike emotions, sensations do not colour thoughts: 'There are care-laden thoughts but no toothache-laden thoughts.'[92] But both emotions and sensations have characteristic expressions.[93]

There are perhaps only two claims here that at least one phenomenologist rejects. First, Scheler argues that one type of emotion is directed towards the entire, extended living body and is given as being diffuse—vital emotion:

> Whereas a sensory feeling is extended and localized, a vital emotion participates in the total extension of the living body but has no special extension 'in' it and possesses no place. A feeling of comfort (*Behaglichkeit*) and its opposite (*Unbehaglichkeit*), e.g feeling healthy (*Gesundheitsgefühl*) and ill, fatigue and vigour, cannot be determined in an analogous way in terms of localisation and of certain organs as when one asks: Where does it hurt? Where do you feel pleasure (*Lust*)? How far does your pain extend? Is your pain piercing or pricking? Nevertheless these emotions are bodily emotions (*Leibgefühle*), in contrast to psychological (*seelisch*) and mental (*geistig*) emotions such as sadness, woe, bliss, despair.[94]

If Scheler is right, the term 'bodily feelings', which is very prominent in accounts of emotions which follow James, is ambiguous. It may refer to affective sensations which are given as occupying a place in the living body and the body-image, have no intentionality, and are in fact merely sensory rather than vital phenomena (pains), or to bodily commotions (thrills), or to bodily emotions proper, vital emotions directed towards the entire living body.[95]

When Wittgenstein says that both emotions and sensations have characteristic expressions, he may have in mind not only organic sensations but also what he calls pain sensations. In the latter case, Scheler once again disagrees. Sensory feelings, he argues, unlike the emotions of suffering or enjoyment of which sensory feelings may be the object, cannot be expressed. They do not show themselves in the way in which emotions show themselves. Affective sensations are essentially private entities, emotions are essentially public objects.[96]

The final difference between sensations and emotions noted in the Brentanian tradition has some interesting implications for the philosophy of emotions.

In 1938 Sartre objects to James's identity thesis that whatever disorders of the body one imagines, one cannot understand how consciousness of these could ever be atrocious or horrifying:

> Terror is an extremely distressing (*pénible*) state, even an intolerable state, and it is inconceivable that a bodily state grasped in and of itself could appear to consciousness with the character of atrociousness (*atroce*).[97]

Similarly, Wittgenstein points out that we say of fear or uncertainty that it is 'schrecklich', terrible, frightful, or horrible, but do not say this of sensations, feelings in one's stomach or the trembling associated with fear.[98]

What sort of a property is atrociousness or terribleness? What Sartre calls 'characters' and 'affective qualities' are what Geiger in 1911 had baptized 'feeling characters' and Scheler 'emotional, qualitative characters'—the cheerfulness of a colour, the sadness of a landscape, the plaintiveness of a melody, the bleakness of a situation.[99] They are neither emotions nor value-properties. If Geiger and Sartre are to be believed, it is not enough to say that fear of a dog is 'about' both the dog and its dangerousness, a vital disvalue for the subject. It is also 'about' the fearfulness of the situation. It has three objects, a proper object, an improper object, and a feeling character. Feeling characters play a much more important rôle in Sartre's phenomenology of emotions than values. In his criticism of James, Sartre's point is that feeling characters may be properties of emotions and not only of their objects but cannot be properties of sensations or bodily commotions.[100]

As we have seen, Brentanian philosophy of emotions relies heavily on the category of mental modes. Such a philosophy faces many choices. The possibility that modes are degreeless has already been mentioned. If mental acts and states do not have token contents, then the distinction between modes and attitudes may seem to be a distinction without a difference. Are modes simple or complex? Are there dependent modes? If Brentano and his heirs, to whom we owe the first philosophy of modes, are right, there are many dependent modes corresponding to different types of value. James was familiar with Brentanian philosophies of mental modes and it is instructive to consider his account of attitudes. James's account of belief, willing, and emoting seems to contain two strands. In one mood, he says that belief is 'a state of consciousness *sui generis*, about which nothing more can be said in the way of internal analysis'.[101] In his account of the will, the 'consent' peculiar to volition is said to be 'one of the peculiar attitudes of consciousness which it is vain to seek to explain', 'a subjective experience *sui generis*, which we can designate but not define'; he says 'we stand here exactly where we did in the case of belief'.[102] Are, then, the emotions, like belief and consent, indefinable attitudes? Is feeling bodily changes an indefinable attitude? What answer does the identity thesis give to these questions? There seems to be a sharp contrast for James between belief and consent, on the one hand, and the complexity of the different emotions. But in another mood James says that will and belief are in fact the same psychological phenomenon and that 'belief consists in an emotional reaction of the entire man'.[103] Willing and believing are, then, emotional reactions. If such a reaction is an emotion, it is a feeling of bodily commotions. Such passages suggest that for James there is just one mode, a simple mode—feeling, which has a complex object or content.[104] But he also, in his first mood, frequently talks of both belief and willing as 'welcomings' and 'rejectings' (an echo, perhaps, of Brentano's terms for what he took to be the two modes of judging, accepting and rejecting) and it is not clear whether he always takes these to be feelings. Marty therefore suggests that James employs, perhaps without realizing it, two different concepts of emotion: a narrow concept of emotions as feelings of sensory pleasure and unpleasure and a wider concept of emotions comprising such feelings and also welcoming and rejecting.[105]

11.6 Scheler and James's Grain of Truth

Wittgenstein made familiar the idea that philosophical claims often possess a grain of truth which is then blown up out of all proportions, which is, for example, overgeneralized or otherwise misunderstood. A more specific version of this claim is that philosophical accounts of some type of phenomenon are often true of, and fit perfectly, pathological or otherwise abnormal cases and false of normal cases. The main exponent of this view is Scheler. One of his examples concerns theories of perception. Many accounts of perception assume that illusion is the normal case. This is the view Taine memorably summed up in the slogan that perception is a hallucination which happens to be true. Nowadays it is often called 'conjunctivism'. A second example given by Scheler is that family of theories of the will and action which make means more basic than ends. This type of theory, argues Scheler, is true of the pathologically indecisive and of stutterers.[106] A third example he gives is theories of action which take the reproduction of an earlier movement to be essential to action. This, Scheler claims, is true of child idiots.[107] Similarly, the associationist theory of thinking is true only of the flights of ideas of schizophrenics.[108]

Another example, he argues, is the Jamesian account of emotions, which is true only of certain abnormal cases. What is the grain of truth in the theory? 'The affects', he says, referring to James's *Psychology*, 'do not *consist* of' visceral sensations, 'as a familiar theory asserts' but these sensations do

> form an essential component in hate, anger, envy, revenge etc... The particular quality and direction of the intention bound up with the affect and of that feature of the affect which is an impulse are independent of these sensations. It is only that aspect of an affect which is its being a state, which varies according to the affect—and is for example much greater in the case of anger than in the case of hate and envy, which are more 'spiritual'—which is based on sensations. These intensified, negatively accentuated visceral sensations... frequently lead to a change in direction of the affective impulses.[109]

It is precisely the phenomenological prominence of affective and visceral sensations which is the source of a distinctive kind of illusion of inner perception: 'we are *born* psychologists of organic sensations (*Organempfindungspsychologen*)'.[110] Hence a psychology unwilling to convert a general inclination to self-deception into the *principle* of its research must not strive to *reduce* psychic facts as far as possible to elements of the state of the body, organic sensations, and sensory feelings. On the contrary, it must strive to *peel these away* from the concrete fact and investigate the nature and the special legitimacy of *what remains*. It is thus merely a consequence of that source of illusion in inner perception when someone wants to reduce the abundant qualities of the *emotions* to pleasure and unpleasure, together with their objective correlates. Certainly, what we all first pay attention to in emotions is not their radically different qualities but only the terminal point at which they flow into the *sensory* feelings of pleasure and unpleasure (the sphere of the sensorily pleasant) and into the body-self, thereby indicating what promotes or hinders the inner life-processes of the organism. But already *the feeling of life* is *not* a sum of sensory feelings. Its modifications, such as *healthy* and *ill*, *languid* and *vigorous*, *rising* and *falling* (*ascent* and *descent*), etc., cannot be represented by the *subtraction* and addition of sensory feelings.[111]

Scheler in this passage is directly addressing James's subtraction argument or challenge. Scheler tells us that if we peel away the sensory feelings and organic sensations from an episodic emotion, something remains, the qualities—that is to say, modes—of emotions, vital, psychological or mental, which have the property of intentionality. Employing his account of properly vital emotions (introduced in §11.5), he claims that when I feel ill, subtraction of all affective and organic sensations leaves the quality of the vital emotion intact.

'The so-called James-Lange theory of affects', Scheler says, 'is a clear example of' the illusion which takes what is most prominent, sensory feelings, to be all there is to an emotion. Here Scheler repeats the mistake made by Stumpf and Marty; James identifies (felt) organic sensations but not sensory feelings with emotions. But in the following passage Scheler addresses James's actual view. It takes, he says, as its starting point a natural tendency:

It is unquestionably important to bring to light the significance of the sensations involved in the discharge of an affect in expressive movements, and, still more, the inner visceral sensations which are even more intense when the external expression of the affect is suppressed. Nevertheless, the qualitative abundance of the affects and the intention governing them, for example 'being-angry-about-something', together with the focus of this intention, which is subject to such far-reaching individual variations, remain completely unexplained. Those cases in which the theory fits the facts are not cases of the normal manifestation and discharge of the affect, but *pathological* cases.

The James–Lange theory *does* correctly describe one sort of affective phenomenon. It is, Scheler argues, a true description of the hearts of hysterics:

It seems to me that the fact emphasized by all who are acquainted with hysteria, namely, that the intensity of the expression of the affects is not in proportion to the inner state (for instance, the individual appears much . . . sadder than he really is to judge from his . . . effusive tears, so that the uninitiated will always be deceived), indicates that the inner quality of feeling and intention on which those expressions are normally based is not present or has been added only afterward as an as-if emotion (*Gefühlsvorstellung*). But just this reveals the mistake this theory of affects makes in the *normal* case. The hysterical patient is actually 'pleased *because* he laughs and sad *because* he cries,' as someone has paradoxically expressed this theory. The normal man behaves *in the opposite way*. The patient's concern for the impression he makes on a spectator, for example the doctor, or for the 'social image' he presents, immediately and, as it were, automatically, induces the discharge of the affect; the patient's own feeling and intention are introduced only afterward. Thus the deception of the observer is always a result of an antecedent self-deception, and this fact distinguishes hysterical behavior from any comedy or simulation which begins in the conscious sphere of will and judgment and aims directly at the observer.[112]

Scheler agrees with James (cf. §11.2 above) that, in the normal case, the more one weeps the more one feels sad but thinks that this is compatible with the claim that we weep because we are sad.

But James in fact intends his account of emotions to apply to both normal and pathological cases and, once again, partially anticipates later criticisms:

I am inclined to think that in some hysteriform conditions of grief, rage, etc., the visceral disturbances are less strong than those which go to outward expression. We have then a tremendous verbal display with *a hollow inside*. Whilst the bystanders are wrung with compassion, or pale with alarm, the subject all the while lets himself go, but *feels his insincerity*, and wonders how long he can keep up the performance…These are the cases of apparently great bodily manifestation with *comparatively little real subjective emotion*, which may be used to throw discredit on the theory advanced in the text.—It is probable that the *visceral* manifestations in these cases are quite disproportionately slight, compared to those of the vocal organs. The subject's state is somewhat similar to that of an actor who does not feel his part.[113]

The real disagreement between James and Scheler concerns not so much what they say about 'hysteric' or 'hysteriform' conditions (however they conceive of these) but rather their views about abnormal cases which may be thought to threaten the identity thesis. Scheler describes subjects who feel nothing until well into their expressive display; the tremendous display of James's subjects coexists with a 'hollow inside', but James also says that there are very slight visceral manifestations in his subjects. Scheler's subjects deceive themselves, they are not deliberately simulating; James's subject, on the other hand, 'feels his insincerity, and wonders how long he can keep up the performance'. So long as slight visceral manifestations and expressive behaviour such as weeping and moaning coexist, the identity thesis is not threatened. But if Scheler is right in thinking that there are cases in which such expressive behaviour is not preceded but followed by and explains emotions (or as-if emotions) and visceral manifestations, then in such cases the subject is indeed sad, or rather make-believedly sad, because she weeps. But this is not true in the normal case.[114]

11.7 Conclusion

The analysing descriptions of affective phenomena given by Brentano's heirs and by Wittgenstein are, as we have seen, often reactions to James's views. Some of these reactions, as in the case of Stumpf, are arguably based on misunderstandings of James. They all appeal to a large number of distinctions, in particular between affective phenomena which are and those which are not directed; between perceptual, organic, and affective sensations; between modes, in particular, attitudes, and contents or objects; between the different types of objects of emotions—natural objects, values, and emotional qualities—; and between different types of reasons or justification. These distinctions are employed in order to argue, against what are taken to be James's views, that emotions are not to be identified either with organic sensations or with affective sensations. Brentano's heirs, unlike Wittgenstein and James, employ these distinctions within a philosophy of the mind which attributes distinctive types of intrinsic complexity to mental phenomena. But Stein and Scheler, as we have seen, make important concessions to James.

Notes

1. Edmund Husserl, *Logische Untersuchungen*, Husserliana XIX/1, edited by Ursula Panzer (The Hague: Martinus Nijhoff, 1984): Investigation II, Appendix, p. 211. This work has been translated as *Logical Investigations* by J. Findlay (Routledge and Kegan Paul: London, 1973); the different Investigations and sections therein will be referred to in the following style: 'LU III §1'.
2. Cf. Kevin Mulligan, 'Scheler: Die Anatomie des Herzens oder was man alles fühlen kann', in *Klassische Emotionstheorien von Platon bis Wittgenstein*, ed. Hilge Landweer and Ursula Renz (Berlin: de Gruyter, 2008), pp. 589–612.
3. The three papers were published together in Carl Stumpf, *Gefühl und Gefühlsempfindung* (Leipzig: Barth, 1928). On Stumpf and Brentano on James, cf. Denis Fisette, 'Mixed Feelings. Carl Stumpf's Criticism of James and Brentano on Emotions', in *Themes from Brentano*, ed. Denis Fisette and Guillaume Fréchette (Amsterdam: Rodopi, 2012), pp. 281–306; on Brentano on sensory feelings, cf. Olivier Massin, 'The Intentionality of Pleasures and other Feelings. A Brentanian Approach', in *Themes from Brentano*, ed. Denis Fisette and Guillaume Fréchette, pp. 307–38. Brentano, at one point, sides with James against Stumpf.
4. Cf. Kevin Mulligan, 'Musils Analyse des Gefühls', in *Hommage à Robert Musil*, ed. Bernard Böschenstein and Marie-Luise Roth (Bern: Lang, 1995), pp. 87–110, and Sabine Döring, 'What is an Emotion? Musil's Adverbial Theory', *The Monist* 97 (2014): 47–65.
5. Not all of Brentano's pupils took James on the emotions seriously. Thus Freud, in his *Vorlesungen zur Einführung in die Psychoanalyse* (Leipzig: Internationaler Psychanalytischer Verlag, 1926, ch. XXV, p. 418), says of the James–Lange theory that it is 'unintelligible for us psychoanalysts' and 'not worth talking about'. This reaction may be thought to confirm a remark by yet another student of Brentano's, the Austrian philosopher-psychologist Alois Höfler: the problem with psychoanalysis is that it contains so little analysis.
6. Jean-Paul Sartre, *Esquisse d'une théorie des émotions* (Paris: Hermann, 1938).
7. Carl Stumpf, 'William James nach seinen Briefen. Leben, Charakter, Lehre', review of *The Letters of William James*, *Kant-Studien* 32 (1927): 205–41 (p. 226). Marty was not German but Swiss and taught in Prague. Husserl and Musil were Austrians. Brentano was a German who taught Husserl and Meinong in Vienna, Stumpf a German who taught in Prague and

then Berlin, where he trained the Berlin Gestalt psychologists. Wittgenstein, another Austrian, was a great admirer and close critic of James. (See, for example, the list of passages parallel to Wittgenstein's *Philosophical Investigations* and *Zettel* in James's *Principles* in Christopher Coope, Peter Geach, Timothy Potts, and Roger White, *A Wittgenstein Workbook* (Oxford: Basil Blackwell, 1970), p. 48.) Scheler, like the other early, realist phenomenologists who figure in what follows—Pfänder, Reinach, Geiger, Stein, and von Hildebrand—were Germans associated with Munich and Göttingen.

8. Stumpf suggests 'emotional sensation' as a translation of '*Gefühlsempfindung*'. Edward Bradford Titchener, in his *Lectures on the Elementary Psychology of Feeling and Attention* (New York: The Macmillan Company, 1909), p. 338, points out that this translation is 'hardly possible' and suggests 'affective sensation' or 'algedonic sensation'.
9. William James, *The Principles of Psychology* (Chicago: The University of Chicago, 1952 [1890]), ch. XXV, p. 743.
10. Wittgenstein gives a negative answer to this question in his *Lectures on Philosophical Psychology 1946–7*, ed. Peter Geach, K. J. Shah, and A. C. Jackson (New York, London: Harvester, 1988), pp. 45, 289.
11. James, *Principles*, ch. XXI, p. 652, p. 750.
12. Carl Lange is the Danish author of an account of the emotions which has some similarities with James's account. James discusses the two accounts in ch. XXV of the *Principles*, and refers to the German translation of Lange's book *Über Gemüthsbewegungen. Eine psycho-biologische Studie* (Leipzig: Thomas, 1887).
13. William James, 'The Gospel of Relaxation', in *Selected Papers on Philosophy* (London: Dent, 1947), pp. 22–39 (pp. 22–3).
14. Another piece of the puzzle prominent in one type of account of episodic emotions is the category of long-lasting sentiments, dispositional desires, preferences, and projects which, according to the account, determine many of the features of episodic emotions. Cf. Richard Wollheim, *On the Emotions* (New Haven: Yale University Press, 1999), Kevin Mulligan, 'Emotions and Values', in *The Oxford Handbook of Philosophy of Emotion*, ed. Peter Goldie (Oxford: Oxford University Press), pp. 475–500. James's view about the relation between instincts and emotions, which will not be considered here, amounts to a version of such an account.
15. Karl Bühler, *Ausdruckstheorie. Das System an der Geschichte aufgezeigt* (Stuttgart: Fischer 1968 [1933]), pp. 223–4. Cf. Carl Stumpf, 'Über den Begriff der Gemütsbewegung', in *Gefühl und Gefühlsempfindung* (orig. pub. 1899), pp. 1–54 (p. 38), Malcolm Budd, *Wittgenstein's Philosophy of Psychology* (London, New York: Routledge, 1989), p. 160.
16. As Stumpf points out in his 'Apologie der Gefühlsempfindungen', in *Gefühl und Gefühlsempfindung*, pp. 103–40 (p. 104), he had read Husserl's account of affective sensations before it was published (in 1901) in the latter's *Logical Investigations*.
17. Stumpf, 'Über den Begriff der Gemütsbewegung', pp. 23–8.
18. Ibid., p. 2.
19. Ibid., p. 3.
20. Carl Stumpf, 'Über Gefühlsempfindungen', in *Gefühl und Gefühlsempfindung*, pp. 54–102 (p. 55); the translation is a modified version of that given by Titchener 1908, pp. 265–6.
21. Ibid., p. 66.
22. Stumpf, 'Über den Begriff der Gemütsbewegung', pp. 2, 17–18.

23. William James, 'The Physical Basis of Emotion', *Psychological Review* 1 (1894): 516–29 (pp. 523–4). Stumpf's misunderstanding is pointed out by Titchener in his *Lectures* (p. 329).
24. Jesse Prinz, *Gut Reactions: A Perceptual Theory of Emotion* (Oxford: Oxford University Press, 2004), p. 178, Julien A. Deonna and Fabrice Teroni, *The Emotions: A Philosophical Introduction* (London, New York: Routledge, 2012), p. 64. Prinz contrasts the view that valence markers are just felt pleasantness and unpleasantness with the view that they are 'inner reinforcers' and argues for the latter view in *op. cit.*, pp. 160–78. Two interesting, recent critical discussions of aspects of neo-Jamesianism are John Deigh, 'Recent Philosophical Interest in James's Theory of Emotions', *Emotion Review*, 6, 1 (2014): 4–12; Barnaby D. Dunn, Tim Dalgleish, and Andrew D. Lawrence, 'The somatic marker hypothesis: A critical evaluation', *Neuroscience and Biobehavioural Reviews* 30 (2006): 239–71.
25. Husserl, LU V §15(b) p. 406.
26. Husserl, LU V §15(b) p. 406.
27. Edmund Husserl, *Ideen zu einer reinen Phänomenologie und phänomenologischen Philosophie*, bk. II, Husserliana IV, ed. M. Biemel (Haag: Martinus Nijhoff, 1952), §39, pp. 152–3.
28. Max Scheler, *Der Formalismus in der Ethik und die materiale Wertethik. Neuer Versuch der Grundlegung eines ethischen Personalismus, Gesammelte Werke*, II (Bern: Francke, 1966 [1913–1916]), p. 335.
29. Ibid., pp. 261–2; cf. Scheler, *Schriften zur Soziologie und Weltanschauungslehre, Gesammelte Werke*, VI, (Bern: Francke, 1963), pp. 191–382 (p. 37); *Formalismus* p. 334; *Schriften aus dem Nachlass, Gesammelte Werke*, X (Bern: Francke, 1957), p. 106; *Wesen und Formen der Sympathie, Gesammelte Werke*, VII (Bern: Francke, 1973 [1923]), p. 177. Scheler thinks that sensory pains and pleasures are not always felt; see his *Formalismus*, pp. 261–2 and *Schriften zur Soziologie und Weltanschauungslehre*, p. 37). On 'orgiastic' pleasantness, cf. C. D. Broad, *Examination of McTaggart's Philosophy*, Volume II, Part 1 (Cambridge: Cambridge University Press, 1938), pp. 130–1.
30. Scheler, *Formalismus*, p. 335.
31. Ibid., p. 79.
32. Max Scheler, 'Erkenntnis und Arbeit', in *Die Wissensformen und die Gesellschaft, Gesammelte Werke*, VIII (Bern: Francke, 1960), p. 285.
33. Husserl, LU V §15 p. 401. There are therefore psychological items, experiences, which lack intentionality. Stumpf seems to have been of this persuasion in 1899. But in 1907 he thinks affective sensations are sensory qualities and so not psychological items.
34. Scheler, *Formalismus*, p. 335.
35. The 'principal target' of Wittgenstein's investigation of the concept of emotion 'is the James–Lange theory of the emotions', according to Budd, *Wittgenstein's Philosophy of Psychology*, pp. 151–2.
36. Ludwig Wittgenstein, *Bemerkungen über die Philosophie der Psychologie*, Vol. II (Frankfurt: Suhrkamp, 1984), pp. 7–346 (§148).
37. Alexander Pfänder, *Einführung in die Psychologie* (Leipzig: Barth, 1904), p. 230. The term '*Stimmung*', later made popular by Heidegger, was sometimes used to describe affective sensations.
38. Scheler, *Formalismus*, p. 345.

39. Husserl, LU V §16 (a). James, too, sharply distinguishes between emotions which have an object and 'objectless' emotions and claims that it is an advantage of his theory that it provides a plausible account of the latter (cf. James, *Principles*, ch. XXV p. 749).
40. Ludwig Wittgenstein, *Bemerkungen über die Philosophie der Psychologie*, vol. I (Frankfurt: Suhrkamp, 1984), pp. 7–346 (§836).
41. The related term, '*Einstellung*', used by psychologists, has often been translated by psychologists as 'set'. At one point, Wittgenstein distinguishes between emotions (*Gemütsbewegung*) and emotional 'sets' or stances (*Gemütseinstellung*) such as love (Wittgenstein, *Bemerkungen II*, §152); on this distinction according to Reinach, Scheler, and Wittgenstein cf. Mulligan, 'Scheler'.
42. Is enjoyment really an attitude? In his 'Beiträge zur Phänomenologie des ästhetischen Genusses', in *Jahrbuch für Philosophie und phänomenologische Forschung*, I, 2 (1913): 567–684 (p. 608), Moritz Geiger argues that it is not: 'If I say: "This picture pleases (*gefällt*) me" or "I like (*schmeckt*) this wine" there lies in the "pleases" an attitude of the self towards the object... But... in enjoying one can discover no such attitude'. In his *Die Bedeutung der Kunst. Zugänge zu einer materialen Wertästhetik*, ed. Klaus Berger and Wolfhart Henckmann (Munich: Wilhelm Fink, 1976), p. 428, he also says: 'In the case of being pleased the right question to ask is: "*How* did the picture, the performance please you—how is your attitude to it?". In the case of enjoyment: "*Did* you enjoy the picture, the performance?"' One argument Geiger gives is that enjoyment, unlike liking and being pleased, has no polar opposite. But this is also true of surprise, which is an attitude.
43. Dietrich von Hildebrand, 'Die Idee der sittlichen Handlung', *Jahrbuch für Philosophie und phänomenologische Forschung*, III (1916): 126–251 (p. 134).
44. Ibid., p. 137.
45. Ibid., p. 138.
46. Adolph Reinach, *Sämtliche Werke*, 2 volumes, ed. Karl Schuhmann & Barry Smith (München: Philosophia Verlag, 1989), p. 109, p. 123.
47. Timothy Williamson, for example, asserts that knowledge-that is an attitude in his *Knowledge and its Limits* (Oxford: Oxford University Press, 2000), pp. 33–41.
48. Stumpf, *Gefühl und Gefühlsempfindung*, pp. 10–11. But on one occasion, in his 'Über Gefühlsempfindungen' (p. 68), Stumpf describes emotions as attitudes.
49. David Irons, 'Prof. James' Theory of Emotion', *Mind* 3 (1894): 77–97 (pp. 93–4). The idiom 'feeling towards' figures prominently in one contemporary account of emotions, Peter Goldie's *The Emotions: A Philosophical Exploration* (Oxford: Oxford University Press, 2000), ch. 3.
50. James, 'The Physical Basis of Emotion', p. 521.
51. James, *Principles*, ch. XXI, p. 638. James also says here that 'the new psychic act' Brentano calls 'judgement' is something he prefers to call 'belief'. His preference was to be widely shared in twentieth-century philosophy.
52. Cf. Husserl, LU V §41, §30, §32, §42. On modes, cf. Tim Crane, *The Objects of Thought* (Oxford: Oxford University Press, 2013), pp. 102–4, and John Searle, *Intentionality. An Essay in the Philosophy of Mind* (Cambridge: Cambridge University Press, 1983), p. 6.
53. Husserl, LU V §15(a) p. 402.
54. Husserl, LU V §15(a) p. 404.

55. Edmund Husserl, *Vorlesungen über Ethik und Wertlehre (1908–1914)*, Husserliana XXVIII, ed. Ulrich Melle (Dordrecht, Boston: Kluwer), p. 106.
56. Ibid., p. 252.
57. Wittgenstein, *Bemerkungen II*, §160. In his *Logische Untersuchung* VI, §55, Husserl says that a dependent or founded act pervades (*durchdringt*) the act it is founded on.
58. Husserl, LU V §15(a) p. 403, cf. tr. 570. On contemporary 'add-on' accounts of emotions, cf. Deonna and Teroni, *The Emotions*, pp. 56–8.
59. Husserl, LU V §18 p. 418.
60. Cf. Ludwig Wittgenstein, *Philosophische Untersuchungen*, ed. Joachim Schulte (Frankfurt: Suhrkamp, Wissenschaftliche Buchgesellschaft, 2001), §22.
61. In Kevin Mulligan, *Wittgenstein et la philosophie austro-allemande* (Paris: Vrin, 2012), I argue that many of the claims made by Brentano's heirs about the nature of mental and linguistic phenomena occur in Wittgenstein's later writings as claims about the ways words are or ought to be used.
62. Anton Marty, 'Anzeige von William James' Werk: The Principles of Psychology', *Gesammelte Schriften* I 1, ed. Josef Eisenmeier, Alfred Kastil, and Oskar Kraus (Halle: Niemeyer, 1916 [1892]), pp. 105–56 (p. 142).
63. Wittgenstein, *Bemerkungen I*, §836, cf. §§747, 804, 834–6, *Bemerkungen II*, §§153, 306, *Zettel*, ed. G. E. M. Anscombe and G. H. von Wright (Oxford: Blackwell, 1988), §§493–4.
64. Peter Geach, *Truth, Love and Immortality. An Introduction to McTaggart's Philosophy* (Berkeley, Los Angeles: University of California Press, rd), p. 119. Geach is here expounding the views of McTaggart and Moore, as found in G. E. Moore, 'Critical Notice' [of Messer 1908], *Mind*, 19 (1910): 395–409, a review of a primer of Husserl's views, viz., August Messer, *Empfindung und Denken* (Leipzig: Quelle & Meyer, 1908); another Cambridge philosopher, C. D. Broad, in his 'Critical Notice' of John Laird's *Problems of the Self*, Mind 27 (1918): 234–43 (p. 239), endorses Meinong's view of the relation between emotions and cognitions, which resembles Husserl's view. The history of early analytic philosophy is very complicated.
65. The metaphor is used by Frege. And many of Brentano's heirs say that emotions colour not only thoughts but also other intentional states and episodes: there is, says Pfänder, a *Gefühlston* which is a 'colouring' of 'consciousness of objects' (Alexander Pfänder, *Einführung in die Psychologie*, p. 237); enjoying is a colouring of concentration, says Geiger (*Beiträge*, p. 642). A distinct use of the metaphor is to be found in claims to the effect that sensations can colour. Rudolph Lotze, for example, speaks of the 'peculiar power to colour' (*kolorierende Gewalt*) of bodily sensations in his *Medizinische Psychologie* (Leipzig: Weidmann'sche Buchhandlung, 1852), §438. Cf. Husserl, LU V §15(b) pp. 408–9.
66. Cf. Husserl, LU V §15(b) pp. 404–5, cf. tr. pp. 571–2. Similarly, Stumpf in his 'Begriff der Gemütsbewegung', p. 12, denies that 'intellectual functions belong only to the genetic conditions (*Entstehungsbedingungen*) of affects', they are rather 'immanent to the affects': 'Envy includes the presentation and judgment of the relevant good as belonging to someone else and exists only as long as these intellectual elements exist; they belong to its substance'.
67. Wittgenstein, *Philosophische Untersuchungen*, §476, cf. Wittgenstein, *Bemerkungen, I*, §801.
68. Ludwig Wittgenstein, *Wittgenstein's Lectures. Cambridge 1930–32*, ed. Desmond Lee (Oxford: Blackwell, 1980), p. 112. Smith seems to have been unpopular in Cambridge: the

example of anger with Smith is employed by Broad in his account of the distinction between directed and undirected feelings in his 'Critical Notice', pp. 238–9.

69. Malcolm Budd, *Wittgenstein's Philosophy of Psychology*, pp. 152–3, cf. Wittgenstein, *Bemerkungen, II*, §148. For judicious remarks about the limitations of what Wittgenstein has to say about directedness, cf. Budd, *op. cit.*, pp. 153–4, and Tim Crane, 'Wittgenstein on Intentionality and Mental Representation', *The Harvard Review of Philosophy*, 17 (1): 88–104, 2010.
70. Husserl, LU V §15(b) p. 410.
71. Cf. Kevin Mulligan, 'Acceptance, Acknowledgment, Affirmation, Agreement, Assertion, Belief, Certainty, Conviction, Denial, Judgment, Refusal & Rejection', in *Judgement and Truth in Early Analytic Philosophy and Phenomenology*, ed. Mark Textor (London: Palgrave/ Macmillan, 2013), pp. 97–137.
72. Husserl, *Ideen*, bk. I, §37.
73. Edmund Husserl, *Einleitung in die Ethik. Vorlesungen Sommersemester 1920/1924*, Husserliana XXXVII, ed. Henning Peucker (Dordrecht: Kluwer, 2004), p. 117.
74. Husserl, *Vorlesungen über Ethik und Wertlehre*, p. 127.
75. Ibid., pp. 240–1, cf. p. 278.
76. Marty also came to the conclusion that mental acts and states are correct in virtue of the way the world of facts, values, and norms is. On the correctness of beliefs, cf. Davide Fassio, *Belief and Correctness* (Ph.D. thesis, Geneva, 2012); on the correctness of desires, cf. Federico Lauria, *'The Logic of the Liver'. A Deontic View of the Intentionality of Desire* (Ph.D. thesis, Geneva, 2013).
77. Edith Stein, *Beiträge zur philosophischen Begründung der Psychologie und der Geisteswissenscahften. Eine Untersuchung über den Staat* (Tübingen: Max Niemeyer, 1970), p. 144. She also gives an account of knowledge by description of value and value-bearers (pp. 145–7).
78. Ibid., p. 144.
79. Ibid., p. 147, cf. p. 240, p. 244.
80. Ibid., p. 144, p. 147.
81. James, *Principles*, p. 757.
82. Cf. Note 24.
83. Scheler, *Formalismus*, p. 335. There is, Scheler, thinks, one important similarity between affective sensations and emotions. They both exemplify the value-properties of pleasantness or unpleasantness.
84. Ibid., p. 337.
85. Ibid., p. 256, cf. p. 264. This notion of requirement, which is also employed by Husserl, was employed later by the Berlin Gestalt psychologists such as Kurt Lewin ('Aufforderungscharaktere') and then appears in English as 'affordances' (Gibson) and 'object-valence' (Tolman).
86. The clearest account of reasons by a phenomenologist is given by Stein, *Beiträge*, pp. 34–6. Cf. also Geiger, *Beiträge*, pp. 588–90, on the distinctions between the causes, grounds, motives, and justifications of emotions. On defeasible reasons and motives cf. Husserl, *Ideen* I, §138.
87. Husserl, LU V §15(b) p. 409.
88. Wittgenstein, *Bemerkungen* I, §836, *Bemerkungen* II, §§148, 325.

89. Ibid., §325; *Zettel*, §510.
90. Wittgenstein, *Bemerkungen* II, §148; *The Blue and the Brown Books* (Oxford: Blackwell, 1972), p. 103.
91. Wittgenstein, *Bemerkungen* II, §161.
92. Wittgenstein, *Bemerkungen* I, §747.
93. Wittgenstein, *Bemerkungen* II, §148.
94. Scheler, *Formalismus*, p. 340, cf. p. 342.
95. David Lapoujade, commenting on William James and the fictions of his brother Henry in his *Fictions du pragmatisme: William et Henry James* (Paris: Minuit, 2008), p. 53, says that in their writings 'the body is not flesh, it is all nerves and brain. It is not incarnated but innervated and cerebralised (*cérébré*)' (also cf. pp. 51–73). From Scheler's point of view, many contemporary accounts of 'embodiment' also fail to appreciate the differences between the sensory and the vital.
96. On this view and on Scheler and Wittgenstein on the internal relation of expression, cf. Mulligan, 'Scheler' and idem, *Wittgenstein*, ch. 3.
97. Sartre, *Esquisse*, p. 22.
98. Wittgenstein, *Bemerkungen* II, §148, *Bemerkungen* I, §728. Budd, in his *Wittgenstein's Philosophy of Psychology*, p. 160, calls this Wittgenstein's 'principal' argument against James's identity thesis.
99. Moritz Geiger, 'Zum Problem der Stimmungseinfühlung', *Zeitschrift für Ästhetik und allgemeine Kunstwissenschaft*, 6 (1911): 1–42 (p. 20); Scheler, *Formalismus*, p. 263. On feeling characters according to the phenomenologists and Wittgenstein, cf. Kevin Mulligan, 'Secondary Meaning, Paraphraseability & Pictures', in L'expression des émotions: Mélanges dédiés à Patrizia Lombardo, ed. Martin Rueff and Julien Zanetta, http://www.unige.ch/lettres/framo/melangeslombardo.html (Geneva, 2015).
100. On Wittgenstein's use of 'schrecklich', cf. Uwe Meixner, *Defending Husserl: A Plea in the Case of Wittgenstein and Company versus Phenomenology* (Berlin: de Gruyter, 2014), p. 131. James, in the long passage quoted in §11.3, mentions two exemplifications of feeling-characters: a fearful situation and an astonishing object. Feeling-characters have not been prominent in contemporary Anglophone philosophies of the emotions. In Germany, they have staged a comeback under the name of 'atmospheres', cf. Kerstin Andermann and Undine Eberlein, eds, *Gefühle als Atmosphären. Neue Phänomenologie und philosophische Emotionstheorie* (Berlin: Akademie Verlag, 2011).
101. James, *Principles*, ch. XXI, p. 638.
102. Ibid., ch. XXVI, p. 820.
103. Ibid., p. 661.
104. On Scheler on the differences between the modes of feeling and emoting, cf. Mulligan, 'Scheler'.
105. Marty, 'Anzeige', p. 127. But, as we have seen, James explicitly rejects what Marty calls the 'narrow conception'.
106. Scheler, *Formalismus*, p. 258.
107. Ibid., p. 261.
108. Ibid., p. 259; cf. p. 179.

109. Ibid., p. 62.
110. Ibid., p. 275.
111. Ibid., p. 276, some emphases mine—KM; cf. Scheler, *Wesen und Formen*, p. 77.
112. Scheler, *Vom Umsturz der Werte, Gesammelte Werke*, III (Bern: Francke, 1955 [1913]), pp. 276–7, cf. Scheler, *Formalismus*, pp. 77–8; Stumpf, too, in his 'Über Gefühlsempfindungen', p. 48, notes that James's theory is true of abnormal cases. The positivist theory of shame, Scheler also argues (*Nachlass*, pp. 76, 78, 92–3), is an application of what is in effect the James–Lange theory.
113. James, *Principles*, pp. 750–1, some emphases mine—KM; cf. p. 747.
114. This paper derives from a talk at a 2010 Geneva workshop on James on the emotions. I am grateful to the participants for many helpful criticisms, in particular to Julien Deonna, Olivier Massin, Fabrice Teroni, and Claudia Wassermann, and also to Philip Gerrans, Uwe Meixner, and Uriah Kriegel. Thanks, too, to Riccardo Braglia, CEO, *Helsin Health Care*, and the *Fundazione Reginaldus* (Lugano) for the financial support which made this paper possible.

Bibliography

Andermann, Kerstin and Undine Eberlein (eds). *Gefühle als Atmosphären: Neue Phänomenologie und philosophische Emotionstheorie* (Berlin: Akademie Verlag, 2011).

Budd, Malcolm. *Wittgenstein's Philosophy of Psychology* (New York: Routledge, 1989).

Broad, C. D. 'Critical Notice' [of John Laird, *Problems of the Self*], *Mind* 27 (1918): 234–43.

Bühler, Karl. *Ausdruckstheorie: Das System an der Geschichte aufgezeigt* (Stuttgart: Fischer, 1968).

Crane, Tim. 'Wittgenstein on Intentionality and Mental Representation', Crane, Tim *The Harvard Review of Philosophy* 17 (1): 88–104, 2010.

Crane, Tim. *The Objects of Thought* (Oxford: Oxford University Press, 2013).

Coope, Christopher, Peter Geach, Timothy Potts, and Roger White, *A Wittgenstein Workbook* (Oxford: Basil Blackwell, 1970).

Deigh, John. 'Recent Philosophical Interest in James's Theory of Emotions', *Emotion Review* 6 (2014): 4–12.

Deonna, Julien and Fabrice Teroni. *The Emotions: A Philosophical Introduction* (London, New York: Routledge, 2012).

Döring, Sabine. 'What is an Emotion? Musil's Adverbial Theory', *The Monist* 97 (2014): 47–65.

Dunn, Barnaby D., Tim Dalgleish, and Andrew D. Lawrence, 'The Somatic Marker Hypothesis: A Critical Evaluation', *Neuroscience and Biobehavioral Reviews* 30 (2006): 239–71.

Fassio, Davide. *Belief and Correctness* (Geneva PhD, 2012).

Fisette, Denis and Guillaume Fréchette (eds). *Themes from Brentano* (Amsterdam: Rodopi, 2012).

Fisette, Denis and Guillaume Fréchette (eds). 'Mixed Feelings: Carl Stumpf's Criticism of James and Brentano on Emotions', in *Themes from Brentano*, ed. Denis Fisette & Guillaume Fréchette (Amsterdam: Rodopi, 2012), pp. 281–306.

Freud, Sigmund. *Vorlesungen zur Einführung in die Psychoanalyse* (Leipzig: Internationaler Psychanalytischer Verlag, 1926).

Geach, Peter. *Truth, Love and Immortality: An Introduction to McTaggart's Philosophy* (Berkeley, Los Angeles: University of California Press, 1979).

Geiger, Moritz. 'Zum Problem der Stimmungseinfühlung', *Zeitschrift für Ästhetik und allgemeine Kunstwissenschaft* 6 (1911): 1–42.

Geiger, Moritz. 'Beiträge zur Phänomenologie des ästhetischen Genusses', *Jahrbuch für Philosophie und phänomenologische Forschung* I, 2 (1913): 567–684.

Geiger, Moritz. *Die Bedeutung der Kunst. Zugänge zu einer materialen Wertästhetik*, ed. Klaus Berger and Wolfhart Henckmann (Munich: Wilhelm Fink, 1976).

Goldie, Peter. *The Emotions: A Philosophical Exploration* (Oxford: Oxford University Press, 2000).

Husserl, Edmund. *Ideen zu einer reinen Phänomenologie und phänomenologischen Philosophie, Erstes Buch*, Husserliana III, ed. Walter Biemel (The Hague: Martinus Nijhoff, 1950).

Husserl, Edmund. *Ideen, Zweites Buch*, Husserliana IV, ed. Marly Biemel (The Hague: Martinus Nijhoff, 1952).

Husserl, Edmund. *Logische Untersuchungen*, Husserliana XIX/1, ed. Ursula Panzer, Investigations I–V (The Hague: Martinus Nijhoff, 1984) (English tr.: *Logical Investigations*, trans. by John Findlay (Routledge and Kegan Paul: London, 1973).

Husserl, Edmund. *Vorlesungen über Ethik und Wertlehre (1908–1914)*, Husserliana XXVIII, ed. Ulrich Melle (Dordrecht, Boston: Kluwer, 1988).

Husserl, Edmund. *Einleitung in die Ethik. Vorlesungen Sommersemester 1920/1924*, Husserliana XXXVII, ed. Henning Peucker (Dordrecht: Kluwer, 2004).

Irons, David. 'Prof. James' Theory of Emotion', *Mind* 3 (1894): 77–97.

James, William. 'What is an Emotion?', *Mind* 9 (1884): 188–205.

James, William. 'The Physical Basis of Emotion', *Psychological Review* 1 (1894): 516–29.

James, William. *The Principles of Psychology* (Chicago: The University of Chicago, 1952).

James, William. 'The Gospel of Relaxation', in *Selected Papers on Philosophy* (London: Dent, 1947), 22–39.

Lange, Carl Georg. *Über Gemüthsbewegungen. Eine psycho-biologische Studie* (Leipzig: Thomas, 1887).

Lapoujade, David. *Fictions du pragmatisme: William et Henry James* (Paris: Minuit, 2008).

Lauria, Federico. *The Logic of the Liver: A Deontic View of the Intentionality of Desire* (Geneva Ph.D., 2013).

Lotze, Rudolph Hermann. *Medizinische Psychologie* (Leipzig: Weidmann'sche Buchhandlung, 1852).

Marty, Anton. 'Anzeige von William James' Werk: The Principles of Psychology', in *Gesammelte Schriften*, I, 1, ed. Josef Eisenmeier, Alfred Kastil, and Oskar Kraus (Halle: Niemeyer, 1916), pp. 105–56.

Massin, Olivier. 'The Intentionality of Pleasures and other Feelings. A Brentanian Approach', in *Themes from Brentano*, ed. Denis Fisette and Guillaume Fréchette (Amsterdam: Rodopi, 2012), pp. 307–38.

Meixner, Uwe. *Defending Husserl: A Plea in the Case of Wittgenstein and Company versus Phenomenology* (Berlin: de Gruyter, 2014).

Messer, August. *Empfindung und Denken* (Leipzig: Quelle & Meyer, 1908).

Moore, G. E. 'Critical Notice' [of Messer 1908], *Mind* 19 (1910): 395–409.

Mulligan, Kevin. 'Musils Analyse des Gefühls', in *Hommage à Robert Musil*, ed. Bernard Böschenstein & Marie-Luise Roth (Bern: Lang, 1995), pp. 87–110.

Mulligan, Kevin. 'Scheler: Die Anatomie des Herzens oder was man alles fühlen kann', in *Klassische Emotionstheorien von Platon bis Wittgenstein*, ed. Hilge Landweer and Ursula Renz (Berlin: de Gruyter, 2008), pp. 589–612.

Mulligan, Kevin. 'Emotions and Values', in *The Oxford Handbook of Philosophy of Emotion*, ed. Peter Goldie (Oxford: Oxford University Press, 2010), pp. 475–500.

Mulligan, Kevin. *Wittgenstein et la philosophie austro-allemande* (Paris: Vrin, 2012).

Mulligan, Kevin. 'Acceptance, Acknowledgment, Affirmation, Agreement, Assertion, Belief, Certainty, Conviction, Denial, Judgment, Refusal & Rejection', in *Judgement and Truth in Early Analytic Philosophy and Phenomenology*, ed. Mark Textor (London: Palgrave/Macmillan, 2013), pp. 97–137.

Mulligan, Kevin. 'Secondary Meaning, Paraphraseability & Pictures', in *L'expression des émotions: Mélanges dédiés à Patrizia Lombardo*, ed. Martin Rueff and Julien Zanetta (Geneva, 2015, http://www.unige.ch/lettres/framo/melangeslombardo.html).

Pfänder, Alexander. *Einführung in die Psychologie* (Leipzig: Barth, 1904).

Prinz, Jesse. *Gut Reactions: A Perceptual Theory of Emotion* (Oxford: Oxford University Press, 2006).

Sartre, Jean-Paul. *Esquisse d'une théorie des émotions* (Paris: Hermann, 1975).

Scheler, Max. *Vom Umsturz der Werte, Gesammelte Werke*, III (Bern: Francke, 1955).

Scheler, Max. *Schriften aus dem Nachlass*, Gesammelte Werke, X, (Bern: Francke, 1957).

Scheler, Max. 'Erkenntnis und Arbeit', *Die Wissensformen und die Gesellschaft*, Gesammelte Werke, VIII (Berne: Francke, 1960).

Scheler, Max. *Schriften zur Soziologie und Weltanschauungslehre*, Gesammelte Werke, VI (Bern: Francke, 1963), pp. 191–382.

Scheler, Max. *Der Formalismus in der Ethik und die materiale Wertethik. Neuer Versuch der Grundlegung eines ethischen Personalismus*, Gesammelte Werke, II (Bern: Francke, 1966).

Scheler, Max. *Wesen und Formen der Sympathie*, Gesammelte Werke, VII (Bern: Francke, 1973).

Searle, John. *Intentionality: An Essay in the Philosophy of Mind* (Cambridge: Cambridge University Press, 1983).

Stein, Edith. *Beiträge zur philosophischen Begründung der Psychologie und der Geisteswissenscahften. Eine Untersuchung über den Staat* (Tübingen: Max Niemeyer Verlag, 1970).

Stumpf, Carl. '"William James nach seinen Briefen: Leben, Charakter, Lehre", review of *The Letters of William James*, 1920', *Kant-Studien* 32 (1927): 205–41.

Stumpf, Carl. *Gefühl und Gefühlsempfindung* (Leipzig: Barth, 1928).

Stumpf, Carl. 'Über den Begriff der Gemütsbewegung', in *Gefühl und Gefühlsempfindung* (Leipzig: Barth, 1928), pp. 1–54.

Stumpf, Carl. 'Über Gefühlsempfindungen', in *Gefühl und Gefühlsempfindung* (Leipzig: Barth, 1928), pp. 54–102.

Stumpf, Carl. 'Apologie der Gefühlsempfindungen', in *Gefühl und Gefühlsempfindung* (Leipzig: Barth 1928), pp. 103–40.

Titchener, Edward Bradford. *Lectures on the Elementary Psychology of Feeling and Attention* (New York: The Macmillan Company, 1908).

Williamson, Timothy. *Knowledge and its Limits* (Oxford: Oxford University Press, 2000).
Wittgenstein, Ludwig. *The Blue and the Brown Books* (Oxford: Basil Blackwell, 1972).
Wittgenstein, Ludwig. *Wittgenstein's Lectures. Cambridge 1930–32*, ed. D. Lee (Oxford: Blackwell, 1980).
Wittgenstein, Ludwig. *Bemerkungen über die Philosophie der Psychologie*, vols I–II (Frankfurt: Suhrkamp, 1984), pp. 7–346.
Wittgenstein, Ludwig. *Zettel*, ed. G.E.M. Anscombe and G.H. von Wright (Oxford: Blackwell, 1988).
Wittgenstein, Ludwig. *Wittgenstein's Lectures on Philosophical Psychology 1946–7*, ed. Peter Geach, K. J. Shah, and A. C. Jackson (New York, London: Harvester, 1988).
Wittgenstein, Ludwig. *Philosophische Untersuchungen.* Kritisch-genetische Edition, ed. Joachim Schulte (Frankfurt: Suhrkamp, Wissenschaftliche Buchgesellschaft, 2001).
Wollheim, Richard. *On the Emotions* (New Haven: Yale University Press, 1999).

12

Methodological Anxiety

Heidegger on Moods and Emotions

Sacha Golob

In the context of a history of the emotions, Martin Heidegger presents an important and challenging case. Emotions, broadly construed, play a central role in his thinking; particularly boredom, fear, and anxiety.[1] This role is, however, highly distinctive: Heidegger is critical of much of the standard ontology of emotions and he is uninterested in many of the philosophical debates within which emotions usually figure. My purpose in this article is to sketch these aspects of Heidegger's work, highlighting both the innovative nature of his views and the distinctive problems he faces as a consequence.

Before getting underway, two preliminary remarks. The first concerns the scope of this chapter. Heidegger was a prolific writer: the *Gesamtausgabe* edition runs to over one hundred volumes. Furthermore, during the course of his lifetime, his work undergoes a series of complex stylistic and philosophical shifts—for example, during the early 1930s, and then again in the aftermath of the war. There is no scholarly consensus on the exact nature of these developments or on the degree of continuity or change that they imply. Given these facts, it would be impossible to address Heidegger's views on 'emotions' or indeed any other topic in a single chapter without radically restricting the chronological range of the discussion. I will therefore focus on Heidegger's best-known work, *Sein und Zeit* (1927), and on the account developed there and then refined in subsequent texts such as Ga29/30, the 1929 lecture series *Die Grundbegriffe der Metaphysik*. In this sense what follows is a study of 'early Heidegger'; for stylistic reasons, I will speak simply of 'Heidegger', taking the restriction as understood. The second preliminary remark concerns my aim: I want to present Heidegger's views in a way that allows one to make sense of where he agrees with, and where he departs from, the other thinkers in this volume. In order to do this within the space available, I will have to sidestep certain exegetical issues pertaining to the internal structure of Heidegger's own system. For example, I will look very closely at his treatment of anxiety, but I will say comparatively little about the larger story in which it is embedded: for example, his theory of 'affectivity' [*Befindlichkeit*], or his idea of 'care' [*Sorge*].[2] I will also focus on the links between Heidegger and other philosophers, rather than, say, psychoanalysts or psychiatrists.[3]

12.1 Heidegger and the Structure of Moods

I want to begin by outlining the concept which dominates Heidegger's discussion of emotions: that of *Stimmung*, which I will translate as 'mood'.[4]

Heidegger is highly suspicious of the apparatus in terms of which previous thinkers have understood what we could loosely call the 'human subject'. This suspicion often manifests in a dismissive rejection of traditional ontologies, and the complaint that these ossify philosophical thought. So, for example, discussing affects, he laments that:

> What has escaped notice is that the basic ontological interpretation of the affective life in general has been able to make scarcely one forward step worthy of mention since Aristotle. On the contrary, affects and feelings come under the theme of psychical phenomena, functioning as a third class of these, usually along with representation [*Vorstellen*] and volition. They sink to the level of accompanying phenomena.[5]

Elsewhere, he states bluntly that 'we must dismiss the psychology of feelings, experiences and consciousness'.[6] Underpinning remarks such as these are broader worries about many of the oppositions used to frame the discussion of emotions: for example, he is insistent that we avoid characterizing matters in terms of rational or irrational states.[7] One immediate consequence is that Heidegger himself does not speak of 'emotions' or 'affects' or 'passions'; instead, for reasons I will unpack below, he frames the discussion in terms of 'moods'. However, at an extensional level, one can see immediate overlap between the phenomena in which he is interested and those found in standard treatments of emotion: the three cases on which he focuses are anxiety [*Angst*], fear, and boredom.[8] Given this extensional overlap, Heidegger can be legitimately seen, at least to begin with, as providing a new account of what we call 'emotions', rather than simply changing the topic. The task now is to introduce the distinctive way in which he frames these cases; what follows is only preliminary and I will come back to many of these points below.

Heidegger sees moods as defined by a number of general features which I will take in turn. First, moods are ever-present: we are always in some mood or other: 'we are never free of moods'.[9] In a characteristic tactic, he suggests that the putative counterexample of 'an evenly balanced lack of mood' is in fact itself a quite specific mood; he speaks of a mood of 'satiation', but one might also call it a mood of indifference.[10] Second, moods shape and inform our experience: the lover in a jealous mood is struck by aspects of the scene he would never normally notice (why is her phone there?). Moods also restrict or distort what we notice: the person in an aggressive mood blindly construes the casual gesture as a provocation. In this sense a mood can 'close the world off more stubbornly than any non-perceiving'.[11] In Heideggerian terms, moods thus play a disclosive role—they make manifest the world in a certain way.[12] One of Heidegger's most striking claims, and one I will analyse in Section 12.4 is that this epistemic function is not a secondary one, not a mere 'gut instinct' substitute for more considered rational cognition. Instead 'from an ontological point of view', it plays an explanatorily fundamental and irreducible role.[13] Third, in moods the world is manifest as mattering in various ways. Underlying this is Heidegger's idea of affectivity. Prior to any kind of rational calculation as to what I should do, there must be an initial assignment of values to the various options: affectivity refers to the fact that we 'always already' find ourselves operating against the backdrop of some such assignment.[14] For Heidegger, moods make this fact manifest: parts of the world can only appear as threatening, for example, insofar as they pose a risk to projects I care about.[15] In contrast, he emphasizes that 'pure beholding' cannot not play the same role: his point is that no set of natural facts are sufficient to establish that something is a threat without some additional premises about what matters to me, premises made available by moods, by what I fear or what bores me, for example.[16] Fourth, in illuminating the world, moods simultaneously illuminate our own situation: so, for example, the body of the stressed or the bored is manifest to them as taut or leaden. Thus, a mood makes manifest 'how one is, and how one is faring'.[17] Fifth, moods illustrate the 'thrown' aspect of our experience. There is a limit to how much control we have over them: as Heidegger puts it, 'a mood assails us'.[18]

This initial sketch sets up a number of lines of possible development. At the macro-level, Heidegger takes moods to support his rejection of the traditional opposition between 'inner' states and an 'external' world. As he puts it, a mood 'comes neither from "outside" nor from "inside", but arises out of Being-in-the-world, as a way of such Being'.[19] He is particularly fond of examples which problematize inner/outer distinctions; consider Ga29/30's appeal to phrases such as a 'cheerful room' or a 'melancholy landscape'.[20] Many commentators see this as part of a larger project within which Heidegger seeks to move beyond familiar categories such as that of 'mental states'.[21] At the micro-level, there is much exegetical work to be done in making clear the details of Heidegger's story: for example, with respect to fear and his claim that 'that about which we fear' is always ourselves.[22]

I am not, however, going to pursue either of these lines here. The macro issue in particular is far too broad. This is because Heidegger's stance on the 'inner' and the 'outer' is not directly a function of his views on the emotions, but rather of his stance on 'content' and on topics like scepticism more broadly.[23] Instead, I want to focus on the question of how Heidegger's theory of moods relates to the broader discussion of emotions in the canon. To see that, I need to say a little more about some of the various roles which such states might play.

12.2 The Role of Emotions within Modern Philosophy

I want to begin by highlighting a few of the varied roles which emotions have played in modern Western philosophy.[24] I will take four examples—these are, of course, not intended to be either exhaustive or exclusive; my aim is rather to provide a backdrop against which the distinctive contours of Heidegger's view can be seen.

First, one might locate emotions in the context of debates surrounding motivation. A classic case here is Hume's treatment of the passions in book two of the *Treatise*, but this approach is also very visible in readings of Kant which emphasize his relationship to Hume.[25] So, for example, Guyer argues that Kant follows Hume in assuming that only 'suitable feelings' can move us to action; the difference between the two is that Kant holds the necessary feelings are in some sense a function of the moral law.[26] The conclusion, Guyer summarizes, is that 'even when pure practical reason is efficacious, it works by modifying our feelings and desires and by determining our actions through them'.[27] Second, one might allot a normative role to emotions: by this, I mean that undergoing a particular emotion is taken to be a necessary condition on being the type of agent whom the author valorizes. A good example here is Hegel, unsurprisingly due to his Aristotelian heritage. On the Hegelian picture: 'It is required not only that we know God, right and the like... but that these things should be in our feelings, in our hearts.'[28] Family members, for example, should thus relate to each other with 'love', members of corporations via 'fellow-feeling'.[29] Possession of the relevant affects is thus a necessary condition on being the type of agent found in Hegel's ideal society. Third, emotions might play a subversive role. Perhaps the best example of this is Nietzschean genealogy. By exposing the emotions, such as *ressentiment*, underlying certain philosophical or political positions, Nietzsche intends to weaken or subvert those views.[30] Fourth, emotions might play a methodological role: the idea here is that only through the experience of certain emotions can the philosopher proceed correctly. Whilst this idea obviously has its roots in the ancient world, post-Nietzschean thinkers often hold specifically that extreme emotions are needed to shatter or shake us out of comforting assumptions in order to see things aright. This idea is particularly visible in twentieth-century French thought, where it is often associated with talk of 'limit experiences', and where it is present even in writers otherwise suspicious of first personal reports on emotional states. Thus, for example Foucault.

> [E]xperience according to Nietzsche, Blanchot, and Bataille has rather the task of 'tearing' the subject from itself in such a way that it is no longer the subject as such, or that it is completely 'other' than itself so that it may arrive at its annihilation, its dissociation. It is this de-subjectifying undertaking, the idea of a 'limit-experience' that tears the subject from itself, which is the fundamental lesson that I've learned from these authors.[31]

The experience to which he refers here are largely emotions, such as Bataille's 'states of ecstasy, of rapture'.[32]

If we now turn back to Heidegger, a few preliminary points can be made. There is no real treatment of the first of these issues in his work, the question of motivation. Whilst, as we will see, Heidegger is extremely interested in the effects of certain emotional experiences, his model of the subject prevents him from framing the issue along the standard belief–desire lines. In particular, the primitive Heideggerian 'action state' is understanding—which simultaneously includes taking a particular stance on myself and on the world by and through realizing certain possibilities.[33] As a consequence, the classic post-Humean question of the relationship between judgement and the 'passions' cannot arise in the same way: to understand in Heidegger's sense is already to act.[34] By extension, he shows no interest in the familiar cast of characters used to frame the motivational debate, such as the psychopath who purports to make moral judgements but finds them unmoving.[35] Likewise, I think that the third strand discussed—the use of emotions for debunking or subversive purposes—is also largely absent from Heidegger's work. Heidegger does hold, for reasons which will become apparent, that inauthentic agents exhibit problematic relationships to their moods (for example, suppressing anxiety).[36] But his strategy is overwhelmingly focused on the further claim that such problems reflect an attempt to hide from deep facts about ourselves: his complaint, unlike the Nietzsche of the *Genealogy*, is not primarily that his opponents are driven by certain emotions, but rather that their emotions serve as an index of their underlying failure to face up to ontological truths. This is of a piece with Heidegger's broader hostility to psychological explanation. In the first volume of the infamous '*Schwarze Hefte*', for example, he suggests that the pre-Socratics are so philosophically significant partly because there is no possibility of 'rooting about' in their characters or letters.[37]

With respect to the other two strands of the traditional debate which I discussed, however, matters are very different. Consider what I called the 'normative' view of emotions: there is clearly a very close tie between anxiety and the form of agency valorized in texts such as *Sein und Zeit*, namely authenticity.[38] Likewise, Heidegger also exemplifies the fourth approach I considered, one on which that certain emotions are methodologically necessary in order to wrench us out of the 'tranquilised' and misguided views in which we typically operate. Thus 'anxiety brings [*Dasein*] back from its absorption in the "world". Everyday familiarity collapses.'[39] By extension, philosophy requires the author to enter into the specific moods that characterize and enable it: thus Ga29/30 states simply that: 'our fundamental task now consists in awakening a fundamental mood which is to sustain our philosophizing'.[40]

I have identified two points of contact between Heidegger and the canonical debate on the emotions: the experience of certain moods is a necessary condition both on the type of agency he privileges and on a rigorous philosophy. However, to understand exactly how he develops these ideas, we need to look simultaneously at the other central role which he allots to mood: that of 'disclosing' or making manifest aspects of the world and of ourselves. The task of Section 12.3 will be to bring together and flesh out these points via a specific case study: his treatment of anxiety.

12.3 A Case Study: *Sein und Zeit* on Anxiety

Sein und Zeit's discussion of anxiety is undoubtedly Heidegger's best-known analysis of an emotional state broadly construed. The other obvious candidate for use as a case study would be Ga29/30's treatment of boredom; that, however, hangs directly on Heidegger's complex views about the metaphysics of time and would require a separate essay on those.[41] I will therefore focus on anxiety, noting parallels to the later discussion of boredom as appropriate.[42]

Anxiety for Heidegger is a mood, where 'mood' is defined by the specific vectors of that term which I discussed in Section 12.1. More specifically, we can think of Heideggerian anxiety along several ontological dimensions. For Heidegger, anxiety is an inescapable dispositional state. As will become clear, he thinks that the features about which we are anxious are necessary and omnipresent aspects of human existence.[43] It is also an incipient state, by which I mean that Heidegger takes all agents to have a peripheral phenomenological awareness of it and yet to have suppressed or distracted themselves from that awareness.[44] In at least some cases, it will further become manifest as a full-blown episodic state with attendant implications, to be discussed below, for the phenomenology and content of any co-occurring experiences; this episodic version of anxiety is what Heidegger is referring to when he talks of it as 'arising in even the most innocuous situations'.[45] Finally it is possible for agents who have experienced episodic anxiety to adopt a particular stance on it and on the incipient awareness of its possible return: such agents, labelled 'authentic' by *Sein und Zeit*, have a 'readiness for anxiety'.[46] I cannot discuss Heidegger's treatment of self-deception and what he calls 'inauthenticity' here; instead, I am going to focus on the relation between dispositional and episodic anxiety, and on the resultant view of things which authentic agents supposedly have. I am going to pick out four central features of Heidegger's discussion.

First, anxiety lacks a specific intentional object. Whereas my fear is directed at a particular target—the snarling dog, the oncoming train—anxiety is 'indefinite'.[47] Phenomenologically put, Heidegger sees episodic anxiety as a state in which one feels a pervasive unease: this unease colours and affects the tempo and dynamics of each interaction, without itself having a clear locus. In the language of *Sein und Zeit* 'that in the face of which one has anxiety is Being-in-the-world as such'.[48]

Second, in this state, the agent feels a particular kind of detachment from the goals and standards by which he or she has previously lived their life. As Heidegger puts it 'the world has the character of completely lacking significance'.[49] Underlying this claim is a distinctive vision of the structure of human agency. Heidegger operates with a picture of experiential space, the 'world', as teleologically structured around the self-identities of agents. The notions of self-identity and world here are often illustrated with quasi-institutional examples (being a doctor), but I think Heidegger must intend it more broadly too (consider, for example, the way one might talk of the world of fashion or of machismo). The basic idea is that in virtue of understanding oneself in a certain way various means and goals show up as salient, as appropriate or as inappropriate.[50] So, to adapt an example of Heidegger's own, the monumental sculpture appears very differently to the critic and to the team whose job is to work out how to crate the thing up: the long protruding arms, that the former sees as a bold departure from modernism, are manifest to the latter as an obstacle, a reason why a standard number 5 crate won't work. These self-understandings, what Heidegger calls our 'for-the-sake-of-which', thus structure the normative landscape; they determine, at least in large part, what we have reason to care about.[51] Now, in a moment of anxiety, Heidegger argues that our identification with and investment in these various identities is suspended: they no longer exercise a pull over us. The world, the network of teleological links, remains intact, but the familiar teleological and social chains that define it seem unmotivating and insignificant. To get into Med School Tom still needs to pass these tests with this score, but that goal, around which his life had previously turned, now appears uncompelling.[52] Yet this is not because Tom suddenly wants to be a racing driver or whatever else. Instead, anxiety globally discolours his experience, it is an extreme state in which Dasein finds itself alienated not just from one particular identity, but from all of them.[53] The result is a global suspension of normativity, resulting from a disengagement with the identities which grounded it: Philipse talks of the 'universal meaninglessness we experience in [anxiety]'.[54] As Heidegger puts it:

> The world in which I exist has sunk into insignificance; and the world which is thus disclosed is one in which entities can be freed only in the character of having no involvement.[55]

Third, Heidegger takes this experience to have profound implications: agents who are authentic recognize these, and in that recognition, their 'readiness for anxiety' characterizes their future conduct. But it is less clear what exactly those implications are. Blattner describes anxiety as the 'the condition in which nothing matters'.[56] Yet, as McManus notes, if anxiety so described is taken straightforwardly as a veridical experience, Heidegger seems to be left with the conclusion that there is no good reason to adopt any particular course of action rather than another: after all, if the world has been exposed as 'insignificant', why do this rather than that? As Tugendhat, perhaps the best-known of critic of this aspect of Heidegger, observes, this seems to undercut the very idea of choice and of personhood: 'A choice…that is not made in the light of reasons…is a choice in which I leave how I choose to accident; and in this respect we have to say that it was not I who chose.'[57] There are various possible responses to this concern.[58] I think that the most plausible is this: anxiety does not show that none of our goals matter. Instead it shows two things. On the one hand, it serves as a shock, a way of viscerally calling in to question the familiar norms into which we have been educated and within which we have lived unquestioningly. For Tom previously going to Med School may have been just 'what one did'—what his siblings did, what his parents did, what he had always assumed he would do; anxiety questions this goal from a new, radically detached perspective. On the other hand, anxiety reveals some quite *specific* kind of disconnection between the subject and the norms and goals which structure its world: it shows that none of these are *necessarily* or *essentially* binding on us. As Thomson puts it:

> [T]he fundamental existential homelessness that follows from the fact that there is no life project any of us can ever finally be at home in, because there is ultimately nothing about the ontological structure of the self that could tell us what specifically we should do with our lives.[59]

A more formal way to put the point is this: anxiety is a state in which we come to recognize not that there are no norms, but that norms are merely hypothetical imperatives.

Contra Kant, there is no norm binding simply on me *qua* agent, a fact made graphic in anxiety as I survey the world in its stark irrelevance. Instead, what we have reason to do is a function of our self-identities and of a gradual piecemeal transition from one such identity to another; stripped of these, as we are in the anxious state, we can find no firm normative ground. One consequence of this move, incidentally, is that one can see how delicate the interplay is between the episodic state and the subsequent attitude to that state held by authentic agents. It is implausible that the phenomenology of the anxiety attack itself contains anything like this type of fine-grained distinction between hypothetical and categorical imperatives. The idea is rather that, following the initial shock, the authentic agent comes to see things in these terms—comes to learn from, and reflect on, and internalize the experience.[60] At a textual level, the details are closely tied to Heidegger's claim that 'anxiety individualises' by 'throwing Dasein back' on its 'ownmost potentiality for being'.[61] In anxiety Dasein experiences itself as cut off from all worldly source of normativity, left in what Ga29/30 calls 'limbo'; this inability to act, this 'impossibility of projecting' in SZ's terms, supposedly makes manifest the absence of norms inhering simply in agency per se, the absence of an non-worldly authority to fall back on.[62]

Fourth, Heidegger argues that agents who face up to such anxiety will ultimately possess a number of distinctive features, features which he valorizes. For example, in line with the point just made, they possess and manifest in their lives a fuller understanding of the normative landscape in which they live.[63] As I have argued elsewhere, Dasein is Heidegger's name for the normative standpoint, and so one can equally express this view by stating that they are more aware of and so more fully manifest the nature of Dasein: as he puts it, they 'liberate' the Dasein within themselves.[64] More broadly, Heidegger takes such agents to possess a refined capacity for decision-making in the future: they are, for example, presented as specifically attentive to the nuances of each individual situation.[65] The most natural way to read this is in terms of an increased recognition that the received norms and practices which they had unthinkingly followed are in fact open to challenge and criticism. Thus Blattner, for example, characterizes the aftermath of anxiety as follows:

> Once I encounter anxiety, I am temporarily alienated from the public norms in the light of which I live, and I thereby come to see them as negotiable in a way I had not before. I can respond to this disclosure in one of two ways: I can flee from it by rushing back to the public world of my everyday existence and aggressively rejecting challenges to public norms, thereby burying myself in an aggravated form of conformism. Or I can return to the everyday world of public norms loosened up and flexible, able to entertain challenges to these norms and imagine alternative ways of living.[66]

12.4 Critical Assessment

We can now see how Heidegger's treatment of anxiety connects to the lines of thought identified in Section 12.2. For Heidegger, anxiety plays a central methodological role: it forces Dasein out of the 'complacency and tranquilized obviousness' in which it characteristically lives.[67] By extension, he valorizes agents who are open to anxiety and who face up to its implications.[68] Heidegger then embeds these claims within his larger system: through anxiety Dasein is disclosed to itself as it truly is: it 'becomes "essentially" Dasein in that authentic existence', fulfilling the ancient injunction to 'become what you are', and making possible a philosophy based on recognition of that nature.[69] As Heidegger puts it:

> If the existential analytic of Dasein is to retain clarity in principle as to its function in fundamental ontology, then in order to master its provisional task of exhibiting Dasein's Being, it must seek for one of the most far reaching and most primordial possibilities of disclosure—one that lies in Dasein itself....As a [mood] which will satisfy these methodological requirements, the phenomenon of anxiety will be made basic for our analysis.[70]

The task now is to offer some assessment of Heidegger's account; we can identify, I suggest, four key questions.

First, why does Heidegger appeal to a mood, to what most authors would class as an emotion, to play this role? Part of the answer will be highly specific. Heidegger uses anxiety to illustrate the structural aspect of our existence which he dubs 'affectivity'—and this, defined in terms of notions like 'throwness' and 'mattering', has obvious links to the basic topology of moods set out in Section 12.1.[71] But I think a broader point can also be made if one asks why Heidegger identifies a mood as that which 'brings Dasein face to face with...the authenticity of its being'.[72] After all, there are clearly many other mechanisms which might shake people out of an assumed belief system and bring them to a new self-understanding: Socratic questioning is an obvious example. I suspect the answer hangs in part on a fundamental suspicion Heidegger has about the nature of dialogue and debate, which he tends to see as progressively obscuring a topic, rather than illuminating it. Thematized in *Sein und Zeit* under the label of 'idle talk' [*Gerede*], this assumption is present throughout Heidegger's work.[73] Thus pre-*Sein und Zeit* texts such as the 1925 lecture course '*Geschichte des Zeitbegriffs*' present academic conferences as devices for 'covering up' ideas through parroting them out.[74] By the time of the *Schwarze Hefte*, Heidegger has applied the lesson to the reception of his own work: scholarly exegesis of *Sein und Zeit* is treated as a derailment device by which academics serve to distract themselves and the public from the book's real import.[75] Of course, Heidegger thinks that anxiety can easily be suppressed and 'explained away' by inauthentic agents.[76] But here even the urgency of this flight still betrays an incipient grasp of Dasein's true nature.[77] So my suggestion is that Heidegger sees the immediacy of moods as providing a superior access to point to Dasein's nature in part because he takes the obvious alternative, discourse and debate, to systematically obscure whatever it treats.

Second, one might ask why Heidegger appeals to this particular mood to play the relevant role. Depending on the comparison one has in mind, this question can take several forms. One issue is why Heidegger offers *this* account of anxiety and not some other. After all, his treatment of it is clearly at odds with many alternate such accounts. To take a simple example, the *Diagnostic and Statistical Manual* used in much contemporary psychiatric practice lists a host of 'anxiety disorders', many of which lack the distinctive features Heidegger stresses. So, for example:

> The individual with separation anxiety disorder is fearful or anxious about separation from attachment figures to a degree that is developmentally inappropriate. There is persistent fear or anxiety about harm coming to attachment figures and events that could lead to loss of or separation from attachment figures and reluctance to go away from attachment figures, as well as nightmares and physical symptoms of distress.[78]

This state clearly has an intentional object—it is about a particular individual or individuals—in a way that Heideggerian anxiety is not; but it still seems reasonably described as a type of anxiety. So the question might be 'why focus on this mode of anxiety and not others?' Alternately, one might mean something more like 'why focus on anxiety as *opposed to* say, joy or depression or contempt or amusement?' As I noted in Section 12.2, the idea that emotions play a central methodological role is a common one, particularly in twentieth-century French philosophy, and its defenders typically each have their own preferred candidate for the key emotion: Bataille, to use the same example as above, emphasizes a form of ecstatic laughter.[79] This raises the question: might not Heidegger's existential analytic have looked very different if he had begun from another emotion? Given this, one might well ask on what basis he chose anxiety rather than, say, joy?

Third, supposing we grant Heidegger's focus on this particular brand of anxiety, why should we take such an experience so seriously? Blattner describes Heidegger's position, as one where '[n]o self-understanding is immune to being undercut by anxiety; anything we take for granted about ourselves can be dissolved by the corrosive effects of anxiety'.[80] But why, to take an Aristotelian worry, is the person for whom this is true not simply incontinent or badly brought up? Above I discussed McManus's concern about whether anxiety was veridical. There I suggested that the problem could be at least postponed by reading anxiety such that it didn't imply complete meaninglessness, but only that no norms were binding on Dasein merely *qua* Dasein. Yet the worry will reoccur—even if this is what the state shows, why should we take it as veridical? The fear is no longer that doing so will deliver us straight into Tugendhat's challenge. Rather, it is broader—why should we regard such states as good evidence? After all, one might think that this kind of foundational normative question needs to be settled by argument—by ruling out, perhaps, the various Kantian programmes which would reach a very different conclusion.

Fourth, suppose we grant that there exists a mood of roughly the type Heidegger describes and which has roughly the methodological and evidential status he claims—is his account of it internally plausible? There seem to me several points on which to press. Consider the supposedly global scope of anxiety—a state in which, as Blattner put it, 'nothing matters to you'.[81] One might object, following Okrent, that whilst we can be alienated from each individual identity, it does not follow that we can be alienated from all of them at once: 'pace Heidegger, the contingency of every one of our identities does not imply the contingency of the fact that each of us has some identity'.[82] One way to put the worry is that we have good Heideggerian reasons to think that even an anxious person sees themselves in terms of some, culturally complex, identity with its own patterns of salience and norms—that of the sufferer of anxiety, in some ways a distinctively modern trope.[83]

I have sketched here four possible lines of attack.[84] Yet these questions are not easy to answer in any direct fashion due to the systematic and holistic character of Heidegger's method. His basic claim is that anxiety allows 'the structural totality of the Being we seek [to] come to light in an elemental way'.[85] But whether it does this or not, and whether it does it better than various other means, will clearly be a function of one's view as to what that totality is and what an 'elemental' approach is—that is even before one gets into familiar Heideggerian controversies such as that over 'Being'.[86] More broadly, to challenge him one would need to show not simply that there are other forms of anxiety (something he explicitly concedes), nor that there are other moods which might equally play a key philosophical role (a point he accepts and utilizes when discussing boredom), but that the results he derives from anxiety are biased or misleading—and it is hard to see how one might do that outside a global valuation of his work.

Perhaps the most that can be said in the current context then is this: I have raised a number of serious questions for Heidegger's analysis, and suggested where he may face problems. I want to conclude by highlighting a final issue. Suppose everything that Heidegger says is right—anxiety thus becomes a state with a profound philosophical importance. Yet Heidegger is clear, particularly in Ga29/30, that we cannot control the onset of moods in any straightforward sense. He writes:

> Moods—are they not something we can least of all invent, something that comes over us, something that we cannot simply call up? Do they not form of their own accord, as something that we cannot forcibly bring about but into which we slip unawares? If so, then we cannot and may not forcibly bring about such a mood artificially or arbitrarily...It must already be there. All we can do is ascertain it.[87]

Moods thus 'assail' us, and their sudden descent is intended to exhibit what he calls our 'throwness', our finding ourselves in a situation not of our choosing. The result is that Heidegger's work on the emotions mandates that we take up a very particular stance. Whilst we cannot induce them, we must be highly attentive to their onset and remove any factors which would block or overcome them. As he puts it when discussing boredom, the upshot is that we must 'not let boredom fall asleep... a strange and almost insane demand'.[88] Han-Pile, analysing the closely related case of the 'call of conscience' puts it like this:

> [T]he choice is neither fully active nor fully passive: it involves a particular kind of agency, which, following Greek grammarians, I shall call 'medio-passive'... Ultimately, hearing the call is not up to me: yet I can take some responsibility for doing so in the sense that, unless I try to attune myself in the right way, it may never be heard at all.[89]

This new problematic links very naturally with Heidegger's theological interests: Dasein's need to be attentive is, for example, the secular analogue of the Pauline injunction to watchfulness.[90] The result is that in identifying the distinctive methodological role for emotions which I have discussed, Heidegger also comes to need a distinctive methodology by which we might cultivate and foster them. This methodology in turn feeds back into the rest of his philosophy. By the time of texts like Ga65, the *Beiträge*, Heidegger's ideal relationship to '*Seyn*'—ceaselessly elusive, resisting any deliberate attempt to grasp it, requiring constant attentive expectation—*mirrors* in many ways this delicate balance of activity and passivity through which we must awaken to moods. In line with the quasi-poetic tenor of Ga65, Heidegger exploits the full gamut of meanings for terms like '*Stimmung*'. But what I want to stress is that we must keep in mind the paradigm provided by the attentive awaiting of moods when we encounter remarks such as this:

> This preparation [for a new kind of philosophy] does not consist in acquiring preliminary cognitions as the basis for the later disclosure of actual cognitions. Rather, here preparation is: opening the way, yielding to the way—essentially, *attuning* [*Stimmung*].[91]

I have argued that Heidegger possesses a sophisticated and innovative philosophy of the emotions. But one might also speak, in the years after *Sein und Zeit*, of an 'emotionalised philosophy'.[92]

12.5 Conclusion

My aim in this chapter has been to trace the profile of Heidegger's innovative treatment of the emotions, and to indicate some of the consequent problems he faces. I have argued that he is uninterested in, and even unable to formulate, a number of the canonical debates in this area: the classic early modern and enlightenment dispute over motivation and the 'passions' is one such case. Simultaneously, however, he makes moods central to both his normative vision and to his methodological programme. Ultimately, I have suggested, there is at least a strand of his thought within which emotions are not simply a necessary condition on philosophizing, but a paradigm for it.

Notes

1. I discuss the relation between Heidegger's preferred characterization of these states and the usual idea of an emotion in Section 12.1. In citing Heidegger, I refer to the standard *Gesamtausgabe* edition (Frankfurt: Klostermann, 1975–; abbreviated as Ga), with the exception of SZ, where I use the standard text (Tübingen: Max Niemeyer, 1957). I employ the following abbreviations and I list any translations consulted below: all translations show the German pagination in the margins.

   SZ *Sein und Zeit* (Tübingen: Niemeyer, 1957); *Being and Time*, trans. J. Macquarrie and E. Robinson (New York: Harper & Row, 1962)

Ga3 *Kant und das Problem der Metaphysik* (1998); *Kant and the Problem of Metaphysics*, trans. Richard Taft (Bloomington: Indiana University Press)

Ga9 *Wegmarken* (1976); *Pathmarks*, trans. William McNeill (Cambridge: Cambridge University Press, 1998)

Ga20 *Prolegomena zur Geschichte des Zeitbegriffs* (1979); *History of the Concept of Time*, trans. Theodore Kisiel (Bloomington: Indiana University Press, 1992)

Ga26 *Metaphysische Anfangsgründe der Logik im Ausgang von Leibniz* (1978)

Ga29/30 *Die Grundbegriffe der Metaphysik* (1983); *The Fundamental Concepts of Metaphysics*, trans. William McNeill and Nicholas Walker (Bloomington: Indiana University Press, 1995)

Ga60 *Phänomenologie des religiösen Lebens* (1995)

Ga65 *Beiträge zur Philosophie (Vom Ereignis)* (1989)

Ga94 *Überlegungen II–VI (Schwarze Hefte 1931–1938)* (2014)

2. Macquarrie and Robinson render *Befindlichkeit* as 'state of mind'; I follow most contemporary authors in avoiding this since it risks prejudging Heidegger's stance on mental states.
3. For an excellent treatment of Heidegger's relationship to Freud, for example, see Havi Carel, *Life and Death in Freud and Heidegger* (Amsterdam: Rodopi, 2014).
4. As with all Heideggerian terminology, translation is a contentious issue. Many commentators now use 'attunement' for *Stimmung* to capture both the play on *stimmen*, meaning 'to tune' (a *Klavierstimmer* is a piano tuner), and some of the themes I discuses below, in particular Heidegger's attempt to subvert models on which moods are inner states projected onto a blankly valueless world. In the current context, however, where the focus is as much on emotions themselves as on Heidegger exegesis, I have decided to employ the simpler 'mood'. In this I follow the standard translation of *Sein und Zeit* by Macquarrie and Robinson.
5. SZ, p. 139. See similarly Ga29/30, pp. 98–9. One of the targets Heidegger has in mind here is Kant, who defends a tripartite analysis of the mind along these lines (*V-MP/Mron*, pp. 877–8). All references to Kant are to the standard edition, *Kants gesammelte Schriften*

GMS *Grundlegung zur Metaphysik der Sitten* (Ak., vol. 4)
MS *Die Metaphysik der Sitten* (Ak., vol. 6)
V-MP/Mron *Metaphysik Mrongovius* (Ak., vol. 29)

(Berlin: de Gruyter, 1900–; abbreviated as Ak.). I employ the following abbreviations:

6. Ga29/30, p. 100.
7. SZ, p. 136.
8. I will say something about the question of whether these examples are all well characterized as moods in Section 12.2.
9. SZ, p. 134; 136.
10. SZ, p. 134. On the general tactic compare SZ, p. 34.
11. SZ, p. 136.
12. SZ, p. 137.
13. SZ, p. 138.

14. Thus Dreyfus's classic formulation: affectivity 'is the condition of the possibility of specific things showing up as mattering'. Hubert Dreyfus, *Being-in-the-world* (Cambridge, MA.: MIT Press, 1991), p. 175.
15. SZ, p. 137.
16. SZ, p. 138.
17. SZ, pp. 134–5.
18. SZ, p. 136. On the link to throwness see especially SZ, p. 135. I'll return to the question of to what degree we might be able to control moods in Section 12.4.
19. SZ, p. 136.
20. Ga29/30, pp. 127–8.
21. For an extremely influential modern formulation of how exactly this might work see Dreyfus, *Being-in-the-world*. Dreyfus thus places particular stress on Heidegger's remarks on the public nature of moods—for example, SZ, p. 138 (Dreyfus, *Being-in-the-world*, p. 171).
22. SZ, pp. 141–2. To see why this is problematic consider the following. I am standing at a viewing platform on top of a mountain. Through the telescope, I see the restaurant across the valley—and a small child cycling right on the edge. It seems natural to express this by saying that I fear that the child will fall. Yet it is not immediately obvious in what sense this fear is about me—the child may be a complete stranger. There are of course responses that might be made—my point is just that some kind of development of the idea is necessary.
23. In Heideggerian terms, the issue of the 'inner' and 'outer' arises at the level of being-in-the-world, of which affectivity is only one aspect. I discuss this issue in detail elsewhere: see Sacha Golob, *Heidegger on Concepts, Freedom and Normativity* (Cambridge: Cambridge University Press, 2014), pp. 70–103.
24. Each philosopher of course has their own preferred taxonomy of emotions/feelings/passions/drives and so on; my goal in this section is simply to sketch some very broad, but I hope useful, patterns of coalescence.
25. For Hume's own famous formulation, see David Hume *A Treatise of Human Nature*, ed. L.A. Selby-Bigge (Oxford: Clarendon Press, 1975), 2.3.3.4.
26. Paul Guyer, *Knowledge, Reason, and Taste: Kant's Response to Hume* (Princeton: Princeton University Press, 2008), p. 181. The key primary passage is this:

    > Every determination of choice proceeds from the representation of a possible action to the deed through the feeling of pleasure or displeasure, taking an interest in the action or its effect. The state of feeling here (the way in which inner sense is affected) is either pathological or moral. (MM 6:399)

27. Guyer, *Knowledge, Reason, and Taste*, p. 183.
28. G.W.F. Hegel, *Lectures on the Philosophy of Religion*, trans. Peter Hodgson, 3 vols (London: University of California Press, 1984–5), vol. I, p. 391.
29. Hegel, *Elements of the Philosophy of Right*, trans. H. Nisbet (Cambridge: Cambridge University Press, 1991), sections 163; 207; 253.
30. Friedrich Nietzsche, *Genealogy of Morals*, trans. Carol Diethe (Cambridge: Cambridge University Press, 2006), 1.10.
31. Michel Foucault. *Remarks on Marx*, trans. J. Goldstein and J. Cascaito (New York: Semiotext, 1991), pp. 31–2.
32. Georges Bataille, *Inner Experience*, trans. Leslie.Boldt (Albany: SUNY Press, 1988), p. 3.
33. SZ, pp. 146–7.

34. SZ, p. 145. For an extremely helpful analysis of this aspect of Heidegger's system, see William Blattner, *Heidegger's Temporal Idealism* (Cambridge: Cambridge University Press, 1999), pp. 40–2.
35. One might try to align such cases with inauthentic Dasein, and there are some very general communalities: both are in an important sense 'defective' judges. But the defects are different. The usual worry in the ethics literature is about agents who are capable of tracking the extension of moral predicates and even offering some account of why they apply, but don't act on the verdicts reached. Inauthentic Dasein, in contrast, systematically misapplies many of the concepts, death, the future, the past, in which Heidegger is interested (SZ, pp. 167–71).
36. SZ, p. 186.
37. Ga94, p. 198.
38. SZ, p. 266 or SZ, pp. 295–6.
39. SZ, p. 189.
40. Ga29/30, p. 89.
41. See, for example, Ga29/30, p. 190. I think SZ's treatment of fear is also interesting, but it is clearly intended by Heidegger as a foil for the methodologically much more significant case of anxiety (SZ, p. 140). I also share widely voiced concerns about how well the episodic fear he discusses actually fits into his taxonomy of moods (see, for example, Dreyfus, *Being-in-the-world*, p. 169).
42. Heidegger embeds anxiety within a complex web of existential and quasi-theological concepts such as death, guilt, authenticity, and the 'call of conscience' (see, for example, SZ, pp. 269–71). The exact role of these concepts within his system is disputed, as is the connection between his use of terms like death and their ordinary meaning. Any treatment of such larger aspects of Heidegger's system would take us well beyond the current chapter, and I will not attempt one here. For a good overview of many of the issues see Iain Thomson, 'Death and Demise in Being and Time', in *The Cambridge Companion to Heidegger's Being and Time*, ed. Mark Wrathall (Cambridge: Cambridge University Press, 2013). For a detailed presentation of my own take on these issues, please see Golob, *Heidegger on Concepts, Freedom and Normativity*, ch. 6.
43. SZ, pp. 186, 187. Thus death, which is closely bound with Heideggerian anxiety, is likewise 'a way to be, which Dasein takes over as soon as it is' (SZ, p. 245; on the close links between death and anxiety see SZ, p. 266).
44. SZ, pp. 185–6; 189.
45. SZ, p. 189.
46. SZ, p. 260, 296. As Blattner observes, Heidegger is ambiguous as to precisely what relation authentic agents need to anxiety (Blattner, 'Essential Guilt and Transcendental Conscience', in *Heidegger, Authenticity and the Self*, ed. Denis McManus (London: Routledge, 2015), pp. 116–35, p. 127. The exact details of the relationship, whilst important to the description of 'resoluteness', do not matter here.
47. SZ, p. 187.
48. SZ, p. 186.
49. SZ, p. 186.
50. SZ, p. 86 (see also Ga29/30, p. 333).
51. In Heidegger's own terms:

    > Why is there anything such as a why and a because? Because Dasein exists... The for-the-sake-of-which, as the primary character of world, i.e. of transcendence, is the primal phenomenon of ground as such... (Ga26: 276)

There is a broader question here as to whether all normativity is a function of these 'for-the-sake-of-whichs'. This will depend on how exactly one specifies 'function', and how one cashes the details of the story about self-understanding. One can, for example, easily imagine identities that give me a reason not to recognize biological needs as reasons. But it is less clear why agents who just unreflectively take biological impulses to be reasons are doing so because of any self-understanding. For a very helpful discussion of these issues, drawing on a comparison with Korsgaard's work on practical identity, see M. Okrent, 'Heidegger and Korsgaard on Human Reflection', *Philosophical Topics* 27 (1999): 47–76.

52. SZ, p. 186.
53. Heidegger makes similar claims about 'profound boredom'. It is an experience in which 'beings as a whole do not disappear, however, but show themselves precisely as such in their indifference' (Ga29/30, p. 208).
54. Herman Philipse, *Heidegger's Philosophy of Being* (Princeton: Princeton University Press, 1998), p. 395.
55. SZ, p. 343. Crowell seems to me to have the idea right when he summarizes that: 'anxiety in Heidegger's sense reveals something like a global incapacity vis-à-vis the normativity of all laws and oughts: existing norms present themselves as mere facts'. Steven Crowell, 'Conscience and Reason', in *Transcendental Heidegger*, ed. Jeff Malpas and Steven Crowell (Stanford: Stanford University Press, 2007), pp. 43–62, (p. 55).
56. Blattner, *Heidegger's Temporal Idealism*, p. 80.
57. Ernst Tugendhat, *Self-Consciousness and Self-Determination*, trans. P. Stern (Cambridge, MA.: MIT Press, 1986), p. 216.
58. For an alternative response which places great stress on the nature of 'making' decisions, see Dreyfus, *Being-in-the-world*, p. 319.
59. Thomson, *Death and Demise*, p. 270.
60. This would be my response to McManus's powerful challenge as to whether anxiety is veridical or not: a positive answer lands one facing Tugendhat's problem, whilst a negative answer makes the importance which Heidegger attaches to it puzzling. My view is that Heidegger does regard it as conveying something accurate about the normative landscape, but it requires subsequent reflection to understand precisely what: the answer, the absence of categorical norms, avoids Tugendhat's threat, whilst still being of obvious import. For an extremely helpful discussion of the underlying issues, and his own solution to the challenge, see D. McManus, 'Anxiety, Choice, Responsibility', in *Heidegger, Authenticity and the Self*, ed. D. McManus (London: Routledge, 2015), pp. 163–86.
61. SZ, p. 191; pp. 186–7.
62. Ga29/30, p. 123; SZ, p. 343. For a full discussion see Golob, *Heidegger on Concepts, Freedom and Normativity*, pp. 229–33.
63. Again, this mirrors the upshot of Heidegger's treatment of profound boredom; see Ga29–30, pp. 254–5.
64. Ga29/30, pp. 246–8.
65. SZ, pp. 298–300.
66. Blattner, 'Essential Guilt and Transcendental Conscience', p. 132.
67. SZ, p. 311.
68. SZ, pp. 296–7.

69. SZ, p. 323; SZ, p. 145.
70. SZ, p. 182.
71. SZ, p. 184.
72. SZ, p. 308.
73. SZ, pp. 167–70.
74. Ga20, p. 376.
75. GA94, p. 74; see similarly p. 39.
76. SZ, p. 185, 187.
77. SZ, p. 185, 187.
78. The American Psychiatric Association, *The Diagnostic and Statistical Manual of Mental Disorders, Fifth Edition* (Arlington VA.: American Psychiatric Association, 2013), p. 189.
79. Bataille, *Inner Experience*, p. 34.
80. D. McManus, 'Anxiety, Choice, Responsibility', in *Heidegger, Authenticity and the Self*, ed. D. McManus (London: Routledge, 2015), pp. 163–85 (p. 155).
81. Blattner, *Heidegger's Temporal Idealism*, p. 80.
82. Mark Okrent, 'Heidegger and Korsgaard on Human Reflection', p. 73.
83. The worry here would be that even in anxiety individuals retain much more of a culturally specific, worldly identity than Heidegger allows—so, for example, something thicker that the bare awareness of one's own being which Blattner calls 'purely thin facticity and existentiality' (Blattner, *Heidegger's Temporal Idealism*, p. 77).
84. When considered in the larger context of Heidegger's work, further worries emerge which I cannot adequately discuss here. For example, as Tobias Keiling perceptively noted in comments on an earlier draft of this material, the central methodological role which Heidegger allots to successive moods (anxiety, boredom, or later what one might call 'restraint' [*Verhaltenheit*]) leads a structural neglect of their phenomenological differences: very crudely put, they all 'do' the same basic thing. I am indebted to Tobias for helping me see this more clearly.
85. SZ, p. 182.
86. Heidegger himself sometimes tries to offer more specific defences of the choice of anxiety, but these are largely couched in terms which require an antecedent acceptance of his system. So, for example, Ga3, pp. 283–4 makes much play of the fact that we are anxious about 'nothing'. Heidegger's intent is to link the supposed absence of a target object in anxiety to his broader doctrine of the 'Nothing' [*Das Nichts*]—the plausibility of this move is entirely a function of the plausibility of that other commitment.
87. Ga29/30, pp. 89–90.
88. Ga29/30, p. 119.
89. Beatrice Han-Pile, 'Freedom and the Choice to Choose Oneself in Being and Time', in *The Cambridge Companion to Heidegger's Being and Time*, ed. M. Wrathall (Cambridge: Cambridge University Press, 2013), pp. 291–319 (pp. 308–9).
90. Ga60, pp. 104–5.
91. Ga65, p. 86 (original emphasis).
92. I would like to thank Denis McManus, Sasha Mudd, and audiences in Southampton and Oxford for extremely helpful discussion of these issues. I would also like to thank the editors of the volume and Tobias Keiling for their insightful comments on an earlier draft.

Bibliography

American Psychiatric Association, *The Diagnostic and Statistical Manual of Mental Disorders, Fifth Edition* (Arlington VA.: American Psychiatric Association, 2013).

Bataille, Georges. *Inner Experience*, trans. Boldt, Leslie (Albany: SUNY Press, 1988).

Blattner, William. *Heidegger's Temporal Idealism* (Cambridge: Cambridge University Press, 1999).

Blattner, William. 'Essential Guilt and Transcendental Conscience', in *Heidegger, Authenticity and the Self*, ed. Denis McManus (London: Routledge, 2015), pp. 116–34.

Carel, Havi. *Life and Death in Freud and Heidegger* (Amsterdam: Rodopi, 2014).

Crowell, Steven. 'Conscience and Reason', in *Transcendental Heidegger*, ed. Jeff Malpas and Steven Crowell (Stanford: Stanford University Press, 2007), pp. 43–62.

Dreyfus, Hubert. *Being-in-the-world* (Cambridge, MA.: MIT Press, 1991).

Foucault, Michel. *Remarks on Marx*, trans. J. Goldstein and J. Cascaito (New York: Semiotext, 1991).

Golob, Sacha. *Heidegger on Concepts, Freedom and Normativity* (Cambridge: Cambridge University Press, 2014).

Guyer, Paul. *Knowledge, Reason, and Taste: Kant's Response to Hume* (Princeton: Princeton University Press, 2008).

Han-Pile, Béatrice. 'Freedom and the Choice to Choose Oneself in Being and Time', in *The Cambridge Companion to Heidegger's Being and Time*, ed. Mark Wrathall (Cambridge: Cambridge University Press, 2013), pp. 291–319.

Hegel, Georg. *Lectures on the Philosophy of Religion*, trans. Peter Hodgson, 3 vols (London: University of California Press 1984–85).

Hegel, Georg. *Elements of the Philosophy of Right*, trans. H. B. Nisbet (Cambridge: Cambridge University Press, 1991).

Heidegger, Martin. *Sein und Zeit* (Tübingen: Niemeyer, 1957); *Being and Time*, trans. John Macquarrie and Edward Robinson (New York: Harper & Row, 1962).

Heidegger, Martin. *Wegmarken* (Frankfurt: Klostermann, 1976); *Pathmarks*, trans. William McNeill (Cambridge: Cambridge University Press, 1998) (Ga9).

Heidegger, Martin. *Metaphysische Anfangsgründe der Logik im Ausgang von Leibniz* (Frankfurt: Klostermann, 1978) (Ga26).

Heidegger, Martin. *Prolegomena zur Geschichte des Zeitbegriffs* (Frankfurt: Klostermann, 1979); *History of the Concept of Time*, trans. Theodore Kisiel (Bloomington: Indiana University Press, 1992) (Ga20).

Heidegger, Martin. *Die Grundbegriffe der Metaphysik* (Frankfurt: Klostermann 1983); *The Fundamental Concepts of Metaphysics*, trans. William McNeill and Nicholas Walkes (Bloomington: Indiana University Press, 1995) (Ga29/30).

Heidegger, Martin. *Beiträge zur Philosophie (Vom Ereignis)* (Frankfurt: Klostermann, 1989) (Ga65).

Heidegger, Martin. *Phänomenologie des religiösen Lebens* (Frankfurt: Klostermann, 1995) (Ga60).

Heidegger, Martin. *Kant und das Problem der Metaphysik* (Frankfurt: Klostermann, 1998); *Kant and the Problem of Metaphysics*, trans. Richard Taft (Bloomington: Indiana University Press, 1997) (Ga3).

Heidegger, Martin. *Überlegungen II-VI (Schwarze Hefte 1931–1938)* (Frankfurt: Klostermann 2014) (Ga94).

Hume, David. *A Treatise of Human Nature*, ed. L.A. Selby-Bigge (Oxford: Clarendon Press, 1975).

Kant, Immanuel. *Kants gesammelte Schriften: Grundlegung zur Metaphysik der Sitten* (Berlin: de Gruyter, 1911).

Kant, Immanuel. *Kants gesammelte Schriften: Die Metaphysik der Sitten* (Berlin: de Gruyter, 1914).

Kant, Immanuel. *Kants gesammelte Schriften: Metaphysik Mrongovius* (Berlin: de Gruyter, 1980).

McManus, Denis. 'Anxiety, Choice, Responsibility', in *Heidegger, Authenticity and the Self*, ed. Denis McManus (London: Routledge, 2015), pp. 163–85.

Nietzsche, Friedrich. *Genealogy of Morals*, trans. Carol Diethe (Cambridge: Cambridge University Press, 2006).

Philipse, Herman. *Heidegger's Philosophy of Being* (Princeton: Princeton University Press, 1998).

Okrent, Mark. 'Heidegger and Korsgaard on Human Reflection', *Philosophical Topics* 27 (1999): 47–76.

Thomson, Iain. 'Death and Demise in Being and Time', in *The Cambridge Companion to Heidegger's Being and Time*, ed. Mark Wrathall (Cambridge: Cambridge University Press, 2013): 260–90.

Tugendhat, Ernst. *Self-Consciousness and Self-Determination*, trans. Paul Stern (Cambridge, MA.: MIT Press, 1986).

13

Sartre on Affectivity

Anthony Hatzimoysis

Emotion has proven resistant to the standard categorizations of psychological states. Indeed, even the term 'state', with its connotations of fixity and stability, appears to assume too much about the nature of emotional experience. Highlighting the active side of emotion, its engagement with those aspects of reality which give rise to affective experience, should be a welcome corrective to the traditional emphasis on emotional passivity. Sartre's work has been pivotal in bringing the active side of emotions to the foreground. Instead of treating behaviour as an optional concomitant of emotion, Sartre appears to approach affectivity as a particular class of conduct.[1] Emotion, for Sartre, is the conscious transformation, by means of one's body, of a situation. What is transformed, though, is not reality itself, but how the world is experienced by the subject, and, consequently, how the subject responds to a thus transformed world.[2] Correspondingly, what drives the Sartrean analysis of affectivity is the desire to make proper sense of the *signification* of emotion in a twofold sense: what it signifies for the life of the agent who experiences the emotion, as well as which aspect of reality is manifested when the agent is emotionally engaged with the world. Sartre's 'phenomenological'[3] approach to affectivity is outlined in the *Sketch for a Theory of the Emotions* (1939), yet it is not restricted to that essay. Remarks about the phenomenology of affectivity are included in Sartre's seminal paper on 'Intentionality', written around 1934, and are further developed in his long essay on the *Transcendence of the Ego* (1936).[4]

Here, however, I would like to explore the relation between the account given in the *Sketch* and the views expressed in a work published shortly afterwards, *The Imaginary* (1940). Each of the two books presents a bold analytical approach to affective phenomena. Both of them bear testament to Sartre's unique capacity to pose philosophical questions through an astute narration of human experience. What is not so clear, though, is whether those texts can be read as parts of a harmonious theory.

The question of consistency between the two texts bears upon an issue in the contemporary understanding of emotions. One the one hand, it has been claimed that emotions are closely akin, if not identical, to perceptual states through which the world is revealed to us. That approach underlines the epistemic dimension of affective content, either as a bare experiential datum, or as conceptually structured evidence on which evaluative judgements can be grounded.[5] On the other hand, it has been argued that emotions may be seen not as perceptual takes on the environment, but as functional alterations of the whole organism whose strategic role is to secure for the agent a utility cost-reduction, or a socially mediated preference satisfaction. That approach highlights the behavioural aspects of affectivity, and its intimate relation to the way an agent responds emotionally to the world.[6]

Accordingly, emotion has been thought to function as a direct cause of behaviour, or as part of the agent's motivational background, or simply as a contributing or hindering force.[7] Sartre is often thought to occupy the extreme position of seeing emotion not merely as connected to a piece of behaviour but as, in a sense, identical to it. For some scholars, Sartre's theory in the *Sketch* entails that 'emotions are actions'.[8] However, as I will argue in section 13.1, that entailment does not hold. Despite the apparent connotations of some phrases in the *Sketch*, Sartre sees emotion as very different from action. Does this difference imply that, for Sartre, emotion is better approached as a type of perceptual experience? *The Imaginary* lends itself to an analysis of affectivity as in many respects similar to perception. In contrast to the account offered in the *Sketch*, the focus of *The Imaginary* is set on emotional feelings, with the behavioural dimension of emotions receding in the background. Is this merely a change in emphasis, or an indication of a deeper tension between the claims made in the two books? And if the latter, does it imply that Sartre saw the error of his old ways, and decided to move on to a different philosophical path?

My answer to those questions will be that Sartre does indeed offer a different set of claims in the two works; the difference lies mainly in the *perspective* from which those claims are made. That difference, in my view, is quite substantial for raising worries about the consistency of the Sartrean theory of emotion. Hence, the success of that theory depends on the possibility of combining the views expressed in the two books into a coherent philosophical outlook. I will first outline the theory offered in the *Sketch* (Section 13.1). I shall then introduce the view developed in *The Imaginary* (Section 13.2) and, after articulating and assessing a possible response to Sartre's critique of subjectivist accounts of emotional feeling (Section 13.3), I will explore in detail the points of similarity and contrast between the views encountered in the two books (Sections 13.4 to 13.6).

13.1 Affectivity in the *Sketch*

In his *Sketch for a Theory of the Emotions*, Sartre presents emotion as the conscious transformation, by means of one's body, of a situation: what changes is how the world is experienced by the subject and, consequently, how the subject responds to a thus transformed world.[9]

The world is understood as a totality of phenomena linked in a network of mutual references. The way in which each phenomenon relates to others defines the type of world encountered by the subject. We should distinguish between at least two worlds: the world of action and the world of emotion.[10] In the former, we experience reality as a combination of demands and affordances; the link between demands and affordances is itself perceived as governed by deterministic processes between causes and effects. The instrumental world of action is captured in the pragmatic intuition of the situation that makes certain moves available for the subject, while denying her others.

The emotional apprehension of the world, on the other hand, hooks on to those qualities or aspects that carry affective meaning for the agent. The joyful, hateful, or bleak world, far from being identical to the word of action, is clearly distinguished from the instrumental world. What appears to bring forth the emotional stance towards the world, is that the situation presents the agent with demands that she is unable to meet—and her emotional response (be it joyous, angry, or sad) consists in a pattern of cognitive and physiological changes which reduce the urgency, lower the intensity, or neutralize the force of those demands.

That is, in rough outline, Sartre's sketch for a theory of the emotions.[11] The issue I would like to raise here is of a different character: it concerns Sartre's claim that 'emotion is a certain way of apprehending the world'.[12] In the *Sketch*, that claim is introduced in the course of Sartre's analysis of affectivity as a distinct class of conduct. In *The Imaginary*, the idea of affectivity as a mode of apprehension returns, though it is not quite evident how exactly it relates to the view outlined in the *Sketch*. Let us look closely at that issue.

13.2 Affectivity in 'The Imaginary'

The accurate interpretation of how a philosopher understands a phenomenon is facilitated by a proper understanding of the expression with which the philosopher purports to capture that phenomenon. The expression 'emotion as apprehension', though, is not by itself easy to comprehend. A first obstacle to a correct understanding of the phrase comes from the fact that cognitive states, such as apprehension, and affective states, such as emotion, are traditionally conceived as sharply different. That difference may permit, at most, the consecutive occurrences of apprehension and emotion. The notion of 'emotional apprehension' might then be thought to denote two states rather than one, with the emotion component following upon the neutral apprehension of reality.

In *The Imaginary* Sartre will probe the validity of the division between the affective and the cognitive by inviting us to think of 'feeling... as a species of knowledge'.[13] Let me call that view 'cognitivist', to be contrasted with the 'non-cognitivist' view of feeling to which Sartre's view is strongly opposed.[14]

Non-cognitivism conceives of feeling as an affective state whose being is exhausted in an ineffable shiver experienced by a subject, in isolation from the surrounding world.[15] The non-cognitivist view may of course be expanded so as to accommodate the connection between what one apprehends and how one feels. The links between feeling and what lies outside the subject are supposedly established through the mechanics of psychological association. Those connections, though, are treated as optional concomitants of what is essentially a phenomenal state that is lived in pure interiority. The overall picture turns feelings into 'an ensemble of capricious appearances that are somehow fortuitously united with representations but which at bottom have no real relation with their objects'.[16] This approach leads inescapably to what Sartre aptly calls 'a sort of solipsism of affectivity'.[17]

The subjectivist may attempt to articulate a response to the Sartrean critique by drawing on the notion of representation. She may claim, for instance, that although there is nothing more to a feeling than what it is like for a subject to undergo that feeling, it might be possible to draw some indirect links between emotion and the world, by means of the representational function of affective experience.[18] If the representationalist manoeuvre is successful, we might have an account of the intentionality that sidesteps Sartre's objections to subjectivism. It is worth considering, therefore, whether the subjectivist appeal to the representationalist model of intentionality can be effective against Sartre's argumentation. The issues here are quite technical, but for the purposes of our discussion we may focus only on the question that exercises Sartre himself, concerning the phenomenological credibility of the subjectivist account of emotional feeling. As I will argue, instead of connecting feeling with the world, the representationalist approach multiplies the problems for subjectivism, as it disconnects feeling from emotion.

13.3 A Critique of Subjectivism about Emotional Feeling

Subjectivists who rely on representationalist models of mental content may link feeling with reality through the following route. Emotional episodes—as Sartre would be the first to insist—are not disembodied.[19] They almost invariably come with changes in heart rate, skin temperature, body posture, tightening of muscles, and so on.[20] Information processed at a neural, sensory, perceptual, or epistemic level, on the one hand, and the goal directedness of volitional or desiderative states, on the other, may set in train autonomic responses preparatory for action (of strike in the case of anger, withdrawal in the case of sadness, reparation in the case of guilt, etc.). The feeling of fear, according to this view, is the intentional state of sensing changes in one's body generated by the autonomic responses preparatory for fight-or-flight, caused by the broadly construed cognitive and conative states of the agent. The emotional feeling registers how one's body stands as a whole in a particular situation. Representationalists may assert that the intentional content of a feeling is what it represents, and what an emotional feeling represents is a bodily gestalt, a patterned web of physiological changes.[21]

However, from a Sartrean perspective, this claim raises a dilemma about the relation between emotion and emotional feelings, neither horn of which is particularly attractive.

If emotions and emotional feelings have the same intentional object, then emotions are directed towards one's bodily state: what I dread is not the murderer catching up with me, but my pulse rate and stomach muscles. This view sounds absurd at worst, and strongly revisionary at best: absurd, because it implies that we are amused, afraid, joyous, or guilty about, say, our body temperature, rather than about the people, actions, or events that make up our social environment. At a minimum, this view demands that we understand ourselves and others as being capable of emotions with just one type of objects, namely the physiological changes that constitute our bodily gestalt. Though not logically incoherent, such a revision would require an immense effort of mental manoeuvring, as it runs counter to both social scientific and folk psychological thinking about emotions.

If, on the other hand, emotional feelings and emotions have different objects, then we are owed an explanation of why such feelings should bear the title of emotions at all. The representationalist might venture an explanation by showing what it is about certain bodily feelings, which makes us identify them as emotional. The answer, perhaps, may invoke a chain of representation: certain feelings represent bodily changes; bodily changes represent certain of the changes in the world that impinge on the body; therefore bodily feelings represent certain changes in the world. Some of those changes in the world relate to matters of concern to us, sources of frustration or satisfaction, actual or forthcoming threats, secured or withdrawn rewards. They are precisely the kind of events that constitute the object of human emotions. Some of our bodily feelings are called emotional because they represent events in the world towards which emotions are directed.[22]

Despite its advantages over traditional forms of subjectivism about emotion, the representationalist line of reasoning encounters some important difficulties. Starting at a rather general level, the representationalist approach draws on the notion of a representational chain that is made possible by the nature of representation as a relation of a state's standing in for something else. However, this view contrasts sharply with the core feature of the Sartrean view of intentionality as a relation of directedness between a state and that towards which that state aims.[23] Take the simpler case of my perceiving dark clouds gathering in the sky. Clouds are caused by various chemical processes on water surfaces of the earth, and, according to the theory under consideration, clouds thus represent such processes. However, the intentional content of my perception is that of clouds in the sky, not of chemical activities of water on earth. It is simply false to equate intentionality with representationality when the latter is understood as a causally determined relation of entities or events that could be interpreted (for all sorts of scientific or practical purposes) as conveying information about each other.

At an explanatory level, the representationalist approach presupposes that we possess the rather unique ability of identifying for each occasion what the object of an emotion is independently of how we feel towards it. It is not sufficient to assert that certain feelings are emotional because they unfailingly happen to co-occur with one's emotions. In order to test the explanatory power of the theory that claims that the object of feeling and emotion coincide, even though they reach their object through totally different routes, we should be in a position to state whether something is for us frightening or amusing irrespective of how we feel about it. Otherwise it would be simply vacuous to claim with representationalism that each time one experiences emotional feelings, both the feeling and the emotion are about the same thing.

It is worth noting finally, that separating the intentional object of feeling from that of emotion does not avoid the revisionist trap. According to the representationalist version of subjectivism, to feel is to perceive changes in one's body. This implies that any locution of the form 'A feels *x* (an emotion) with/about/towards B', should be understood along the lines of 'A perceives *y* (a bodily state) and he has also *x* (an emotion) with/about/towards B'. Although Pierre says that he feels angry with his neighbours, what he means is the conjunction of two contingently related things, the second of which is devoid of feeling: that he perceives his blood boil, and that he is angry with his neighbours. It might perhaps be possible for representationalism to map ordinary thought and talk onto a two-tier model of bodily reports and statements about one's emotion, though how this is possible in practice remains to be seen.

All of the above problems are symptomatic of the conflict between the phenomenology of emotional experience and its purported representationalist explanation. Being emotionally engaged with something is experienced as a unitary state directed towards that thing. This is what makes possible the sense of seeing things as appealing or appalling, and the suggested parallel between emotional and perceptual states so apposite.

The main moral to be drawn from the preceding discussion is that subjectivism either in its naïve traditional version, or its sophisticated representationalist forms, appears to fail to account for the phenomenology of emotional feeling. The links devised by the subjectivist, 'are established from the outside. It is not a living synthesis of representation and feeling: we remain in the mechanical domain of associations.'[24]

13.4 The Reflective Standpoint on Emotional Experience

For Sartre, the subjectivist approach results in a solipsism of affectivity. The culprit for that solipsism is the severing of the feeling from its *signification*, in two senses of that term: which is the worldly *object* signified in an affective episode, and what that episode signifies for the life of the agent who experiences the feeling.[25] The question is how we may reconnect the affective to its signification; and Sartre's answer in *The Imaginary* is that we should appeal to the deliverances of reflection.

Appealing to reflection sounds like an unobjectionable starting point, but, in my view, it is not. In fact, that methodological stricture brings to light some underlying assumptions of Sartre's own conception of his project as phenomenological.[26] Phenomenology purports to be the unprejudiced study of phenomena to the extent that, and exactly as, they present themselves in our experience.[27] Nevertheless, reflection is but one of the ways in which experience can be approached.

Reflection privileges a first person perspective on affectivity, over an 'impersonal' or, at least, 'third personal' description of the phenomena. Given that affectivity is something that is 'lived'—what German phenomenologists call an 'Erlebnis', and what Sartre's French contemporaries refer to as 'le vécu'.[28] I believe that it is right of Sartre to adopt the reflective standpoint; but it is not philosophically neutral. In fact, the problems we shall encounter as we proceed in our reconstruction of his theory of affectivity may stem from the kinds of standpoint Sartre occupies in different works. Let us see what reflective exploration reveals, according to Sartre, before we assess its methodological significance.

The first datum offered by reflection is that phenomena like joy, hate, melancholy, or indignation are not *states* but *consciousnesses*.[29] To appreciate the bearing of that distinction for Sartre's view of affectivity, let me outline his view of mental life before reflection takes off.

Pre-reflective consciousness is the ordinary consciousness of objects in the world; reflective consciousness is the consciousness of being conscious of an object. Pre-reflective consciousness is a positional consciousness of a certain object, in the sense that consciousness posits, sets before itself, the object as a target of its intentional activity. However, when one is positionally conscious of a particular object, one is non-positionally conscious of being conscious of that object. Pre-reflective consciousness is thus non-positionally aware of itself as being directed towards its objects. For Sartre, every positional consciousness of an object is at the same time a non-positional consciousness of itself.[30]

When we think and talk about our experience, the life of consciousness is considered under certain headings, such as 'qualities of character', 'physical acts', and 'affective states'.[31] Those headings impose some order into past conscious experience, transforming continuous instances of activity into isolable states. However, according to Sartre, this picture tends to present conscious experience the wrong way round. In reality, what comes first is the conscious activity directed at the world; the psychological state follows, as the outcome of grouping—by means of reflection—several activities under one heading. That grouping generates psychological categories which transcend consciousness, in the sense that those states appear as fixed entities with set boundaries, which share nothing of the fluid and luminous character of conscious activity. Those transcendent psychological states are then erroneously conceived as pre-existing members of one psychological whole, which embraces and governs every aspect of our mental life.

Sartre asserts that affective states make their appearance when one reflects on one's past mental or physical activities, on one's actions, judgements, or feelings. Take for instance the relation between the feeling of lust and the state of love. Feeling lust at the sight of a particular person is an experience absorbed with the attractive qualities of that individual. Experienced as a direct engagement with the world, the upheaval of a particular feeling towards someone marks the intentional connection between my consciousness and that being. The feeling of lust is a conscious activity occurring instantaneously or through a limited time span, and one that meets Sartre's absolute principle of consciousness, i.e., to be an instant of lust and to feel as an instant of lust are one and the same thing: there is no gap within the 'consciousness (of) lust' between appearing and being.[32]

The genitive construction 'consciousness (of) lust' might give the impression that in the course of ordinary encounter with the world, there is a thing called 'lust' to which consciousness pays attention. That interpretation is misleading. Lust is not an object for consciousness; it is consciousness itself as it experiences its intentional object. The genitive participle 'of' is put in brackets so as to signal that the grammatical construction purports to characterize what a particular consciousness is (namely, lust), not what the consciousness is about (its intentional object, the particular person who has arrested my sexual attention). However, if we were to move from the plane of emotional encounter with the world, to the higher level of reflection upon that type of encounter, our consciousness could take in its purview the emotion-consciousness. At that level, lust or other emotional experiences would themselves become an object of conscious examination and, thus, the locution 'consciousness of lust' (free of internal brackets) would denote the second-order activity of consciousness focusing upon its conscious activities. The confusion of the first-order level of the (lustful, despairing, or joyous) experience of the world, with the second-order level of the consideration of such an experience by the (reflective) subject is a major source of difficulties for the adequate analysis of affective phenomena.

13.5 Affectivity as a Distinctive Mode of Intentionality

In *The Imaginary*, Sartre contrasts *states* with *consciousnesses* and places the affective phenomena in the latter category. As we just saw, however, Sartre's detailed discussion of that issue in previous works provides a different or, at least, more fine-grained mapping of the affective domain. To take one of his favourite examples: hate is not a *consciousness* but a *state* produced by one's reflection on one's past feelings of disgust or repulsion towards the person who was the intentional object of the 'consciousness (of) repulsion'. Repulsion is not an object for pre-reflective consciousness; it is consciousness itself as it experiences its intentional object (the particular detestable person). When consciousness turns its attention back unto itself, trying perhaps to make sense, narrate, or evaluate its past behaviour, consciousness may group certain activities under the heading of 'hate', attributing thus to itself a state out of which particular instances of repulsion supposedly emanate. Note, moreover, that such an attribution is not produced from a neutral description of isolated mental events; rather, it expresses a commitment as to how the agent is to stand towards the detestable person. To move from the claim 'I am feeling a violent repulsion while looking at Pierre' to the claim 'I hate him' is to perform 'a passage to infinity'.[33] To state that you hate someone is, in essence, to judge what your feelings towards him meant in the past and to express a commitment as to how you are to stand, in feeling, thinking and action, towards that person in the future.

A feeling, according to this picture, forms the ground of affectivity: it is a distinct manner in which consciousness is directed at the world, while a state is the reflective product of consciousness's taking purview of its past activities. To the activity of feelings, we may contrast the passivity of states, and to the fluidity and lucidity of the former, we should counterpose the fixity and opacity of the latter. Affectivity is first and foremost a consciousness, and all consciousness is directed at an object. Sartre's account of feeling is premised on those two claims. Before we see how his account of feeling concludes, it is worth inquiring about the relation between the two claims: are they independent of each other, and if not, which one forms the basis for the other?

The opening lines of the long paragraph from the section of *The Imaginary* that we examine at present, appear to favour the former option. Sartre states that 'Reflection delivers us affective *consciousnesses*.... And we must apply to them the great law of consciousness: all consciousness is consciousness of something.'[34] It seems therefore that the former phenomenological claim stands independently of the latter nomic statement, which comes to validate an important step towards the cognitivist view Sartre wishes to uphold: 'Feelings have special intentionalities', they represent a way of consciousness transcending itself towards the world. 'To hate Paul is to intend Paul as a transcendent objet of consciousness.'[35] However, in earlier works Sartre presents the nomic statement as itself a product of phenomenological reflection: intentionality is revealed as the essence of consciousness, each time consciousness purports to make sense of itself.[36]

I think that the different statements on intentionality raise the following issue for Sartre: *either* he means that affectivity is intentional because it is given to the reflexive gaze as a type of conscious activity, *or* he maintains that it is a type of conscious activity because it is shown, upon reflection, to be always intentional. The former horn of the dilemma is what appears to be chosen when the paragraph under examination opens. As the text unfolds, though, it is the latter horn for which Sartre opts—and that is all for the best, I think, for two reasons. First, it offers Sartre a sound basis on which to develop his account; instead of importing into his discussion an extraneous dogma about mental life in general, he attends to the special character of affective experience. Secondly, it sets for Sartre the task of providing an independent consideration in support of his claim that affectivity in general, and feeling in particular, are intentional phenomena.

Sartre discharges that task with a masterful move against his subjectivist opponent. A standard contention of the subjectivist camp is that once you remove the psychological manifestations of emotion, affectivity vanishes, and all you are left with is an intellectual grasp of the situation or an abstract judgement. Sartre turns the tables, by inviting his opponent to consider a thought experiment: 'Try to bring about in yourself the subjective phenomena of hate, of indignation without these phenomena being oriented *on* a hated person, *on* an unjust action, and you can tremble, hammer your fist, blush, but your inner state will be devoid of indignation, of hate.'[37] Affectivity for Sartre is a conscious 'aiming at' an object; remove the object, and the affective will vanish, as well. Affectivity in other words is necessarily a world-directed, intentional phenomenon.

The picture of affectivity Sartre draws in *The Imaginary* contains two further important elements concerning, on the one hand, the intentional activity and, on the other, its intentional object. First, affectivity is irreducible to other forms of intentionality. In particular, the fact that feelings are directed at something should not be taken as grounds for rendering affectivity a subspecies of whatever is taken as the standard form of intentionality. Attempts to assimilate the intentionality of feelings to some other form of directedness at the world include the analysis of emotion as similar to desire,[38] or as identical to a kind of judgement,[39] or as a variation on propositional attitudes that do not involve acceptance of the relevant content as true, such as imaginings, thoughts, or construals.[40] Sartre is sharply opposed to all those attempts: 'We must not commit the intellectualist error... Feeling aims at an object but it aims in its own manner, which is affective.'[41]

Secondly, my feeling towards the qualities of the object (say, the long, white fine hands of the loved person) is not an optional add-on, subsequent to the neutral representation of those hands; rather, the feeling itself 'is a certain way that finesse, whiteness, vivacity have of appearing to me'.[42] That statement is, in my view, the clearest and nearest Sartre ever gets in *The Imaginary* to illustrating the claim, made in the *Sketch*, that emotion is a certain way of apprehending the world.

13.6 A Problem of Consistency

Here is the problem which, to my knowledge, has gone unnoticed in the literature. In the *Sketch*, the claim about emotion as a mode of apprehension purports to capture Sartre's novel approach to affectivity as a particular class of conduct. Yet nothing in the account of affectivity we encounter in *The Imaginary* involves any claim about human conduct. The discussion, in the section we have examined, proceeds without a reference to how affectivity relates to how one engages, stands towards, or behaves in a demanding situation. Moreover, no indication is given that the account articulated in that section is, in any important sense, incomplete. In *The Imaginary*, affectivity is approached from a first-person perspective, through an analysis of feelings as intentional phenomena, in which certain qualities of an object are given to the subject, in a distinctive way, such that the subject acquires a non-intellectual knowledge of the world. By contrast, the *Sketch* purports to analyse affectivity in terms of the functions served by our emotive reactions to a situation. We should underline here two features of the functionalist account given in the *Sketch*, one concerning its content, the other the perspective from which it is articulated.

The situations that give rise to an affective response are characterized in the *Sketch* as *difficult*.[43] Faced with a situation that makes strong or unbearable demands, the agent responds bodily and mentally not in order to effect changes in the world (that would be a practical response), but with a view to alter the conceptual parameters of the situation, so that the demands raised by the situation are diffused. We could be allowed to think that Sartre views affective phenomena as a repertoire of 'defence mechanisms', if that label were not reinterpreted along Freudian lines.[44]

Most importantly, though, we should note that, in the *Sketch*, the description of the relevant phenomena, the examples chosen, as well as the moral drawn from the proposed interpretation, are all in principle available to a third-person standpoint. The first person perspective from which the phenomenological account in *The Imaginary* is articulated is not prominent in the relevant part of the *Sketch*, except for the sections where Sartre attacks some classic theories of emotion for their failure to make sense of the relation between affectivity and the world.[45]

The difference of methodological standpoints marks one important distinction between the accounts of affectivity presented in the two works. Another significant difference is that the negative characterization of affectively relevant situations in the *Sketch* is absent in *The Imaginary*. That absence may not be attributed to an oversight, or to a desire not to go through again an issue already covered in previous works; rather, there is reason to believe that the absence is indicative of a deeper tension. On the one hand, there is no evident link between the intentionalist account of feelings offered in *The Imaginary*, and the evaluative claim that feelings may be directed only towards negative aspects of the world. On the other hand, the intentionalist view appears to entail for Sartre that a situation in which things fail to present affective qualities is a situation of reduced positive significance: the affective qualities of object in a situation '... entirely permeate the object; when they disappear... perception remains intact, things are not touched, and yet the world is singularly impoverished'.[46]

13.7 Conclusion

I think there is a tension between the accounts of affectivity presented in the *Sketch* and *The Imaginary*. The tension could be reduced through a division of theoretical labour, with the earlier work offering us an account of emotion sketched from a third-person perspective, and the later work providing us with an account of feeling narrated from a first-person standpoint. However, unless those accounts are shown to be compatible, they can hardly be thought to stem from a consistent philosophical outlook.

Perhaps such a coherent and explanatory powerful outlook on affectivity requires the inclusion of the functionalist and intentionalist proposals, in a theory of the human way of being. That is the task that Sartre will eventually try to carry out, a few years later, in his elaborate analysis of *l'homme en situation*.[47] Even though the facts that comprise a situation are not of one's own making, the significance they carry for each agent is dependent on the ways she projects herself in the world. Accordingly, the emotions will figure as parts of the agent's response to a situation whose affective qualities are correlated to the values that inform the agent's project. Affectivity will thus find its place in an ontology of what is 'truly concrete', that is neither the world in itself, not consciousness for itself, but 'the man within the world'.[48,49]

Notes

1. '...une classe particulière de conduite', in *The Imaginary: a phenomenological psychology of the imagination* (London: Routledge, 2004)—cited as *IPPI*—a translation by Jonathan Webber of *L'Imaginaire: Psychologie phénoménologique de l'imagination* (Paris: Gallimard, 1940) —cited as *Ire*: *IPPI* 199, n. 25/*Ire*, p. 92, fn. 2. In that note, Sartre refers to the French psychologists Pierre Janette and Henri Wallon, whose theories form the backdrop of his own approach to emotional phenomena; see *Sketch for a Theory of the Emotions* (London: Routledge Classics, 2004)—cited as *STE*—a translation by Philip Mariet of *Esquisse d'une Théorie des émotions* (Paris: Hermann, 1939)—cited as *ETE*: *STE*, pp. 17–26/*ETE*, pp. 37–55. Cf. my discussion in *The Philosophy of Sartre* (Durham: Acumen, 2011) section 4.VII, regarding Sartre's attempt to transcend those theories towards a phenomenologically sound account of emotion.
2. *STE*, p. 41/*ETE*, p. 79.
3. *STE*, p. 34/*ETE*, p. 69.
4. 'Intentionality: A Fundamental idea in Husserl's Phenomenology', *Journal of the British Society of Phenomenology* 1, 2 (1970): 4–5—cited as *IHP*—a translation by Joseph Fell of 'Une Idée fondamentale de la phénoménologie de Husserl: L'intentionnalité', in *Situations I* (Paris: Gallimard, 1947), pp. 31–4—cited as *I*. *The Transcendence of the Ego* (London: Routledge, 2004)—cited as *TE*—a translation by Andrew Brown of *La Transcendence de l' ego* (Paris: Vrin Librairie Philosophique, 1988)—first published in *Recherches Philosophiques* (1937)—cited as *LTE*. On the question of the exact dating of the composition of the two drafts see Van de Coorebyter's detailed discussion in 'Introduction et notes', *in La transcendence de l'ego et autres textes phénomenologiques, by Jean-Paul Sartre*, introduits et annotés par Vincent de Coorebyter (Paris: Vrin, 2003), pp. 7–81.
5. See Ronald de Sousa, *The Rationality of Emotion* (Cambridge, MA: MIT Press, 1987), chs. 4–5; Catherine Elgin, *Considered Judgment* (Princeton: Princeton University Press, 1996), ch. 5; Christine Tappolet, *Emotions et Valeurs* (Paris: Presses Universitaires de France, 2000); Mark Johnston, 'The Autonomy of Affect', *Philosophy and Phenomenological Research* 63 (2001): 181–214; Robert Roberts, *Emotions: An Essay in Aid of Moral Psychology* (Cambridge: Cambridge University Press, 2003); Jesse Prinz, *Gut Reactions* (New York: Oxford University Press, 2004); Linda Zagzebski, *Divine Motivation Theory* (Cambridge: Cambridge University press, 2004); Julien Deonna, 'Emotion, Perception and Perspective', *Dialectica* 60 (2006): 24–49; Sabine Döring, 'Seeing What to Do: Affective Perception and Rational Motivation', *Dialectica* 61 (2007): 363–94.
6. Paul Griffiths acknowledges the Sartrean roots of current work on the strategic role of emotions in 'Basic Emotions, Complex Emotions, Machiavellian Emotions', in *Philosophy and the Emotions*, ed. Anthony Hatzimoysis (Cambridge: Cambridge University Press, 2003), pp. 39–68; cf. D. M. Buss, *The Dangerous Passion: Why Jealousy is as Essential as Love and Sex* (New York: Simon and Schuster, 2000); S. Chevalier-Skolnikoff, 'Facial expression of emotion in nonhuman primates', in *Darwin and Facial Expression: A Century of Research in Review*,

ed. P. Ekman (New York and London: Academic Press, 1973), pp. 11–89; L. Cosmides, and J. Tooby, 'Evolutionary Psychology and the Emotions', in *Handbook of the Emotions*, ed. M. Lewis and J. M. Haviland-Jones (New York and London: Guildford Press, 2000), pp. 91–115; Paul Ekman, 'Biological & cultural contributions to body & facial movement in the expression of emotions', in *Explaining Emotions*, ed. A. O. Rorty (Berkeley: University of California Press, 1980), pp. 73–102; J. M. Fernandez-Dols, and M.-A. Ruiz-Belda, 'Spontaneous facial behaviour during intense emotional episodes: Artistic truth and optical truth', in *The Psychology of Facial Expression*, ed. J. A. Russell and J. M. Fernandez-Dols (Cambridge: Cambridge University Press, 1997), pp. 255–94; R. H. Frank, *Passions Within Reason: The Strategic Role of the Emotions* (New York: Norton, 1998); R. A. Hinde, 'Expression and Negotiation', in *The Development of Expressive Behaviour*, ed. G. Zivin (New York: Academic Press, 1985), pp. 103–16.

7. Important discussions, which address issues already raised in Sartre's work, involve Rosalind Hurshouse, 'Arational Actions', *Journal of Philosophy* 88 (1991): 57–68; Antonio Damasio, *The Feeling of What Happens: Body and Emotion in the Making of Consciousness* (New York: Harcourt, Brace & Co, 1999); Aaron Ben-Ze'ev, *The Subtlety of Emotions* (Cambridge, MA: MIT Press, 2000); Peter Goldie, *The Emotions: A Philosophical Exploration* (Oxford: Oxford University Press, 2000); Craig Delancey, *Passionate Engines: What Emotions Reveal about the Mind and Artificial Intelligence* (New York: Oxford University Press, 2002); Sabine Döring, 'Explaining Action by Emotion', *Philosophical Quarterly* 53 (2003): 214–30; Bennett Helm, *Emotional Reason* (Cambridge: Cambridge University Press, 2003); Christine Tappolet, 'Emotion, Motivation, and Action: The Case of Fear', in *Oxford Handbook of the Philosophy of Emotion*, ed. Peter Goldie (Oxford: Oxford University Press), pp. 325–45.
8. Jerome Neu, *A Tear is an Intellectual Thing: The Meanings of Emotion* (New York: Oxford University Press, 2000); cf. G. Mazis, 'A New Approach to Sartre's Theory of Emotions', *Philosophy Today* 27 (1983), pp. 183–99; D. Weberman, 'Sartre, Emotions, and Wallowing', *American Philosophical Quarterly* 33, 4 (1996): 393–407.
9. *STE*, p. 34–61/*ETE*, p. 69–117. Sartre calls this type of transformation 'magical' (*STE*, p. 55/*ETE*, p. 107). For a careful analysis of that notion see Sarah Richmond, 'Magic in Sartre's Early Philosophy', in *Reading Sartre*, ed. Jonathan Webber (London: Routledge, 2010), pp. 145–61, as well as my attempt to respond to her insightful remarks about Sartre's views on that topic, in 'Consistency in the Sartrean analysis of emotion', *Analysis* 74, 1 (2014): 81–3.
10. *ETE*, p. 74–8. The distinction is not exhaustive: in *Being and Nothingness* Sartre will discuss a third type, in between the world of action and the world of emotion, that he will call 'the world of desire'; see *Being and Nothingness* (Oxon: Routledge Classics, 2003)—cited as *BN*—a translation by Hazel Barnes of *L'être et le néant: Essai d'ontologie phénoménologique* (Paris: Gallimard, 1943—édition corrigée avec index d'Arlette Elkaim-Sartre, 1976)—cited as *EN*: *BN*, pp. 412–15/*EN*, pp. 431–43; for a detailed interpretation of the Sartrean approach to the worlds of desire and action, see Thomas R. Flynn, *Sartre, Foucault, and Historical Reason: Toward and Existentialist theory of History, Vol. 1* (Chicago, IL and London: University of Chicago Press, 1997), chs. 1 and 4, and for informative discussions Joseph Catalano, *A Commentary on Jean-Paul Sartre's Being and Nothingness* (Chicago, IL: University of Chicago Press, 1974), ch. 6, and Sebastian Gardner, *Sartre's Being and Nothingness* (London: Continuum, 2009), Part III.

11. A detailed interpretation of that theory is attempted in *The Philosophy of Sartre*, secs. 4.XII–4.XIV. His approach illuminates some puzzling emotional phenomena and helps to resolve problems encountered in emotion research Cf. my paper on 'Passive Fear', *Phenomenology and the Cognitive Sciences*, 14 (2015), for the articulation of a Sartrean approach to the phenomenon of fear-involved tonic immobility, that is of major interest to contemporary emotion science. Yet Sartre's approach has not been free of criticism. Most of those criticisms are directed against the intimate link that Sartre's account seems to postulate, between emotional states and personal responsibility. Some of the most astute criticisms come from readers otherwise sympathetic to Sartre's overall philosophical outlook, such as Iris Murdoch, *Sartre: Romantic Rationalist* (New Haven, CT: Yale University Press, 1953); Hazel Barnes, *An Existentialist Ethics* (New York: Knopf, 1967); Robert Solomon, 'Sartre on Emotions', *Journal of Philosophy* 72, 17 (1975): 583–4; and Greg McCulloch, *Using Sartre: An Analytical Introduction to Early Sartrean Themes* (London: Routledge, 1994).
12. 'L'émotion est une certaine manière d'appréhender le monde' (*STE*, p. 35/*ETE*, p. 71). Independently of exegetical issues in Sartrean scholarship, this claim can be illuminated from two perspectives. One perspective would enable us to see what is distinctive of emotion as opposed to other manners of apprehension, while the other perspective would highlight the fact that emotion is an apprehension as opposed to other kinds of mental activity; both perspectives may also fuse so as to throw light on the nature of the objects apprehended by emotion.
13. 'le sentiment se donne donc comme une espèce de connaissance' (*IPPI*, p. 69/*I*[re], p. 94). I follow Jonathan Webber in his translation of the French *sentiment* as 'feeling', even though that word lacks the connotations of the English word 'sentiment', thus making the reader unaware of the underlying connections between the French school of psychology (to which Sartre often refers in the course of his analysis), and the tradition of sentimentalism in English-language philosophy—see for instance, a fine application of insights from both traditions in *La psychologie des sentiments*, by Theodule Ribot (Paris: Felix Alcan, 1896).
14. Note that Sartre's own term for the view he criticizes is 'subjectivism'. Given, though, the multiple philosophical connotations of that term and of its contrary, 'objectivism', I think it is more accurate—and closer the spirit of the claim that feeling is a kind of '*connaissance*'—to call that view 'cognitivist'. The cognitivist view I attribute to Sartre should not be confused with a realist understanding of the values featuring in the intentional content of emotional feeling. A realist conception of evaluative qualities is apparent in Sartre's early paper on 'Intentionality'—see, e.g. 'To hate another person is one more way of bursting towards him; it is to find oneself suddenly faced with a stranger whose objective "hateful" quality one experiences', and more explicitly: 'Fearsomeness is a property of this Japanese mask, an inexhaustible, irreducible property that constitutes its very nature-not the sum of our subjective reactions to a piece of carved wood' (*IHP*, p. 4–5/*I*, pp. 32–3). To be sure, in that paper, Sartre aims at a phenomenologically accurate narration of the relevant experiences, rather than an ontological explanation of the arising of the qualitative aspects of things in themselves; cf. my *The Philosophy of Sartre*, sec. 2.IV for further discussion. In general, it is worth preserving the distinctions between the epistemic and the metaphysical level of analysis, on pain of bypassing important alternatives that purport to articulate a way of justifying evaluative judgements without succumbing to extravagant ontological claims about the referents of the concepts involved. The best context of debating this issue

is contemporary meta-ethics, where the relation between emotional feeling and evaluative qualities has been explored. For related discussion see my paper 'Ontology and Axiology', *Philosophy* 72, 280 (1997): 293–6, and Justin D'Arms and Daniel Jacobson, 'Sentiment and Value', *Ethics* 110 (2000): 722–48. For reasons that will gradually unfold, another label for Sartre's position could be 'intentionalism', i.e., the view that feelings are essentially intentional, in the sense that they are necessarily directed at some object; cf. Alex Byrne, 'Intentionalism Defended', *Philosophical Review* (2002): 199–240, for background discussion. However, intentionalism itself is subject to alternative interpretations, depending on the role attributed to intentional *content* in accounting for the totality of the intentional *experience*. It is not clear, to me at least, that Sartre would be happy to treat the content intended as the exclusive source of the main characteristics of the intentional event; see *The Philosophy of Sartre*, ch. 5 for further analysis.

15. *IPPI*, pp. 68–70/*I*[re], pp. 92–5.
16. *IPPI*, p. 68/*I*[er], p. 93.
17. *IPPI*, p. 68/*I*[er], p. 93.
18. For an original attempt to retain a subjectivist account of feeling with a representationalist account of intentionality see Jesse Prinz, 'Emotion, Psychosemantics, and Embodied Appraisals', in *Philosophy and the Emotions*, ed. Anthony Hatzimoysis (Cambridge: Cambridge University Press, 2003), pp. 69–96; for background discussion see J. C. Speisman, and R. S. Lazarus, A. M. Mordkoff, and L. A. Davison, 'The experimental reduction of stress based on ego-defense theory', *Journal of Abnormal and Social Psychology* 68 (1964): 367–80; K.R. Scherer, 'On the Nature and Function of Emotion: A Component Process Approach', in *Approaches to Emotion*, ed. K. R. Scherer and P. Ekman (Hillsdale, NJ: Erlbaum, 1984), pp. 293–318; and R. S. Lazarus, *Emotion and Adaptation* (New York: Oxford University Press, 1991).
19. 'There are no feelings without an ensemble of corporeal phenomena' (*IPPI*, p. 137). Emotional experience, according to Sartre, cannot be dissociated from the body on pain of 'falsity' of the professed emotion: 'the physiological phenomena... represent the seriousness of the emotion, they are the phenomena of belief' (*STE*, p. 50/*ETE*, p. 96—translation altered).
20. Cf. *STE*, pp. 15–17/*ETE*, pp. 33–7.
21. See, for instance, Peter Carruthers, *Phenomenal Consciousness* (Cambridge: Cambridge University Press, 2003); Craig DeLancey, *Passionate Engines: What Emotions Reveal about the Mind and Artificial Intelligence* (New York: Oxford University Press, 2002).
22. Cf. Jesse Prinz, *Gut reactions: a perceptual theory of emotion* (New York: Oxford University Press, 2004), ch. 2.
23. On Sartre's phenomenological view of intentionality, see my analysis in *The Philosophy of Sartre*, secs. 2.III and 5IV. Alternative accounts of the notion of intentionality involved in emotional experience are offered by Anthony Kenny, *Action, Emotion and the Will* (London: Routledge & Kegan Paul, 1976); Ronald de Sousa, *The Rationality of Emotions* (Cambridge, Mass: MIT Press, 1987); Robert Gordon, *The Structure of Emotions* (Cambridge: Cambridge University Press, 1987); Peter Goldie, *The Emotions* (Oxford: Oxford University Press, 2000); Robert Roberts, *Emotions* (Cambridge: Cambridge University press, 2003); Robert Solomon, 'Emotions, Thoughts and Feelings: What is a "Cognitive Theory" of the Emotions and Does It Neglect Affectivity?', in *Philosophy and the Emotions*, ed. Anthony Hatzimoysis

(Cambridge: Cambridge University Press, 2003), pp. 1–18; and F. Teroni, 'Emotions and Formal Objects', *Dialectica* 61, 3 (2007): 395–415.

24. *IPPI*, p. 68/*I*^{er}, p. 93.
25. *IPPI*, p. 68/*I*^{er}, p. 93.
26. *STE*, pp. 3–15/*ETE*, pp. 7–30; cf. *IHP*, p. 4/*I*, pp. 32–3; *TE*, pp. 2–20/*LTE*, pp. 13–44; *The Imagination* (London: Routledge, 2012)—cited as *TI*—a translation by Kenneth Williford and David Rudrauf of *L'Imagination* (Paris: Presses Universitaires de France, 1936)—cited as *I*^{on}: *TI* ch. IV/*I*^{on} ch. 4.
27. Sartre's reception and eventual transformation of Husserl's phenomenological project is exhaustively explored by Vincent de Coorebyter, *Sartre face à la phénoménologie* (Brussels: Ousia, 2000), pp. 50–83, 276–9, 393–9; cf. Stephen Priest, *The Subject in Question* (London: Routledge, 2000) for a concise and illuminating discussion.
28. *TE*, p. 1/*LTE*, p. 13.
29. *IPP*, p. *I* 69/*I*^{er}, p. 93.
30. Cf. *TE*, pp. 9–16/*LTE*, pp. 26–37; cf. *BN*, p. 9/*EN*, p. 18. We may express the distinction by stating that positionally we are aware of objects, and that non-positionally we are aware of our experience of those objects; cf. Dan Zahavi, *Subjectivity and Selfhood: Investigating the First-Person Perspective* (Cambridge, MA: MIT Press, 2008). For the bearing of that distinction on the contemporary discussion about the relation between self-consciousness and self-knowledge, see my paper 'A Sartrean Critique of Introspection', in *Reading Sartre*, ed. Jonathan Webber (London: Routledge, 2010), pp. 90–9.
31. *TE*, p. 21–6/*LTE*, pp. 45–51.
32. *TE*, pp. 22–3.
33. *TE*, pp. 22–4/*LTE*, pp. 46–9.
34. *IPPI*, pp. 68–9/*I*^{e}, p.^{r} 93.
35. *IPPI*, p. 69/*I*^{re}, p. 94; cf. Sartre's characterization of affective consciousnesses as ways of 'discovering the world' in what is probably his very first discussion of that issue: 'haine, amour, crainte, sympathie... elles ne sont que des manières de découvrir le monde' (*IHP*, p. 5/*I*, p. 34).
36. *IHP*, p. 4/*I*, pp. 32–3; *TE*, pp. 2–16/*LTE*, pp. 14–37; *TI*, pp. 125–42/*I*^{on}, pp. 139–60.
37. *IPPI*, p. 69/*I*^{re}, p. 93. The main philosophical target here is, of course, William James; cf. *ETE*, pp. 33–43, and my application of the Sartrean critique on neo-Jamesian variations of the peripheric theory, in *The Philosophy of Sartre* secs. 4.V–4.VI.
38. See the seminal discussions by Elizabeth Anscombe, *Intention* (Ithaca: Cornell University Press, 1963), pp. 70–3; Donald Davidson, 'Intending', in *Essays on Actions and Events* (Oxford: Oxford University Press, 1980), pp. 83–102; Graham Oddie, *Value, Reality and Desire* (Oxford: Clarendon Press, 2005) sec. 3.9.
39. Robert Solomon, *The Passions* (New York: Anchor/Doubleday, 1976); William Lyons, *Emotion* (Cambridge: Cambridge University Press, 1980); Martha Nussbaum, *Upheavals of Thought* (Cambridge: Cambridge University Press, 2001).
40. Patricia Greenspan, *Emotions and Reasons* (London: Routledge, 1988); for criticisms of that approach see Justin D' Arms and Daniel Jacobson, 'The Significance of Recalcitrant Emotion', in *Philosophy and the Emotions*, ed. Anthony Hatzimoysis (Cambridge: Cambridge University Press, 2003), pp. 127–46, and Michael Brady, *Emotional Insight* (Oxford: Oxford University Press, 2013), sec. 1.4.3.

41. *IPPI*, p. 69/*I*[re], p. 93.
42. *IPPI*, p. 69/*I*[re], p. 94.
43. 'Ce monde est *difficile*.' (*ETE*, p. 78.)
44. See ch. 4 of *The Philosophy of Sartre* for the critique of Freudianism in the *Sketch*.
45. *STE*, pp. 15–27/*ETE*, pp. 33–67.
46. *IPPI*, p. 69/*I*[re], p. 94.
47. *EN*, pp. 95–7, 333–6, 489–90.
48. *EN*, pp. 37–8.
49. I am indebted to Alix Cohen, Robert Stern, and two anonymous referees for comments on an earlier draft.

Bibliography

Anscombe, Elizabeth. *Intention* (Ithaca: Cornell University Press, 1963).

Barnes, Hazel. *An Existentialist Ethics* (New York: Knopf, 1967).

Ben-Ze'ev, Aaron. *The Subtlety of Emotions* (Cambridge, MA: MIT Press, 2000).

Brady, Michael. *Emotional Insight* (Oxford: Oxford University Press, 2013).

Buss, D. M. *The Dangerous Passion: Why Jealousy is as Essential as Love and Sex* (New York: Simon and Schuster, 2000).

Byrne, Alex. 'Intentionalism Defended', *Philosophical Review* 110 (2002): 199–240.

Carruthers, Peter. *Phenomenal Consciousness* (Cambridge: Cambridge University Press, 2003).

Catalano, Joseph. *A Commentary on Jean-Paul Sartre's Being and Nothingness* (Chicago, IL: University of Chicago Press, 1974).

Chevalier-Skolnikoff, Suzanne. 'Facial Expression of Emotion in Nonhuman Primates', *Darwin and Facial Expression: A Century of Research in Review*, ed. Paul Ekman (New York and London: Academic Press, 1973), pp. 11–89.

de Coorebyter, Vincent. *Sartre face à la phénoménologie* (Brussels: Ousia, 2000).

de Coorebyter, Vincent. 'Introduction et notes', *La transcendence de l' ego et autres textes phénomenologiques, by Jean-Paul Sartre*, introduits et annotés par Vincent de Coorebyter (Paris: Vrin, 2003), pp. 7–81.

Cosmides Leda, and John Tooby. 'Evolutionary Psychology and the Emotions', in *Handbook of the Emotions*, ed. Michael Lewis and Jeanette M. Haviland-Jones (New York and London: Guildford Press, 2000), pp. 91–115.

Damasio, Antonio. *The Feeling of What Happens: Body and Emotion in the Making of Consciousness* (New York: Harcourt, Brace & Co, 1999).

D'Arms, Justin and Daniel Jacobson. 'Sentiment and Value', *Ethics* 110 (2000): 722–48.

D'Arms, Justin and Daniel Jacobson. 'The Significance of Recalcitrant Emotion', *Philosophy and the Emotions*, ed. Anthony Hatzimoysis (Cambridge: Cambridge University Press, 2003), pp. 127–46.

Davidson, Donald. 'Intending', *Essays on Actions and Events* (Oxford: Oxford University Press, 1980), pp. 83–102.

Deonna, Julien. 'Emotion, Perception and Perspective', *Dialectica* 60 (2006): 24–49.

De Sousa, Ronald. *The Rationality of Emotion* (Cambridge, MA: MIT Press, 1987).

Döring, Sabine. 'Explaining action by emotion', *Philosophical Quarterly* 53 (2003): 214–30.

Döring, Sabine. 'Seeing What to Do: Affective Perception and Rational Motivation', *Dialectica* 61 (2007): 363–94.

Ekman, Paul. 'Biological & Cultural Contributions to Body & Facial Movement in the Expression of Emotions', in *Explaining Emotions*, ed. Amelie O. Rorty (Berkeley: University of California Press, 1980), pp. 73–102.

Elgin, Catherine. *Considered Judgment* (Princeton: Princeton University Press, 1996).

Fernandez-Dols, José M. and Maria-Angelès Ruiz-Belda. 'Spontaneous Facial Behaviour during Intense Emotional Episodes: Artistic Truth and Optical Truth', in *The Psychology of Facial Expression*, ed. J. A. Russell and J. M. Fernandez-Dols (Cambridge: Cambridge University Press, 1997), pp. 255–94.

Flynn, Thomas R. *Sartre, Foucault, and Historical Reason: Toward and Existentialist theory of History*, Vol. 1 (Chicago, IL and London: University of Chicago Press, 1997).

Frank, R. H. *Passions Within Reason: The Strategic Role of the Emotions* (New York: Norton, 1998).

Gardner, Sebastian. *Sartre's Being and Nothingness* (London: Continuum, 2009).

Goldie, Peter. *The Emotions: A Philosophical Exploration* (Oxford: Oxford University Press, 2000).

Greenspan, Patricia. *Emotions and Reasons* (London: Routledge, 1988).

Griffiths, Paul. 'Basic Emotions, Complex Emotions, Machiavellian Emotions', in *Philosophy and the Emotions*, ed. Anthony Hatzimoysis (Cambridge: Cambridge University Press, 2003), pp. 39–68.

Hatzimoysis, Anthony. 'Ontology and Axiology', *Philosophy* 72 (1997): 293–6.

Hatzimoysis, Anthony. 'A Sartrean Critique of Introspection', in *Reading Sartre*, ed. Jonathan Webber (London: Routledge, 2010), pp. 90–9.

Hatzimoysis, Anthony. *The Philosophy of Sartre* (Durham: Acumen, 2011).

Hatzimoysis, Anthony. 'Consistency in the Sartrean Analysis of Emotion', *Analysis* 74 (2014): 81–3.

Hatzimoysis, Anthony. 'Passive Fear', *Phenomenology and the Cognitive Sciences* 13 (2014): 613–23.

Helm, Bennett. *Emotional Reason* (Cambridge: Cambridge University Press, 2003).

Hinde, R. A. 'Expression and Negotiation', in *The Development of Expressive Behaviour*, ed. G. Zivin (New York: Academic Press, 1985), pp. 103–16.

Hurshouse, Rosalind. 'Arational Actions', *Journal of Philosophy* 88 (1991): 57–68.

Johnston, Mark. 'The Autonomy of Affect', *Philosophy and Phenomenological Research* 63 (2001): 181–214.

Kenny, Anthony. *Action, Emotion and the Will* (London: Routledge & Kegan Paul, 1976).

Lazarus, R. S. *Emotion and Adaptation.* (New York: Oxford University Press, 1991).

Lyons, William. *Emotion* (Cambridge: Cambridge University Press, 1980).

Mazis, Glen. 'A New Approach to Sartre's Theory of Emotions', *Philosophy Today* 27 (1983): 183–99.

McCulloch, Greg. *Using Sartre: An Analytical Introduction to Early Sartrean Themes* (London: Routledge, 1994).

Murdoch, Iris. *Sartre: Romantic Rationalist* (New Haven, CT: Yale University Press, 1953).

Neu, Jerome. *A Tear is an Intellectual Thing: The Meanings of Emotion* (New York: Oxford University Press, 2000).

Nussbaum, Martha. *Upheavals of Thought* (Cambridge: Cambridge University Press, 2001).

Oddie, Graham. *Value, Reality and Desire* (Oxford: Clarendon Press, 2005).

Priest, Stephen. *The Subject in Question* (London: Routledge, 2000).

Prinz, Jesse. 'Emotion, Psychosemantics, and Embodied Appraisals', *Philosophy and the Emotions*, ed. Anthony Hatzimoysis (Cambridge: Cambridge University Press, 2003), pp. 69–96.

Prinz, Jesse. *Gut Reactions: A Perceptual Theory of Emotion* (New York: Oxford University Press, 2004).

Ribot, Theodule. *La psychologie des sentiments* (Paris: Felix Alcan, 1896).

Richmond, Sarah. 'Magic in Sartre's Early Philosophy', in *Reading Sartre*, ed. Jonathan Webber (London: Routledge, 2010), pp. 145–61.

Robert, Gordon. *The Structure of Emotions* (Cambridge: Cambridge University Press, 1987).

Roberts, Robert C. *Emotions: An Essay in Aid of Moral Psychology* (Cambridge: Cambridge University Press, 2003).

Sartre, Jean-Paul. 'Intentionality: A Fundamental Idea in Husserl's Phenomenology', trans. Joseph Fell, *Journal of the British Society of Phenomenology* 1 (1970): 4–5.

Sartre, Jean-Paul. *Being and Nothingness*, trans. Hazel Barnes (Oxon: Routledge Classics, 2003).

Sartre, Jean-Paul. *Sketch for a Theory of the Emotions*, trans. Philip Mariet (London: Routledge Classics, 2004).

Sartre, Jean-Paul. *The Imaginary: A Phenomenological Psychology of the Imagination*, trans. Jonathan Webber (London: Routledge, 2004).

Sartre, Jean-Paul. *The Transcendence of the Ego*, trans. Andrew Brown (London: Routledge, 2004).

Sartre, Jean-Paul. *The Imagination*, trans. David Rudrauf (London: Routledge, 2012).

Klaus R. Scherer, 'On the Nature and Function of Emotion: A Component Process Approach', in *Approaches to Emotion*, ed. Klaus R. Scherer and Paul Ekman (Hillsdale, NJ: Erlbaum, 1984), pp. 293–318.

Solomon, Robert. 'Sartre on Emotions', *Journal of Philosophy* 72 (1975): 583–4.

Solomon, Robert. *The Passions* (New York: Anchor/Doubleday, 1976).

Solomon, Robert. 'Emotions, Thoughts and Feelings: What is a "Cognitive Theory" of the Emotions and Does It Neglect Affectivity?', in *Philosophy and the Emotions*, ed. Anthony Hatzimoysis (Cambridge: Cambridge University Press, 2003), pp. 1–18.

Speisman, J. C., R. S. Lazarus, A. M. Mordkoff, and L. A. Davison. 'The Experimental Reduction of Stress based on Ego-defense Theory', *Journal of Abnormal and Social Psychology* 68 (1964): 367–80.

Tappolet, Christine. *Emotions et Valeurs* (Paris: Presses Universitaires de France, 2000).

Tappolet, Christine. 'Emotion, Motivation, and Action: The Case of Fear', in *Oxford Handbook of the Philosophy of Emotion*, ed. Peter Goldie (Oxford: Oxford University Press, 2010), pp. 325–45.

Teroni, Fabrice. 'Emotions and Formal Objects', *Dialectica* 61 (2007): 395–415.

Weberman, David. 'Sartre, Emotions, and Wallowing', *American Philosophical Quarterly* 33 (1996): 393–407.

Zagzebski, Linda. *Divine Motivation Theory* (Cambridge: Cambridge University Press, 2004).

Zahavi, Dan. *Subjectivity and Selfhood: Investigating the First-person Perspective* (Cambridge, MA: MIT Press, 2008).

14

In Pursuit of Emotional Modes

The Philosophy of Emotion after James

Fabrice Teroni

> I predict: The 'will' has virtually passed out of our scientific psychology today; the 'emotion' is bound to do the same. In 1950 American psychologists will smile at both these terms as curiosities of the past. (M. Meyer, *The Whale Among the Fishes—The Theory of Emotions*)

Max Meyer could not have been more wrong, and the eighty years that have elapsed since he ventured his prognosis have been a whale of a time for philosophers interested in emotions—a period ripe with original insights, arguments, and accounts to which it is utterly impossible to do justice in the space of a single chapter. I will therefore not attempt to do so and will rather try to remain faithful to the spirit of this research by concentrating on a series of sectional views of debates that have continually animated it. These debates centre on contrasts that govern most of the philosophical thinking regarding the nature of emotions at least since the publication of William James' seminal and extremely contentious view about them. Focusing on these contrasts will not only allow me to introduce some dramatic turning points in the recent history of theorizing about emotions; it will also hopefully serve to bring to light some fundamental constraints bearing on emotion theory.

Let me start with a straightforward observation. When we describe someone as undergoing an emotion, we describe her as being in a given psychological *mode* or *attitude* towards a given object, event or state of affairs (I shall use the term '*content*' to refer to what the emotion is about). This is what we do when we claim that Raymond is angry at the Swiss government, that Monique is sad that her old friend is sick, that Cio Cio San is ashamed of herself, and so on. Observe that descriptions of this nature are slightly ambiguous since they may attribute psychological episodes or dispositions—as when one says that Joanna is sad about her father's death while her mind is wholly absorbed in a game. Since it has become usual to conceive of the emotions as affective episodes, however, our attention will be exclusively directed to situations in which it is correct to say that an emotion fills in one's stream of consciousness, that it takes place or occurs.[1] Now, philosophers have quite naturally been led to consider the elucidation of the psychological modes and contents at stake in emotions as one of their main duties. For that reason, the central thread in recent theorizing about the emotions is constituted by attempts at conceiving of emotional modes in terms of other modes like feeling, believing, desiring, and perceiving, or combinations of these, and to adjust their contents accordingly. This is why my discussion is organized around a series of contrasts that play a fundamental role in shaping one's approach to the underlying issues. These contrasts are those between *emotions and feelings*, between *specific and unspecific phenomenology*, and between *dependent and independent modes*. Since these contrasts are best approached in the wake of James' account, it will do no harm to open our discussion by briefly reminding ourselves of its key features.

14.1 James' Account

It takes little reflexion to realize that undergoing an emotion is an event that possesses a bodily facet: being afraid, sad, joyful, proud or ashamed are all characterized by a variety of physiological changes. Very few approaches to the emotions have been bold enough to deny this obvious fact, which is of course not to say that they have agreed on the role one should allocate to these physiological changes.

James has proven to be, if not the first, at least the most persuasive and influential advocate of the idea that physiological changes are key to the understanding of emotions.[2] To cut a long story short, James' fundamental contention is that an emotion consists in the subject's being proprioceptively aware of (i.e. feeling) the relevant physiological changes. This is to say that these physiological changes not only take place, but are felt by the subject undergoing the emotion—more precisely, according to James, a subject's undergoing an emotion simply consists in his feeling these changes. Being afraid comes down to, say, feeling one's heartbeat accelerating, one's breathing quickening and so forth. As is well known, the reconfiguration of the role played by physiological changes recommended by James led him to champion some surprising claims regarding the explanatory relations in which they stand to emotions—according to him, it is because one's heartbeat accelerates that one is afraid, and in the same way it is because one cries that one is sad. The pros and cons of this apparent consequence of his view is not what matters most for the present discussion, however.[3]

What does matter is the specific way James attempts to understand emotional modes, on the one hand, and their contents, on the other hand. In his account, there is just one emotional mode—*feeling*—and the relevant contents are provided by *specific physiological changes*. As regards the mode, James does not tire of emphasizing that feeling is what distinguishes emotions from cold, intellectual states—it is what makes for the emotionality of emotions, so to speak. Yet at the same time, he is keen to insist that his account avoids any appeal to additional psychological modes: the mode characteristic of emotions is nothing else than that of feeling. In so doing, he provides us with the first example of a recurrent strategy in post-Jamesian thinking about the emotions: that consisting in assimilating emotional modes to other psychological modes.[4] As far as James is concerned, the consequences regarding the content are quite obvious: the different types of emotions—fear, anger, joy, shame, admiration, and so on—have to be distinguished from one another in terms of the different types of physiological changes that one comes to feel. This is particularly manifest in his insistence on the profusion of possible physiological changes as well as on their impact on our conscious lives.

Now, in the words of a contemporary of James, the position he ends up advocating 'suggest[s] rather a good joke than a serious scientific hypothesis'.[5] If so, then the fact that his appeal to bodily feelings has become one of the main axes around which subsequent theorizing has revolved betokens a singular lack of humour on the part of philosophers interested in emotions. Regardless of what it reveals about them, their attitude has usually led them to underline the first contrast that will interest us, that between sensations and other psychological modes.

14.2 Emotions vs Feelings

As we have seen, James claims that the psychological mode characteristic of emotions is that of feeling: to undergo an emotion is to feel specific physiological changes from the inside. I shall be exclusively concerned with feelings understood in this way, and hope in so doing to keep clear of the ambiguities that so often surround uses of the term 'feeling' in discussions of the emotions.[6] That being said, let us now turn our attention to James' contention. It has been met, until quite recently at least, with almost universal disapproval and has led philosophers to insist on a contrast that continues to play a major role in theorizing about the emotions—what I will refer to as the contrast between the mode of emoting and that of feeling. That such a contrast exists is made manifest, it is claimed, by the fact that some fundamental attributes of the former mode distinguish it from the latter. Let me emphasize two of them.

First, as opposed to emotions, sensations or feelings are not mental states that we are tempted to assess as reasonable or unreasonable, rational or irrational, justified or unjustified.[7] True, one may declare a person irrational or unreasonable insofar as she has put herself in a situation that, as she surely should have anticipated, was going to elicit some painful, unwanted, or distracting sensations in her. The same holds for the emotions, as when we disapprove of somebody aware of his arachnophobia for having agreed to watch *Spider City 3D*. Still, emotions are assessed for rationality or reasonableness in a different way that fails to apply to sensations: not because of what the subject did or did not do in order to put herself in a position to feel or avoid feeling them, but because they themselves make it manifest that he is being irrational or unreasonable.[8] This is revealed in our propensity to assess an episode of fear of, say, a harmless tiny bug as irrational or unreasonable, while such assessments fail to get a grip on a shiver down the spine or a chest pain.[9] Incidentally, observe how admitting that emotions are subject to standards of rationality or reasonableness opens up the possibility that at least some of them are rational or reasonable responses to the circumstances in which the subject finds himself. Growing insistence on the rational aspects of the emotions rather than on their being at best pleasant, at worst disruptive and dysfunctional, is certainly a significant development in the literature during the period covered by the present discussion.[10]

Second, it has proven very tempting to locate the source of the variance in how emotions and feelings get assessed in the diverging representational or intentional properties of these two psychological modes. A passage obligé for a significant portion of post-Jamesian investigations of the emotions indeed consists in emphasizing that by contrast with emotion, feeling is not an intentional mode.[11] Sensations, it is maintained, are not about anything—something which is made manifest in the fact that it hardly makes sense to ask someone 'What do you have a shiver about?' or 'Do you feel nausea for this, or for that?' Things could of course not be more different in the case of the emotions: one does after all understand a person's psychological condition very incompletely if one is merely convinced that she is angry, sad, or afraid without having any inkling as to what she is angry at, sad about, or afraid of.[12]

To insist on these two attributes of emoting is of course to go against a venerable tradition whose most prominent figures arguably are Descartes and especially Hume, according to which emotions are 'original existences' that do not possess any sort of 'representative quality'.[13] As far as James is concerned, he was happy to deny that emotions are intentional, something he agreed was a consequence of his account.[14] Now, these thinkers have certainly failed to motivate such a substantial departure from the way we commonly think and talk about the emotions. One may even be tempted to suggest at this stage that James was simply wrong if he indeed thought that his theory should lead him to embrace such a conclusion. After all, many contemporary advocates of what often goes by the name of Brentano's thesis—the claim that all and only mental states are intentional—have repeatedly and, in my opinion, convincingly laid emphasis on the fact that most if not all sensations and feelings have (more or less diffuse) spatial content.[15] Even if a shiver may not be about anything in the sense implied by the above question, it is a distinctive experience that is 'of' or 'about' a given part of the body. As such it is intentional, and so assimilating emotions to feelings, as James does, does not imply the unpalatable conclusion that emotions are about nothing.

Still, even if one is ready to grant that much, the substance of the objection to James is left almost intact. Feelings may be intentionally directed towards parts of the subject's body, yet the emotions that have the same directedness—as when one is ashamed of one's nose or hopes that an acne pimple will heal—are the rare exceptions that prove that, as a rule, emotions are directed at objects, events, or states of affairs that lie outside one's body.[16] How could feeling one's body parts being variously affected even begin to make sense of, say, a Frenchman's sadness that Napoleon lost the Battle of Waterloo? In addition, and as Kenny persuasively argues, various restrictions bear on the sorts of objects emotions can take—one can no more be grateful for being harmed than proud of a defect.[17] This stands again in sharp contrast to sensations and is difficult to make sense of other than by agreeing that emotions are not about bodily changes.[18]

It is worth observing at this juncture how the disparity between sensations and emotions at the level of intentionality is made manifest in the sorts of behaviour that are typically explained by reference to them. Reference to sensations is almost exclusively made in order to explain behaviour that is aimed at getting rid of them (scratching being an obvious example) or at continuing to feel them. Emotional behaviour, on the other hand, is much more exceptionally aimed at maintaining or changing one's emotional condition as opposed to maintaining or modifying a relation with the relevant object.[19]

We are led to conclude, with Solomon, that James erred in exclusively focusing on the emotions' 'red-in-the-face and visceral cramp symptomatology' at the expense of their central intentional features.[20] And while we shall come to realize that there are extremely different ways of trying to explain or explain away the fact that emotions concern themselves with the world beyond the body, one conclusion has at least been accepted by the vast majority of philosophers: to undergo an emotion cannot be wholly assimilated to feeling one's body.

14.3 Specific vs Unspecific Phenomenology

The second contrast on which I wish to focus is rooted in another remarkable aspect of James' account. Recall that James is keen on emphasizing that reference to bodily feelings allows his account to harness the richness of physiological changes and their conscious repercussions in order to tell the different types of emotions apart from one another. In fear, say, one feels one's heart's accelerated pace, one's muscles getting tense, and cold sweat running down one's spine, whereas shame will be characterized by feeling one's face reddening and feeling 'small'. More generally one may say that a Jamesian approach is likely to insist on the subject's consciousness of the facial expressions, changes in skeletal muscles, as well as alterations in vocal expression and in the autonomic nervous system.

It is important to realize that these aspects of emotions are, according to James and his heirs, crucial for understanding their nature. This betrays their conviction that emotional phenomenology is sufficiently rich to individuate at least a substantial number of emotion types.[21] This richness is due to the fact that the psychological mode appealed to—feeling—can alternately target the bodily changes characteristic of fear, those characteristic of shame, etc. The distinction between these types of emotions is manifest at the phenomenal level.

Until quite recently, most if not all philosophers had convinced themselves that James' contention was completely off track. One may even say that the so-called 'cognitive revolution' that swept away so many disciplines after the heyday of behaviourism led philosophers to build with a surprising consistency their approaches around the following two affirmations. First, that emotions are intentionally directed towards objects outside the body, something I already commented upon, and, second, that emotional phenomenology is relatively if not extremely unspecific in the sense that it cannot tell apart different types of emotions from one another.[22]

It is on this second point that I now want to concentrate. We should surely wonder what explains this insistence that emotional phenomenology is impoverished. Is it due to discrepancies in the deliverances of introspection—was James endowed with an atypically acute form of bodily awareness in which later philosophers did not partake? Partly, perhaps, but the situation can alternatively and more reassuringly be construed as being the upshot of different lines of thought that all make it seem as if James' emphasis on the richness of bodily feelings is seriously amiss. I will consider four such lines of thought and then proceed to explain the theoretical approaches they have helped support.

The first line of thought is constituted by the worry that an emphasis on phenomenology would make it difficult if not impossible to account for the fact that we spend a good part of our waking lives sharing and discussing about our emotions with others.[23] It is obvious that, in so doing, we do not systematically speak past one another but rather refer to the same sorts of entities without having had the opportunity to check whether we enjoy the same phenomenal states. This observation has encouraged the thought that our shared concepts of (different types of) emotions do not make any substantial reference to their felt aspect. Needless to say, this is the emotion-oriented version of a more encompassing suspicion of unobservable entities. Yet it has cast its shadow over emotions for a much longer time than over other types of mental states.

It has done so because, second, neglect of phenomenology has also been encouraged by the considerations set forth in the previous section and emphasized by most of the leading players in the cognitive turn. As we have observed, emphasis was laid on the fact that we assess emotions as being (un)reasonable, (ir-)rational, or (un-)justified. What is so assessed are of course specific emotional reactions; it is, for instance, irrational to feel proud of a hungry tiger coming towards you and quite rational to feel afraid of it. Now, the paradigm mental states that we assess along such dimensions are beliefs, on the one hand, and desires, on the other hand.[24] This has led many philosophers to subscribe to the following line of thought: insofar as we strive to elucidate the nature of world-directed psychological modes that lend themselves to assessments of reasonableness or justification, reference to bodily phenomenology is out of place.

Third, the same conclusion has been stimulated by the fact that many philosophers have given barely a passing thought to an important and rather traditional contrast: that between emotion types that are nowadays frequently described as basic and the non-basic ones. It is right to emphasize that the traditional contrast—the one we see at work in Descartes' *Les passions de l'âme* or in Spinoza's *Ethica*, for instance—is quite different from the one many contemporary philosophers and psychologists have in mind.[25] Still, the details matter less than the ultimate aim of that contrast, which has always been to tell apart a number of emotional primitives from derivative constructs.

Philosophers have quite consistently conceived of the latter as being the result of basic emotions interacting with states such as beliefs and desires. Overlooking the contrast, then, means that the following kind of reasoning appears much more compelling than it really is.

Consider an episode of anger and one of indignation. Try to concentrate on their felt aspects as you live them and ask yourself whether the emotions differ in this regard. If the deliverances of your inner sense fall into line with those of most emotion scholars, you will answer with a resounding 'No!'. The only substantial difference, you will insist, is one of belief. Anger is a response to one's believing to have been, say, treated without due respect, and it so happens that we speak of indignation when that very same response is occasioned by a slightly different belief, i.e. that others have been so ill-treated. It should now be obvious that if one overlooks the contrast between basic and non-basic emotions—i.e. does not conceive of the emotional domain as being layered, so to say—one may be tempted to generalize the lesson here. One then concludes that the distinction between types of emotions—whether basic or non-basic—owes nothing to their respective phenomenology and all to the distinct beliefs they contain or presuppose.

Fourth and finally, neglect of another traditional distinction makes the same conclusion appear inescapable. I have in mind the distinction between sentiments (love, hate, etc.) and character traits (honesty, courage, etc.), on the one hand, and emotions, on the other hand.[26] The former should be understood in terms of dispositions to, amongst other things, undergo a variety of emotions depending on the circumstances in which one finds oneself. The latter, despite the already acknowledged fact that many emotion terms can be read dispositionally, are episodic. Some have taken advantage of the failure to draw this distinction in the following way. Consider love and ask yourself what feelings of love may be. You are supposed to appreciate that love not only outlives any feeling, but also that it does not have any privileged links with any. After all, feelings of almost any kind may manifest love if one provides the relevant circumstances. This is to say that the expression 'feelings of love'—even when it is understood in its specifying sense (see note 6)—does not refer to a specific set of feelings, but serves instead to indicate those feelings, which may be of any sort, that occur because of love. Again, one may be tempted to generalize the conclusion. There are no feelings of fear, sadness, hope, admiration, or anger in the sense of feelings distinctive of these emotions, only less specific feelings whose occurrence is sometimes explained by such emotional conditions.[27]

These four lines of thought have conspired to make phenomenology seem of minor import for theorizing about emotions in general as well as about specific emotion types. We are now in a position to realize that the crux of the debate between James and his opponents is not the richness of bodily feelings, but the role these play in emotional states. According to the latter, bodily feelings are completely disconnected from the emotions. Perhaps we should acknowledge that unspecific feelings sometimes accompany emotions, but this is in any case not to probe into what makes emotions what they are. This goes some way towards explaining the unexpected popularity, from Meinong's early insights to Gordon's sensitive distinctions, of approaches to the emotions that assimilate them to beliefs, desires, or combinations of these.[28] More specifically, these approaches can be divided into two broad families: those that proceed to analyse emotions in terms of combinations of beliefs and desires, and those that restrict themselves to beliefs. According to the first family of approaches, Michel would be, say, afraid of a tiger when he believes that he is near one and desires to avoid this situation (perhaps because he does not want to be torn to pieces). According to the second, his fear consists rather in his judging that the situation he faces is dangerous. This amounts to saying that emotions come down to a mode or a combination of modes (*believing* or *believing plus desiring*) that takes a *propositional content*, whose nature is either left *unspecified* or specified as being *evaluative*.

I shall neither explore the differences between these approaches in any detail here, nor the substantial problems with which they are confronted.[29] Let me emphasize only that the second at least attempts to make good on the important connections between emotions and evaluative properties that are already apparent in ordinary language—e.g. when objects or events are described as being dangerous, disgusting, happy, fearful, sad, admirable, shameful, and so on. This speaks to Kenny's aforementioned stricture against feeling approaches and to his emphasizing that given types of emotions can only take objects within a suitably restricted set. At the core of the evaluative belief approach, we can indeed recognize an attempt to heed Kenny's insightful observation by defining each emotion type in terms of the representation of a given evaluative property. As we shall see, the fact that emotions intentionally relate to evaluative properties is insisted upon by most mainstream theories, despite the fact that virtually no one still believes in the viability of belief approaches.[30]

For the time being, though, the important point is that the two families of approaches under discussion constitute clear attempts to account for emotional modes in terms of other psychological modes. Now, what should strike us is the fact that the modes appealed to have nothing phenomenal about them.[31] The net effect of the different lines of thought reviewed in the foregoing is indeed that the felt aspect of emotions has been a dead weight during a significant period in emotion theory—roughly, between the 1920s and 1980s. This is certainly not to say that philosophers failed to mention it. Still, looking at it in retrospect, one feels as if they were, we might say, embarrassed by it, not knowing exactly what to do with it.

We are now in a position to make sense of this otherwise surprising attitude. Insofar as the underlying phenomenology is conceived of as being unspecific and unrelated to the world beyond the subject's own body, it cannot play any substantial theoretical role. In particular, it can no more be recruited to tell types of emotions apart from one another than to make sense of their rationality and intentionality. Hence the idea that feelings are mere 'ornamentation[s] of emotion', 'epiphenomenal coda to judgement', contingent effects of what is essential, something that comes in any case a day after the fair.[32] This is a consequence of the wish to integrate the emotions within the realm of reason and to tell them apart from sensations. Let me observe that this contributes significantly to explaining the aforementioned fact that many philosophers have moved from a traditional emphasis on the dysfunctional dimension of emotions to an almost exclusive insistence on their 'cognitive' aspects.

There are at least two reasons to think that this is to substitute one distorting portrayal for another similarly distorting one, however. The first is that it turns out to be difficult to assimilate the rationality of emotions entirely to that of beliefs and desires. As regards the conative aspects of the approaches under discussion, there seem to be rational constraints on desires that fail to apply to the emotions. It is often insisted that one cannot desire something while believing it to be impossible, to lie in the past or to be for whatever reason unattainable. Yet, a variety of emotions (regret, guilt, joy, etc.) can constitute rational responses to such events. These observations have led many to appeal to less rationally constrained conative states like wishes.[33] As regards their cognitive aspects, a more significant group of worries concerns whether emotions have the right format even to be assimilated to judgements and so to be subject to comparable rational constraints. It has thus been repeatedly emphasized that emotions do not depend on sophisticated cognitive capacities. In particular, it would be wrong to require a subject to master and deploy the concepts of dangerousness or offensiveness in order to be afraid or angry.[34] In addition, many emotional reactions exhibit a sort of imperviousness to evidence that prevents direct assimilation to judgements—one may think here of a variety of more or less automatic emotional syndromes, of different kinds of phobias, of socially instilled fears, and so on.

Second, and perhaps most obviously, the attempted analyses are distorting because of the subservient role they devote to the felt aspects of emotions. Do we really want to end up claiming that fearing a tiger or being angry at a remark is to intentionally relate to these entities in exactly the same mode as one does when one passes an evaluative judgement about them, and to feel something merely as a result? If one subscribes to such a sharp division of labour between a 'cold' intentional aspect and a 'hot' felt consequence, is it still possible to make sense of the manner in which emotions present themselves from the first person perspective, namely as intentional relations to specific external objects or events?[35]

The vast majority of the participants in the debates about the nature of emotions during the past twenty years or so have answered these questions negatively. This appears reasonable: insisting on the fact that emotions are not feelings should not lead us to deny the obvious by claiming that their nature can be understood in complete isolation from their phenomenology. We shall consider in Section 14.4 the sort of approaches to the emotions that have tended to be favoured as a result. But let me first bring the present discussion to a close.

Various lines of thought have conspired to push the felt aspect of the emotions into the background: it is impoverished, unspecific, and not key to understanding what is essential, namely the emotions' rational and intentional dimensions. The price paid consists in ending up with an account that is likely to leave the very emotionality of emotions out of the picture, or at least to make it play a very subservient role. So, while the approaches under discussion have been right to emphasize the rational aspects of emotions, they have gone much too far in disregarding their phenomenology. Accounting for emotional modes in terms of beliefs or desires proves no more satisfying than doing so in terms of body-directed feelings.

14.4 Dependence vs Independence

The third and last contrast that shall concern us is that between dependent and independent intentional modes. Examining it will put us in an ideal position to assess the sort of approaches to the emotions that has dominated the field since the dismissal of the accounts discussed in Section 14.3. Like the two first contrasts, it can be profitably approached in the light of another striking aspect of James' account.

As we already emphasized, emotions are, according to James, bodily feelings; they are experiences that are intentionally directed towards events occurring at the relevant bodily locations. To home in on the contrast I wish to discuss, consider the following question: do bodily feelings rely on the subject's having another sort of access to the relevant events and body parts? The answer plainly is negative. Feeling something happening in one's body need not rely on any other access to its intentional object and is in this sense an independent intentional mode. By contrast, remembering constitutes a good example of a dependent intentional mode insofar as it relies on one's having had another sort of access to what one remembers, e.g. one must have seen it. What about the emotions? Are they really, as James suggests, independent intentional modes?[36] Is it possible to agree with him on this count while rejecting his contention that they are about body states?

Diverging answers to these questions create another fundamental rift within emotion theory. To chart the possible answers, we have to make use of two distinctions: that between merely *causal* and *more substantial* dependence, on the one hand, and that between *partial* and *total* dependence, on the other. Let us consider these distinctions in this order.

The distinction between *causal* and *more substantial* forms of dependence becomes especially significant once we realize how the apparent implication of the considerations against James' account put forward in Section 14.2 has frequently been resisted. Recall that these considerations seem to imply that emotions are intentionally directed beyond the subject's own body. Yet, this implication may be resisted if the dependence at stake is conceived as being merely causal. This is worth considering in some detail. Resistance to the Jamesian picture starts with common sense: we talk as if emotions were directed toward a variety of objects—one is said to be sad at a rail accident or ashamed of a misdeed. Clearly, the subject's original access to these objects cannot be provided by the emotions she feels. Feeling sad is not an independent mode of access to a rail accident, but presupposes beliefs, perceptual states, or memories with the relevant content. Let us call these the cognitive bases of emotions.[37]

The fact that emotions have such cognitive bases does not imply that they themselves have the very same content. One may maintain instead that the relation between them is merely causal. This is a well-trodden road that we have already had the opportunity to consider from another perspective in Section 14.3: it consists in explaining the (apparent or real) intentionality of emotions by their being based on intentional modes that cause nonintentional feelings. In the present context, the addition of 'apparent or real' is needed, because one still faces the task of deciding what to call an emotion within the relevant causal sequence. If one's coming to believe that a rail accident took place causes a feeling to occur, is sadness identical with the whole 'cognitive state causing a feeling' sequence (in which case it is about the accident), or only with the feeling part of it (in which case it is not)? This is not the place to consider the resulting accounts of emotions in any detail.[38] What is significant for us is that the two sorts of accounts endorse the same claim: insofar as it reaches beyond the confines of the subject's body, the intentionality of an emotion is that of its cognitive base, while a feeling unrelated to the world takes care of its phenomenal aspect.

At this stage of our discussion, however, we already know why this has not met with universal approval. Such attempts at accommodating the felt or hot aspect of emotions within any of the cognitivist accounts of their intentional aspect discussed in Section 14.3 are indeed not very attractive. They rely on an unpersuasive error theory about emotional intentionality as far as it reveals itself from the first person point of view. After all, when one is afraid of a tiger, it seems to one as if one's fear is intentionally directed to the tiger. Many have dug in their heels here, insisting that it would grossly betray the phenomenological facts to describe this in terms of one's perception of the tiger causing a feeling that is not about the tiger. This is the cash value of Goldie's famous attacks against what he tellingly describes as 'add-on' approaches to emotional phenomenology.[39]

In addition to these claims about the way it feels like to undergo an emotion, philosophers have insisted on two further liabilities of a (merely) causal account of the relations between emotions and their cognitive bases. First, such accounts have the consequence that a subject would have to learn that her feelings are caused by the relevant thoughts. If feelings did relate to thoughts only causally, then the subject would have to learn of the relation specific types of feelings have to specific types of thoughts in the same way he has to learn of the causal origin of skin lesions in order to understand that they are sunburns (i.e. caused by expositions to solar rays). This epistemological consequence has struck many as being absurd.[40] Second, whereas effects can always in principle outlive their causes, emotions cannot subsist in the absence of a representation of the relevant events or objects.[41] Emotions are not simply launched by their cognitive bases, they inherit their contents: fearing is an attitude that is intentionally directed at something one sees, believes, remembers, etc.

All this militates in favour of the conclusion that the relation of dependence between emotions and their cognitive bases is more than causal: emotions inherit the contents of their bases, they are, so to say, extra intentional modes directed towards these contents. This in turn suggests that emotions can be viewed as independent modes of access to their objects only to the extent that these objects are confined to changes within the subject's own body.

Consideration of the second distinction, that between *partial* and *total dependence*, will lead us to amend this conclusion, however. The relevant question now becomes the following one: do emotions inherit their complete content from their cognitive bases, or do they contribute something original to it? The issue is important, since it concerns whether emotions supply subjects capable of undergoing them with original intentional capacities. Now, approaches to emotional intentionality in exclusively *factual* terms appear bound to endorse total dependence. After all, they would otherwise have to endorse the claim that emotions inform us about the shapes, colours, texture, weight, and so on of their objects without relying on other mental states—and Kenny is certainly right to insist that there is no plausibility to this claim.[42] One may speculate that this is why approaches that conceive of emotional intentionality in purely factual terms are those that defend the idea that emotions are admixtures of beliefs and desires with the possible addition of unintentional feelings.[43] In any case, advocates of the idea that emotional intentionality is only partially dependent have been exclusively recruited among those who emphasize its *evaluative* dimension. They have been alone in attempting to endorse James' independence claim while taking exception to his contention that emotions are about nothing beyond the subject's body. Let us try to understand why.

If emotions represent evaluative properties, claiming that this aspect of their intentionality is also inherited from their cognitive bases would amount to the idea that emotions are always prefixed by states delivering the required evaluative information. This gives rise to the following dilemma. The prefix states are either evaluative beliefs or evaluative intuitions. If the former, then the resulting theory is cognitively much too demanding, as we have already realized above in connection with a different approach to the emotions identifying them with evaluative beliefs. An additional worry is that many emotions simply do not appear to be prefixed by such beliefs, which makes it difficult to see how they could inherit their contents from them. The other horn of the dilemma has not been especially popular, perhaps because no convincing account of the relevant evaluative intuitions has been so far forthcoming.[44] It is also fair to point out that, to many, the idea that emotions are prefixed by such mysterious intuitions has nothing to be said in its favour either from the first- or from the third-person perspective.

All this makes it seem that only one avenue is left for those who insist on the evaluative dimension of emotional intentionality: to conclude that this is an original contribution of the emotions themselves (thereby dispensing with intuitions), without this implying that they are evaluative judgements (thereby eschewing too demanding accounts). This explains the attractiveness of partial intentional dependence.[45]

Together with the worries raised by the accounts discussed in Section 14.3, these considerations helped give rise to an alternative approach to the emotions. Indeed, these two lines of thought suggest that we should understand the emotions as independent and cognitively quite undemanding modes of access to evaluative properties. Yet, is it possible to steer such a middle course between a feeling theory à la James, which appears to emphasize the felt aspect of emotions at the expense of their intentional and rational aspects, and the cognitivist accounts many have been led to defend in reaction to it and which suffer from the opposite flaw? In fact, it is possible, and fleshing out the proposal means assimilating emotions to perceptual experiences as opposed to judgements and desires.

Some aspects of perceptual experiences encourage this idea. They prove to be as difficult to assimilate to conceptual states as emotions are; they are likewise impervious to counter-evidence—as any subject apprised of a variety of well-known optical illusions can testify; and they possess intentional and phenomenal aspects that are hard to disentangle from one another. Why not conclude, then, that undergoing an episode of fear is to perceive a danger, undergoing an episode of admiration to perceive an instance of admirableness, and so on? We are invited to approach the emotions primarily through their felt aspect, but this time in a resolutely non-Jamesian way. We should rather conceive of this felt aspect as a perception-like access to the domain of values.[46] Since emphasis is primarily laid on this aspect of the emotions and its intentional role, the contrast to the cognitive accounts examined in Section 14.3 could not be greater.

Now, there are very different ways of applying the model of perception, and this is not the place to examine them all.[47] It will be more profitable for our discussion to consider the following more general question. Is it more appealing to understand emotions in terms of a combination of the *mode of perceiving* and *nonconceptual evaluative contents* than to do so in terms of the other combinations of modes (feeling, believing, desiring) and contents we have considered in the foregoing? Here are two reasons to doubt that this is the case.

First, the dependence of emotions that I insisted upon at the outset of this section makes it difficult to assimilate them to perceptual states. After all, perceiving is an independent intentional mode: irrespective of the sensory modality, perceiving objects and their properties requires no other access to them. Hearing is an independent access to sounds and some of their properties such as loudness and pitch, vision an independent access to middle-sized objects, their colours and forms.

In addition, we have been led to think that emotions inherit their contents from other mental states. This already makes for an atypical form of perception, in particular because emotions are states for which we ask reasons and which we assess as justified or not in light of these reasons. This important aspect of the emotions, which was key to motivating accounts in terms of belief, tends to be overlooked within perceptual approaches. Because of this, advocates of the latter give priority to situations in which emotions behave in the light of the evidence at the subject's disposal in the way perceptual states do, namely by remaining impervious to it. Hence the emphasis on phobia and reflex-like emotions, which is a striking feature of many recent discussions. As we have acknowledged above, emotions certainly do sometimes remain impervious to evidence. This should not distract us from the bigger picture, however: they are typically sensitive to the evidence at the subject's disposal, and this brings them much closer to beliefs than to perceptual states.

Still, is it not possible to capitalize on the contrast discussed above so as to maintain that the intentional dependence of emotions on their bases is only partial and does not affect their relation to evaluative properties—which is after all the basic contention of a perceptual approach? This is possible, but the specific form of dependence displayed by the emotions makes the strategy difficult to implement. On the one hand, this dependence pertains to properties that are closely connected to the specific value at stake. Suppose you suddenly spot a tiger ready to rush upon you and feel afraid as a result. In this case, you seem to be visually acquainted with what constitutes, in the circumstances, a specific danger. Considered in this light the claim that the emotions themselves are perceptual experiences of evaluative properties appears to make room for a very atypical form of perception indeed. One would perceive an instance of a property (danger) thanks to another perceptual relation to the properties that constitute it in the circumstances in which one finds oneself. On the other hand, the fact that emotions can inherit their contents from a variety of mental states places perceptual approaches under pressure. Suppose a person is afraid because she conjectures that an event will take place, or becomes angry after having heard a witness report an offensive remark made in her absence. Is it convincing to hold that, despite having no perceptual access to any further properties of the relevant events, the person is nonetheless well placed to perceive their values? Given how hard it is to make sense of such an unconstrained form of perception, one may well hesitate to say that it is.

Let me now turn my attention to the second reason why one may resist perceptual approaches. You may recall that we brought Section 14.3 to a close by observing that to assimilate emotions to beliefs is arguably to leave their emotionality or 'hot' aspect out of the picture. The question is whether the same observation carries over to the perceptual approaches under discussion. Here is one argument to answer this question in the affirmative.

What is fundamentally incorrect in the appeal to belief is that undergoing an emotion is not or not merely accepting or acquiescing to the representation of a certain event as occurring or of a certain state of affairs as obtaining. It rather consists in a relation to it in the specific intentional mode that is fear, a specific attitude towards it that differs from believing. This line of thought is made tempting by the fact that a belief that something is dangerous or offensive may, for a variety of reasons, leave one completely cold. However, if this is a correct diagnosis, then it seems to tell likewise against perceptual approaches. After all, if perceiving is a specific psychological mode, it is one that is difficult to gloss in terms of the taking of a certain attitude. This is perhaps why perceiving is sometimes claimed not to be in itself any sort of attitude towards its object, but rather a precondition for taking any one of a range of different attitudes towards it.[48] It is certainly unclear why tampering with the content—moving from the perception of colours, sounds, etc. to that of evaluative properties—improves the situation in this respect. If at all possible, the perception-like representation of an evaluative property would seem not only to be susceptible to occur in the absence of any emotion, but to potentially give rise to a variety of different and incompatible emotional reactions to it.[49] This may in turn lead one to think that James was to a certain extent right to insist on bodily feelings: this reveals his striving to conceive of the felt aspect of emotions as an experience of being engaged in responding to worldly events as opposed to one of non-committing perceptual registration of them.[50]

All in all, then, it appears that conceiving of emotional modes as being perception-like does not significantly improve on conceiving of them as being identical to believing. The benefit is that emotions are rightly taken as being cognitively less demanding than beliefs, but the cost is that one ignores the fact that they are justified or unjustified reactions to what we represent.[51]

14.5 Conclusion

In the foregoing, I have explored three fundamental contrasts that have played leading roles within philosophical discussions since James' seminal contribution to the field became available. We unquestionably know much more about the emotions than ever before. Still, it seems fair to say that the philosophical approaches to the emotions that have dominated the field and continue to do so have failed in their attempt to assimilate emotions to other psychological modes. I have reviewed some reasons to conclude that undergoing an emotion consists neither in bodily feeling, nor in believing (alone or in combination with desiring), nor in perceiving. Perhaps the cautious lesson to be drawn is that we have to live with the fact that they are distinct and basic psychological modes after all, which can be fruitfully compared to other modes but not reduced to them. These other modes have by definition nothing emotional about them, and the fact that they target specific contents does not magically turn them into emotions. This makes it apposite to conclude with a reference to Brentano,[52] who correctly saw that affective states do not provide us with new objects or predicate anything of them but are rather original ways of relating to them.[53]

Notes

1. Two notable exceptions are Richard Wollheim, *On the Emotions* (Yale: Yale University Press, 1999) and Peter Goldie, *The Emotions: A Philosophical Exploration* (Oxford: Oxford University Press, 2000), who favour an alternative way of categorizing the domain, emphasizing the dispositional nature of emotions and conceiving of the relevant affective episodes as emotional experiences. This issue, which is at least in part terminological insofar as everybody should accept that there exist emotional episodes as well as emotional dispositions, will not play a central role in what follows.
2. See William James, 'What is an Emotion', *Mind* 9 (1884): 188–205 and *The Principles of Psychology* (New York: Dover, 1890/1950), ch. 25.

3. An illuminating discussion of James' theory is Gerald Myers, 'William James' Theory of Emotion', *Transactions of the Charles S. Peirce Society* 5 (1969): 67–89, who assesses many classical objections to it. See also Mulligan, this volume, pp. 223–52.
4. This is not to say that this strategy is exclusive to this period. It has been, on the contrary, common since the dawn of theorizing about the emotions, as the views of Aristotle and the Stoics testify. Still, the strategy has played an especially dominant role in post-Jamesian philosophical discussions.
5. H. N. Gardiner, 'Recent Discussion of Emotion', *The Philosophical Review* 5 (1896): 102–12.
6. One important ambiguity is that between what we may call respectively the 'transitive' and the 'specifying' sense of 'feeling' used in connection with names of emotions (see Olivier Massin, 'The Intentionality of Pleasures and Other Feelings, A Brentanian Approach', in *Themes from Brentano*, ed. Denis Fisette and Guillaume Fréchette (Amsterdam: Rodopi, 2013), pp. 307–38, who draws this distinction in connection with pleasure). Expressions such as 'feelings of fear' may be understood as a description of feelings intentionally directed towards fear, suggesting in the process that fear itself, as opposed to the feeling of it, need not be conscious—or at least that it is not felt until feelings distinct from it are directed towards it (for emphasis on this transitive sense, see William Alston, 'Feelings', *Philosophical Review* 78 (1969): 3–34). Yet, these expressions have typically a different function, namely that of referring to sensations conceived of as being characteristic of or perhaps even unique to fear, and this without implying that emotions need not be felt. Uses of the expression to that specifying effect may be motivated by Kenny's observation that emotions are not the sorts of things we perceive by feeling; to feel anger is to feel angry, but to feel the roughness of the table is certainly not to feel rough (Anthony Kenny, *Action, Emotion and Will* (London: Routledge, 1963)). In any case, as Myers acutely observes, James did not want to leave room for unfelt emotions (Myers, 'William James' Theory', pp. 77–9). For an influential endorsement of the opposite view, see Anthony Damasio, *Descartes' Error: Emotion, Reason, and the Human Brain* (New York: Putnam, 1994), ch. 7.
7. This distinction is highlighted in Errol Bedford, 'Emotions', *Proceedings of the Aristotelian Society* 57 (1957): 281–304 and George Pitcher, 'Emotion', *Mind* 74 (1965): 326–46. For a more recent discussion, see Stephen R. Leighton, 'A New View of Emotion', *American Philosophical Quarterly* 22 (1985): 133–41.
8. The observations that follow should not be read as implying that there is only one dimension to the reasonableness of emotions. Quite the contrary, in fact, since emotions are subject to a variety of normative considerations. On this topic, see Gordon's insightful distinction between reason for an attitude and epistemic reasons (Robert Gordon, *The Structure of Emotions: Investigations in Cognitive Philosophy* (Cambridge: Cambridge University Press, 1987), pp. 34–6), as well as Rabinowicz and Rønnow-Rasmussen's emphasis on the difference between epistemic and prudential reasons bearing on emotions (Wlodek Rabinowicz and Toni Rønnow-Rasmussen, 'The Strike of the Demon: On Fitting Pro-attitudes and Value', *Ethics* 114 (2004): 391–423).
9. Here and in what follows, I skip over some possible complications having to do with the fact that pains may well have an emotional component (see e.g. Roger Trigg, *Pain and Emotion* (New York: Oxford University Press, 1970) and Michael Tye, 'The Experience of Emotion: An Intentionalist Theory', *Revue internationale de philosophie* 62 (2008), pp. 25–50). As far as I can see, this has no significant impact on my discussion.

10. That being said, this development certainly has as much to do with changing attitudes towards the nature of rationality as with changing attitudes towards that of emotions. On this topic, see Robert W. Leeper, 'A Motivational Theory of Emotion to Replace "Emotion as Disorganized Response"', *Psychological Review* 55 (1948): 5–21, who documents the impact of the traditional emotion-disturbance equation in the literature up to the time of his writing, and the more recent survey of the debates in Michael Lacewing, 'Moral Intuitions and its Development: A Guide to the Debate', *Topoi* 34 (2013): 1–17. An influential book-length treatment of the relation between emotions and rationality is Ronald De Sousa, *The Rationality of Emotion* (Cambridge, Mass.: MIT Press, 1987).
11. See Robert Gordon, 'The Aboutness of Emotions', *American Philosophical Quarterly* 27 (1974): 11–36; Kenny, *Action, Emotion*, p. 14; Pitcher, 'Emotion'; Jean-Paul Sartre, *Sketch for a Theory of the Emotions*, trans. B. Frechtman (New York: The Philosophical Library, 1948); and Irving Thalberg, 'Emotion and Thought', *American Philosophical Quarterly* 1 (1964): 45–55. De Sousa, *The Rationality of Emotion*, ch. 5 is a helpful discussion of the issues related to the fact that emotions may have a variety of objects. The idea that emotions are intentional mental states is not universally accepted, however, and we shall have the opportunity to come back to this claim in Section 14.4.
12. Two observations are in order. First, it is often claimed that the main difference between emotions and moods lies in the intentional aspect of the former. I shall have no more to say about moods in what follows. Second, insisting on the intentionality of emotions in no way implies that their objects are always transparent to one. On the contrary, this makes room for errors of a specific type, i.e. those consisting in misidentifying these objects.
13. For Descartes, see *Les passions de l'âme* and the illuminating discussion in Amélie Rorty, 'From Passions to Emotions and Sentiments', *Philosophy* 57 (1982): 159–72. The relevant passage in Hume is *Treatise* II.3.3, but see Lilli Alanen, 'The Powers and Mechanisms of the Passions', in *The Blackwell Guide to Hume's Treatise*, ed. Saul Traiger (Oxford: Blackwell, 2005), pp. 179–98 for a nuanced discussion of Hume's understanding of the intentionality of the passions.
14. This is emphasized in Myers, 'William James's Theory'.
15. For discussion, see Tim Crane, 'Intentionality as the Mark of the Mental', in *Contemporary Issues in the Philosophy of Mind*, ed. Tim Crane (Cambridge: Cambridge University Press, 1998), pp. 229–51.
16. One may also insist on the fact that emotions are not localized in the body, whereas sensations are essentially individuated in terms of a more or less diffuse bodily location. In Kenny's unforgettable words, it is 'impossible to imagine [...] the discomfort of constipation in the cheek' (Kenny, *Action, Emotion*, p. 58).
17. See Kenny, *Action, Emotion*, ch. 9.
18. Observations of this nature constitute Kenny's main reason for introducing the idea that emotions have evaluative properties as their 'formal objects' (on this notion, see Fabrice Teroni, 'Emotions and Formal Objects', *Dialectica* 61 (2007): 395–415). We shall have opportunities to come back to the relations between emotions and evaluative properties in Section 14.4.
19. See William Lyons, *Emotion* (Cambridge: Cambridge University Press, 1980), p. 7.
20. See Robert Solomon, 'Emotions and Choice', in *Explaining Emotions*, ed. A. Rorty (Berkeley: University of California Press, 1980), pp. 251–81 (p. 274).
21. One influential neo-Jamesian theory that shares this conviction is put forward in Jesse Prinz, *Gut Reactions: A Perceptual Theory of the Emotions* (New York: Oxford University Press, 2004).

22. This is of course not to say that the idea originated during this so-called revolution, as it can for instance be found in the writings of Wundt, Stumpf, and Meinong. Later, it is endorsed by e.g. Bedford, 'Emotions'; Lyons, *Emotion* (pp. 81, 127, 137) and Pitcher, 'Emotion'. In psychology, it plays a vital role within constructionist approaches (see e.g. James Russell, 'Core Affect and the Psychological Construction of Emotion', *Psychological Review* 110 (2003): 145–72).
23. See in particular Ludwig Wittgenstein, *Philosophical Investigations* (Oxford: Blackwell, 1953) and Bedford, 'Emotion'.
24. Needless to say, philosophers inspired by Hume insist that only instrumental desires can be assessed in this way. I shall not be further concerned with this issue in what follows.
25. This is particularly the case insofar as the contemporary distinction associates basic emotions with universal affective responses that have a signature facial expression and a clear evolutionary function.
26. Kenny, *Action, Emotion*, p. 14 provides a telling example of such confusion, while Moreland Perkins, 'Emotion and Feeling', *The Philosophical Review* 75 (1966): 139–60 offers a diagnosis in terms of the contrast between episodes and dispositions (see also Gordon, *The Structure of Emotions*, pp. 72, 92–3). One outstanding exception to the claim under discussion is Shand's book-length treatment of the underlying issues (Alexander Shand, *The Foundations of Character* (London: Macmillan, 1914)). His contribution has, however, been almost completely forgotten, and still awaits rediscovery.
27. Three philosophers who have succumbed to the temptation are Ryle (Gilbert Ryle, *The Concept of Mind* (London: Hutchinson, 1949)), obviously, Kenny, *Action, Emotion*, pp. 98–9 and Lyons, *Emotion*, pp. 130–43. A similar conclusion has been driven by Schachter and Singer's famous experiments, on the basis of which many have endorsed the idea that phenomenal states have the 'feel' of emotions insofar as the subject undergoing them accepts a specific explanation of their occurrence (Stanley Schachter and Jerome Singer, 'Cognitive, Social, and Physiological Determinants of Emotional State', *Psychological Review* 69 (1962): 379–99). For discussion, see Gordon, *The Structure of Emotion*, ch. 5 and Julien Deonna and Fabrice Teroni, 'Getting Bodily Feelings into Emotional Experience in the Right Way', Emotion Review 9 (2016): 55–63.
28. See Alexius Meinong, *Psychologisch-ethische Untersuchungen zur Werttheorie*, in *Alexius Meinong Gesamtausgabe Band III*, ed. Rudolf Haller and Rudolf Kindinger (Graz: Akademische Druck- und Verlagsanstalt, 1968), pp. 3–244 and Gordon, *The Structure of Emotion.* Two detailed approaches in terms of belief are Martha Nussbaum, *The Therapy of Desire: Theory and Practice in Hellenistic Ethics* (Princeton: Princeton University Press, 1994) and Robert Solomon, *The Passions: Emotions and the Meaning of Life* (Indianapolis: Hackett Publishing, 1993).
29. A rich discussion can be found in Rainer Reisenzein, 'Arnold's Theory of Emotions in Historical Perspective', *Cognition and Emotion* 20 (2006): 920–51. See also Julien Deonna and Fabrice Teroni, *The Emotions: A Philosophical Introduction* (New York: Routledge, 2012), chs. 3 and 5.
30. So doing allows these theories to explain the fact that emotional rationality is first and foremost evaluative. We assess an episode of anger at a remark as irrational when there is no hint of offensiveness in the remark, and so on. The fact that this is left unexplained within the first family of approaches (which proceed in terms of combinations of non-evaluative beliefs and desires) may suggest that those who subscribe to them have some

misgivings about the ontological standing of evaluative properties and/or about their role in emotion theory.

31. I do not mean to deny that desiring does sometimes have consequences for the way one feels. This is unquestionably the case if one faces a situation that one perceives as satisfying or frustrating one's desire. There is actually one approach to the emotions that conceives of them as representations of the satisfaction or frustration of desires, but I shall not discuss it any further here. See Deonna and Teroni, *The Emotions*, ch. 3.
32. The first expression is Solomon's (*The Passions*, p. 97). The second I take from Geoffrey C. Madell, 'Emotion and Feeling', *Proceedings of the Aristotelian Society*, Suppl. Vol. 71 (1997): 147–62 (p. 147), who offers an illuminating discussion of this aspect of 'cognitivism', which he spots in the writings of Alston, Lyons, and Gordon.
33. See in particular Gordon, *The Structure of Emotion*, pp. 30–1 and Richard Peters, 'Emotions and the Category of Passivity', *Proceedings of the Aristotelian Society* 62 (1961): 117–34 (p. 127).
34. On this issue, see John Deigh, 'Cognitivism in the Theory of Emotions', *Ethics* 104 (1994): 824–54; Sabine Döring, 'Seeing What to Do: Affective Perception and Rational Motivation', *Dialectica* 61 (2007): 363–94; and Christine Tappolet, *Emotions et valeurs* (Paris: Presses universitaires de France, 2000).
35. An extensive list of contrasts between belief-like states and emotions can be found in Leighton, 'A New View', p. 134. See also Geoffrey C. Madell, 'Emotion and Feeling', *Proceedings of the Aristotelian Society*, Suppl. Vol. 71 (1997): 147–62.
36. On this issue, see Teroni, 'Emotions and Formal Objects'.
37. This kind of dependence characteristic of emotions is nicely emphasized by, amongst many others, Meinong (Alexius Meinong, *On Emotional Presentation*, trans. M.-L. Schubert Kalsi (Evanston: Northwestern University Press, 1971)) and Stumpf (see Rainer Reisenzein and Wolfgang Schönpflug, 'Stumpf's Cognitive-Evaluative Theory of Emotion', *American Psychologist* 47 (1992): 34–45). For doubts regarding the need for the relevant contents to be available before the emotion is undergone, see Max Scheler, *Formalism in Ethics and Non-formal Ethics of Values*, trans. M. Frings and R. Funk (Evanston: Northwestern University Press, 1973), pp. 17–18).
38. An example of the first type of approach is to be found in Lyons, *Emotions*. In conceiving of the passions as 'delight or uneasiness' consequent on a thought, Locke endorsed an approach of the second type, more recently adopted in Irwin Goldstein, 'Are Emotions Feelings? A Further Look at Hedonic Theories of Emotions', *Consciousness and Emotion* 3 (2002): 21–33; Uriah Kriegel, 'Towards a New Feeling Theory of Emotion', *European Journal of Philosophy* 22 (2014): 420–42; and Demian Whiting, 'The Feeling Theory of Emotion and the Object-directed Emotions', *European Journal of Philosophy* 19 (2011): 281–303. For an informed discussion that favours the second type of approach, see Rainer Reisenzein, 'What is an Emotion in the Belief-Desire Theory of Emotion?', in *The Goals of Cognition: Essays in Honor of Cristiano Castelfranchi*, ed. Fabio Paglieri, Luca Tummolini, Rino Falcone, and Maria Miceli (London: College Publications, 2012), pp. 181–211. One reason for thinking that the onus of proof is on the shoulders of those who advocate that the relation is that of a whole to its parts is the following one. We are prone to explain why emotions occur by mentioning the relevant belief–wish pairs or evaluations—Mary is afraid of the lion because she believes that she is facing one and does not want to be torn into pieces. Such explanations look more like explaining why someone believes that there

is an apple in the cupboard by saying that he saw one there than like explaining why someone believes that the apple is red and round by mentioning his beliefs that it is red and that it is round. Basically the same debate takes place in psychology and concerns the role of appraisal. See Magda Arnold, *Emotion and Personality* (New York: Columbia University Press, 1960) and, for discussion, Agnes Moors, 'On the Causal Role of Appraisal in Emotion', *Emotion Review* 5 (2013): 132–40 and Rainer Reisenzein, 'Arnold's Theory of Emotions in Historical Perspective', *Cognition and Emotion* 20 (2006): 920–51.

39. Peter Goldie, *The Emotions: A Philosophical Exploration* (Oxford: Oxford University Press, 2000).
40. See in particular Wittgenstein, *Philosophical investigations*: I, 476 and Kenny, *Action, Emotion*, p. 72. An application of basically the same point to Prinz's neo-Jamesian account of the emotions is attempted in Deonna and Teroni, *The Emotions*, ch. 6.
41. This is nicely emphasized in Irving Thalberg, 'Emotion and Thought', *American Philosophical Quarterly* 1 (1964): 45–55.
42. Kenny, *Action, Emotion*, p. 56.
43. Gordon, *The Structure of Emotion*, pp. 63–4 makes it especially clear that he conceives of emotional intentionality as being reducible to that of the relevant belief–wish pairs.
44. But see Kevin Mulligan, 'Intentionality, Knowledge and Formal Objects', *Disputatio* 2 (2007): 205–28.
45. See e.g. David Pugmire, *Rediscovering Emotion: Emotions and the Claims of Feeling* (Edinburgh: Edinburgh University Press, 2004), who endorses this idea under the name of the 'primacy of affect'.
46. Emphasis on the perceptual nature of emotional phenomenology is frequent in the writings of Scheler, and is nowadays associated with Goldie's 'feelings towards' (Goldie, *The Emotions*). For discussion, see Joel M. Potter, 'Arguments From the Priority of Feeling in Contemporary Emotion Theory and Max Scheler's Phenomenology', *Quaestiones Disputatae* 3 (2012): 215–25.
47. Goldie, *The Emotions* and Tappolet, *Emotions et valeurs* develop accounts according to which emotions are direct perceptions of evaluative properties, whereas Robert Roberts, *Emotion: An Essay in Aid of Moral Psychology* (New York: Cambridge University Press, 2003) appeals instead to aspectual perception. See also De Sousa, *The Rationality of Emotion*; Julien Deonna, 'Emotion, Perception and Perspective', *Dialectica* 60 (2006): 29–46; and Döring, 'Seeing What to Do'. Several variants of the perceptual approach are discussed in Deonna and Teroni, *The Emotions*, ch. 6, as well as in Jérôme Dokic and Stéphane Lemaire, 'Are Emotions Perceptions of Value?', *Canadian Journal of Philosophy* 43 (2013): 227–47.
48. See John McDowell, *Mind and World* (Cambridge, Mass.: Harvard University Press, 1994), who speaks somewhat metaphorically of perception as being an 'invitation' to endorse a content.
49. Armon-Jones makes this point forcefully in relation to approaches appealing to aspectual perception (Claire Armon-Jones, *Varieties of Affect* (Toronto: University of Toronto Press, 1991), p. 25). See also Mulligan, 'Intentionality, Knowledge'.
50. This invites probing into the nature of emotional phenomenology and whether it differs from that of perceptual experiences. For discussion, see Deonna and Teroni, *The Emotions*, ch. 6.

51. On that issue, see in particular William McDougall, *An Outline of Psychology* (London: Methuen, 1923), ch. 11.
52. See Franz Brentano, *Psychology from an Empirical Standpoint*, trans. A. Rancurello, D. Terrell, and L. McAlister (London: Routledge, 1974/1995) and, for discussion, Roderick Chisholm, *Brentano and Intrinsic Value* (New York: Cambridge University Press, 1986). This line of thought is pursued in Deonna and Teroni, *The Emotions*, ch. 7.
53. I am grateful to Julien Deonna, Olivier Massin, and Cain Todd for their helpful comments on a previous version of this paper.

Bibliography

Alanen, Lilli. 'The Powers and Mechanisms of the Passions', in *The Blackwell Guide to Hume's Treatise*, ed. Saul Traiger (Oxford: Blackwell, 2005), pp. 179–98.

Alston, William. 'Feelings', *Philosophical Review* 78 (1969): 3–34.

Armon-Jones, Claire. *Varieties of Affect* (Toronto: University of Toronto Press, 1991).

Arnold, Magda. *Emotion and Personality* (New York: Columbia University Press, 1960).

Bedford, Errol. 'Emotions', *Proceedings of the Aristotelian Society* 57 (1957): 281–304.

Brentano, Franz. *Psychology from an Empirical Standpoint*, trans. A. Rancurello, D. Terrell, and L. McAlister (London: Routledge, 1974/1995).

Chisholm, Roderick. *Brentano and Intrinsic Value* (New York: Cambridge University Press, 1986).

Crane, Tim. 'Intentionality as the Mark of the Mental', in *Contemporary Issues in the Philosophy of Mind*, ed. Tim Crane (Cambridge: Cambridge University Press, 1998), pp. 229–51.

Damasio, Anthony. *Descartes' Error: Emotion, Reason, and the Human Brain* (New York: Putnam, 1994).

Deigh, John. 'Cognitivism in the Theory of Emotions', *Ethics* 104 (1994): 824–54.

Deonna, Julien. 'Emotion, Perception and Perspective', *Dialectica* 60 (2006): 29–46.

Deonna, Julien and Fabrice Teroni, *The Emotions: A Philosophical Introduction* (New York: Routledge, 2012).

Deonna, Julien and Fabrice Teroni, 'Getting Bodily Feelings into Emotional Experience in the Right Way', *Emotion Review* 9 (2016): 55–63.

De Sousa, Ronald. *The Rationality of Emotion* (Cambridge, MA: MIT Press, 1987).

Dokic, Jérôme and Stéphane Lemaire. 'Are Emotions Perceptions of Value?', *Canadian Journal of Philosophy* 43 (2013): 227–47.

Döring, Sabine. 'Seeing What to Do: Affective Perception and Rational Motivation', *Dialectica* 61 (2007): 363–94.

Gardiner, H. N. 'Recent Discussion of Emotion', *The Philosophical Review* 5 (1896): 102–12.

Goldie, Peter. *The Emotions: A Philosophical Exploration* (Oxford: Oxford University Press, 2000).

Goldstein, Irwin. 'Are Emotions Feelings? A Further Look at Hedonic Theories of Emotions', *Consciousness and Emotion* 3 (2002): 21–33.

Gordon, Robert. 'The Aboutness of Emotions', *American Philosophical Quarterly* 27 (1974): 11–36.

Gordon, Robert. *The Structure of Emotions: Investigations in Cognitive Philosophy* (Cambridge: Cambridge University Press, 1987).

James, William. 'What is an Emotion?', *Mind* 9 (1884): 188–205.

James, William. *The Principles of Psychology* (New York: Dover, 1890/1950).

Kenny, Anthony. *Action, Emotion and Will* (London: Routledge, 1963).

Kriegel, Uriah. 'Towards a New Feeling Theory of Emotion', *European Journal of Philosophy* 22 (2014): 420–42.

Lacewing, Michael. 'Moral Intuitions and its Development: A Guide to the Debate', *Topoi* 34 (2015): 409–25.

Leeper, Robert W. 'A Motivational Theory of Emotion to Replace "Emotion as Disorganized Response"', *Psychological Review* 55 (1948): 5–21.

Leighton, Stephen R. 'A New View of Emotion', *American Philosophical Quarterly* 22 (1985): 133–41.

Lyons, William. *Emotion* (Cambridge: Cambridge University Press, 1980).

Madell, Geoffrey C. 'Emotion and Feeling', *Proceedings of the Aristotelian Society, Suppl. Vol.* 71 (1997): 147–62.

Massin, Olivier. 'The Intentionality of Pleasures and Other Feelings, A Brentanian Approach', in *Themes from Brentano*, ed. Denis Fisette and Guillaume Fréchette (Amsterdam: Rodopi, 2013), pp. 307–38.

McDougall, William. *An Outline of Psychology* (London: Methuen, 1923).

McDowell, John. *Mind and World* (Cambridge, MA: Harvard University Press, 1994).

Meinong, Alexius. *Psychologisch-ethische Untersuchungen zur Werttheorie*, in *Alexius Meinong Gesamtausgabe Band III*, ed. R. Haller and R. Kindinger (Graz: Akademische Druck- und Verlagsanstalt, 1968), pp. 3–244.

Meinong, Alexius. *On Emotional Presentation*, trans. M.-L. Schubert Kalsi (Evanston: Northwestern University Press, 1971).

Meyer, Max. 'The Whale Among the Fishes: The Theory of Emotions', *Psychological Review* 40 (1933): 292–300.

Moors, Agnes. 'On the Causal Role of Appraisal in Emotion', *Emotion Review* 5 (2013): 132–40.

Mulligan, Kevin. 'Intentionality, Knowledge and Formal Objects', *Disputatio* 2 (2007): 205–28.

Myers, Gerald. 'William James' Theory of Emotion', *Transactions of the Charles S. Peirce Society* 5 (1969): 67–89.

Nussbaum, Martha. *The Therapy of Desire: Theory and Practice in Hellenistic Ethics* (Princeton: Princeton University Press, 1994).

Perkins, Moreland. 'Emotion and Feeling', *The Philosophical Review* 75 (1966): 139–60.

Peters, Richard. 'Emotions and the Category of Passivity', *Proceedings of the Aristotelian Society* 62 (1961): 117–34.

Pitcher, George. 'Emotion', *Mind* 74 (1965): 326–46.

Potter, Joel M. 'Arguments from the Priority of Feeling in Contemporary Emotion Theory and Max Scheler's Phenomenology', *Quaestiones Disputatae* 3 (2012): 215–25.

Prinz, Jesse. *Gut Reactions: A Perceptual Theory of the Emotions* (New York: Oxford University Press, 2004).

Pugmire, David. *Rediscovering Emotion: Emotions and the Claims of Feeling* (Edinburgh: Edinburgh University Press, 2004).

Rabinowicz, Wlodek and Toni Rønnow-Rasmussen. 'The Strike of the Demon: On Fitting Pro-attitudes and Value', *Ethics* 114 (2004): 391–423.

Reisenzein, Rainer. 'Arnold's Theory of Emotions in Historical Perspective', *Cognition and Emotion* 20 (2006): 920–51.

Reisenzein, Rainer. 'What is an Emotion in the Belief-Desire Theory of Emotion?', in *The Goals of Cognition: Essays in Honor Of Cristiano Castelfranchi*, ed. F. Paglieri, R. Falcone and M. Miceli (London: College Publications, 2012), pp. 181–211.

Reisenzein, Rainer and Wolfgang Schönpflug, 'Stumpf's Cognitive-Evaluative Theory of Emotion', *American Psychologist* 47 (1992): 34–45.

Roberts, Robert. *Emotion: An Essay in Aid of Moral Psychology* (New York: Cambridge University Press, 2003).

Rorty, Amélie. 'From Passions to Emotions and Sentiments', *Philosophy* 57 (1982): 159–72.

Russell, James. 'Core Affect and the Psychological Construction of Emotion', *Psychological Review* 110 (2003): 145–72.

Ryle, Gilbert. *The Concept of Mind* (London: Hutchinson, 1949).

Sartre, Jean-Paul. *Sketch for a Theory of the Emotions*, trans. Bernard Frechtman (New York: The Philosophical Library, 1949).

Schachter, Stanley and Jerome Singer. 'Cognitive, Social, and Physiological Determinants of Emotional State', *Psychological Review* 69 (1962): 379–99.

Scheler, Max. *Formalism in Ethics and Non-Formal Ethics of Values*, trans. Manfred S. Frings and Roger L. Funk (Evanston: Northwestern University Press, 1973).

Shand, Alexander. *The Foundations of Character* (London: Macmillan, 1914).

Solomon, Robert. *The Passions* (New York: Doubleday, 1977).

Solomon, Robert. 'Emotions and Choice', in *Explaining Emotions*, ed. A. Rorty (Berkeley: University of California Press, 1980), pp. 251–81.

Solomon, Robert. *The Passions: Emotions and the Meaning of Life* (Indianapolis: Hackett Publishing, 1993).

Tappolet, Christine. *Emotions et valeurs* (Paris: Presses Universitaires de France, 2000).

Teroni, Fabrice. 'Emotions and Formal Objects', *Dialectica* 61 (2007): 395–415.

Thalberg, Irving. 'Emotion and Thought', *American Philosophical Quarterly* 1 (1964): 45–55.

Trigg, Roger. *Pain and Emotion* (New York: Oxford University Press, 1970).

Tye, Michael. 'The Experience of Emotion: An Intentionalist Theory', *Revue internationale de philosophie* 62 (2008): 25–50.

Whiting, Daniel. 'The Feeling Theory of Emotion and the Object-directed Emotions', *European Journal of Philosophy* 19 (2011): 281–303.

Wittgenstein, Ludwig. *Philosophical Investigations* (Oxford: Blackwell, 1953).

Wollheim, Richard. *On the Emotions* (Yale: Yale University Press, 1999).

Index